HOW TO TALK TO KIDS ABOUT ANYTHING

"Dr. Robyn's *How to Talk to Kids About Anything* joins the handful of ever-green parenting books that every parent should have at the ready and on their shelf—one that will be repeatedly referenced, dog-eared, and reused throughout the stages of childhood."

—Tina Payne Bryson, LCSW, PhD, *New York Times* best-selling co-author of *The Whole-Brain Child* and *No-Drama Discipline*, and author of *The Bottom Line for Baby*

"It's hard to overstate how good this book is. If you've found yourself stuck or stammering in responding in the moment to those oh-so-important questions children seem to lob at you when your defenses are down... This. Is. The. Book. Imagine if Jiminy Cricket, Mr. Rogers, and ChatGPT got together to craft the truest words for the trickiest situations, all in one book. Yeah, *How to Talk* is that and more."

—Ned Johnson, co-author of *The Self-Driven Child* and *What Do You Say?: How To Talk with Kids to Build Motivation, Stress Tolerance, and a Happy Home*

"Talking to our kids about tough topics is one of the hardest—and most important—parts of parenting. In her wise, thoughtful, and accessible book, Dr. Robyn Silverman walks readers through some of the most challenging conversations and offers the insights, strategies, and scripts we need to connect with our kids about everything from friendship and mistakes to divorce and death. I highly recommend this book to any parent looking for the right words at the right time—which is to say, all of us."

—Carla Naumburg, PhD, author of *How to Stop Losing Your Sh*t with Your Kids*

"Dr. Robyn has created a step-by-step manual with real-life examples of what to say to children on any subject. Her scripts are actionable and essential. A sorely needed resource for parents."

—Jessica Lahey, bestselling author of *The Gift of Failure*

"In today's Internet-soaked culture, it has become not only important but imperative to be our children's first source of information. In *How to Talk to Kids About Anything*, Dr. Robyn shows us how."

—Michele Borba, bestselling author of *Thrivers* and *Unselfie*

"Robyn Silverman is a treasure, and this book is a great gift to parents and to professionals who talk with kids about hard things. Dr. Silverman combines her own experience as a development psychologist, as a mother, and even as a child, with important research and the wisdom of the hundreds of professionals she has spoken to over the years about talking with kids. *How to Talk* is filled with language that will help adults communicate with children in ways that make them feel understood, loved, and safe. If you'll ever need to talk with kids about sex, death, hard feelings, gender issues, or other difficult topics, this book is for you. You'll keep coming back to it again and again as children bring you new challenges to discuss."

—William Stixrud, PhD, co-author of *The Self-Driven Child* and *What Do You Say? How to Talk with Kids to Build Motivation, Stress Tolerance, and a Happy Home.*

"Robyn Silverman shares insights from a broad range of experts to help parents meet the many challenges of raising children."

—Joanna Faber and Julie King, co-authors of *How to Talk So LITTLE Kids Will Listen* and *How to Talk When Kids Won't Listen*

"Dr. Robyn Silverman distills decades of research and experience and hundreds of expert interviews into a warm, wise, clear, and comprehensive guide that really does explain *How to Talk to Kids About Anything*. Reading this book feels like having an enjoyable conversation with a deeply knowledgeable friend. It's a gift to parents everywhere."

—Lisa Damour, PhD, author of *Untangled*, *Under Pressure*, and *The Emotional Lives of Teenagers*

"As they grow into adults, children will have questions on virtually every topic—sex, love, death, divorce. Dr. Robyn guides parents through the turbulent waters of conversation during the delicate, impressionable years of childhood. A must-read!"

—Rosalind Wiseman, bestselling author of *Queen Bees & WannaBes*

"Dr. Robyn Silverman distills decades of research and experience and hundreds of expert interviews into a warm, wise, clear, and comprehensive guide that really does explain *How to Talk to Kids About Anything*. Reading this book feels like having an enjoyable conversation with a deeply knowledgeable friend. It's a gift to parents everywhere."

—Lisa Damour, PhD, author of *Untangled*, *Under Pressure*, and *The Emotional Lives of Teenagers*

Robyn Silverman's steady, encouraging, and compassionate voice is just what parents and caregivers need. In *How to Talk to Kids About Anything*, she provides both contextual science and a treasure chest of accessible conversational strategies, tips, and scripts for everyday topics such as friendship and money to tougher topics such as sex, death, and diversity. Readers can dip in to find a solution for their pain point du jour and come away with a feeling of agency and direction for their next conversation.

—Christine Koh, PhD, co-author of *Minimalist Parenting* and host of the *Edit Your Life* podcast

"Get ready to dog-ear lots of pages in How to Talk to Kids About Anything, a thoughtful and practical book that covers all bases for parents in need of talking points when kids have big emotions, ask tricky questions or make uncomfortable comments."

—Nefertiti Austin, Amazon bestselling author of *Motherhood So White: A Memoir of Race, Gender, and Parenting in America*

"*How to Talk to Kids About Anything* is *the* definitive guide to having tough, critical conversations with children. Author Robyn Silverman's magic is her ability to simplify the most complex topics, including sex, body image, money, and divorce. Along the way, she offers parents all the scripts, tips, research, and tools they need to keep the lines of communication open and confidently answer their kids' most challenging questions. I can't overstate how much I love this book—it's a reassuring must-read for anyone who seeks to raise an emotionally healthy human being!

—Phyllis L. Fagell, LCPC, author of *Middle School Matters* and *Middle School Superpowers*

"*How to Talk to Kids about Anything* is a treasure trove of advice, encouragement and comforting phrases that helps parents know what to say when their kids need them the most. Dr. Robyn's suggestions reflect her compassion, firsthand experiences, and mastery of the child psychology/development research to produce a handbook that will help guide parents and make the most difficult conversations easier to have.

—Mona Delahooke, author of *Brain-Body Parenting* and *Beyond Behaviors*

"If you've ever chickened out of having a conversation with your kids about a topic like friends, money, sex, or divorce, this is the book for you. Dr. Silverman presents solid information on these and other touchy subjects, and then—through intriguing sections like Talking Points, Truth Bombs, and Scripts in a Pinch—she holds your hand as you imagine and prepare for the discussion with your child. A real parental anxiety reducer!"

—Thomas W. Phelan, PhD, bestselling author of *1-2-3 Magic*

"In *How to Talk to Kids about Anything*, Dr. Robyn has gifted parents with the ultimate 'cheat sheet' so we can confidently engage in even the trickiest of conversations with our kids in a way that builds self-respect, agency, and connection."

—Debbie Reber, founder & CEO of Tilt Parenting, author of *Differently Wired*

GOOD GIRLS DON'T GET FAT: HOW WEIGHT OBSESSION IS MESSING UP OUR GIRLS AND HOW WE CAN HELP THEM THRIVE DESPITE IT

"In this straightforward guide, Silverman explores weight obsession in teenage girls, outlining ways that parents can help their daughters succeed in a 'thin-is-in' world."

—*Publishers Weekly*

How to
TALK TO KIDS ABOUT ANYTHING

Tips, Scripts, Stories, and Steps to Make Even the Toughest Conversations Easier

ROBYN SILVERMAN PhD

Published by Sourcebooks
P.O. Box 4410, Naperville, Illinois 60567-4410
(630) 961-3900
sourcebooks.com

Cataloging-in-Publication Data is on file with the Library of Congress.

Printed and bound in the United States of America.
VP 10 9 8 7 6 5 4 3

To my children, Tallie and Noah. Let's keep talking.

Contents

Introduction: Can We Talk?

I was sitting on a park bench with the mother of one of my daughter's friends when she turned to me and said, "My youngest has been asking me about death recently. 'Are you going to die? Am I going to die?' Half the time, I have no idea what to say to these kinds of questions, so I stammer through some incoherent answer and then wind up changing the subject entirely to, you know, 'Who wants ice cream?'"

Tricky conversations with kids present themselves all the time (one minute, I'm talking with my son about breakfast cereal, and the next, he's asking how babies are made). These conversations can be carefully crafted or come out of nowhere. In the back seat of the car. In the middle of the grocery store. Before bed. In line at the movie theater. Life lobs 'em up, and we're meant to take a shot—sometimes with no feeling of preparation, no warning, no words, but all the emotions they never prepare you for when you don't have kids yet and think you know everything.

Believe me, I always knew just what to say before I had kids. Without any emotional stake, I was clear, calm, collected, and an expert on every aspect of parenting. I wondered why anyone would have trouble talking to their own children about key topics such as courage, responsibility, making mistakes, or even death. Just open your mouth and let it rip, right?

Um, no. Now that I have my own kids, I thank goodness nobody's keeping score, since there have been many days when I have had this little voice inside my head saying, *Really? Was that the best you could do?*

The truth is that we're all humans with varied experiences, knowledge, and comfort levels, not Google or Wikipedia. And when we are smack-dab in the middle of a parenting moment, it's not always easy to come up with sparkling words of wisdom on the fly. Yet as parents, teachers, and mentors, we want to ensure we can answer our children's questions confidently and completely, even when they seem to come out of left field and hit us square in the nose.

And then do it again and again.

Critical conversations are not one big talk. They are a series of little talks that build on one another over time. A topic may pop up when your children are four ("Why is the bug not moving?") and not again until they're seven ("Who will take care of me when you die?"), nine ("What happened to Rover's body when he died?"), and fourteen ("What is the meaning of life and death?"). Or your child may become hyperfocused on a singular subject, peppering you with questions and realizations during a marathon exchange over several hours, days, or weeks. The key is to stay open whenever opportunities present themselves. Research has shown most young people do not feel like they have at least three people to turn to in a time of need or challenge.[1] Let's ensure we are one of the three.

After all, conversations are key to our children's development. They teach them how to function in a grown-up world—how to describe, how to ask for help, how to understand, and how to feel okay (particularly about what's happening in their own bodies and minds or in the world around them when they're away from us). Conversations give them the opportunity to learn, connect, discover, understand, reflect, and grow.

Unfortunately, many parents don't talk to their kids about tough topics; they may want to but feel unsure of what to say. Others talk to their kids about one critical issue but not another—or talk about a topic once and then never again, assuming the work is done. But the truth is that tough conversations are not ones to check off a list. We don't have "The Death Talk," "The Sex Talk," or "The Diversity Talk" and then move on. If it were like that, I'd be handing you a pamphlet, not a whole book!

There are so many parenting guides out there on discipline (and we are grateful for the help!) but not many focused on communication, which is why I wanted to write this book. Instead of simply telling parents, teachers, and coaches to broach conversations about important topics, I wanted to show them how. I wanted to provide scripts and tips and share my own struggles as well as the stories other parents have told me—the good, the bad, the ugly. I wanted to share the incredible insights of so many experts I've had the pleasure of working with and interviewing for my podcast, *How to Talk to Kids about Anything*. I wanted a whole chorus of people to come together and say, *Yes, we can do this.* Skills in action!

Life is messy, and we don't always have the time, the headspace, or the patience to deal with tough topics exactly when we need to. But if we don't take the reins of these conversations, we allow strangers—some kid in gym class or a random social media influencer—to take the first crack at it, so let's take aim and do the best we can. There are awkward discussions at every turn and more nuanced conversations at every stage of life. We need to be ready.

Who Am I?

For the past thirty years, I've been reading, writing, presenting, and talking about children. As a child- and teen-development specialist, I've worked with kids from preschool age to college bound and beyond, including non-disabled kids, deaf kids, autistic kids, and kids with all kinds of mental disabilities and physical challenges. I've also founded girls' groups to discuss body image and friendship and created classes to talk about bullying and character development.

Yet when I look back, I think my interest in conversations came not from my career but from an ugly experience in fifth grade—I was bullied and ostracized, and none of the key adults in my life knew quite what to say to me or the other kids involved. As you can imagine, feeling like you're on your own at age ten, even when you are surrounded by adults who want to help you, can feel devastating. I decided I wanted to become the adult I needed when I was a child—the one who not only knew what to say but could also help other key adults know what to do and say when their kids needed them the most.

When I was completing my PhD at Tufts University at the Eliot-Pearson Department of Child Study and Human Development, focusing a great deal on children's friendships, bullying, sense of self, and body image, I wrote a character education curriculum, "Powerful Words." It is a system of scripts and support materials to help teachers, coaches, and after-school educators talk to children about everything from respect and responsibility to courage and perseverance. We used it in classes (my husband and I owned and ran a martial arts and fitness academy in Massachusetts for ten years), and it was used in other facilities worldwide. It still is.

But even a deep dive into the research and curriculum for kids didn't fully prepare me for the real thing. Having your own wide-eyed child ask you why a friend doesn't have a daddy or needs a wheelchair can put marbles in your mouth. I was (and am!) always finding ways to synthesize information across experts and translate their tips into scripts to be used on the fly. I've developed a reputation as a "scriptician," and some parents have asked if I make house calls since "it would be so much easier if you could just talk to my kids for me!" Comments such as these are what led me to start the *How to Talk to Kids about Anything* podcast, where I am able to learn and disseminate the scripts I know parents, like myself, want and need, and it led me to this book.

How to Read This Book

Clearly, you can read this book any way you'd like. You can read it in its entirety and then go back to certain chapters when you need a refresher, or you can read it front to back or on a need-to-know basis. The chapters in this book represent nine of the topics I get asked about most often when I'm presenting at conferences or just sitting and talking to friends:

- "My son is so scared about the first day of school. What should I do?" (Chapter 1)
- "My daughter's complaining about being fat. Why? I've never told her she was or that it's a bad thing." (Chapter 2)
- "I blew it. My son came out to me as gay, and I was totally tongue-tied. Did I mess him up for life?" (Chapter 5)
- "My child has trouble making friends. How can I engage him to want to try?" (Chapter 8)
- "My daughter said, 'Mom, what does "sex" mean?' Dr. Robyn, help!" (Chapter 3)

Many answers to these complex questions, as you'll read, have science behind them, but they have also been battle-tested within my own family. I've done 'em wrong, and I've done 'em right, but the important part is that I've done them and learned a lot about what works for my brood and what doesn't.

In this book, I'm giving you everything I've got—the mistakes I've made, the conversations I've had, and the studies out there to help guide you through all these wonderful and difficult conversations, big and small, with your children. By the end, you'll not only have an anthology of tips, scripts, stories, and steps, but you'll also have your own notes on what works and your own stories to share.

While this book is for you, our kids gain so much from all this as well. Yes, they gain insight and answers as well as the language they need to talk about these topics with others, but most importantly, they learn that the adults in their life are always a trusted source for information. We don't bail when things get awkward or difficult. We show up. We pull up a chair. We listen and advise as needed. And in a world where communication has become increasingly muddied and sporadic, that's really saying something.

Only *we* can offer our children the truth while keeping their developmental readiness in mind and their best interests at heart. As key adults in the lives of our children, we are their safe places, their buffers, their soundboards, their teachers, their best listeners, and their dependable advisers. When they are with us, we want them to know they can ask us anything— tell us anything—and we will step into that conversation with both feet, prepared with what they need in the moment.

And the best part? You don't have to go it alone. We're in this together. So let's get talking.

Chapter 1

How to Talk to Kids about Anger, Sadness, and Other Big Feelings

"How Can I Tell You How I Feel?"

A boy took my son's ball away from him on the playground. Being six years old and, in that moment, full of frustration, confusion, and anger, my son did the first thing that came to mind: he shoved the boy. When the initial rage subsided, my son's irritation turned inward. "My hands were so mad, and I couldn't stop them from pushing," he grumbled to me later.

Big feelings happen, and when they do, they are often paired with intense, reflexive reactions that burst out without any thought or planning—hot, swirling, pitted, pent-up energy that can make people act in ways they never would under normal circumstances.

And I'm not just talking about children.

Angry parents and caretakers can scream, stomp, grunt, or slam the door better than any child. There are stretches of time when I feel like I need a sign that reads: *It's been* x *number of days since I lost my shit*. We all have these moments. Why? Because we're all human, we're not perfect, and we all have our triggers. Dirty dishes in the sink? Check. Wet towels on the floor? Check. Rolled eyes, sharp tongues, and short tempers? Check, check, and check. For me, it's the constant sibling bickering. There have been times when I've gotten so frustrated with my children for yelling at each other that I start to yell at them for yelling!

Of course, anger isn't the only big feeling. There are many: sadness, fear, disgust, surprise, happiness—and a mishmash of everything in between. All told, there are some thirty-four thousand different emotions that can be felt and experienced in the human body.[1] The more we can experience, respond to, and get comfortable with them, the more we can

- express and connect with others,
- become emotionally agile,[2] and
- reduce the *intensity* of unpleasant big feelings such as anxiety, fear,[3] and loneliness.

That last point is important. Big feelings are how our bodies react to and cope with what is happening in the moment. They are *hardwired* into our brains, which means we can't *stop* them. We need to feel them, express them, and regulate them in productive ways. "The secret to being an emotionally intelligent parent," Dr. John Gottman, author of *Raising an Emotionally Intelligent Child*, writes, "lay in how parents interacted with their children when emotions ran hot."[4] I would add that the secret is also in understanding what's happening in our children's brains when they act out. As I've said to my own children, we must learn how to manage our big feelings so our big feelings don't manage us!

"It's Not My Fault!": The Science behind Big Feelings

You might have heard that when our brains sense we are under attack, they throw us into fight-or-flight mode. That's because the amygdala or "feeling part" of our brains (or the "downstairs,"[5] primitive lower region, as neuropsychiatrist Dr. Dan Siegel and parenting coach Dr. Tina Payne Bryson refer to it), sounds an alarm, sends down a gate, and puts the "upstairs," "thinking part" of the brain on hiatus for a little while. When that amygdala gate is down, it blocks off the "stairs" between the two levels, leaving the downstairs (feeling) part in charge. This is what Daniel Goleman, author of *Emotional Intelligence*, calls "emotional hijack" (previously coined "amygdala hijack")[6] and what Dr. Dan Siegel refers to as "flipping your lid."[7]

The "hijacking" is typically a good thing because we don't have time to problem-solve and think through possible solutions in an emergency—when, for example, someone is setting fire to a building or taking a bat to a nearby beehive. We only have a short time to flee to safety.

Because the thinking part of our brains isn't finished developing until our late twenties, our children's brain alarm systems can be a little faulty. They can't well distinguish the difference between an angry arsonist, a beehive basher, and their little sister taking their favorite toy away from them. Therefore, the lid gets flipped no matter how many times you say, "It's your sister's turn. You already had a turn, so you shouldn't be upset." In that moment, you're using your upstairs thinking brain to reason with your children's downstairs feeling brain—and your kids are not hearing you! You might as well be speaking a different language!

Emodiversity

While we may wish our kids could be happy all the time, as it turns out, they wouldn't be healthy if they were. Studies show that those who experience emodiversity, a range and abundance of both negative and positive emotions, are happier and healthier than those who remain numb or tend to fixate on any one emotion for a long period of time. Additionally, in environments that place a premium on expressing *only positive* emotions, those who experience negative feelings tend to falter. As Susan David, PhD, psychologist and bestselling author of *Emotional Agility* says in her TED Talk,

"Tough emotions are part of our contract with life. You don't get to have a meaningful career or raise a family or leave the world a better place without stress and discomfort."[8]

When we attempt to suppress emotional thoughts, feelings, and expressions, there can be negative consequences. Studies show that emotional inhibition and invalidation contribute to children becoming dysregulated, distressed, depressed, anxious, and more negative over time.[9] When we try to reject, dismiss, and prematurely urge our children to move away from tough feelings, they can wind up with *more* of them. Plus, if we ignore or minimize our children's feelings, we could hurt our relationship with them and make them feel lonely or even worthless.

Conversely, when parents accept their children's feelings and view emotional displays as opportunities to empathize, connect, and strategize, kids tend to have fewer emotional and behavioral problems, including issues with anger, anxiety, and acting out. "Feelings are just a message to us," Dr. Laura Markham, psychologist and author of *Peaceful Parent, Happy Kids: How to Stop Yelling and Start Connecting*, told me. "When you allow yourself to feel an emotion, it begins to dissipate and heal."[10]

Parents often ask me if they should be sharing their own negative feelings with their children. The knee-jerk reaction, of course, is to say no—we want to protect our kids from the unpleasant things in life. But research shows that parents and key adults who hide their negative feelings from their children may not only confuse them but also appear less emotionally available. In a recent study of 107 parents and their children, researchers at Washington State University found that when parents pretended everything was fine, the kids exhibited more signs of stress and, in fact, both parents and kids were less warm and engaged with one another.[11] Also, parents who admit to and cope with common negative feelings such as anger, sadness, and fear show kids how to handle these emotions, regulate them, and make a situation better.

The key to emodiversity is to feel a whole host of emotions—and express them in healthy ways. We don't want them to build up and lie dormant. As

Marc Brackett, PhD, author of *Permission to Feel*, so beautifully told Brené Brown on her podcast *Unlocking Us*, "Hurt feelings don't vanish on their own. They don't heal themselves. If we don't express our emotions, they pile up like a debt that will eventually come due."[12]

Bottom line? Every feeling has a purpose. Talking about uncomfortable emotions and embracing them can result in better mental and physical health and, potentially, greater happiness in our kids and ourselves.

Game

One, Two, Three, Feeling Face!

In my Powerful Words character curriculum, a comprehensive character education system I write for educators who work with children, when the powerful word is "empathy," we do a game called "One, Two, Three Feeling Face." It's a game in which one child is the "emoter" and the other child/children are the "guessers." The emoter faces away from the others, and we yell, "One, two, three, feeling face!" The emoter turns around, showing the "feeling face" of their choice, and the other kids have to guess which emotion it is. You can add in body language as well! The game is typically done in "rapid fire" and often leads to peals of laughter while kids learn about reading emotions.

Feelings at a Glance

When you're teaching kids about emotions, it's important to give them labels to choose from that pinpoint the nuances of the many emotions people can feel. Clearly, a child who is a little miffed needs a different label than one who is furious, just as a teen who feels a bit grouchy warrants a different label than one who is feeling distraught, depressed, or miserable.

Dr. Gloria Willcox, who invented the well-known feeling wheel, posits there are six core emotions: mad, sad, scared, peaceful, powerful, and joyful.[13] Each one of these is then split into more specific feelings that vary in definition and intensity. Sad, for example, is split into words like "depressed," "ashamed," and "guilty" and then further split into labels such as "remorseful," "isolated," and "inferior."

There are more simplified wheels or alternative images that provide somewhat different emotions, like that of Dr. Robert Plutchik, who proposed eight primary emotions: joy, sadness, disgust, fear, anger, anticipation, trust, and surprise (some of these you may recognize from the Disney/Pixar animated film *Inside Out*).[14] The wheel shows variations of intensity and relatedness (like opposites sadness and joy or anger and fear) as well as mixed combinations of feelings (disgust + anger = contempt). These can all be used to help your child put names to a variety of emotions.

We can use the wheels by asking our kids to label how they are feeling, then pointing out how we think they are feeling based on their visual cues, how *we* are feeling, and how *others* are feeling:

- "You look quite serene, sitting there by the water, relaxing."
- "You're banging your fists on the table—you must feel frustrated!"
- "She's sitting by herself and crying quietly. I wonder if she's feeling lonely."
- "Your sister didn't feel prepared for the test, so she was anxious about taking it."
- "There are so many kids in our new neighborhood. I'm hopeful we'll all make a lot of new friends!"
- "I know you were both surprised and sad to hear about your friend moving away."

Allowing your children to learn more precise ways to describe their feeling helps them gain understanding of what they're experiencing.

Also, according to educator and bestselling author Rosalind Wiseman, "getting granular,"[15] or specific, about emotions allows young people to get the right help at the right time, especially when they're anxious, depressed, distraught, lonely, suicidal, or otherwise troubled and in need of help.[16] And it allows them to develop better social skills and peer relationships.

Print out a feelings chart, table, or wheel, and put it where your kids can see it, use it, and ask questions about it. Simple questions (such as "How are you feeling right now?" or "When you look at your baby cousin's face, can you guess how Sammy is feeling?") can increase your children's emotional vocabulary.

Parenting Out Loud: Big Feelings

Modeling different feeling words can be a useful way to expand your child's emotional glossary.

- **Say** "I'm feeling sad right now because I miss Grandma, so I'm going to spend some time baking and listening to music because that makes me feel a little happier."

- **Say** "I can feel myself getting angry inside my body, so I'm taking some deep breaths while I go for a walk to calm myself down."

This lets our kids know that we all have permission to feel and the power to positively cope with negative emotions in ways that make us feel better. We can even tell them we're not "failing for feeling," as emotional development expert Alyssa Blask Campbell said on my podcast.[17] We all feel—including parents! Here are some other ways to provide the language our kids need to describe the feelings that are troubling them.

🗩 *Scripts in a Pinch*

- **Situation:** Your child's best friend moved away, and your child is crying. This friend won't be able to come to your child's birthday party and/or they won't be in class together next year.
  - **Script:** "It's okay to feel **sad** when your friend moves away. [Child's name] was a very good friend to you, and you feel so **disappointed** that your friend won't be at your birthday party or in your classroom next school year. These kinds of feelings **hurt**. I'm here for you whenever you need me!"

- **Situation:** Your child is yelling, "I hate you!" or "You're a bad parent!" or "You're a poopy head!" in the supermarket because you wouldn't buy them the cereal they wanted.
  - **Script:** "You are clearly very **angry** with me! You wanted that cereal very badly, and you are **furious** that I am saying no to your request.

It's okay to feel **frustrated,** but I don't like being called names, and when you yell, it's hard to hear what you're trying to tell me. I'm right here if you want to talk more about it calmly and pick out a cereal from this area."

- **Situation:** Your child is hiding behind you when meeting the new teacher and pulls you toward the hallway. Your child says, "I want to leave and go home. I hate it here."
  - ○ **Script:** "I'm getting the idea that you feel **nervous** about being here and meeting your new teacher. What's going on? Are you **worried** about something? You can tell me how you feel!"

ARE YOU AN EMOTION SUPPRESSOR OR EMOTION EXPRESSER?

Be sure to declare your home (or classroom or sports field) a safe place to feel. Ask yourself these questions:

- **Do I** show an awareness of my child's emotions, whether positive or negative?
- **Do I** label and share my feelings with my children in age-appropriate ways so they can see how to handle them in healthy ways?
- **Do I** use my child's emotional expression as an opportunity to connect and teach or discourage and punish?
- **Am I** an empathetic and supportive listener who validates my children's feelings?
- **Do I** actively label my children's emotions so they have the language to express themselves?
- **Do I** make myself available to assist my child to discuss, problem-solve, and cope with a frustrating situation in an age-appropriate, positive way?
- **Do I** show my child that I feel a range of emotions, positive and negative, and I am able to express them in healthy ways?

Quick Tip

WIG-ing

Psychologist and communication expert Eran Magen, PhD, developed an ingenious way to reflect our children's feelings and show them that we're listening and working to understand their tough emotions. It's summed up in the acronym WIG (short for "what I got"),[18] as in, "What I got from what you said is that you are really upset that Morgan told Taylor your secret."

As Ned Johnson, coauthor of *What Do You Say*, explained on my podcast, WIG-ing can

- show our children that we "get them," which is the single most important way to calm hard emotions and make sure someone feels heard.
- stop us from jumping into problem-solving, blaming, and advice giving. Instead, WIG-ing gives us time to "count to ten in our heads" before moving into action.[19]

Big Feeling: Anger

I remember when my then-eight-year-old son picked up my daughter's protractor, which she had borrowed from one of her beloved fourth-grade teachers for her math assignment. He just wanted to look at it but also, with the telling smirk of a little brother, wanted to bother his sister—you know, just a little bit. While my daughter barked, "Don't touch it," called her brother "*so* annoying," and chased him through the kitchen, my son impulsively flicked the flimsy piece of plastic onto the ground, where it broke it into four jagged pieces.

The result wasn't intentional, and he bellowed in his defense, "I didn't know it would *break!*" My daughter, red-faced and furious, yelled, pointed, and cried at the injustice. She swore she'd never, *ever* talk to him again.

Perhaps you might call me delusional, but I thought (fantasized?) that by the time my kids were in upper elementary school, it would be pretty much smooth sailing for a while, but feelings don't take a hiatus. Anger doesn't evaporate as children get older. However, starting when they're young, we can teach children to cope with anger in ways that allow them to express it, manage it, and deal with it when it gets out of control.

What makes children escalate or melt down?[20]

- **Unmet needs:** They're thirsty, but they forgot to take their water bottle to the park.
- **Unmet expectations:** They thought they were going to spend the afternoon playing with friends, but you need to take them to the dentist.
- **Cognitive inflexibility:** They want to wear their favorite sweatshirt to school, but it's wet and in the wash. They insist that no other sweatshirt will do.
- **Inattention:** You have a big deadline that has to be met, and you're unable to play with them at that moment.
- **Impulsivity:** They take their little sister's new stuffed animal. She screams and hits them, so they shove her.
- **Fatigue:** They stayed up late last night and woke up early this morning. Even brushing their teeth is a hassle.
- **Hunger or poor nutrition:** They skipped breakfast and picked at their lunch, and now it's almost 2:00 p.m., and they're *hangry*.
- **Traumatic life experiences:** They've just been through something upsetting and/or hurtful, such as a messy divorce, an abusive home situation, or the loss of a loved one.

These underlying causes can frame meltdowns and help us both understand the triggers and address them.

Quick Tip

Eye Level Tantrum Taming

It's not unusual for a young child to have as many as nine tantrums per week, according to Denis Sukhodolsky, a clinical psychologist at Yale Child Study Center.[21] That entails fits of crying, kicking, stomping, hitting, and pushing for five to ten minutes.

It's normal to get frustrated with your children in these moments, bark orders, and make yourself sound and appear "large and in charge." But this can backfire by escalating the very behaviors you are trying to squelch. Instead of derailing your child further with an intimidating presence or loud voice, use eye level empathy and quiet understanding:

1. Crouch or sit down to get to eye level.

2. Take some deep breaths to help encourage coregulation.

3. Validate all feelings while confirming that you understand the situation. Say softly, "I can see you're upset. You wanted to pick the movie tonight, but it's your sister's turn. You want it to be your turn. You're clearly very frustrated."

As author L. R. Knost says, "When little people are overwhelmed by big emotions, it's our job to share our calm, not join their chaos."[22]

When Your Children Feel Angry

Anger gets expressed in many ways. Sometimes it's quiet and brooding, and other times it can be loud, in your face, or even coupled with unsafe or unkind behaviors. When anger brings potentially dangerous or emotionally harmful actions with it, follow the **CARES** formula.

CONFIRM AND COMFORT

- **What to do:** When children are angry, validate their feelings. This helps to calm people down, as they feel seen, heard, and understood. You can offer a hug or simply be a calming presence.
- **What to say:**
  - "It's okay to feel angry. It's hard when your brother comes into your room without knocking and you want your privacy. I'm here to listen."
  - "How frustrating! You and your friend planned to play after school today, and now she's unavailable. I get why you feel angry. That stinks!"

ASSERT

- **What to do:** In a recent podcast interview, Deena Margolin, LMFT, and parent coach Kristin Gallant—the creators of the company and curriculum Big Little Feelings—talked about "okaying the feeling" but also upholding the boundaries (or bumpers, as they call them) of kindness and safety consistently and unwaveringly.[23]
- **What to say:**
  - "While it's normal to feel many different emotions, it's not all right to act on those feelings in a mean, unfair, or unsafe way."
  - "It's okay to be mad at your brother, but it's not okay to use angry hands to hit or hurt." (Or, as Margolin and Gallant structure the communication, "I can't let you hit him.")

REMIND AND RESULT

- **What to do:** Use natural or related consequences rather than unwarranted or unrelated punishment to teach. It's important to keep others safe and unharmed while we help our children cope with intense emotions.
- **What to say:**
  - "We can't throw sand at our friends, even if we're angry [reminder], so we'll need to leave the sandbox to calm our body and keep our friends safe [result]."

○ You can also remind your child, "Remember, when you get angry, you can take three deep breaths, pound your Play-Doh, or listen to the music you put aside for this on your iPad."

EXPLAIN AND EMPATHIZE

- **What to do:** Later, when your child is calm, willing, and able to talk, link the natural or related result to what happened (or could have happened).
- **What to say:**
  ○ "We needed to leave the sandbox to calm our body because throwing sand can hurt someone's eyes."
  ○ "We needed to put the game away because hitting is unsafe and hurtful. It can be frustrating when you're playing a game and your little brother isn't sticking to the rules." (This can also be used to convey different perspectives: "Remember when you threw sand at Olivia because you were feeling angry? What could have happened to her eyes? What is a safe action to take next time you're feeling angry?")

SCHEDULE

- **What to do:** Remember to try again! Kids learn how to cope with anger by practicing. Schedule another opportunity for your children to regulate their emotions in real time.
- **What to say:**
  ○ "We can try playing with this toy again after dinner."
  ○ "We can come back to the park tomorrow and try again."

While our knee-jerk reaction may be to punish unsafe or unfair behaviors in the moment, using the **CARES** format can help build connection, create understanding, and relay learning over time.

The format is also helpful when our own anger gets the best of us:

- "It's okay that I felt angry when your brother wasn't following directions before school." (**Confirm/Comfort**)
- "It isn't okay that I screamed at him." (**Assert**).
- "Saying mean words in that tone makes people feel small and sad. I needed to leave the room so I could cool my temper, wash my face, and take a few deep breaths. Next time, I'll try to do that." (**Remind/Result**)
- "It's important that I apologize to you now because yelling is not a kind way to communicate my feelings to others—even when I get angry and when I'm worried we'll be late. I imagine that my loud voice scared you too, so I want to say 'I'm sorry.'" (**Explain/Empathize**).
- "Next time I start feeling frustrated, I'll give myself a big hug and tell myself, 'It's not an emergency. I'm okay,' so I have a better chance of keeping my temper in check. Let's come up with a plan to leave for school a little earlier tomorrow so we can get in the car without all the yelling and have a pleasant ride. We can even have a dance party in the car!" (**Schedule**)

The **CARES** formula keeps empathy for ourselves and others at the forefront while also providing the opportunity for a new understanding. It allows us to model that (1) it's okay to make mistakes, (2) we need to acknowledge how our actions impact others, and (3) we can give all of us some grace to try again without a penalty. Each one of us is learning and growing each day.

Quick Tip

Don't Ride the Emergency Brake

Here's the strange truth: Yelling often works. It stops our children in their tracks and sometimes even scares them right out of a tantrum. "Yelling is like pulling the emergency brake on the attention system," Dr. Dehra Harris said during a presentation on neuroscience for Systems Success Mastermind, a consultant group founded by my husband, Jason, for after-school activity center owners. "But just like driving your car on the emergency brake, parenting on the emergency brake just wears everything out." If used over and over, this strategy no longer works. After all, it's only designed to be used in a true emergency—it's not for everyday use!

Anger Management for Kids

The key to defusing angry outbursts in the moment is to help children decide what to do *in advance*—before intense emotions are triggered. What follows are techniques children can employ to help ease their bodies and brains when big feelings arise.

- **Brain breaks:** Remember the stress gate that was closing off the thinking brain? "On average," according to Dr. Dehra Harris, "if you remove a child from a triggering situation, it takes around twenty minutes to reopen the thinking part of the brain."[24] We call that period a "brain break." While time-outs can feel like a punishment (as they are framed as removing the child due to "bad behavior"), brain breaks can be framed as self-care when in a heightened emotional state. During a brain break, children can get their emotional energy out and get back to a state of calm. They might take out their "mad box" (see next bullet) or enlist other coping mechanisms provided in this chapter.

- **Mad box:** Imagine having a calm-down kit with child-approved, prese-lected items that can help your child cope with anger in a productive, safe way. When I interviewed Wendy Young and Dr. Lynne Kenney, coauthors of the book *Bloom: 50 Things to Say, Think and Do with Anxious, Angry and Over-the-Top Kids*, we discussed using a "mad box" that allows your child to have an always-ready basket of coping mechanisms to get their "angries" out.[25] What might be in your child's mad box? You could try Play-Doh, calming music on an MP3 player, a favorite book, a soft blanket, crayons and paper, a writing journal, a joke book, a stress ball, and popping paper. Whatever will do the trick for your child.

- **"I feel":** When we're angry, our knee-jerk reaction is often to start our feedback with the word "you" ("You did this!"), which can be viewed as an attack. Flipping things around and starting off our reaction with "I feel" can completely change the experience. For example, instead of "you barged into my room—how dare you!" we can teach our children to use "I feel angry when you walk into my room without knocking first."

- **A simple note:** Sometimes our children aren't ready to say anything out loud to the person they are angry with in that moment. Teach your children to write their "I feel" statement on a piece of paper and slip it under the other person's door! As Joanna Faber and Julie King, authors of *How to Talk When Kids Won't Listen* and *How to Talk So Little Kids Will Listen*, told me, the good thing about writing things down is that "notes don't get louder."[26]

- **A bug and a wish:** To make the "I feel" concept memorable for young children, child and adolescent therapist and founder of Kidlutions Wendy Young, LMSW, created "a bug and a wish," which she talked about on my podcast: "It **bugs** me when you knock over my blocks, and I **wish** you would stop." I've tried this with my own kids—it works! Not only are you helping your children say what's bothering them, but you're giving them the tools to express what they want done differently. You are helping them convey information *and* set limits.

After the Storm

Once the tantrum dust has settled and calm has been restored, talk to your child about what happened in order to prepare him or her for the next time—and you *know* there will be a next time! Consider it shifting the starting point so they can move forward and think through the emotion with more insight, using these strategies that you practice:

- **Ask powerful questions:** Celeste Headlee, author of *We Need to Talk: How to Have Conversations That Matter*, told me on my podcast, "Don't forget how powerful questions are… Your best tool to get your kids to talk to you is a well-designed question…a simple, direct question starting with who, what, where, when, why or how."[27] If your child yelled, pushed, bit, or threw a tantrum, help them to home in on what happened before the proverbial volcano erupted. Ask these questions:
  - "What happened right before you got angry?"
  - "What did you see? Hear? Feel? Think?"
  - "How did you feel inside your body?"
  - "What is your anger trying to tell you?"

  Remember the story in the beginning of the chapter? My six-year-old son shoved another boy who took his ball during recess. Using these prompts, my son was able to tell me, "He took my ball. I saw him take it! He laughed at me. I felt angry. I was thinking, 'Give it back! You're mean! I don't like you!'" While it may take several minutes to get a full understanding of what happened, once you both recognize the triggers, you can help your child gain useful coping skills to manage the anger properly.

- **Anger Mountain:** Angry outbursts tend to have a ramp up (escalation), a peak (crisis), and a decline (recovery and cool-down). Dr. Lynne Kenney calls this "Anger Mountain."[28] You can sketch out a line-drawing of a mountain so that they have a concrete illustration of what's happening with their anger. Using this visual cue, you and your child can probe 1) what they thought (point to the bottom of the mountain and glide your finger going upwards), 2) what they felt and what made them feel that way (glide your finger further up the mountain), 3) what happened as they escalated (point to the upper part of the mountain), and 4) what they did to calm down (glide your finger down the mountain on the other side). By breaking down the process, you can help your child make amendments to any area where they struggled, provide additional support, or put strategies in place for next time that may work better. They can even learn how to bypass the peak by employing calming methods before "flipping their lid."

- **Where in my body do I feel my anger?** Big feelings are personal, and we all experience them differently. Anger can feel like a knotted stomach, a fast-beating heart, sweaty palms, clenched fists, a tight jaw, tense shoulders, a hot face, quickened breathing, or even a headache or dizziness. These physical feelings can then become our own personal warning signs that we're heading up Anger Mountain. If we teach our children to pay attention to these kinds of physiological indicators, they can learn to employ a coping technique that bypasses the peak and provides them with a "shortcut" to the decline of the mountain. You might say, "You know how you get a tickle in your throat before you get sick? It's a little clue that tells you to slow down, get more sleep, and maybe load up on some vitamin C! Well, you also get a clue before you get angry. You told me that your face gets hot and your belly gets tight when you're angry—those are your personal clues! As soon as you feel them, you can take some deep breaths, go to your mad box, or come over and get a hug from me to help you calm your body and tell your brain that you're okay."

Truth Bomb!

Other big feelings such as sadness, vulnerability, and loneliness often present as anger, which is known as an "iceberg emotion" because you often only see a small amount of what's happening "above the surface." The "Anger Iceberg," coined by Julie and John Gottman of the Gottman Institute,[29] can be a visual tool to help kids name their hidden emotions so they can process them in a healthy way. It may be helpful, in a quiet moment, to ask your child, "What are you really feeling underneath all the anger?" Then name it: "Sometimes when I feel left out and sad, it comes out as anger for me too."

Big Feeling: Sadness

Children may be sad for many reasons. Losing a baseball game. Losing their dog. Losing their beloved grandpa to cancer. Sometimes sadness looks like frowns and tears, but other times the signs are more covert—hidden behind blank stares or even fake smiles. Sadness can feel heavy, lonely, numb, or even infuriating.

While society may call sadness a "negative emotion," it's normal and healthy. It can be very powerful to give your children permission to be sad in a world where happiness is highlighted, coveted, posted, and celebrated. They need to know, "Nobody can be happy all the time. Sadness is part of being human. Just like you get sad sometimes, so do I. So does your sister, your brother, your uncle—even pets get sad sometimes too! It's okay to be sad."

Sadness offers us some key benefits:

- **It provides a catharsis by getting our internal pain out of our physical bodies.** Emotional distress can cause headaches, stomachaches, muscle soreness, and even addiction.[30] Studies show that by getting sadness out, such as through crying, we can release stress and tension, regulate our moods, and regain a sense of emotional balance.[31]

- **It alerts us that something feels wrong, missing, or meaningful.** Our sadness can lead us to determine that a loss or a missed person, opportunity, or situation might be more important to us than we initially realized. This realization can be the impetus for us to correct the problem. The key is to consider: What is this feeling trying to tell me?

- **It allows us to adjust, get help, or cope with a challenge.** Sadness, in the movie *Inside Out*, says wisely, "Crying helps me slow down and obsess over the weight of life's problems." By paying attention to this feeling, sadness teaches us that we can employ techniques that help us feel better and deal with the challenges ahead.

- **It connects us with others in a time of need.** Studies show that sadness has the power to rally support from those around us and that expressions of sadness, like crying, elicit care and comfort for the one in need.[32] It is important to note, however, that studies also suggest that girls, especially once they get into middle school, tend to cry more and seek more help when sad than boys do. Boys also receive less encouragement and more disapproval in response to outward expressions of sadness than girls (see box).

- **It shows us that we can handle hard emotions.** Sadness can be a tough, uncomfortable emotion, but by experiencing how it feels when it settles in, noticing when it dissipates, and realizing that we can employ techniques to help us feel better, we grow and mature as emotionally aware individuals.

When children understand that sadness isn't a feeling that must be immediately overturned to get back to happiness, they can learn to pay attention to the emotion, in both themselves and others, and also learn that they have the power to sit with the discomfort, address it, and move through it. As Dr. Susan David, author of *Emotional Agility*, advises parents to say and model for their children, "This is what sadness feels like. This is what it feels like after it passes. This is what I did that helped it pass."[33] By honoring sadness, we are less likely to get stuck in it.

Truth Bomb!

Boys Cry

For a long time, our culture has provided a toxic narrative that "boys don't cry" and that expressing emotions is "soft," "weak," "girly," or "feminine." These kinds of attributes have created the "Man Box," or the "Act Like a Man Box,"[34] as authors Paul Kivel and Rosalind Wiseman call it—a collection of rigid rules (i.e., strong, confident, moneyed, tall, gets girls, always relaxed, independent) that tell us what "a real man" does, is, or must pretend to be.

According to "The Man Box," a study which surveyed men in the United States, United Kingdom, and Mexico between the ages of eighteen and thirty, a whopping 72 percent said they have been told "a real man behaves a certain way"; 59 percent agree with the statement that guys should act strong, even if they feel scared or nervous inside, and 40 percent agree that "men should figure out their personal problems on their own without asking others for help."[35]

But here's the kicker: Michael Reichert, the author of *How to Raise a Boy*, says this message of toxic masculinity is extremely harmful to boys and men. "Boys and men who subscribe to the man box are the ones most likely to be depressed and anxious, harass others, bully, be bullied, and feel suicidal," he said. "If you are hiding who you are in the man box, and you are unable to express yourself, you feel very alone."[36]

The only way to change the narrative and adjust the outcome for boys is to alter the way we educate them about what it means to be a strong boy and a real man. We must tell them:

- "It's okay to cry."
- "It's normal and healthy to feel sad or scared or any other emotion."
- "It's okay to show people how you feel. I sometimes feel sad or scared, and it helps to talk about it." (Especially coming from men in the boy's life.)

Validating Sadness

A child's sadness can be as uncomfortable for the parent as it is for the child. Therefore, to move their child to a more comfortable state, parents may attempt to "lessen" children's sad emotions, inadvertently invalidating them. Instead, we must use compassionate language so we can send our children these messages:

- Their upsetting feelings are valid and matter.
- They deserve to be around others who are supportive, patient, and kind while they are coping with uncomfortable emotions.
- They can be compassionate and patient with themselves as they move through their sad emotions in whatever timeline feels right for them.
- They gain the ability to sit with their sadness and the choice to use available strategies to help the feelings pass when they're ready.

Avoid	Don't Say	Say This Instead
Minimizing/ Invalidating	• "It's not a big deal." • "This won't matter later on in life."	• "I hear you are really disappointed about what happened."
Dismissing	• "I've been through that too. It works out fine. Move on." • "It's all in your head."	• "You sound really disappointed. Can you tell me more about what's upsetting you?" • "I want to understand."
Condescending	• "You think you have problems? Just wait until you're older!"	• "This feels really big for you. Would you like me to sit with you, or would you prefer to be alone?"
Contradicting	• "You don't really feel that way!" • "You're fine." • "It's not that bad."	• "It's normal to feel upset by that."
Toxic Positivity	• "Look at the bright side!" • "Just be our happy kid!" • "Cheer up!"	• "Take all the time you need. There's no need to rush through your feelings."
Ignoring	• "No, you actually have a lot of [friends, good grades, etc.]." • "Let's talk about happy things instead."	• "I'm here to listen." • "Let me see if I'm hearing you correctly. You are feeling really down because..."

Avoid	Don't Say	Say This Instead
Fixing	• "Here's what I think you should do."	• "Would you like me to simply listen, or are you hoping for some advice?"
Exacerbating	• "I warned you not to do that!"	• "It's so hard when things don't go the way you hoped."
Sarcasm	• "Oh, boo-hoo! Clearly you have the biggest problem of them all!"	• "I care about you. Is there anything I can do to help?" • "You're not alone in this. If you want to talk, I'm here."
Shaming	• "Big kids/boys don't cry." • "Don't be a crybaby." • "You're too sensitive." • "What's wrong with you?!"	• "Let it out." • "Crying is normal and healthy." • "Many people in your situation would feel just as you do." • "You are not weak or defective."
Blaming	• "It's your fault that you feel this way."	• "You never intended this to happen. You feel so hurt because things turned out this way."

Remember, even if you don't agree with your children, their interpretation of the circumstances, or how they handled the situation they were in, you can still be kind, encouraging, and supportive as they cope with sadness, disappointment, and distress.

🏠 In My Home

When my daughter was younger, she was so inspired by our discussion of what we were grateful for during our Thanksgiving holiday that she wanted to do it year-round.

And we did.

The activity wound up morphing into "Roses and Thorns." At the end of each day, we would have conversations about our "roses" (what went well during the day). These might include instances that made us smile, the kind people in our lives, the pets we adore, or the people we helped. We also talked about our "thorns" (things that might have been a bummer), such as striking out during the ball game, loneliness, or witnessing something sad.

By doing so, we provide a distinct time to celebrate the good...and acknowledge the bad. We show our children that there are always negatives and positives in life—and that's okay.

Is It Childhood Depression?

As we go through the ups and downs of life, experiencing periods of sadness is completely normal. However, some children and teens develop depression, a serious clinical mood disorder that is characterized by pervasive feelings of hopelessness, powerlessness, fatigue, irritability, and loneliness. According to a recent *New York Times* article, children as young as eight years old are being admitted to emergency rooms for undiagnosed mental health conditions such as depression and thoughts (or attempts) of suicide—especially after stressful events like the death of a loved one, parental divorce, and unpredictable times, such as a pandemic.[37]

It's important to know the difference between sadness and depression. Depression can look different for different people. Katie Hurley, LCSW, author of *The Depression Workbook for Teens*, says, "Many people think depression means crying all the time, but actually it's more like a combination of anger, loneliness, helplessness, and exhaustion. Depression is tricky because it wears a lot of disguises."[38]

LOOK FOR THE SIGNS

- **Would I characterize what my child is going through as uncomfortable or as unsafe/unhealthy?** Uncomfortable emotions, problems, and situations are part of life. However, once something becomes unsafe or unhealthy, it can put your child in danger.
- **Are these emotions temporary and transitory, or do they seem more pervasive and long-lasting?** Typical feelings come and go, responding to distraction and comfort. Depression is persistent. Your child can't just "snap out of it."
- **Are my child's moods getting in the way of normal life?** Are you seeing marked negative changes in eating (too much or too little), sleeping (too much or too little), relationships (dropping key friendships), favorite activities (avoiding involvement), or personality (incredibly irritable, forlorn, or full of rage)? If so, these may be indicators that there's a larger problem.

While, as parents and caregivers, we may not always know if our children are truly depressed by looking at them, trust your gut. You know your child best! If the voice inside your head is telling you that something isn't right, it's better to ask a professional to check your child out than to leave it to chance.

🗩 *Scripts in a Pinch*

My Child Might Be Depressed

- **Approach and broach:** "I've noticed you don't seem quite yourself lately."
- **Care and concern:** "I care about you and want you to know I am here for you. What would be most helpful to you right now? There's no issue too big for us to work through together."
- **Divulge the evidence:** "I've also noticed you haven't been eating or seeing any of your friends, and you've been sleeping a whole lot more than usual."

- **Empathize:** "Things have been really tough on you lately, and it makes sense that you've been feeling down. I wish I could take this pain away from you!"
- **Focus on getting help:** "Do you feel like you could use some help to get through this difficult time?" Or "Many people benefit from getting help when they're coping with big feelings. You deserve to have that help too. I'll be by your side every step of the way."
- **Get the help you need:** Depression doesn't resolve itself on its own. See a professional to assess the situation and provide next steps. If your child is attending school, get school counselors involved, as they are a wealth of information and can offer additional support to your child during the school day.

Suicide

Nearly eight hundred thousand people die by suicide in the world each year, which is roughly one death every forty seconds.[39] Suicide is the second leading cause of death in the world for those aged fifteen to twenty-four years. These are the statistics—but when it comes to suicide and talking to kids, the statistics don't give us the words, the feelings, the weight of the loss, the answers. Given that this is such an emotionally charged and scary topic, many parents and educators worry that discussing it with their kids might be doing more harm than good—giving life to ideas that might be lying dormant in their child's mind.

But does asking directly about suicide put the idea inside a person's head? The research says absolutely not. According to a classic 2005 study by Madelyn Gould, PhD, MPH, high-risk students (those who showed signs of depression, had substance-use issues, or who attempted suicide previously) did not show more distress when asked about suicide—in fact, they appeared less distressed after talking about it.[40]

One big caveat: if you are divulging that someone has died by suicide, steer clear of talking about the details. Discussing method has been linked to copycat tragedies in high-risk populations, according to Dr. Dan Reidenberg, executive director of Suicide Awareness Voices of Education (SAVE) and managing director of the National Council for Suicide Prevention. "Whether you are talking about social media, traditional news media, blogging, podcasts, billboards, radio, or TV ads, it is *how* you talk about suicide, not *if* you talk about it. When we communicate about suicide safely, it does not harm someone or put someone at greater risk. However, when we communicate about suicide in an unsafe way (mode, words, images, and even dose) there can be negative effects from it."[41]

Quick Tip

Safe Discussion of Suicide

1. **Honor the individual relationship:** Jonathan Singer, PhD, LCSW, who specializes in suicide prevention and intervention, reminds us that "people can share the same loss but have a totally different experience of it."[42]

2. **Acknowledge the different ways of grieving:** Everybody grieves in different ways. Sometimes it can be intense and obvious, while other times it can be delayed and covert. There is no wrong way to grieve.

3. **Establish that children are not alone:** Dr. Reidenberg advises that this message be said outright and more than once to those who are hearing about and coping with the news of a suicide. You might say, "We need to have a tough conversation, and before we have it, I just want you to know that we are going to be here for you, and we are going to help you through it."

4. **Provide the facts clearly and gently:** To diminish the chance of contagion, leave out the means and the details while still

being clear and compassionate. Dr. Reidenberg suggests: "We learned today [name] died. We don't know all the reasons or the circumstances, but we know she's gone. This is really hard. We can't imagine the pain you must feel and how difficult it is for you to hear this. We are here for you."

5. **Have what Dr. Singer calls a "post-vention" follow-up:** He says that checking in with young people after a death by suicide can be an "intervention as a form of prevention." You might say, "We wanted to check in with you to see how you're feeling. Are you struggling with the news? Would you like to speak to me or someone else about it? We want you to know we're here for you, now and in the future. There is no rush. Take all the time you need."

🚩 Scripts in a Pinch

My Child May Be Thinking about Suicide

When children are talking about suicide, expressing hopelessness, or alluding to wanting to die, we must talk with them right away. Dr. Singer advises that we do the following:

- **Learn what is distressing to them:** "You've been through so much this year. Nobody should have to go through that."
- **Offer help or to get them the support they need:** "There are people out there who can help. I know it doesn't seem possible, but there are."
- **Actively listen"** "I want to understand what you are going through."
- **Be there to ensure they get the help they need:** "Together, we can find the right people to help you."

Listening and broaching this topic builds trust and reiterates that you are someone who can take on the tough conversations when your child is in need. As Dr. Singer says, "Having a kid feel heard and validated is, in and of itself, protective against suicide."

Big Feeling: Fear

Everyone feels fear and anxiety at times. Even daredevils, soldiers, and first responders. Fear is a normal response to scary or dangerous stimuli.

Like sadness, fear can alert us to moments when we should take caution or action to ensure our safety. When a loud sound is heard from overhead, fear might cause us to look up or duck at a moment's notice. If we see a car speeding down the road just as we are about to cross, fear tells us to freeze or step back. As children are getting used to the world around them and making sense of confusing or frightening things they see, hear, or experience, we can help in these ways

- **Praise fear for its helpfulness:** Say, "I saw the little dog next door escape from the backyard, so I scooped him up right before he ran into the street! The fear of Charlie getting run over by a car really made me move fast and be brave. Thank goodness for fear! Isn't it amazing how fear can be helpful?" or "When you stayed very still after that wasp landed on your shirt, that was your fear keeping you safe!"

- **Normalize fear:** Say, "Fear is a normal emotion." Or "Mom/Dad/ Grammie/Grandpa get scared too sometimes." Or say, "When I get scared, I feel it on the back of my neck and in my tummy. Where do you feel it?"

- **Share your own childhood fears:** Say, "Did you know that when Daddy was your age, he was scared of the dark too?" Or "Want to hear the story of my first day of first grade? I was so scared that I tried to hide behind your grandpa's leg! Would you like to hear what Grandpa did to help me?"

- **Change the goal:** Say, "I know this is scary for you, but I truly feel confident and certain that you can do hard things. Even though you *feel* scared, you can *be* brave. I've seen you do it a hundred times before, like when you rode the bus on the first day of school and started to ride a bike without training wheels. You are fully capable."

- **Offer support:** Say, "Take the first step when you're ready. I am here to support you and love you through it as you go."

Fears ebb and flow, change and grow, over time. However, there are some common fears that many children experience throughout their childhood.

Age	Common Fears
Babies and toddlers	Loud noises (flushing toilets, thunderstorms, slammed doors, shouting), separating from key caregivers, stranger anxiety.
Preschoolers and young school-age children	Loud noises (thunderstorms, big/loud dogs, fireworks, popping balloons), people in costume, magic/imaginary creatures (monsters under the bed, ghosts in the closet, aliens), noises in the night, separating from key caregivers, the dark, nightmares, closed spaces, strangers and "bad people," shots/blood.
Older school-age children	Bodily injuries, physical danger, illness, enclosed spaces, unknown/loud sounds, squeaky doors/floors at night or when home alone, something bad happening to the people they love, something bad happening to them, school shootings, natural hazards, bullies, bugs.
Teens	Being rejected by peers, what peers think of them, something bad happening to them or people they care about, doing poorly in school, not making the team, getting into big trouble at home/school, natural disasters, school shootings, machinery (i.e., guns and other weapons), bullies, death/injury.

While there are many common fears that kids experience throughout childhood, fear looks different in each child. According to Dr. Eli Lebowitz, author of *Breaking Free of Child Anxiety and OCD* and founder of Yale University's SPACE program (Supportive Parenting for Anxious Childhood Emotions), while some children will go in the "flight direction" of fear, other children will go to the "fight side" and exhibit aggression, anger, irritability, temper tantrums, and rigidity.[43] Lebowitz reminds us that we need to "broaden our view of what an anxious child looks like," and by doing so, we can get the help children need when fear becomes overwhelming.

Is It Fear or Something Else?

Fear, anxiety, and phobias are closely related, but they are not the same. In an interview, Dr. Dawn Huebner, author of *What to Do When You Worry Too Much* and *Outsmarting Worry*, admits that most people use the terms interchangeably, so the definitions can get muddied.[44] However, it's useful to untangle these words so we can decipher what is healthy, normal functioning versus what needs to be addressed using coping mechanisms or clinical assistance.

- **Fear:** A natural and desirable response to a real and present danger. "When used correctly," Huebner says, "fear signifies that there is an imminent threat."
- **Anxiety:** Discomfort and nervousness about something that might happen. It's a reaction to a perceived threat rather than an actual one. Anxiety is fueled by what-if thinking that can trigger a fear response or "false alarm" even though the danger is not actually present.
- **Phobia:** A strong specific fear of an object or situation that leads to avoidance and severe stress and ultimately gets in the way of healthy or normal functioning.[45] Huebner says that "phobias are extreme and irrational; they are always out of proportion to the actual danger posed by the object of the phobia." A fear becomes a phobia when you change your lifestyle to accommodate that fear.

FEAR

- **Situation**: The child throws a ball into a bees' nest at the park, and the bees get mad. They're flying toward the child. The child thinks, "I've got to get out of here! I'm so scared!"
- **What to say:** "You were absolutely right to listen to your body and brain and move away from the angry bees before they stung you. Those bees were not happy to have their hive disturbed. Usually, bees keep to themselves and don't bother anyone—but when their hive is hit by an incoming ball, they get defensive and want to protect it."

ANXIETY

- **Situation:** The child wonders, "What if there's a bee at the park?" Perhaps your child saw a bee around the swings the last time your family visited the park. Your child tells you, "My heart pounds really fast when I'm near a bee. It might sting me. Maybe we should go to a different park?"
- **What to say:** "I get that bees can make you feel nervous. When bees are attacked or their hive is disturbed, they can get defensive and sting—like that time when you threw a ball and the hive got hit. That was scary for you, so now your body sounds an alarm when you go back to that park—even if there's not really any danger. After all, bees don't want to sting you. They have better things to do! We also might not see any bees at the park today. If we do see a bee, we can take a deep breath to tell our bodies, 'It's not an emergency. I'm okay,' and walk away."

PHOBIA

- **Situation:** You notice that every time your child sees a bee or even thinks about bees, they're immediately filled with terror. Your child might think, "I won't join my friends to play at the park. There might be bees, and bees sting! That would be horrible! It will hurt so much." They might say, "I'm not going. Bees are scary. I'll just stay inside."
- **What to say:** "It's scary for you to think about bees. Every time you think you might see a bee, your heart starts to pound, and you think about getting stung, and then you want to stay inside. It's like your brain and body are telling you there's a terrible danger, but the chance of being stung is tiny, and even if you do get stung, you'll be okay. What your body is doing is called a false alarm: when you feel like you're in danger but you're not. False alarms about bees are making you miss out on playing with your friends, and that's sad. Let's do something about this. Let's work on getting used to being outside—just a little bit at a time—so your fear doesn't get in the way of having fun."

Our children need to be well versed in how to recognize when anxiety and fear are taking hold, coping mechanisms that work for them, and steps that will help them conquer their anxiety and phobia. A skilled professional could be a wonderful partner to work with your child and family when anxiety and phobias interfere with living a healthy, happy life.

Anxious Thinking

Sometimes our children's brains (as well as our own!) can play tricks on them, telling them that things are worse than they really are. Negative thoughts become exaggerated, laced with blame, and increasingly judgmental. Ruminating on these "cognitive distortions" can make them seem more true and powerful. On the *How to Talk to Kids about Anything* podcast, mental strength expert and author Amy Morin discussed the need to change "blue thoughts" into "true thoughts" so that they showcase what is factual and realistic rather than what is irrational and inaccurate.[46] Here are some heavy-hitting "thinking traps" to discuss with your kids:

- **The Catastrophizer:** "If I don't get an A on this essay, I'm going to fail sixth grade!"
- **The Blamer:** "My dad forgets to remind me to put my homework in my bag."
- **The Fortune Teller:** "I'm going to get onstage, and everyone is going to laugh at me!"
- **The Overgeneralizer:** "I didn't make the team. I'm never going to make any team!"
- **The Labeler:** "I forgot your birthday—I'm the biggest idiot there is!" Or "I got the question wrong when I raised my hand in class. I'm so stupid."
- **The Black-and-White Thinker:** "Well, I already missed this assignment, so I might as well miss them all!"
- **The Judge and Jury:** "I didn't make the goal. I suck at hockey."
- **The Downer:** "I didn't get the part in the play. Nothing ever goes my way in life."

When you hear these, call them out. Ask your child, in a calm moment, "Is this a true thought or a blue thought?" (And eventually, as Morin points out, kids will be able to start asking themselves this question.) Then help them to change the negative thought to a more realistic one. For example: "I know you are disappointed that you didn't get the part in the play that you wanted. But is it accurate that 'nothing ever goes your way'?" Chances are this kind of question will prompt children to generate thoughts about positive friendships, successful accomplishments, and fruitful areas of their lives outside this one disappointment.

Exposure and Fear Ladders

I often tell my own kids that the only way to deal with their common fears is to do the things that scare them. Sometimes that means taking one daring jump off the diving board or willing themselves onto the school bus on the first day of school. Other times, it takes more patience and additional steps to conquer fears.

Dr. Andrea Umbach, a psychologist who specializes in anxiety and the author of *Conquer Your Fears & Phobias for Teens*, explained on my podcast, "We need to take baby steps with fear. Take one step closer, stay a little longer, tolerate the discomfort and the feelings we may have so that we can teach our brain and our body that it is not dangerous and that it's okay. That's the learning experience."[47]

One such way to do this is through exposure.[48] Creating a "fear ladder" can be a great visual way to examine the anxiety.[49]

Ask your child:

- "What is the end goal?"
- "What do you ultimately, in your heart of hearts, truly want to do?"
- "If fear weren't an issue for you, what would you do?"

Then work backward from there. For example, your child's goal might be "to go to my friend's house and play with his new puppy in the backyard." Then brainstorm some *steps* with your child, and organize them from easiest (Step 1) to hardest (Step 10):

STEP 10: RUN AND PLAY WITH MY FRIEND'S PUPPY IN MY FRIEND'S YARD.

STEP 9: LET MY FRIEND'S PUPPY LICK MY HAND AND FACE.

STEP 8: GIVE MY FRIEND'S PUPPY A TREAT IN MY FRIEND'S FENCED-IN YARD.

STEP 7: PET MY FRIEND'S PUPPY WHILE SHE'S NOT ON LEASH IN MY FRIEND'S HOUSE.

STEP 6: HOLD MY FRIEND'S SLEEPING PUPPY AFTER DINER WHEN SHE'S SUPER TIRED.

STEP 5: PET MY FRIEND'S PUPPY ON THE HEAD WHILE SHE'S BEING HELD ON THE SIDEWALK.

STEP 4: STAND ON THE SAME SIDE OF THE STREET AS MY FRIEND'S PUPPY WHILE SHE'S ON A LEASH.

STEP 3: WAVE TO MY FRIEND'S NEW PUPPY FROM ACROSS THE STREET.

STEP 2: WATCH VIDEOS OF DOGS ON SITES LIKE "THE DODO" OR THROUGH INSTAGRAM/TIKTOK INFLUENCERS SUCH AS TUCKER BUDZYN AND HAMMYANDOLIVIA.

STEP 1: LOOK AT PHOTOS OF DOGS, SUCH AS ON INSTAGRAM/TIKTOK'S JIFFPOM, ITSDOUGTHEPUG, TUNAMELTSMYHEART FEEDS.

Children are very concrete—so having a visual way to see the baby steps Dr. Umbach mentioned can help mark their progress toward conquering their fear. With each rung of the ladder, they pull themselves up toward their goal.

The key for parents or mentors is to remain calm and celebrate the small wins. Professor Eli Lebowitz, while on my podcast, encouraged parents to acknowledge the fear and "see the child's experience" ("I know this is feeling frightening for you right now…"). Then express your confidence in your child ("I know you can handle this feeling, so if you want to give it even a little bit of a try, I'm right there with you."). Stick by your child's side, as patiently as you can, as they conquer each step of the fear ladder. Of course, if your child's phobias are extreme, reach out to a medical professional to help you.

Knowledge Is Power: Reality Mantras

Remember when we were talking about the "emotional (amygdala) hijack" and "flipping our lid" in the beginning of the chapter? Help your child apply that knowledge to what's going on in their bodies when dealing with unproductive anxiety. Psychologist Karen Young, founder of the website Hey Sigmund and author of the children's book *Hey Warrior*, which is about finding your inner "brave," suggests we rewire the message that our children repeat in their brains.[50] They might tell themselves:

- "My brain is filling me with special body fuel to get me ready to fight or flee. I don't need to fight or flee, so it's building up."
- "The reason why I have a racing heart is not because something bad is about to happen (or I'm about to have a heart attack) but because my heart is pumping to get that fuel around my body."
- "The reason my legs and arms feel tight isn't because something bad is about to happen (or because I'm sick) but because my brain is making my arms ready in case I need to fight and my legs ready in case I need to flee."

🏠 *In My Home*

My seven-year-old daughter was getting ready for her very first night at camp. She was nervous, scared, excited, and anxious. Each night before bed, she would start a looping monologue. "I'm really scared about the sleepover... I'm going to miss you... What if I want to go home? What if I have to go to the bathroom? What if I'm scared?"

It's hard when we want our child to try new things but fear has taken hold and won't let go. So how can we help our children help themselves when trying constructive new things that excite but scare them?

- **Note the time:** If your child is extremely tired, this might not be the best time to have a serious conversation about fear. You can say, "I know you're nervous about [X], and I'm happy to talk about it with you, but right now, it's very late. How about we talk about it in the morning when your brain is fresh and you've had a good night's sleep?"

- **Help your child realize they are in the driver's seat:** I love what Elizabeth Gilbert said in her "welcoming speech prepared for fear": "Dearest Fear: I recognize...that you are part of this family...but still --your suggestions will never be followed. You're allowed to have a seat, and you're allowed to have a voice, but you are not allowed to have a vote... You're not allowed to touch the road maps... Dude, you're not even allowed to touch the radio. But above all else...you are absolutely forbidden to drive."

- [51]It's vital that our children feel a sense of ownership about their feelings and choices. I told my own daughter a rendition of this letter. "Fear can tag along, but it can't drive your bus!"

- **Ask, "What will make you feel more calm and less scared?":** When you ask this question, it allows your children to be proactive about what will help them rather than focus on the problems. Tallie decided that sleeping next to one of her counselors during the overnight would help. Was that possible? I told my daughter, "You can ask your counselor, Amanda, that question. I believe you can do it yourself." There's something empowering about saying the words yourself and hearing the answer with your own ears. When Tallie came home, she announced she had asked her question and that she would be sleeping next to Amanda.

- **Have your child write down their concerns—and voice them:** I had Tallie take out a piece of paper and write down her questions to ask at the overnight meeting the next day. The following afternoon, I got an email from her camp that said, "Tallie was so articulate at our meeting about the overnight tomorrow. She asked all of her questions!" Tallie left feeling knowledgeable about what to expect on her overnight.

- **Realize that preparation and problem-solving are part of the win:** While we want our children to face their fear and see the end of their journey, there are plenty of wins to celebrate along the way. For example, the process of facing your fear instead of simply saying "I won't do it" is a win! My daughter went from "I'm scared" to "I'll write down my concerns and ask for what I need to feel more calm and less scared." That's another win! Even if she didn't sleep over in the end, she had made progress.

- **Connect the wins to your child's character:** You can say, for example, "One thing I know about you now is that you have the courage to look fear in the face, ask questions, make sound decisions, and get out of your comfort zone. I hope you see that you can believe in yourself. You're courageous. Way to go!"

As it turns out, my daughter made it! I received an email from the person in charge that said, "You can be very proud of your daughter. She was a total superstar on the overnight. She was very respectful when we said it was time to turn out the lights. She had a blast swimming in the lake and was very excited about the ice cream bar! She did it!"

Soothing the Reactive Brain: Giving All Our Feelings a Boost

It's hard to see our children struggle with big feelings. We often want to offer something that will "turn that frown upside down" or settle that anxious stomach. But according to psychologist Dr. Susan David, author of *Emotional Agility*, the parent who manages a child's feeling states is doing the equivalent of "emotional helicoptering," rushing in to provide immediate relief, which can disrupt a child's ability to develop qualities like grit and resilience. Instead, she told the *New York Times*, when it comes to feelings, teach your child to feel them, show them, label them, and watch them go.[52]

By teaching kids to practice healthy coping strategies, we can show them how to employ specific techniques that work for them. According to Janine Halloran, MA, LMHC, who described the calming, physical, distracting, and processing coping categories discussed below on the *How to Talk to Kids about Anything* podcast, "Just like kids have different learning styles, they have different coping styles."[53] The key is to figure out which strategies work best for your children so they can employ them when needed.

CALMING TECHNIQUES

- These techniques soothe the nervous system and can be employed when your child is stressed, overwhelmed, frightened, or angry. They are to replace the very unhelpful statement "just calm down" (since, as the saying goes, never in the history of calming down has anyone calmed down by being told to calm down). Halloran, the author of *Coping Skills for Kids Workbook*, reminds us that when our children use calming techniques, it moves them from "fight or flight" to "rest and digest" so they can self-regulate.

- **Sample calming techniques**
  - Deep breathing
  - Meditating
  - Taking a nature walk
  - Imagining your favorite place
  - Taking a hot shower or bath
  - Tracing patterns with your finger
  - Running your hands through sand

- ○ Drinking a cup of tea
- ○ Mindfully eating a piece of dark chocolate
- **You might say:** "When our bodies feel angry or scared, our breath quickens, our hearts beat faster, and our muscles get tight. This is because, a long time ago, our bodies needed to get ready to fight the bear, flee the tiger, or hide from the lion! But we usually don't have to fight lions and tigers and bears, so when we get angry or scared, we can tell our brains and our bodies, 'It's okay, there's no bear here. I'm safe, just angry at my brother.' We send that message to our brains and our bodies by taking some nice deep breaths."

PHYSICAL TECHNIQUES

- Sometimes our kids just need to get the negative energy out of their bodies through movement, which can help busy the body and focus on kicking the ball into the goal rather than on their sister who won't share her new game. Exercise also reduces levels of the body's stress hormones, such as adrenaline and cortisol, and stimulates the production of mood elevators and natural painkillers in the brain called endorphins. Even engaging in small consistent movements like rocking, swaying, swinging, and bouncing on a ball can help settle your child's vestibular system, which studies suggest plays an important role in your children's well-being and emotion regulation. Find out what your child might like to do when triggered so they can turn to that preselected activity when interactions start to get heated.
- **Sample physical techniques**
  - ○ Gymnastics or hip-hop
  - ○ Running
  - ○ Jumping on the trampoline (or the bed!)
  - ○ Punching a pillow
  - ○ Popping Bubble Wrap
  - ○ Pounding Play-Doh

- ○ Squeezing a stress ball
- ○ Jumping rope
- ○ Taking a hike
- **You might say:** "I know you like to throw things when you get angry! While I can't let you throw the TV remote or hard toys, how about we have a barrel of Nerf balls for you to throw at a target when you get angry?" Or "When you get that nervous energy in your body before you leave for school on big test days like you had yesterday, how about we put on a fun fifteen-minute exercise video (go for a morning run, do a series of jumping jacks, push-ups, and squats) that we can do together before you leave?"

DISTRACTING TECHNIQUES

- Games and activities or taking care of someone or something can be a wonderful way of coping with big feelings. Distracting techniques can interrupt the anxiety spiral since, as Halloran put it on my podcast, "When you've already talked it all through, you don't want to start back at the beginning like the *If You Give a Mouse a Cookie* book!" In other words, we want to steer clear of feeding a rumination pattern. Distractions can take your child away just long enough to provide some perspective and give the body a chance to reset and calm down.
- **Sample distracting techniques**
- ○ Baking
- ○ Cleaning out the closets (one can dream!)
- ○ Writing a letter to a friend
- ○ Planning a birthday party
- ○ Writing a story
- ○ Doing a puzzle
- ○ Walking the dog
- ○ Doing some charity work
- ○ Helping an elderly neighbor

- **You might say:** "I'm so sorry you're feeling sad. How about we take out your favorite puzzle?" Or a simple question like, "Who do you think needs some help?" or "How do you think your love of reading might be a gift to someone else?" could kick off a conversation during a calm, nonconfrontational moment.

PROCESSING TECHNIQUES

- These strategies are designed to help your child work through their thoughts and feelings so they can make sense of them. They can also use these strategies to express their emotions in a safe way. Instead of distracting themselves, they use techniques like singing, drawing, or writing to identify and face their negative feelings and get them out of their bodies.
- **Sample processing techniques**
  - Talking out a problem with someone they trust
  - Singing an emotional song
  - Drawing a picture using fervent scribbles
  - Painting with colors that signify different feelings
  - Writing—perhaps a letter (that your child might never send) to a classmate who "made you feel this way" or even a creative writing prompt such as *If I had a robot that could do anything, I would program it to...*
- **You might say:** "Sometimes it can help us cope with our feelings when we talk them out. But if we don't want to do that right now, we can release those negative feelings by writing, drawing, or painting a picture. You might keep certain questions in mind, such as 'What upset me? What happened right before I yelled/pushed/hid? What do I wish happened instead? How did it make me feel?' and 'What do I want to happen next?' while processing these feelings using one of these techniques. When journaling or doing an art project to release your feelings, you don't have to make it perfect or pretty—it can be big and scribbly or small and curvy or whatever you feel inside. These are just strategies to get your emotions out of your body and onto the paper so you can feel better."

The key to success here is to investigate beforehand which technique is best for your child. Learning how to self-regulate in this way is knowledge that can be used throughout your child's lifetime.

The Big Idea about Big Feelings

Parents and caregivers are such important allies when it comes to helping kids manage big feelings. With time and patience, you can teach children to better regulate and deal with their feelings in healthy ways on their own through the following:

- **Acceptance:** "It's okay to feel your feelings," and "It's healthy to express your feelings."
- **Confidence:** "I know you can cope with these feelings."
- **Support:** "Here are some ways to cope with these feelings," and "I'm here if you need me."

There is no one-size-fits-all strategy to cope with and manage big feelings. Different strategies are not only for different children but for different moments. One day, a hug might do the trick, and the next, your child will respond to singing their favorite song. Plan for these moments so you can preview them and recognize them.

And remember, no feeling lasts forever.

✐ Talking Points

QUESTION	YOUR ANSWER
What messages do I want to send to my children about feeling and managing their emotions?	

QUESTION	YOUR ANSWER
When it comes to emotions, in general, how can I ensure that my children feel and know I am here to support, encourage, listen to, and hold space for them?	
What are my biggest concerns about my children's understanding, expression, or management of their big feelings?	
How can I be more empathetic and supportive of my children as they learn to cope with uncomfortable feelings like anger, sadness, and fear?	
What tip(s) really struck me that I want to integrate in the way I help my children understand or cope with their big feelings?	
Which specific conversation(s) regarding feelings—in general, anger, sadness, or fear—do I want to make sure I cover with my children in the next few months or year?	
Is there any message or behavior around big feelings that I want to address or change within myself so I alter that message or behavior when coping with (or helping my child cope with) my child's big feelings?	

Chapter 2

How to Talk to Kids about Self-Esteem and Body Image

"Am I Good Enough?"

W hen I was in elementary school, I struggled with a lot of the school-work that my older brothers had breezed through just a few years before. Marc and Scott were invited into HAP, an advanced-placement pro-gram for the "smart kids." I was not. They learned all their times tables with-out any help. I did not. They could spell both the easy and hard words for their spelling quizzes on the first try. I could not.

Extrapolating from my everyday perceived mediocrities, I came to the only conclusion that I thought was plausible: I am stupid.

This definitive statement wheedled its way into my decision-making. It became my go-to explanation for why I couldn't possibly do as well as my brothers in school, giving me the proverbial "I told you so" that I pulled out of my pocket any time I tried and fell short.

The impact of self-esteem, defined by author and psychotherapist Nathaniel Branden as "the disposition to experience oneself as being competent to cope with the basic challenges of life and of being worthy of happiness,"[1] has been well documented. In the 1980s and 1990s, California's Task Force to Promote Self-Esteem and Personal and Social Responsibility declared "self-esteem as the likeliest candidate for a social vaccine" that plays "a central role in the social problems that plague our society"[2]—something that stemmed from legislation on the topic. And while other studies, including an exhaustive review of the literature by social psychologist Roy Baumeister and his team in 2003,[3] have shown that high self-esteem isn't the Holy Grail of psychological constructs—that is, it won't solve all the world's problems—researchers (even Baumeister himself) agree that high self-esteem offers distinct and important benefits that impact lifelong well-being, including:

- **A decreased risk for a range of mental health problems like depression and anxiety:** More specifically, research tells us that low self-esteem is related to depression, substance abuse, antisocial behavior, and suicide, while high self-esteem is associated with a sense of well-being and the healthy coping skills needed throughout life.[4]

- **Increased initiative:** People with high self-esteem do more things![5] They are more likely to initiate new relationships, speak up in groups, and work harder. They get better grades and are more willing to change pursuits when they believe the path they are on is unpromising.

- **Greater happiness:** Children with healthy self-esteem are more likely to be happy and make and maintain positive friendships, while children with poor self-esteem are less likely to be happy and more likely to have emotional and social challenges. In addition, when parents attend to and foster a child's positive qualities, that child becomes more aware of their character strengths, which is connected to greater happiness and higher self-esteem.[6]

- **More resilience:** High self-esteem has been shown to strengthen persistence after rejection and failure, which researchers suggest could lead to better outcomes in school, work, relationships, and health.[7]

Given that self-esteem supports kids in crucial ways, helping them develop it is a priority. The irony—as the *How to Talk to Kids about Anything* podcast guest Sue Atkins, a parenting expert and author, so eloquently said—is that it's "an inside job."[8] It's not an easy button we can push from the outside but rather something internal that develops over time as kids learn that they are worthy and matter just as they are. Our role, as key adults in the lives of kids, is to hold up a mirror so they can see their strengths and contributions and step back so they can gain confidence and competence in themselves.

People who have a healthy sense of self-esteem know that

- "Who I am is enough."
- "What I can do is enough."
- "How I show up in the world is enough."

"When we nurture in our children a sense that they are inherently good, lovable, and worthy, they can get out of their own heads, stop worrying about what everyone thinks of them, and lead meaningful lives," says Melinda Wenner Moyer in her book *How to Raise Kids Who Aren't Assholes.*[9] Children and teens play a big role in creating or altering how they see themselves, their strengths, their abilities, their bodies, and their connections—if they know how to do it. And that's where we come in.

Glossary

Body image: How you think, feel, and see your body when you look in the mirror, view yourself in a photo, or picture yourself in your mind.

Body neutrality: An approach that, rather than asking us to love or hate our bodies, fosters acceptance and respect for the body we have and what it can do.

Body positivity: The movement that asserts that all bodies—regardless of size, shape, weight, skin tone, gender, or ability—are worthy of acceptance and positive body image.

Identity: the set of qualities or beliefs that makes you uniquely you.

Self-confidence: *Belief* in yourself; the general level of trust you have in your own abilities, qualities, and judgment.

Self-efficacy: *Task-specific* self-confidence; positive belief that you have the skills, knowledge, and capacity to achieve a specific goal.

Self-esteem: How you *feel* about yourself and perceive your overall value.

Who I Am Is Enough

When my husband's grandfather, "Pa," playfully complained "I am old" on his ninetieth birthday, his wife of nearly seventy years replied in Yiddish, "vau 'ikh bin' iz, du bist," or "Where 'I am' is, you are." Over a slice of homemade apple cake, Ma explained that you have to be careful of the words you "hitch to the backside" of "I am," because "negative or positive, you've now given them permission 'to be.'"

The sentiment hit me like a ton of bricks. Hadn't I been doing exactly that as a child? "I am-ing" myself to death with the declaration that "I am stupid"? Although I had learned, over time, that I was capable in academic settings, I went through years of bowing out of challenges and deferring to others because of how I chose to frame my intellect. "I am stupid" also led me to place additional focus on my appearance, which was something I felt I could control more than my intellect (more on body image later).

As it turns out, there's a whole framework around this called self-affirmation theory[10] which says that when we embrace a positive view of ourselves—that is, when we know who we are and know our value as well as what we value about ourselves—we can maintain a positive view of ourselves (even when things don't go so well or people are giving us negative feedback). "It's about reminding ourselves what matters most to us," as Harvard professor Amy Cuddy states in her book *Presence*, "and, by extension, who we are."[11]

That's powerful stuff. When I toured the country as a child-development specialist and keynote speaker, presenting to large groups of students and mentors, I began structuring this idea of the power of "I am" as an exchange between kids, parents, teachers, administrators, and other key adults.

"Whatever follows 'I am…'" I would call out, letting it hang in the air as the audience answered, "WILL BE!" I began asking the kids to dig deep and voice how they would describe themselves, why those values were important to them, and how they show these positive descriptors of themselves every day. I then asked them to share their "Am-firmations," as I called them, out loud—and some audience members even got onstage with me to share them emphatically.

The answer to "who am I?" becomes our child's identity. Whether the answers are positive, neutral, realistic, or negative can impact how they feel about themselves and their worth. As James Clear relays in his book *Atomic Habits*, "Your identity can hold you back…or build you up."[12] For kids, that might look like this:

IDENTITY CAN HOLD YOU BACK		IDENTITY CAN PUSH YOU FORWARD
"I'm awful in math."	→	"I'm a good reader."
"I am scared of everything."	→	"I am brave when it counts."
"I'm not coordinated."	→	"I am someone who tries new things."
"I am the worst at catching a football."	→	"I'm good at throwing the ball and running."
"I'm not a good artist like you."	→	"I'm a strong performer onstage."
"I'm trash at taking tests."	→	"I study hard and finish what I start."
"I am stupid."	→	"I need some extra help in this class."

When we learn that we can take ownership of how we define ourselves, we sit firmly in the driver's seat of our own identity. These short, powerful, value-based statements can envelop our children like a protective cloak, buffering them when they face discrimination and helping them to achieve better overall well-being and to be more tolerant of others. If our children can learn to define themselves by their assets, then these types of affirmations can become steady reminders and course correctors when they face a challenge.

"I Am" Projects

During my workshops on identity and becoming a "strength finder," I love to do "I Am" projects and exercises that allow kids to get creative and use their hands as well as their minds. Here are two:

- **"I Am" poem:** On the *How to Talk to Kids about Anything* podcast, Julie Bogart, author of *The Brave Learner* and *Raising Critical Thinkers*, noted that our identity often describes much more than one aspect of us.[13] She urged children to write an "I Am From" poem, a template and project born out of a powerful poem by George Ella Lyons,[14] which asks kids to think about the stories they love, the communities they are part of, and the habits they've adopted along the way. Springboarding from this idea, I invite kids, parents, teachers, and students to write an "I Am" poem that captures all the different aspects that make them who they are. You might, for example, encourage your children to write:
  - I am [what I do] a writer, an artist, an athlete, a gamer, a babysitter.
  - I am [what I love] a dog lover, a chocolate lover, a booklover, a beach lover.
  - I am [a role for others] a daughter, a son, a father, a mother, a teacher.
  - I am [where I'm from] a U.S. citizen, a Jersey girl, a proud Australian, a small-town boy.
  - I am [my race, religion, gender] Asian, Jewish, a girl, a Gen Zer, a member of the LGBTQ+ community, a second-generation immigrant.

- ○ I am [character traits] courageous, intuitive, sensitive, persistent, responsible.
- ○ I am [future aspirations] a future doctor, a future leader, a future chef.

  Sit down with your child and discuss their "I Ams" (and yours too!). Ask questions about them: "What does it mean to you to be intuitive? What made you describe yourself as a New Yorker through and through? How do you think it influences how you think, feel, and act when you define yourself as an artist?" Post their "I Ams" on the refrigerator or on a wall, and revisit them from time to time: "Has anything changed?" You might urge them to ask themselves, "Am I being the person I say I am?"

- **Am-firmation wall:** Why not put up a bulletin board in your children's rooms where they can post reminders of who they are and what they can do? "I am a capable student." "I am a kind friend." "I am a motivated and courageous person." I especially like it when kids invite their friends to write a note that asserts that what is written is true. For example, a friend may write, "You are the best friend I could ever have! You are always there when I need you, and you are so much fun. You even helped me learn how to ride a bike!" (Or they may just punctuate an Am-firmation that's already there by, for example, scribbling the word "truth" on a sticky note with an arrow that points to "I am a good gymnast even when I make a mistake.") At a low point, your children can turn to the board for a reminder that they are good enough as they are and have what it takes to do great things.

Quick Tip

Permission to Express the Need for Attention

Children who have a healthy dose of self-esteem can express their needs appropriately. They do not "wait" for parents, teachers, or friends to guess what they need by being passive-aggressive, whiny, manipulative, or rude. If you notice any of these behaviors, say to your child:

- **"You have rights!"** "You have the right to [ask for what you need, request my attention, express a frustration]." Certified parent coach Destini Ann Davis gives this wording when her child resorts to undesirable attention-seeking behaviors: "Do you need attention? It's okay for you to desire my energy. If I can't give you my attention right now, I promise I can give you a double dose later."[15]

- **"You can take action!"** "You can ask a question. For example, 'Mom, can we spend some time together without the baby?'" Or "You can make a plan. For example, 'For our special bonding time, I'd like to read this new library book together.'"

- **"You can ask for a time."** Teach them to ask, for example, "What time works today?" Then you might say, "After I finish putting your sister down for a nap, how about you and I spend twenty minutes together before we have to get ready for your playdate?"

When you tell your children they are worthy of having their needs filled, the likelihood of their having the confidence and skill to express themselves the next time they have a need is much higher—even if they need to wait for a few minutes.

Identity Feedback Loop

When children become confident in who they are, in their identity, they not only know when something feels wrong, but they can also recalibrate and determine how to make themselves feel right again. In this way, identity becomes a checkpoint or home base when making important decisions: "Is this congruent with who I am?" The process creates a feedback loop, according to Jan Stets and Peter Burke at University of California, Riverside, constantly reinforcing how our children define themselves, their behavior, how people evaluate their behavior, and the congruence between all these factors.[16]

For example, children who see themselves as kind will likely choose to exhibit kind behaviors. They will then receive feedback from others who tell them they are a kind person, which reinforces the way they define themselves.

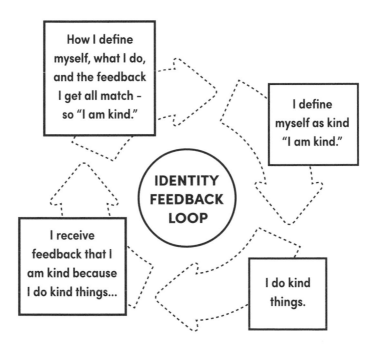

Of course, the opposite is true too. If children who see themselves as mean and rude (even if the label is untrue) choose to take actions that are mean and rude and receive feedback that they are a mean and rude person, this can add fuel to the identity fire.

To get to the root of how your children see themselves, you might try the following:

- **Ask:** "Which three positive words do you think describe you best?" and "When do you think you show examples of those three words?"

- **Reflect the positive descriptors back to them:** "You showed your kindness when you offered your jacket to your friend who forgot hers. You are a kind person."

- **Share how you describe yourself and how you show these parts of your identity to others:** "I'm an organized person, so I keep all my dates on this calendar and also enter in important events right away so I don't forget them."

- **Acknowledge faults as a work in progress rather than as defining characteristics:** "Sometimes I procrastinate on getting things done, but I'm working on that so I don't have to rush through at the last minute. I'm working on being more responsible."

Interrupting the feedback loop at any point can help children redefine who they are and, consequently, what they do, setting them on a different, more positive course. This may take persistent work and awareness, especially when the brain has gotten into the habit of thinking in negative ways. While there are times when negative feelings are healthy and appropriate (I mean, who can blame a child for feeling angry when someone takes his toy?), these brain tricks—or "stinking thinking,"[17] as famed psychologist Albert Ellis famously dubbed them in the 1950s—can create a negative downward spiral that feels inescapable, becoming a form of unintentional self-sabotage.

When children learn the power of their words on their thoughts, feelings, and actions, they may realize that they can be in the driver's seat of their own minds. In fact, the more kids learn to speak to themselves in a way that de-escalates and calms negative feelings, the more they rewire the brain to make productive self-talk easier in the future.

Instead of	You might teach them to say
"My coach didn't ask me to demonstrate the skill. She must hate me."	"My coach didn't ask me to demonstrate the skill. She wanted to give someone else a turn today."
"One of my friends didn't really talk to anyone in school today. She barely looked at me! I bet she doesn't want to be my friend anymore."	"My friend seemed quiet and 'not herself' today when I saw her. Maybe something happened in one of her classes or she got into a fight with her mom at home again. I'll have to check on her."
"I bombed my math test. I'm so stupid. What an idiot!"	"I didn't do as well on my math test as I would have liked. I'll go in for extra help and find out what I can do next time."

Persistent "stinking thinking" habits take time to break. Be gentle in coaxing your child out of the shadows while, at the same time, putting high beams on realistic and positive self-talk habits that can bolster high self-esteem.

Replace "Should" and "Must"

Albert Ellis, who gave us "stinking thinking," also used the direct, humorous phrase "don't should on yourself" (as well as the equally memorable word "musterbation"). Instead of "I should have set my alarm clock," have your child rephrase to "I'd like to make a habit of setting my alarm clock so I don't wake up late and miss the bus. I'll put a sticky note on my pillow so I remember to do it tonight." Similarly, instead of the double dose of "should" and "shouldn't" in "I should have known that I shouldn't have eaten all that ice cream," you can teach your child to replace them with something less guilt-inducing: "I feel better when I eat nondairy desserts, so I'll do that next time."

Other helpful phrases to replace "should" include the following:

- "It would be better if..."
- "I'd appreciate it if..."
- "It would be nice if..."
- "I want to..."
- "If I really wanted to, I could..."
- "I would prefer..."
- "I feel great when I..."
- "I wish that..."
- "It's really important to me that..."
- "It would mean so much to me to..."

Uncovering Our Children's Strengths

Every child has strengths. Some are easy to spot—they are gifted artists, prolific writers, exceptional athletes. Other times, those strengths may not be as obvious. Perhaps they are not developed yet or are buried under piles of what I refer to as "dirty laundry"—unsettling past experiences, ugly labels, and painful scars that leave our children to define themselves by what went wrong or their weaknesses. When they can't see their gifts for themselves, we need to become strength finders and reveal them.

- **Help them to see themselves in a new light:** You may be the first to notice it—their talent as a public speaker, their leadership tendencies, their knack for out-of-the-box thinking. And your words may have a way of reaching that child's ears in a way that nobody else's have in the past. When I was in ninth grade, my teacher Mr. Orsini posed an analytical question about the Shakespeare text we were studying. I raised my hand to answer, and he responded, "I'm saving you for a more difficult one." His confidence in me, in that split second, gave me a moment of intro-spection: "Am I someone who can answer the difficult questions in this class? I guess I am!" I had never seen myself that way—until I was able to look at myself through Mr. Orsini's eyes. To your child, you might say,

"You've got quite the knack for spotting the best fruit and cut flowers at the supermarket. I'm so glad you're coming with me!" or "You have such a gentle way with animals. No wonder dogs and cats come right over to you."

- **"One thing I know about you…(with evidence)":** As parents and educators, we spend many hours with the young people in our lives. We *know* these kids, and we must take the time to comment on the strengths we see in front of us. Be sure to add the evidence:

  - **Identify strength:** "You've shown yourself to be dedicated time and time again."

  - **Evidence:** "Remember when you were in the school musical and the other lead quit halfway through and you kept going to help keep the show together?"

  - **Sum up:** "Being a committed member is one of your real gifts that will serve you throughout your life."

  If your child is still unsure, don't be afraid to add, as my colleague and parenting expert Sue Atkins mentioned on the *How to Talk to Kids about Anything* podcast, "Borrow my belief in you until you find your own belief within yourself."[18]

- **"The overhear":** Imagine your child is in a room nearby and you are on the phone talking to your sister-in-law when you tell her, "I can't wait until you hear April play her piano when you get here! She's worked really hard, and it's so fun to watch her play. She plays with real emotion, which makes her a captivating pianist." Also referred to as "earshot praise"[19] by my friend and colleague Michele Borba, "the overhear" helps kids draw the conclusion that if someone is saying something positive about them when they're not around (particularly when they think they're not supposed to hear it), it must be true!

- **Picture this:** One of my favorite photos I have ever received of my daughter was taken when her back was turned. She has her arm around a friend at overnight camp, her hand cupping her friend's head, comforting her, after all the parents left on visiting day. To me, these kinds of photos—the ones beyond her standing around looking cute or getting ready to head out for Halloween trick-or-treating—are the ones that highlight who she really is. Be sure to take, display, and talk about the kinds of photos that underscore your children's strengths so they can see it—and know that you see it. "I love this photo because it shows your empathy. Your friend must have been so relieved and grateful to have you there during this difficult time. Look at how she has her head on your shoulder and you're comforting her. You're an empathetic person and a kind friend."

- **"Good job" notes:** There's something about a note that does double duty. It provides your children with encouragement, support, and an "I see you" message in the moment while giving them something to go back to again and again when the chips are down and they're feeling low. These "good job" notes can be a small, concrete way to praise our children's effort and highlight a character trait that reflects something you know about them. (And in this visual world, I've been known to do fifteen-second "good job" notes in video form too!)

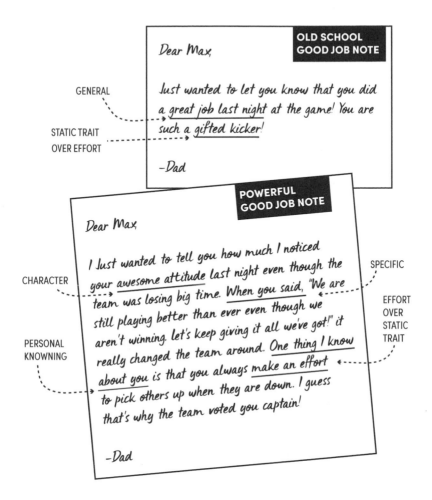

Once our children can "see" their strengths, they can better apply them. Their goals become more possible as they realize they have what it takes to overcome barriers, achieve benchmarks, and persevere to the end.

Replace Their Label

At a BlogHer conference, Sheryl Sandberg, Facebook COO and author of *Lean In*, gave pertinent words of advice: "Next time you want to call your daughter 'bossy', take a deep breath and say, 'My daughter has executive leadership skills.'"[20] (I say, go a step further and *tell* her that too!) When we frame potential strengths as weaknesses, young people are much more likely to try to squelch them rather than develop them. We can reframe and relabel instead:

Bossy	→	Assertive, directive
Quiet	→	Thoughtful, introspective
Talks too much	→	Communicates thoughts effectively and thoroughly
Silly	→	Finds the joy in life
Overly emotional	→	Empathetic, feels deeply

Sometimes our children's hidden assets are simply appointed as weaknesses that need some rebranding. Be the one who helps children see themselves and their attributes in a fresh, new light.

Words Every Child Needs to Hear

You matter.

I'm proud of who you are.

Be Yourself.

You are enough.

You deserve kindness.

I'm here for you.

Trust Yourself.

I'm sorry.

I believe in you.

I'm listening.

You are fully capable.

Thank you.

I forgive you.

You can do hard things.

I love you.

What I Can Do Is Enough

Self-confidence—the belief in our abilities, qualities, and judgment—can also impact self-esteem. It is the job—or, perhaps, gift—of self-confidence to lift us from the inside, urge us forward, and whisper in our ears, "You can do it!" and "You have what it takes!" These inner refrains become part of who we are and translate into very personal and transformative mantras like, "Yes, I can!" and "Yes, I do!" (Conversely, a lack of confidence is an enemy of progress. As activist and writer Brittany Packnett Cunningham says in her viral TED Talk "How to Build Your Confidence—and Spark It in Others." "Without confidence, we get stuck, and when we get stuck, we can't even get started."[21])

Research shows self-confidence

- **Is a strong predictor of learning, achievement, and future success.**[22] Believing in our ability to do something or achieve something can enhance our ability to do it.

- **Helps us to set and go after goals.** People with strong self-efficacy (task-specific self-confidence) are more likely to choose more difficult or more challenging goals,[23] stay committed to those goals, and achieve their goals[24] when compared to those with weak self-efficacy. In fact, research over the past thirty years suggests that self-efficacious people tend to perceive setbacks and obstacles not as a time to attack their low aptitude but rather as an occasion to increase effort and develop their skills.

- **Helps us to recover from adversity.** Self-confidence is correlated with resilience, our ability to bounce back from challenges. Having high self-confidence and a favorable attitude toward ourselves offers a protective factor when dealing with problems or when things don't go our way.[25]

- **Urges us to engage in novel experiences.** When we are confident about ourselves and our abilities, we are more open to trying new things. And when we learn new skills, we become more confident!

- **Protects against anxiety, loneliness, and fear.**[26] Not only does self-confidence become a buffer for athletes in competitive situations where performance anxiety can be triggered, it can protect against anxiety symptoms in extreme situations, such as during a pandemic.[27] Low self-confidence, on the other hand, contributes to feelings of anxiety and depression.[28]

While self-confidence may not be tangible or static, we know it when it walks into the room or when it pulls our shoulders back and keeps our heads held high. As Katty Kay and Claire Shipman write in *The Confidence Code*, "Confidence is…easy to recognize. With it, you can take on the world; without it, you live stuck at the starting block of your potential."[29]

Silencing Your Gremlin

One of the biggest impediments to self-confidence is our inner critic, the voice inside that tells us, "You *can't*." In coaching, we call this naysayer a "gremlin,"[30]—a term coined by author Rick Carson in the 1980s—and we tell clients to give it a name, to otherize the voice in their head so they can speak back to it and challenge it. The name could be general like "the bully" or "the troll," or it could be specific like "Janice" (perhaps the name of the person who put the detrimental thought in your head).

I had one client, Jess, who called her gremlin "Paul"—the name of the boy in fourth grade who tormented her. Jess listed off the many digs he made at her expense. "He told me that I 'can't spell to save my life,' that I 'sound like I'm trying too hard when I read in front of the class,' that I 'play sports worse than my baby brother,' and that 'I'm not really good at anything.'" Paul's voice had become Jess's voice, telling her to stay quiet and to refrain from trying new things for fear of embarrassment. Jess would literally sit on the sidelines of her life—arms and body "pretzeled"[31] as Rachel Simmons, author of *Enough as She Is* and *The Curse of the Good Girl*, says is common among girls—and watch others engage.

I encouraged Jess to write to Paul in her journal whenever she heard the negative thoughts taking hold and to tell him what she really thought of his "opinions." Making positive statements about her abilities—"I read with expression and feeling, which is why I landed a great part in last year's musical!" and "I am trying out for softball this year because I can hit a ball pretty well most of the time"—helped her to declare her confidence in herself. She ended the exercise each time with, "You don't know me, and you can't stop me. I'm no longer listening to you." These proclamations, over time, became her self-talk that she could carry and repeat as needed. She was able to see that Paul's voice was not her own and that she didn't have to accept what the voice was saying.

You can provide your children with a "gremlin" journal so they can push back on both ugly self-talk and cognitive distortions. Ask "If this [gremlin, person] were sitting here right now, what would you want to tell them about what you can do? Is what they have been telling you accurate?" Encourage them to add visual reminders of their abilities: the photo of your daughter overcoming her fear and getting on a horse for the first time, the ticket stub from the time your son volunteered to perform with a visiting theater group, the tally from the first summer reading challenge that your kids completed… All these tell your kids that they *can* do things—and in fact, they did!

Finding Their Voice

Once our children have identified their gremlin, we must help them reclaim their self-confidence by talking back to their gremlin. In the book *Self-Esteem*, authors Matthew McKay and Patrick Fanning call this our children's "healthy voice."[32] Rachel Simmons calls this their "BFF voice."[33] "In your worst moments," she says, "talk back to yourself in the voice of your best friend."[34]

For example, "I stink at math! I should just give up!" complained my daughter, Tallie, trapped in negative thinking at age ten.

I asked, "What would Katie [her best friend in elementary school] say to you right now if she heard you saying these things to yourself?" (Or alternatively, "What would you say to Katie if she were saying these things about herself?")

Tallie answered, "You just need some help in math because you don't get how to make fractions into percentages."

Removing herself from the situation and introducing empathy gave Tallie the perspective she needed. When situations arise where your children are internally bashing themselves, looking at the situation through fresh eyes (like those of a good friend) can be just the help they need to silence their inner gremlins. Eventually, with practice and persistence, this kinder, gentler, and more accurate voice becomes their own healthy voice.

Confidence Comes from Competence!

Self-efficacy, or confidence in one's abilities to accomplish specific tasks, doesn't just come from showing up. It comes from learning, doing, and making progress. It comes from failing, then mastering a skill and getting that "I did it!" feeling. Firsthand experiences tell us we are capable—and that we can be capable in the future—and let us see the connection between our effort and our outcome.

A child who fumbles through dressing himself is eventually going to get better at dressing himself. He will feel more confident with the task as he becomes more competent and perhaps takes on more self-care tasks. A child who isn't given the opportunity to appropriately struggle will (1) glean that he should be dependent on others to do this task, (2) believe that struggling is not a normal part of learning, and (3) if it becomes a pattern, will remain unsure of himself each time he approaches something new or challenging. "You can't do it for them," Carrie Goldman, award-winning author of *Bullied: What Every Parent, Teacher, and Kid Needs to Know about Ending the Cycle of Fear*, told me during an interview. "The best you can do is to be the net." [35]

To master tasks, children need to be given the chance to get out of their comfort zones. You might ask these questions:

- "What have you done that takes you out of your comfort zone and puts you in your courage zone, where you try new things and sharpen your skills?"
- "What skill did you have to keep working on before you mastered it?"
- "How did you feel about it when you first tried it?"
- "How did you feel about it when you were struggling to learn it?"
- "How do you feel about it now?"

As children see that gaining confidence only comes when they stick through challenges, even when uncomfortable, they will recognize it as a result of hard work and perseverance rather than something bestowed on a certain lucky few.

Ways to Praise

"Great helping!" "That's an amazing drawing!" Parents and teachers often want to say the words we think our kids need to hear in hopes that they will start saying them to themselves. And rightfully so! When kids display low self-esteem, negative self-talk, or distorted thinking, recognizing what they do well can feel particularly important.

However, research shows that parents give kids *inflated*—or overly positive—praise about 25 percent of the time. Eddie Brummelman, an associate professor at the University of Amsterdam, and his colleagues found that attempting to augment self-esteem with well-intentioned but inflated praise backfired, especially with children who displayed lower levels of self-esteem.[36] In other words, as parents' praise inflated, children's self-esteem deflated.

"The self-esteem gurus led us to believe we could hand our children self-esteem on a silver platter through our praise, through our words," Carol Dweck, author of *Mindset* and professor of psychology at Stanford University, told *Nightline* back in 2009. "And we thought…almost the definition of being a good parent was to keep handing self-esteem to our child. But it doesn't work that way."[37] Here's what we can do instead.

BE SPECIFIC

"Good job," while nice to hear at times, tends to go in one ear and out the other.

- **Science says:** Research shows that behavior-specific praise explicitly identifies the behavior for which the child is being praised, helping kids to show more engagement in learning, increased classroom participation, less disruptive conduct, and more on-task behavior.[38] The best kind of specific praise is unplanned and, of course, sincere.
- **Sample scripts:**
  - "You included so many thoughtful details in the story you wrote. I enjoyed reading about the characters since you made them so vivid!"
  - "I appreciate the way you waited for me to finish my call before asking me about your playdate. That shows patience. You're a patient person."
  - "You shared your crayons with all your friends!"

PRAISE THE EFFORT

When kids are praised for effort, they are compelled to keep trying to overcome challenges. When they are praised for their smarts or natural ability, they may avoid trying for fear that they are not as smart or able as others think.

- **Science says:** Stanford professor Carol Dweck—along with Claudia Mueller, MD, PhD—showed that when kids were given challenging math problems and praised with "you must have worked really hard" instead of "you must be smart at this," they were more likely to choose to work on challenging problems rather than request "easy" problems in the future and less likely to lie to make themselves look better.[39]
- **Sample scripts:**
  - "You studied so hard, quizzed yourself, and got extra help when you didn't understand. Now that's what I call persistence!"
  - "Let's add one of the most powerful little words to the end of your

statements: 'I can't do this…yet,' 'I don't know…yet,' 'I'm not that good at this…yet.' It'll come with effort and time!"

○ "You remembered the first five steps of the dance! You must have worked hard at learning them."

PRAISE PROGRESS IN RELATION TO THE PRODUCT

It's exciting to see our kids win the award or slay the test, but don't forget what it took to get those results. Character? A skill? We can praise kids for what they're putting into the goal but also recognize what they've achieved so far.

- **Science says:** Dweck says while we "want to take the emphasis off outcomes…[we don't] want to take the emphasis off learning and progress."[40] We want kids to take pride in their progressing skills. Dweck encourages us to help them move forward and bounce back from failure. A child who is praised for effort is much more open to looking at their mistakes as opportunities to learn.

- **Sample scripts:**
  ○ "You didn't finish the whole thing yet, but look at that improvement! You remembered the first three lines of the poem—and almost got the fourth. That takes a lot of concentration. You're making great progress!"
  ○ "You ran around the whole block two times! You've been working so hard on your endurance by playing tag with your brother and doing all those bike rides with friends. Keep going, and you'll be ready to run the 5K in the spring like you've wanted."

REFRAIN FROM COMPARING

When we see our kids outperforming peers, we might feel compelled to point it out. For example, "You are the best one on the team." Or "The chorus would be nothing without you, since you sing like an angel." But research shows there are issues with "social-comparison praise."[41]

- **Science says:** While social comparisons can motivate kids at times,[42] they can also backfire. They can tell children that they are only praise worthy if they remain the top dog. Studies show that when kids receive social-comparison praise, they lose motivation when their competitive edge slips.[43] This kind of praise can also relay to kids that the goal of a task is to beat out other kids rather than achieve mastery or encourage community building. We want kids to look inward (or extend a hand outward) when sharpening skills or accomplishing a task.
- **Sample scripts:**
  - "I noticed how you really hustled today on the field. You passed the ball to your teammates and drove that ball to the goal with determination and focus. You helped the team a lot!"
  - "I really like that you and your sister participate in our dinner discussions. You both have such a unique way of looking at things. When we all participate, the conversation is so much more interesting, don't you think?"

How I Show Up in the World Is Enough

Faces. Bodies. Clothes. Hair. Our children present all different and wonderful "packages" that allow them to connect with, participate in, and experience the world around them. Unfortunately, society has something to say, both overtly and covertly, about what it sees, and the messages society sends out can invite kids to personally examine how best they adhere to what is deemed attractive and worthy of praise.

Surprisingly, this happens from the time kids are babies. I still remember when I was sitting at the hair salon, my infant daughter, Tallie, gurgling beside me in her stroller, and a middle-aged woman came over, peered into the stroller, and exclaimed, "Oh, look at her!" Before I could smile or utter a word of endearment, the woman continued effusively, "Look at those fat thighs! Oh my! Enjoy it now, honey. It's the only time fat is cute." Bombarded with messages like that, is it surprising that by the time kids, especially girls, are three years old, they can be critical of the way they look and the size, weight, or shape of their bodies?

Body dissatisfaction, the discrepancy between the perceived body ideal and how people believe they stack up to it, is experienced by 49 percent to 84 percent of teens,[44] regardless of gender,[45] although girls typically showed more dissatisfaction than boys as they matured.[46] While research has found that many girls often worry about being "thin enough," a significant number of boys are concerned about being "muscular enough." Health advocate Oona Hanson says in Charlotte Markey's book *Being You: The Body Image Book for Boys*, "When it comes to body image, many boys feel competing pressures—not wanting to be 'too small' while also being afraid of being 'too fat.' Because our culture links appearance concerns with girls, many boys wonder if something is wrong with them simply for caring about how they look."[47] Sometimes body dissatisfaction becomes so extreme that it can affect everyday life and put young people at an elevated risk for eating disorders.[48]

"What's going on?" you might ask. "Where is my child learning all this?" The short answer: everywhere. One only needs to look at these examples:

- Gendered and sexualized Halloween costume options and advertisements (thin models, in very little or tight revealing clothing, advertised toward girls)
- Barbie dolls (tiny features that would never hold up in real life)
- Action figures (enormous pecs and biceps)
- Popular actors and actresses (losing weight and getting buff for films)
- Social media influencers (showcasing hashtags like #perfectbody and #shredded)

The message is clear: Girls are valued for thinness. Boys are valued for their muscles. And if you fall somewhere in between those two extremes, you are barely represented at all. (Note: while there has been an attempt to provide some body diversity—e.g., Disney's *Encanto*, Barbie's "curvy" doll, body image books that acknowledge boys who are struggling too—there is still so much work to do.)

But it's more than that. While media is pervasive and buzzy, the people who are closest to our children can either reflect or deflect these messages and uphold or dismantle the impossible standards they see. Friends. Teachers. Coaches. Siblings. *Us*. We need to talk to all kids about body image and how valuing ourselves or others based on their physical appearance sells everyone short. We need to

- Discuss what *really* goes on behind the curtain of perfect.
- Refocus attention on what our bodies can *do* rather than how they look.
- Relay that good people and good bodies come in all shapes and sizes.

When we are proactive about these discussions instead of waiting until our children bring them up, we are arming them with the information they need to repel negative messages they receive from those around them as well as from media. We want them to know, as Dannielle Miller, a teen educator and the bestselling author of *The Butterfly Effect*, said to me on my podcast, "They are not just bodies. They are *somebodies*."[49] Take the plunge and get started today.

🏠 *In My Home*

When Tallie was in third grade, she told me that a boy on the school bus told her to say, "I. M. S." She did, and he told her it meant "I am sexy." She laughed.

"Oh?" I uttered. "And what does that mean?"

"I don't know," she answered. "What does 'sexy' mean?"

"It's an adult word that means you feel attractive to other people and that other people would want to hug and touch and kiss you because of how you look."

She became alarmed. "I am not sexy!" she exclaimed several times with an embarrassed smile on her face.

When it comes to body image development, it is impossible to deny that young girls learn that "sexiness," even before puberty, is a bar they need to clear. Through peer relationships, fashion, social media, and mainstream media (research on girls ages six to eleven shows an average of twenty-four incidents of sexualized content in popular children's shows *per episode*, from sexualized comments to unwanted sexual touching[50]), they get the message that being sexy or hot is a critical part of becoming a valued adult.[51] Being "hurried" in this way can also impact how girls feel about their bodies and normalize the pressure to look and feel sexy at younger and younger ages (not to mention that boys may get the message that girls are sexual objects [52])—laying the groundwork for self-objectification, which has been linked with both body image disturbances and eating disorder symptoms.[53]

It is crucial that not only women talk to their girls about early sexualization but for men to do so as well, since being "sexy" is often couched in a way for girls to get their attention. Try these statements:

- "You do not need to objectify yourself for people to notice you."
- "Do you see that billboard? It shows young women on all fours with almost no clothes on in order to sell [a product]. I don't think that's right. Women are not objects—they are mothers and daughters and friends with feelings. What do you think?"
- "If there were no brand names on this Facebook ad, what would you think they were selling? Why do you think they positioned that actor in that way? If you were going to promote that [movie, TV series], what kind of advertisement would you create?"

Remember, you may not be showing your children media with sexualized images, but they are all around them—in Instagram feeds, magazines, movies, TV shows, and even a stroll through the shopping mall.[54] When you uncover these subliminal messages for what they are, you take away the power of these messages over your children while increasing your children's media savvy and power to deconstruct what they see.

Media Literacy: Pulling Back the Curtain

When I was in my twenties and early thirties, I ran a program for girls ages eight to twelve called Sassy Sisterhood Girls Circle, where we talked through pertinent issues of friendship, self-esteem, and body image. In a memorable discussion, we were gathered around a desktop computer, and I showed the girls how magazine cover photos were altered. They started pointing and shouting out the changes:

"Look! They shaved off part of her arm!"

"They took a huge chunk out of her waist!"

Then one very introspective girl named Megan asked, "Are you telling me that the girl on the cover doesn't even look like the girl on the cover?"

That was close to twenty years ago, and things have only gotten worse. TV watching and reading print magazines may be down among children and teens,[55] but social media is scrolling up. Pew Research Center's recent Teens, Social Media and Technology 2022 Survey[56] shows that 67 percent of teens are using TikTok, 62 percent are on Instagram, 57 percent are on Snapchat, and a whopping 95 percent are using YouTube (one in five admit "almost constantly"), and they are often fooled by the power of Photoshop, Facetune, and other selfie-editing tools on images posted online everyday masquerading as "real life."

We need to teach our kids what's going on behind the scenes, that not everything they see on social media is as it seems. Dr. Lindsay Kite, one of the authors of *More Than a Body*, told me on the *How to Talk to Kids about Anything* podcast, "When you can help kids to realize that most of the images, even from those people who they know and love, are likely filtered, edited, cropped—they are the highlight reel—it sets them up to be more critical."[57] Here are some ideas on how to educate your children about media literacy.

COMPARE THE PHOTOS

- **Science says:** Studies have shown that when young people are continually exposed to images and videos depicting "perfect bodies," they feel worse, and the use of image-driven social media sites like Instagram has been linked to body image concerns such as body dissatisfaction and self-objectification.[58] Research out of Flinders University in Australia shows that seeing "edited vs. real photos" side by side results in decreased body dissatisfaction as compared to the control group.[59]

- **To do:** There's a revealing trend on social media where photos are compared, side by side, to peg heavily retouched, filtered, and photoshopped images against reality. Search "Instagram vs. real life celebrities" or "Photoshop fail" to pull up some of these comparison photos.

- **Conversation starters:** "Let's take a look at these two photos. What do you notice? How does seeing these photos side by side make you feel? Why do you think the [editor, advertiser, celebrity] changed the photo? Do you think your friends change their photos before posting them? What advice would you have for the [advertiser, celebrity, friend] about editing photos? What does this edited photo convey about people's bodies? Remember, edited photos are created—they aren't reality."

CRACK THE TRICKS

- **Science says:** Apps such as Snapchat, TikTok, and Instagram have built-in filters and photoshopping tools that allow users to alter their appearance. When the bulk of faces and bodies that we see in images and videos have been changed, it creates an unrealistic bar that we feel we have to clear. Boston Children's Hospital child psychologist Keneisha Sinclair-McBride says, "There's evidence that supports the observation that while kids are good at noticing filters and Photoshop…they don't necessarily understand exactly how they work."[60]

- **To do:** Expand on the above tip and show your kids accounts (or use your own) that demonstrate how editing software is used to make others look "perfect." Show them that people have cellulite, pores, fat, and wrinkles and how it's possible to "edit out" what they perceive as flaws. Discuss how these functions can dupe us and make us feel inferior.

- **Conversation starters:** "Remember how photos are edited to make celebrities look thinner, more muscular, or more 'perfect'? Would you like to see how regular people do this on their photos too? Just as people can use filters to make them look like a Disney character, they can use them to look like they have no acne and a tiny waist! Why do you think they'd do that? How do you think people think and feel when they view those photos? Remember, there's no such thing as 'perfect'!"

CURATE YOUR FEED

- **Science says:** Research tells us that young women regularly report seeing advertisements, notifications, or videos that push cosmetic procedures, including lip fillers and plastic surgery, to change their face or body to make it appear more "ideal."[61] Many use social media to see how they stack up as well as to gain feedback from others about their appearance. Research shows there are negative consequences for this type of mal-adaptive social media use for people, whether they are Black or white[62] and regardless of gender,[63] though young men weren't as likely as young women to use social media to compare themselves.[64] Young people also see influencers embrace food restriction. Dieting has become synonymous with self-control. As Virginia Sole Smith, author of *The Eating Instinct* and *Fat Talk*, writes, "Food became something to categorize— whole or processed, real or fake, clean or dirty—and to fear."[65] Social media serves it all on a silver platter.
- **To do:** Talk to kids about "digital pruning"[66]—actively unfollowing accounts that make them feel bad—and interacting with body-positive, body-realistic, or positive self-esteem accounts instead. Alternatively, suggest kids use social media to focus on personal interests (climate change, gardening, dogs, etc.) and steer clear of body comparison altogether.
- **Conversation starters:** "What do you see when you open your social media? How do those accounts make you feel? Many people get sucked down a rabbit hole when they scroll, and the feeds they see make them

feel bad about themselves and how they look. Because of the algorithm, you see more of what is popular and what you liked or followed. But you can be in charge of your feed. Who or what would you like to mute or unfollow? What would you like to see more of?" As Dr. Devorah Heitner, author of *Screenwise* and *Growing Up in Public*, said on the *How to Talk to Kids about Anything* podcast, "You can tell your child, 'You don't have to continue to go back to places that make you feel bad.'"[67]

COMMIT TO REAL

- **Science says:** A large body of research suggests that social media activities, such as viewing or uploading unrealistic/edited photos, are associated with body image issues and disordered eating. A recent study out of City, University of London, by Professor Rosalind Gill showed that 90 percent of young women use a filter or editing tools before posting images of themselves to even out or bronze their skin, reshape parts of their face, appear thinner, or brighten teeth.[68] Even when we are the ones altering the photos, researchers find that it can create "Snapchat dysmorphia"[69]—when patients obsess over minor or imagined flaws and bring filtered selfies to surgeons to illustrate the desired surgical changes they want to achieve.[70]

- **To do:** "Commit to real" applies to us too. We can't enhance-to-post our own photos or bury ourselves in accounts that make us feel bad if we want our kids to do the opposite. As Nancy Redd, author of *Body Drama*, wrote in a Mashable article, "We're living in a time when school portraits are offered with Photoshop enhancements."[71] Are we really looking for an edited version of ourselves or our child? Let's make "commit to real" a family act and a family pact.

- **Conversation starters:** "I love you just the way you are, do you know that? There is no reason to change a thing. You know how we've talked about how people change photos to make them appear more 'perfect'? I don't think we should do that because what could be more beautiful and perfect than what's real? Let's refocus our energy on all the real things we get to do with our bodies, all the real places we get to take our bodies, and all the real people we get to spend time with because our bodies make it so. Are you with me? Let's commit to what's real!"

CONTROL YOUR TIME

- **Science says:** The American Academy of Child and Adolescent Psychiatry reports that U.S. children, ages eight to twelve, spend four to six hours a day using screens, and teens spend up to nine hours.[72] The nonprofit research organization Common Sense Media reported a large upswing in social media use from 2019 to 2021 among children ages eight to twelve (even though the platforms were not designed for kids) due in large part to the COVID-19 pandemic.[73]

- **To do:** Diana Graber, founder of Cyberwise, suggests that kids keep a daily log to reveal how much time they spend on screens, create a "bucket list" of things they would do if screens didn't exist, and do a screen-free day filled with carrying out some bucket list items.[74]

- **Conversation starters:** "What did you discover from your log about how you spend your time? Here's what I learned about me. What would you like to do on our screen-free day that you've wanted to do? How exciting! Going forward, what do you think about doing a 'bucket-list day' each week/month so we can tick off some of these items from our lists and focus on what's real and wonderful?"

A recent study found that when university students were exposed to Facebook photos of plus-size models, they had less body dissatisfaction and were in a better mood.[75] In addition, when people made negative comments about the plus-size models, the participant was also more likely to make a negative comment. We need to make sure we're exposing our children to a wide variety of body types and discussing the pile-on effect. Perhaps the adage is best: if you don't have anything nice to say, don't say anything at all!

Focus On What Your Body Can Do

One morning, my fitness trainer, Kevin Gidrey, told our sweaty, panting group that one of our fellow classmates wasn't attending class that morning because she was going in for chemotherapy to fight an aggressive cancerous tumor. "Remember," he said, "you *get* to exercise your body this morning. It's a glorious day to be alive, and it's a privilege to be healthy and able." That same day, I interviewed Drs. Lindsay and Lexie Kite on the *How to Talk to Kids about Anything* podcast, both of whom reiterated several times, "Our body is an instrument, not an ornament."[76]

These comments got me thinking. How often do we brainstorm with our kids about what amazing things their bodies allow them to do daily? It's time to shift our attention to our bodies as tools for enjoyment, connection, progress, health, and well-being. Get out a sheet of paper and some markers, then ask your family these questions:

- **"What are your favorite things that your body allows you to do?"** They may come up with athletic activities, such as hockey and cheerleading, or interpersonal connecting like hugging and cooking meals, which remind our children that our bodies allow us to engage and do and are not just props to be evaluated for how they look.

- **"What wonders have our bodies allowed us to go, see, hear, feel, and experience?"** Your family might talk about being able to feel the cool water of the ocean on their skin, see the Grand Canyon, or hear their baby sister say their name for the first time. Our bodies are wonders that allow us to experience wonders!

- **"Who do you get to spend time with because your body allows you to do so?"** Whether your children tell you that they get to go to the park with their besties, watch the clouds go by with Daddy, or take a plane to visit Grandma, they are seeing that our bodies are vehicles for connection and enjoyment.

Getting the family to think and speak in this way reframes our body discussions away from talking about them as decorative problems that need to be fixed, weighed, redesigned, or picked apart to vehicles that should be embraced with gratitude for the functions we enjoy and rely on each day.

Don't Do This, Do That!

NUTRITION

- Don't encourage kids to engage in restriction or fad diets or stay away from "bad foods," as in, "Don't eat that muffin. It will make you fat," or "You need to eat carb-free."
- Charlotte Markey, author of *The Body Image Book for Girls* and *Being You*, reminds parents to "encourage kids to eat nutritious food most of the time and tell them to listen to their bodies when they feel hungry or thirsty."[77]

SOCIAL MEDIA

- Don't bury your head in the sand when it comes to what your children are following and listening to online. The Dove Self-Esteem Project made an emotional short film titled *Toxic Influence*[78] that showed the kind of detrimental "advice" kids were being given online, such as, "If your teeth are uneven, you can just file them down with a nail file," "Lip filler kits let you inject yourself at home," and "Keep telling yourself you're not hungry."
- Discuss the messages that young people are receiving through social media and ads head-on. You can even use the Dove short film to get the ball rolling. Don't be afraid to ask questions like these:
  - "What messages about looks and beauty have you heard?"
  - "Why do you think this woman is talking about the 'life-changing Botox' she got from this surgeon?"
  - "How do these ads make you feel?"
  - "Is there anything you want to ask?"

FAMILY VALUES

- Don't allow family members to body-shame or tease your children about their body shape, size, weight, or overall appearance. Calling your children names or making derogatory comments about their body, even in jest, can result in them viewing their bodies in a negative way.[79] Research shows that many people who develop low self-esteem and eating disorders report, among other determining factors, that they were once teased about their looks.[80]

- Create a culture within your family and a haven within your home where all bodies are accepted and "fat talk," ritualized derogatory talk focused on fat bashing, weight, and shape (often with a heaping side of self-degradation), is not permitted. When speaking to parents and educators, I often encourage them to create a "fat-talk-free zone," where discussing the latest diets, lost and gained pounds, and the size and shape of friends, family, and celebrities is kept at bay. If needed, stick a note on the door that reads, "Please leave your fat talk at the door. You can pick it up on the way out. You are entering a fat-talk-free zone."

MISINFORMATION

- Don't allow your family, friends, or the media in your home to reflect misinformation about health, weight, and well-being. Good health is not obtained from dieting, restricting, excessive exercising, or taking diet pills. According to the Renfrew Center, a well-known eating disorders treatment center, while those closest to our children can't "cause" eating disorders, they can be powerful contributors to poor body image, which is often seen as the fuel for dangerous eating habits and harmful beliefs about size, weight, body shape, health, and wellness.[81]

- Regardless of weight, talk to your children about what health and well-being really stem from:
  - Eating nutritious foods
  - Drinking enough water each day

- ○ Getting enough sleep
- ○ Exercising and moving your body daily
- ○ Blowing off steam to manage stress in a productive way, such as laughing with a friend

Studies show that engaging in healthy behaviors is highly related to positive body esteem![82]

STEPPING ON THE SCALE

- When speaking about weight and health, I like to give examples: "Imagine a teen, Sarah, is a size two, and another girl, Anna, is a size fourteen. Who is healthier? Now what if I told you Sarah only eats one apple and drinks diet soda all day, does no exercise, and stays up late into the night watching videos. Anna eats a healthy, balanced diet, goes to sleep by nine thirty each night, and runs circles around her friends on the soccer field. Have you changed your mind? Should we tell Anna that she needs to lose weight in order to be healthy? Health and weight are not the same thing."

Enough Is Enough

Self-esteem and body image are inside jobs. In order to develop them, our kids need to see that

- **Who they are is enough.** They have strengths, and they have challenges, and it's okay.
- **What they do is enough.** They are highly capable and can make notable progress with effort.
- **How they present to the world is enough.** Their bodies are a means to experience the world—not to sit idly on the sidelines as the world evaluates their worth.

When kids stop looking outward for validation, they realize they had what it takes to be "enough" all along. Self-esteem is born and cultivated within each of us—not because key adults put it there but because they hold up a mirror and allow kids to see it for themselves. Our kids can then go out into the world and be a full expression of themselves. And that, my sweet friends, is beautiful.

✐ Talking Points

QUESTION	YOUR ANSWER
What are my children's top strengths?	
How have I highlighted my children's strengths so they know they are valued and seen?	
What kinds of identity habits or thinking mistakes have the potential of holding my children back, and how can I talk to them about changing those "blue thoughts" into "true thoughts"?	
Do my children have a "gremlin"? When do I hear it? How can my child catch that gremlin in the act and put it in its place?	

QUESTION	YOUR ANSWER
How do I praise my child? And for what do I praise my child? Are there any changes or enhancements I would like to make?	
What conversations are most crucial to have with my children regarding body image and self-esteem at this point in their lives?	
What messages about self-esteem, identity, confidence, and body image do I feel my children have already learned from me?	

Chapter 3

How to Talk to Kids about Sex

"But How Does the Baby Get *in* There?"

Ah, the talk. You know, *the sex talk*. The one about the birds and the bees? The topic can make us squirm in our seats, go red in the face, or make us leap for the remote control when an innocent surf lands on a premium cable channel's adult movie.

My own sex talk came in the form of an illustrated book, left on my bed at age eight, that showed how different animals made babies and ended with a final page that showed a woman and man in bed, under the covers. My mom peeked her head into my room after I perused the book, inquiring, "Do you have any questions?" I shook my head (although I'm sure I had many), wide-eyed and embarrassed, and that was it. The end.

Talking about sex makes parents feel somewhere between nervous, mentally fleeing the building, and wanting to throw up. Trust me, I understand. There were moments when I thought that if there were a choice between discussing the mechanics of sex with my own children and scaling Mount

Everest, I would give serious consideration to investing in some climbing gear. When I interviewed my first sex expert on my podcast, I slumped at my desk as if to hide myself, stomach clenched, internally urging myself to grow up and put on my big girl pants so I could get through the recording. It was a good thing I did, because it was only a few weeks later that my eight-year-old daughter asked, "But how does the baby get *into* the belly?"

According to a poll released by Planned Parenthood, although 82 percent of parents have talked to their children about issues related to sexuality (such as relationships or about when they believe sex should or should not take place), many don't broach the tougher, more complicated topics, including how to say no to sex or the use of condoms and birth control.[1] Research shows that these deeper conversations make a difference, particularly in the teen years. A *JAMA Pediatrics* study reports that adolescents who have talked to their parents about sex are more likely to communicate with their partners and use condoms and birth control.[2]

A study by the National Institutes of Health adds another nuance: it suggests that parents tend to exclude positive topics associated with sexuality, such as pleasure, love, and healthy relationships, in favor of negative topics and warnings.[3] Additionally, a study of more than six hundred young people, ages twelve to fifteen, reports this whammy: nearly one-third had *never* talked to their parents about sex at all. That's quite a number.

Truth Bomb!

According to a large-scale survey commissioned by the National Campaign to Prevent Teen and Unplanned Pregnancy, teens say that parents (38 percent) *most* influence their decisions about sex. They are more influential than peers (22 percent), the media (9 percent), teachers and educators (4 percent), and others. Nearly nine in ten (87 percent) young people surveyed voiced that it would be much easier for them to delay sexual activity and to avoid teen pregnancy if they had the opportunity to have more open, honest, and informative discussions about these topics with their parents.[4]

While every parent has their reasons for abstaining from the sex talk, most usually fall into one of four categories:

1. **They find talking about sex to be awkward, unpleasant, and embarrassing.**[5]

   This is one of the biggest impediments that parents mention when explaining why they haven't talked to their kids about sex. Many report not knowing what to say, fearing that they will say too much or too little, or feeling unsure how to phrase answers so they don't sound crude.[6] Other parents admit to worrying that they may inadvertently reveal details about their own sex lives they wish they hadn't or, conversely, might learn something about their child's experience with the topic that makes them uncomfortable. And of course, many parents often skirt talking about sex because they feel like the topic is inappropriate and embarrassing for young ears to hear. I remember having a conversation with one of my friends who said her child brought up something related to sex, and she panicked and changed the subject to what they had for lunch. "How about that ham sandwich?" *Divert! Divert! Nothing to see here!*

   Dina Alexander, the founder and president of Educate and Empower Kids, told me on a podcast interview that parents have been conditioned and socialized to believe that talking about sex is awkward.[7] "We've been told dozens of times throughout our lives, 'Oh, you don't want to have that conversation,' when really, when you get down to the heart of it, it's no big deal," Alexander said, adding that parents should really think about what makes them so uncomfortable. "Is it the topic of actual intercourse?

Is it talking about predators? Is it talking about anatomy? Such a self-assessment can help pinpoint and even dilute your discomfort."

2. **Parents don't feel like they're well-versed on the subjects of anatomy or biology.**

The next time your child asks, "Where do babies come from?" and you feel the need to scour the WebMD website for a medically factual answer, don't. Remember, unless we are doctors or health experts, virtually none of us knows everything there is to know about how our bodies function. What we *do* have, though, are our own unique experiences with sex, which are useful and sufficient to begin a discussion. We can also simply listen. "We don't need to have all the answers," noted Richard Weissbourd, a senior lecturer at the Harvard Graduate School of Education and the Kennedy School of Government, in a recent podcast interview. "We should go into these conversations with some insights but also expect to learn a lot too."[8]

3. **Parents believe that talking about sex suggests tacit approval.**

Some mothers and fathers believe the sex talk is code for "you can go out and have sex now!" in the same way as giving someone a recipe means "you can bake a cake now." I get the fear, but the theory doesn't hold water.

Journal of Health Communication research has shown that children who are comfortable talking about sex are actually more likely to *delay* sexual activity and are also older when they first have intercourse.[9] If you think about it, it makes sense: when your children talk to you, they get the benefit of your wisdom and learn how and why to make healthy choices for their bodies. "The curiosity about sex is there no matter what," Alexander notes. "Parents often feel like they're going to be taking away their child's innocence if they talk about these things, and I say that is garbage. This is about empowering your child."

4. **Parents' religious, moral, or value-based beliefs may be contrary to the information their children are receiving.**[10]

Research tells us that religious beliefs can impact the frequency of conversations around contraception, premarital sexual activities, pornography, pregnancy risk, homosexuality, and sexual health choices with kids. Many religious ideologies provide strict rules about sex—delaying intercourse, sex for procreation only, etc.—while popular culture, especially as it's relayed to young people in the media, promotes premarital sex and sex for pleasure. Is it possible to teach kids about sexual health without undermining your own moral or religious views?

I think it is, particularly if you couch some of what you relay in your religious faith: "You were blessed with all these amazing, capable body parts, each with an important function." Or "Sex is part of creating life." And even "You will be receiving a lot of messages about having sex during your teen years. In our religion, we believe..." Of course, be ready to answer if your children want to know why your religion espouses what it does—especially if they are unsure (or have a negative reaction to) how the messaging impacts them and the people they love and respect. If you are uncertain, you can always research the answers together. When kids think critically about sex, relationships, and consent, it not only creates informed individuals but also healthy communities—including healthy faith-based communities.

The Sex Talks

Traditionally, a discussion about sex has been more about how babies are made (see box) rather than a wider view of how sex needs to be defined. While it's true that pregnancy and procreation are important parts of the discussion, they're certainly not the only pieces. By keeping the scope of this discussion so narrow, we miss the opportunity to talk to our kids about information that can help them to become informed, empowered experts of their bodies and their own sexual health.

Instead of one big, pressure-filled lecture, the sex talk should be a series of talks or microdiscussions about a host of sexual topics that might include the following:

- Knowing and understanding your body

- Consent
- Sexual harassment, sexual assault, and sexual abuse
- Exploration and masturbation
- What sex is and how it works
- Pleasure, connection, and relationships
- Pornography
- Risks such as sexually transmitted diseases (STDs) and sexually transmitted infections (STIs)
- Intercourse, including, yes, how babies are made

These conversations can happen over time from babyhood to young adulthood, making them commonplace and frequent.

Wait…babyhood? Yes. Can't we wait until the teen years? No. Even young children need and deserve to learn about their bodies for safety and understanding. No matter what your family values are or when you think it's okay for young people to engage in sexual behavior, puberty can begin, whether we want it to or not, as early as nine years old. Children can come across sexual imagery such as pornography as early as age six or seven, as reported by the *New York Times*.[11]

Most Girl Bodies	Most Boy Bodies
Puberty usually occurs between the ages of eight and fifteen.	Puberty usually occurs between the ages of nine and fifteen.
Possible physical changes: breast development, body hair, vaginal discharge, menstruation, growth spurt (taller, wider hips, thicker thighs, smaller waist, weight gain), acne, body odor, more sweat production, estrogen increases, ovaries send out eggs.	Possible physical changes: facial hair, spontaneous erections, masturbation, wet dreams, larger testicles, growth spurt (taller, broader, body bigger), voice lower, acne, body hair, body odor, testosterone increases, sperm production.
Possible emotional changes: mood swings, sexual interest, desire for more privacy, individuation from parents.	Possible emotional changes: mood swings, sexual interest, desire for more privacy, individuation from parents.

The problem with *not* talking to your kids about sex is that eventually your children will likely learn about it through the lens of popular media, a peer, or a porn site. Plus, at increasingly young ages, many children have access to electronics that keep them connected—often mistakenly—to sexual imagery, pornography, and negative messaging about intimacy and sex. Parental filters only go so far; there's a strong possibility that your child has access to adult-oriented sites *somewhere*. Even if your children don't cart around a phone or tablet, one of their friends probably does.

You are the best source of information because you know your children best. You have your children's best interests in mind. You know what is true and accurate, and if your children have questions, you can help them find the right answer. There are wonderful children's books and age-appropriate videos and podcasts that can provide additional support as you engage in these conversations.

When you normalize the discussion of sex—meaning you make it *normal* to ask, answer, and be curious about sex, the human body, and developing feelings related to sex—it gets easier to discuss. If we can begin a strong dialogue now, when our children are young, by the time they reach sexual maturity, they will be ready to make the right choices for themselves based on real information. Additionally and just as importantly, they will know they can rely on *you* for truthful, sound information, rather than the school bathroom wall or the kid on the bus. That's worth a little discomfort on our part.

Truth Bomb!

Richard Weissbourd of Harvard's Making Caring Common Project reports that young people don't just want to talk about sex—they also want to talk about the feelings and relationships that are tied into it.[12] In fact, 70 percent of young people said they wished they had received more information from their parents about how to manage the complicated emotions that arise in a relationship.[13] More than a third reported they wanted more guidance on how to have a mature relationship and handle breakups as well as how to avoid getting hurt in a relationship. They also wanted to know to how to compromise in a relationship when both partners are stubborn, deal with falling out of love with someone, wait to have sex, and deal with cheating. While sex may be part of dating for some adolescents, when it comes to most teens, it's about more than sex. It's about how to have a meaningful relationship.

How Are Babies Made?

It seems to be a rite of passage that parents are asked this question, no matter what way your family has come to be. It is no secret that my husband and I adopted both of our children. I've been open with them from an early age that the "baby-making machine inside me was broken," and while the doctors tried to help me get pregnant, it was fate that our family would be blessed by adoption.

Therefore, it seemed logical (although I was taken aback) when my daughter asked me one night at bedtime, "So when I want to get pregnant, I'll go to the doctor too?" The answer, of course, was, "It doesn't always work like that. While some couples and single parents go to the doctor to help them get pregnant, other people do not."

Then came *the question*: "But then how does the baby get into the belly?" Here are the highlights of that conversation:

- **The egg and the sperm:** "Well, you remember what I told you about the egg and the sperm—that most women are born with eggs and one is released each month into their womb, and most men have the sperm."

- **How the egg and sperm get together:** "The sperm comes out of the penis, and the eggs are accessed through the vagina. The penis goes into the vagina—they go together like interlocking puzzle pieces."
- **How the penis can get into the vagina:** "You know how cream has a slick and slidey feeling? The woman's body puts out a fluid that makes the inside of her vagina very slick. And the man's penis becomes stiff—that's called an erection—and it just slides in."
- **How the sperm comes out:** "The woman and man move back and forth, and then the sperm comes out of the hole at the top of the penis—kind of like when you shake up a soda bottle and open it. It's called ejaculation."
- **What happens next:** "The sperm go on a long trip through the fallopian tubes, and one single sperm combines with the egg. Only one sperm per egg! Sometimes the sperm and the egg get together, and sometimes they don't. When a sperm penetrates or goes into the egg, that forms what's called a zygote or fertilized egg. That travels over the next few days to the special room, or womb, where it's nice and cushy and safe to develop—if the timing and science are just right—into a baby."
- **What happens to the couple while they are trying to make a baby:** "You show each other how much you love one another. You kiss and hug and can say beautiful things to each other. This is why this act, in many cases, is not just called sex but making love."

I know this conversation seems like it would be really awkward. But I have to say, for me, that's not really how it felt. To my surprise, after this discussion, we talked quite a bit more about important things like consent, mutual respect, pleasure, and love. What I thought would be a quick talk about the mechanics of sex and baby making became so much more, and I came away from the conversation not feeling embarrassed but really lucky to have been able to have these kinds of talks with my daughter. And the best part was what my daughter said as I was walking out: "Mommy, I love having these kinds of conversations with you. I wish we could talk all night." Thankfully, there are always more opportunities.

Truth Bomb!

While rare, not all men have sperm and not all women have eggs. For example, some men have azoospermia, when there is no sperm in their ejaculate, and some women are born with abnormal ovarian development, which compromises egg production. In addition, albeit infrequently, some girls are born without a vagina or uterus (some get hysterectomies as adults), some boys are born without a penis, and some children are born intersex or with external genitalia that do not match their gender.[14]

What's Sex Anyway?

Young people are bombarded with messages about what they should and should not do with their bodies and what they think "sex" is. It turns out that the nuances of this definition are crucial to our choices and beliefs about sexual behavior.

While personal definitions may vary, perhaps it would be helpful to have a sample definition. Sexologist Logan Levkoff defined sex while talking to me on my parenting podcast as "a range of behaviors in which people share their bodies with one another."[15] She details that sex "can be genital-genital, genital-oral, genital-anal" and that it describes something that is "deeply personal and intimate during which comes the capacity for pleasure as well as big responsibilities." I like that definition and would add that sex needs to be completely consensual and voluntary.

Studies show that when young people are told that *only* vaginal intercourse is sex, many believe that oral sex or anal sex, for example, is not "*real* sex." Some even equate oral sex to kissing rather than to sex. When I recently spoke to a sampling of middle school girls in the northeast United States, they explained to me that they used oral sex to satisfy or "hold off" their boyfriends who were interested in vaginal intercourse. They also said that because it was not "the real thing," they considered it safer and something they could do prior to having intercourse because "it's not as big of a deal." When we cultivate our definition of sex, we need to think about these kinds of children's perspectives as well as our own as parents. No matter what your personal values are, here are some questions to consider:

- What were you told about sex and sexuality when growing up?
- How might your life or sexual experiences have been different if the information you received were different?
- What do you wish you knew about sex and your body before you were faced with making decisions about it?
- Do you believe "sex" to be any intimate behaviors that involve the body? Which intimate behaviors are and aren't considered part of sex in your eyes? Which fits into your definition?
  - Self-sex or masturbation
  - Petting or sexual touching of breasts or genitals
  - "Dry sex" (rubbing genitals together while clothed)
  - Manual-genital sex (also called hand jobs, fingering, or "third base")
  - Oral sex
  - Vaginal intercourse
  - Sex-toy play
  - Sexting or cybersex
  - Reproduction
- How do you want your tweens and teens to interpret the messages they receive about sex and their bodies when they are faced with sexual images, videos, or propositions from potential romantic partners?
- What do you want them to know about procreation, romantic connection, consent, and pleasure before they become sexually active?
- How do you want your children to feel when making choices about their bodies, sex, and relationships?

Your answers to these questions can help guide you to have the microconversations that you know your child needs and deserves. Do you want your child to receive information similar to what you received? Different? This exercise can frame your approach and provide the motivation for getting uncomfortable. Let's get started.

▣ Stats in a Pinch

When your tween and teen children express to you that "everyone does it," as it relates to sex, turn to these powerful statistics so they have the right information.

Middle school

- About 88 percent of middle schoolers are *not* having sexual inter-course.
- Only about 8 percent of middle schoolers report having oral sex.
- Only 6.5 percent of middle schoolers engage in anal sex.[16]

High school

- A national Youth Risk Behavior Surveillance System (YRBSS) survey conducted by the CDC on ninth to twelfth graders showed that just under 40 percent of high school students report having had sexual intercourse, which means three-fifths of high school kids have *not* had sexual intercourse.
- While many assume boys are much more sexually active than girls, the YRBSS showed that about 39 percent of boys and 38 percent of girls report having had sexual intercourse in high school.
- The proportion of high school students having sexual intercourse has been trending down over the past few decades.[17]

Conversation #1: Know Your Body

If you want to lay the foundation for open communication with your children about sex and sexuality, then talking about the body is the perfect place to start. The earlier, the better! Diaper changes, baths, and doctor's visits provide easy opportunities to name and discuss all your children's wonderful parts. And genitals? Include them—they're body parts too!

We don't want children to get the idea that any body parts are "unmentionables." Everyone has them, they're normal, and they serve very important functions. As Melissa Pintor Carnagey encourages in the book *Sex Positive Talks to Have with Kids*, go beyond "head, shoulders, knees, and toes."[18] Name the penis, vulva, nipples, and anus as easily as you do an arm, belly button, or chin.

Dina Alexander agrees. "I've recommended, especially for young girls ages eight or nine years old, giving them a mirror and letting them look at their vagina," she says. "They need to know what it looks like. They need to understand the difference between where their urine comes out and where their vagina is. To me, this is the same as showing them their elbow or their eyeball. I can look in the mirror and see my eye, but I can't look straight in the mirror and see all the parts of my vulva and my vagina. And a girl needs to know what she looks like down there."[19]

If you don't take the time to name them, who will? My friend and colleague Dr. Dae Sheridan, a sexologist and professor of human sexuality, notes that many young women in college were never taught that they have three openings: a urethra, a vagina, and an anus.[20] "It's funny because when it comes to sex ed, especially with girls, we talk about it from the inside out—fallopian tubes, uterus, birth canal—which doesn't make a lot of sense. We wouldn't teach a child about her tympanic membrane and the cochlea before we said, 'Hey that's your ear!'"

When kids know the anatomically correct names for body parts, they are better able to talk about them and let key adults know if they have questions or concerns. This knowledge also allows kids to voice if they are experiencing pain or discomfort, such as a urinary tract infection, or even if they are suffering from abuse.

Additionally, when we freely talk about all the body parts in a positive light, it helps children to develop a more positive view of every aspect of their body, its functions, and its amazing capabilities. As Bonnie J. Rough, author of *Beyond Birds & Bees*, challenged parents on a recent *How to Talk to Kids about Anything* podcast episode, "Are you using negative terms [while changing your child's diaper]? What's your demeanor? We don't want to give our children the idea that while their cheeks and their tummies are adorable, there's something yucky between their legs."[21] Every part of the body is worthy of care and curiosity.

Q&A

MY NINE-YEAR-OLD DAUGHTER ASKED ME WHAT IT MEANS TO "GET YOUR PERIOD"? HOW DO I ANSWER?

"During puberty, usually between the ages of ten and fifteen, you will likely get something called a period. A period, or menstruation, is something that happens about once per month. It's a way that your body prepares you and your uterus to get pregnant and have a baby one day if you choose to do so. Your hormones tell your uterus to thicken up its lining so that if a baby is conceived, it can grow in there. One of your two ovaries pushes out an egg. If that egg meets a sperm, it can be fertilized to make a baby. It would then head to the uterus to start growing. Of course, most of the time, there is no baby, so that thick padding in your uterus, made up of blood and nutrients, isn't needed. This lining is pushed out of your body through the vagina. The blood that comes out is your period. It's totally normal! This process usually happens every month, unless you're pregnant, and usually lasts between three and seven days. You can choose to use a pad, tampon, or menstrual cup (and even special period underwear) to keep your clothes clean and fresh when you get your period."

MY TEN-YEAR-OLD SON ASKED ME WHY THE PENIS GETS HARD AND STICKS OUT SOMETIMES. HOW DO I ANSWER?

Sexologist Logan Levkoff suggests that we first describe what is happening during an erection so kids can understand their bodies better:[22] "The reason a penis gets hard is that it's made of this spongy tissue and blood rushes to it. And just as a sponge will absorb water and expand, the penis will absorb the blood and expand, and this causes it to get hard."

You can then go on to say, "When a penis gets hard like that, it's called an erection. Erections can happen throughout your life. It's completely normal if it happens or it doesn't happen. When it occurs during puberty, it's more like a 'systems check' to make sure everything is working right. It may happen at random times, and you can't always control that, but when you get older, you will be able to control it more. Erections can make it possible for you to have intercourse and make a baby when you're older, when and if you're ready and interested in that life choice."

Conversation #2: Consent

Consent, as you likely already know, is saying yes to something. We provide consent for our kids to go on field trips to the museum and for our medical records to be transferred from one doctor's office to another. As it relates to this chapter, consent is saying yes to being physically touched and, more intimately, engaging in sexual behavior.

Sexual consent requires a 100 percent enthusiastic yes from both people involved. Yes can be changed to no at any point, even if both people were on board before. Consent is not consent if it's forced, assumed, or pressured out of a person or if the person giving consent is under the influence of alcohol or drugs or is too young to give consent (laws differ by state).

How do we explain consent to kids? You can start at a young age and use everyday situations:

- When they're seeing a friend, you can encourage your child to ask, "Can I give you a hug?" and wait for an answer.

- When you approach a dog while on a walk around the neighborhood, you can instruct your child to ask, "May I pet your dog?" and then wait for the answer.

- On the days that your children don't want to be hugged but still want to greet their most affectionate friend, you can coach them to offer an alternative that makes them feel comfortable. For example, "Today, I don't want to be hugged. How about a high five?" This kind of consent is a precursor to sexual consent.

Occasionally, the answer is simply no. That's all right too. Teach your child, "Sometimes the answer will be yes. Sometimes it will be no. Either answer is okay and needs to be respected." Similarly, say, "Your body belongs to you. If someone wants to touch, tickle, or hug your body, and it's not okay with you, you can say, 'No, I don't want to be touched.'"

A popular YouTube video quite smartly equates consent to giving someone (or not giving someone) a cup of tea.[23] The main underlying messages are "If someone doesn't want a cup of tea, changes their mind about wanting a cup of tea, isn't sure they want a cup of tea, or falls unconscious before the tea is ready, don't make them drink tea!" Similarly, equating consent to something in your child's world can make it more understandable, such as, "If you asked your friend, 'Do you want a cookie?' and that friend said no, you wouldn't make them eat the cookie, right?" or "If your classmate asked if you wanted one of her pretzels and, at first, you said yes, but then you changed your mind, do you still have to eat the pretzel? Of course not!"

Q&A

MY CHILD ASKED ME IF SEXUAL INTERCOURSE FEELS GOOD. HOW DO I ANSWER?

"At first, when it's new to you, there's a lot of learning about what feels good and right to you and the other person. But when you love someone and you are old enough to make this choice and you have said yes to having sex with this person, it can be wonderful. It can feel great—it should grow to feel great for both people. But if you are with someone you don't want to be with, with someone you did *not* say yes to, it can hurt—it can hurt physically, and it can hurt your feelings. You should only have sex with someone you truly want to be with—someone who respects you and cares for you in a very special way."

Truth Bomb!

Studies show that young people feel pressure to have sex before they're ready because they worry it's expected or that "everyone is doing it." Girls in particular report having trouble saying no, whether it's for a sexy selfie or for sexual favors, for various reasons:

- They worry they will hurt the other person's feelings.
- They are at a "point of no return" where it's easier to just go through with it.
- They need to finish what they started due to shame, guilt, or obligation.

Peggy Orenstein wrote in her book *Girls & Sex* that young women receive the message that "our bodies exist for male sexual pleasure" and "our power is in attracting male desire."[24] It's vital to our children's well-being that we lay any sexual pressures on the table and tell them directly, "These messages are pervasive, but they are garbage. You can say no at any point, and you don't need to justify why. Listen to your gut: if it doesn't feel right to you, stop right away. You are under no sexual obligation at any time for anyone."

Conversation #3: Pornography

I could wish all day long that pornography weren't so accessible to children, but it is. These images, once secured on a high shelf of a magazine stand or under your big brother's mattress, are now only a Google search and click away. In one University of New Hampshire study, 93 percent of boys and 62 percent of girls admitted to seeing online porn during their adolescence. Other studies state that twice as many teenagers watch porn than their parents surmised, with up to one-third of boys and 12 percent of girls having seen rough oral sex and "gang bangs."

"It's either you or UPorn—who is going to educate your kids about sex?" Peggy Orenstein stated plainly on my podcast recently.[25] "Porn shows that sex is something that men do to women. Female pleasure is a performance for male satisfaction—a lot of eroticized violence and humiliation...acts that wouldn't feel good to most people, especially most women. Absent from trusted adults, that's their sex educator now."

According to a recent statement by the American College of Pediatricians, pornography exposure for children and adolescents has become widespread.[26] In a 2010 survey of English students fourteen to sixteen years old, almost one-third claimed their first exposure to internet pornography was at ten years old or younger,[27] while a recent 2021 review of porn research sites found that the tender age of eight was the first point of contact[28] (Other studies have found the age can be even younger.)[29] With so little understanding of what sex is, it's not surprising that after viewing pornography, children report a toxic stew of disgust, shock, embarrassment, and other emotions, and they may suffer the symptoms of anxiety and depression.

Additionally, children under twelve years of age who have viewed pornography are statistically more likely to sexually assault their peers.[30] As noted by Gail Dines, author of *Pornland: How Porn Has Hijacked Our Sexuality* and founding president of the nonprofit Culture Reframed, "The more you are exposed to porn, the less capacity you have for intimacy and relationships, and the more likely for boys to aggress against a girl."[31]

Not to mention, porn is addictive and can alter a child's developing brain—literally—impacting its structure and functionality. According to Neuroscience News, a site that reports on research from labs, universities, and hospitals around the world, "Porn scenes, like addictive substances, are hyper-stimulating triggers that lead to unnaturally high levels of dopamine secretion. This can damage the dopamine reward system and leave it unresponsive to natural sources of pleasure."[32] The fallout is that porn viewers then have difficulty in achieving arousal with a physical partner and are constantly seeking new and harder themes in videos as they build up tolerance for what they've been consuming online—just like drug addicts must do with their next hits.

What do you do if you find evidence that your child has been viewing pornographic material? Whatever their age, it's important to treat the situation with caution and restraint. Even if you are having a panic attack inside or want to throw the computer or phone across the room, "Don't start yelling and screaming," says Dina Alexander.[33] "That doesn't work." Indeed, that only produces shame from your child and can shut down any sexual dialogue you may want to have.

What does work? Patience, tolerance, and understanding.

1. Establish whether your children saw pornographic images without blaming them. "You are not in trouble. You didn't do anything wrong.

Can you tell me if you've seen any pornographic images and, if so, what you've seen?" It's important that you don't make assumptions and that you are clear on the specific images in question so you can address them. Steer clear of shaming them by saying things like, "You're disgusting!" or "There's clearly something wrong with you!" Shame is a conversation ender, not a conversation starter.

2. Ask your children what they think about what they saw. "How did you feel when you saw those images? Have you seen them before? Where?" This is what Alexander calls a "temperature question"—we are taking our children's "temperature" to find out their knowledge of a particular subject. You can also establish when they saw the images, through which means, and with whom so you can better understand the level of exposure and if anyone else was involved who may need some help from their parents or key adults. Gail Dines also adds the question "When you were finished with this image, how did that make you feel?" She reports from her research and interviews that "it makes them feel terrible."

3. Let them know they are being duped. Our kids hate to be "played"—and knowing that adults are trying to gain control over what they do, see, and ultimately spend money on can help them gain perspective. Dines reminds us to cite the manipulation outright and tie the adult industry to a desire for habitual users and money. You might say, "The porn industry is trying to manipulate you by exposing you to free images now so you get hooked. These images trigger the reward center of your brain—similar to when you are playing video games or when a rat gets food pellets for getting to the end of a maze. It makes you want more and more! Their goal is to make you into a habitual, addicted user, just like a dealer to a drug addict, so you eventually have to pay for videos and images that feed that addiction. Believe me, they're not giving you these free images and videos in good faith. They don't care about your well-being. Just your money."

4. Talk about what's real and what's not real. Let them know that pornography is not sex or love—or even real life. It does not represent what people

want, what they should expect, or how sex plays out between two people who love each other. Explain that pornography can skew how kids think about what is true about sex and sexuality. Kind of like a TV commercial. Or a reality show. You might say something like, "Porn is used for adult entertainment and does not show real relationships or real bodies. Real relationships are about love, respect, and intimacy. Real bodies are all different sizes, shapes, weights, colors, and ages. Many pornographic bodies have been modified and enhanced to look the way they do. The people in these videos are being paid to do what they're told—many are being exploited and used—to get people to watch and come back for more. It's fiction masquerading as fact."

5. Discuss the messages porn sends. Porn mistakenly tells our kids that

   ○ Everyone should be available at all times for sex.

   ○ No intimacy, love, or respect is required or desired for sex.

   ○ Violent sexual acts are normal, warranted, and wanted.

   ○ Mutual consent is not necessary for sex to take place.

   ○ Safe sex is not desirable.

   ○ Girls are valued for their hypersexualized looks, their sexual availability, and their willingness to do whatever a man wants, even if it's demeaning or dehumanizing.

   ○ Boys are valued for their hypermasculine looks, their dominating actions, and their aggressive performance.

The topic of pornography is an uncomfortable conversation for most of us, but *not* talking about it won't make it go away.

♠ In My Home

One night, at our dinner table, where we talk about lots of subjects with varying degrees of difficulty, I said to Tallie and Noah, "I've been wanting to ask you both something for a while because it applies significantly to kids who are nine to twelve years old, and you are both right in that age group."

They looked at me attentively. "The researchers are telling us that kids your age sometimes come across websites, videos, and images that show naked bodies. Now...nobody is in trouble, and nobody is mad. Daddy and I just wanted to know if that has ever happened to you?"

My son answered immediately. "Yes, I was looking for a camera app, and there was a picture of a naked woman that popped up, and she was, like, lying down like this..." He put his hand up to his head as if he were posing. "I x-ed out of it right away."

"Okay, as I said, nobody is in trouble," I said. "There's nothing wrong with the human body, but we wanted you to know that sometimes kids your age stumble on these websites and are curious. And it's normal to be curious about the body. But many of these websites don't have your best interests in mind. They want to hook you in and get you to come back again and again for more. And eventually, they want you to pay for it."

"But why would I want to look a random lady's naked body?" Noah asked.

"You may not be so interested now, but as you get older, you might be more curious. Again, this is normal. However, these websites are not healthy. They don't just show naked bodies. They also show sex and often violence, especially against women. Studies show that these kinds of websites, called pornography, or 'porn' for short, can have negative effects on our brains and make us feel depressed and anxious and also make us have a tough time with our relationships when we do want to have a boyfriend or a girlfriend."

"I wasn't going to tell you I saw that because I thought you'd get mad," Noah said.

I shook my head. "You'll never get into trouble for coming to us and telling us about a problem," I reiterated. Kids need to know this as a *fact*.

"What should I do if an image like that comes up again? Should I x it out? Or show it to one of you? Or turn my computer around and bring it over?"

"I think x-ing it out is a good choice. And tell one of us. We want to be able to help you."

My daughter, Tallie, had been listening and told us that she saw something by accident when with a friend. She said the two of them slammed the computer down and never opened whatever it was again. She didn't want to discuss it further and, at this point, asked if it was okay to leave the table. Of course, we let her. These conversations, in addition to showing your children that you are open to the topic of sex, reveal if your children are open as well. Some kids are ready to talk; others might need some more time.

Conversation #4: Body Exploration and Masturbation

Children are naturally curious—especially about the people they care about, their environment, and their bodies. However, when young people touch their private parts, it is often considered taboo, offensive, and even bad or wicked. Yet kids need to be taught that the natural exploration of their bodies is completely normal.

I know this may seem surprising, but when young kids touch their private parts, it's not because they are sexually aroused or interested in sex. Young kids simply touch their bodies because they like the way it feels. This kind of body exploration may be used to relax, fall asleep, or feel less anxious, and it's completely typical for children to do it, or not do it, to do it every once in a while, or to do it every day.

"A lot of parents freak out about the masturbation discussion," Dina Alexander, founder of Educate and Empower Kids, told me on a podcast episode.[34] Seeing this kind of touching through adult eyes might make parents conclude that it is "wrong" or "dirty" or overtly sexual, but "masturbation is not sexual for a five-year-old. They're just feeling good. They're self-soothing. And it's our job to help them understand that they have an amazing body."

Children learn more about themselves through body exploration. They can gain a more positive body image, a stronger sense of ownership, and a deeper understanding of what feels good, okay, or bad to them. This puts them in a positive position of being able to recognize safe or unsafe touch as well. And given that girls' private parts are more tucked away than those of boys, it is common that some girls miss key information about themselves when they don't know their bodies. As long as children understand that exploration should be done in private, it's not only seen as normal but positive.

⌐ *Scripts in a Pinch*

As children enter puberty and hormones become par for the course, you can let them know these facts:

- **It's all completely normal:** "Interest in your body is normal, interest in other people's bodies is normal, self-exploration is normal, and sexual feelings are normal! And if you don't have this interest or these feelings, that's normal too."

- **You are entitled to privacy:** "You have the right to privacy where you can have the freedom to explore your body in ways that feel right to you."

- **We all have the capacity for pleasure—with another person or alone:** "Sex is not simply about making someone else feel good. It should be enjoyable for both people. Your needs are equally as important as your partner's satisfaction." As Logan Levkoff said on my parenting podcast, "None of us has to be dependent on another person to give us pleasure."[35]

Teachable Moments

While there's no specific date on the calendar to start talking about sex, sexuality, menstruation, or maturation, you can start by allowing everyday opportunities for discussions to present themselves. Your children may not respond at first— they may not respond *at all*—but you are opening the door to a conversation that they may have been wanting to broach but weren't sure how.

Teachable Moments	Conversation Starters
A quiet, calm time, one-on-one in the car, walking on the beach, etc.	"When I was your age, we never talked about (sex, masturbation, consent, STDs, pornography, etc.). Have you heard anything about this before? I know it's a bit awkward to talk about, but I really wish someone had told me that…"
Strolling in the park watching the birds.	"Hey, do you see those two birds chasing each other around? Do you know what they're doing?"
Watching a TV show featuring a pregnant character.	"See how big that woman's belly is? Do you know she has a baby in there?"
Reflecting on seeing your children's classmates for the first time in a while.	"Pete looks so tall! And Brianna, she looks so much like her mother! It's amazing how kids' looks and bodies often change so much in middle school, right?"
In the supermarket, passing by menstrual hygiene products, condoms, or other items related to sexuality or maturation.	"I know you've probably passed by these products before, but do you know what they're used for?"
News coverage about sex, sexual assault, sexting, etc.	"I saw a news story today about a sexual harassment case at a school. Have you heard those words before? It's kind of like bullying but when someone says rude or inappropriate comments about another person's body or body parts. Has that ever happened at your school?"
TV shows/movies/ videos depicting romance or a sexual situation.	"What did you think when [Person A] put their arm around [Person B] in the movie-theater scene?" or "I got the feeling that [Person A] was really uncomfortable in the party scene. What did you think? Have you ever felt like that?"

Teachable Moments	Conversation Starters
Magazines, TV shows, or social media sites talking about celebrity relationships, pregnancy, birth, or infidelity.	"I saw the announcement [your favorite actor(s)] made today on their social about their new relationship. They seem happy! What did you think of what they said?"
Highly sexualized images or videos in advertisements, media, etc.	"What do you think they are trying to sell on that billboard featuring the woman in her underwear?" or "I was leafing through this magazine, and I saw that the women are objectified in this ad. Do you know what that means?"
Pregnancy, miscarriage, birth, or adoptions within the family, neighborhood, or community.	"Aunt D is really upset because she had a miscarriage. That means that she's no longer pregnant. While we aren't always sure exactly why, it can happen when the baby isn't developing normally and stops growing. She didn't do anything wrong, and she can go on to have a healthy pregnancy after this. Right now, she's just so sad."
Preteen or teen life event like a first period, buying a first bra, or seeing a sex-education film at school.	"You mentioned that you saw a sex-ed film at school today. What did you think of it? Anything surprise you or confuse you? I'm here to answer any questions."
Overhearing people using sexual slurs like "whore," "slut," etc.	"I just read a research study out of Penn State University that there were 419,000 tweets per day that contained common sex slurs in it like 'whore' or 'slut'! The number surprised me. Does it surprise you? Why do you think people use these words?"[36]
Expectations of affection toward family or friends.	"We're seeing your cousins next Friday. I heard you say that you didn't want to hug them when you saw them, and that's okay. Did something happen that made you feel uncomfortable? How would you feel best greeting them?"

Truth Bomb! ——

Some young people falsely believe that the first time they engage in sexual activity, they have some kind of "first-timers protection." One of my friends relayed to me that her fifteen-year-old daughter, who had a boyfriend, was shocked to hear that a girl could get pregnant right away—even if they stopped having intercourse in the middle of the act. Be straightforward with your child: "You can get pregnant [or an STD] the very first time you have sex. Even if the penis is pulled out before ejaculation, some sperm can come out during the earlier part of intercourse that could result in pregnancy." Talk about protections people use, such as condoms, birth control, or delaying sex.

Conversation Starter: Discussing Risks of Early or Casual Sex

- **Early pregnancy risks:** The North Carolina School Health Training Center has an exercise they do with middle schoolers where they investigate the health, legal, financial, and social consequences of adolescent and unintended pregnancy.[37] They ask teens to write down what they want to become, do, or be in the next five to fifteen years, then ask how those future goals would be affected if an unintentional pregnancy occurred. You might do the same: "One of the biggest risks that comes with early sex between teen boys and teen girls is pregnancy. What would change in your lives if you (or your girlfriend or your friend) got pregnant? How would it impact finishing school? How would it impact the ability to become a [doctor, engineer, teacher, entrepreneur, etc.]?" Opening this conversation based on what-ifs can be enlightening.

- **Physical risks:** Pregnancy isn't the only possible result but it's important to note that, according to the World Health Organization, "adolescent mothers (aged 10–19 years) face higher risks of eclampsia, puerperal endometritis and systemic infections than women aged 20–24 years, and babies of adolescent mothers face higher risks of low birth weight, preterm birth and severe neonatal condition."[38] In addition to pregnancy and the physical risks it poses for teens, people can get STDs or STIs such as chlamydia, gonorrhea, HIV, and syphilis from unprotected oral, vaginal, and anal sex—and according to the American Academy of Pediatrics[39] as well as various studies,[40] many adolescents are unaware of this fact. A whopping one in four teens contracts an STD every year.[41] Say, "Some teens don't realize that they can get an STD, STI, or HIV from any kind of unprotected sex: vaginal, oral, or anal. And while some are treatable with antibiotics, some have no cure, so it's important to know these physical risks." This can be a perfect lead in to discussing (and answering questions about) different types of contraception: from external and internal condoms to the pill and birth control implant, their levels of protection, how they're used, and your opinions about them.

- **Emotional risks:** Research reveals that early sexual behavior with a partner as well as casual hookups are correlated with negative reactions such as regret, disappointment, confusion, embarrassment, guilt, low self-esteem, and even anxiety and depression. While some studies suggest that girls are more likely than boys to report feeling bad about themselves or feeling used after participating in oral sex and vaginal intercourse, other research shows high distress scores, lower life satisfaction, and decreased happiness after casual sex, regardless of gender. Say, "So often, people talk about the physical side of sex, but they don't think about the emotional investment and the need for connection, understanding, communication, trust, and mutual respect. You want to be ready for all aspects of sex—it's not just something you do with your body. It's also a real invest-ment of your heart and your emotions. It's a big step and feels best when you are doing it with someone who is truly special to you—who is kind, respectful, and cares deeply about you. It's not something that should be taken lightly or done casually."

Conversation #5: Sexual Assault

You might be thinking: Do we really need to be talking about consent, sexual assault, and the Bill Cosbys, Larry Nassars, and Harvey Weinsteins of the world, for goodness' sake?

Yes, we do.

Children need to know, from a young age, that their bodies are their own, their words are powerful, and nobody has the right to take advantage of them simply because they are bigger or stronger or because they outrank them. A few sobering statistics: according to the U.S. Department of Health and Human Services' Child Maltreatment Survey, every nine minutes, Child Protective Services substantiates or finds evidence for a claim of child sexual abuse.[42] In fact, in 2016 alone, Child Protective Services agencies indicated that 57,329 children were victims of sexual abuse. And both girls and boys are affected: one in four girls and one in six boys in the United States are sexually abused before the age of eighteen.[43]

This is serious. We don't have the leisure of putting off these conversa-tions until our children are adolescents—or worse, not having them at all. "Early efforts at prevention are necessary," Dr. Sandy Wurtele, psychologist, child sexual abuse prevention expert, and author of the *Body Safety Training Workbook for Parents*, told me recently. "As parents, the most important thing you can do is engage your child in discussions, often." Not sure how to start? Here are some things to keep in mind as you broach the topic.

Truth Bomb!

While the words "sexual assault" might conjure up images of "dirty old men" and "creepy-looking strangers" lurking behind the trees, most child molesters are people the child knows. Only 7 percent of those who sexually abuse children are strangers.[44]

- **Give age-appropriate facts:** While it's unnecessary to explain the sordid details of a high-profile sexual assault case or local predator's convictions to our children, ensuring they understand the basic facts and why abusive behavior is wrong and detrimental to others can be helpful. Say, "A person [in Hollywood, in Washington, DC, in your neighborhood, etc.] behaved in a way that made other people feel uncomfortable, powerless, and terrible inside. He bullied them and hurt their bodies [or touched them without their consent] and made them feel like if they told anyone about it, they'd get in trouble." You can get more specific, depending on what happened, and still remain age appropriate, such as, "A man in Aunt Jen's building said some very insulting and rude words to her about her body, and it turns out he's been doing this to her neighbors as well." Or "A coach for DJ's team touched some of the players' private body parts and told them to keep it a secret."

- **Relate it to being a victim:** Many young children know what it feels like to be sad, angry, and powerless. Ask "Have you ever felt like you couldn't speak up when someone was being mean or inappropriate? Sometimes it feels difficult because the other person is bigger, stronger, older, or more popular than you. Even if you feel alone in those moments, you are never alone. Even if that person tells you to keep it a secret, you can come and tell us right away. We're here for you, and we will listen."

- **Ask powerful questions:** Pose questions that allow your children to think through how this information pertains to them:

- ○ "Who can you talk to if someone is making you feel this way?"
- ○ "What if the first person you tell doesn't really listen to you?"
- ○ "What can you say to the person making you feel this way?"
- ○ "What if the person is much bigger, older, or more popular than you? What can you do then?"
- ○ "What if the person making you feel this way is someone you know or thought you could trust—like a teacher, coach, babysitter, or family member?"

- **Offer suggestions or role-play:** Talk about how you'd like your child to handle these situations. Discuss whether you want them to, for example,
  - ○ Shout, "Back off!" or "Don't put your hands on me!"
  - ○ Assertively say, "What you're saying is making me feel uncomfortable. Please stop." Or "You're creeping me out" or "You're making me feel unsafe."
  - ○ Walk toward a person of safety.

- **Relate it to being a person with power:** Children understand power discrepancies. They are often aware that they are not the ones making the rules or calling the shots in many areas of their lives, so it should resonate with them when you explain, "When we are older, bigger, or stronger than someone else, we should not use our power to hurt others. That's not okay. We should use our power for good." Children need to know that they get a say in what happens with their bodies—even when they are not the most powerful person in the room.

- **Take blame and manners out of it:** We hear this argument often: that someone has somehow "brought on" sexual harassment or assault by dressing in a certain way or giving a person extra attention. Talk about it:
  - ○ "You are not to blame when someone makes the choice to say rude or unwarranted words to you about your body or touches you in a way that makes you feel uncomfortable or unsafe."

○ "Nobody is allowed to touch you or say rude words about your body simply because you're 'being nice.'"

○ "I want to be clear here. I never want you to feel that you have to let someone touch your body because you don't want to be rude. This is not about good manners. If you don't want to be touched, you should not be touched."

- **Speak up when you see it or hear it:** When you see misogynistic or degrading behavior by adults or young people, whether in song lyrics, on TV, or in film, point it out. For example, you might say, "It really makes me feel angry when I hear people speaking like that about others. How does it make you feel?"

- **Relate it to being an "upstander":** We all have the ability to make a difference, and our kids need to know that they must speak up when they see sexual harassment, intimidation, bullying, or assault happening. Say, "If you see something, say something. Stand up for the person being victimized, or make sure to let a trusted adult know what's going on so the behavior is stopped as soon as possible."

The Five (or Six!) Rs

Sometimes it's easier to have a specific way to remember how best to talk about a tough topic. Psychologist Dr. Sandy Wurtele explains the prevention of child sexual abuse this way:[45]

- **Recognize:** Teach kids to recognize potentially abusive situations or potential abusers. Say, for example, "Nobody should take pictures of your private parts or touch you where your bathing suit covers (barring doctors' visits and help with bathing/dressing from an approved parent or grandparent, etc.). This is your private body."

- **Refuse:** Encourage children to say no to sexual requests. Say, "If someone tries to touch your private body or tells you to touch their private body parts, tell them clearly and loudly, 'No!'"

- **Resist:** Help kids understand how to get away from a potential perpetrator. Say, "If someone refuses to stop touching your private body even after you tell them no, try to run, kick, or scream."

- **Report:** Urge children to tell someone about the abuse. Say, "If anyone tries to touch your private body or asks you to touch their private body, tell me, your teacher, or Aunt Jen. You will never get in trouble for reporting this—even if the person told you to keep it a secret!"

- **Responsibility:** Explain that secret or inappropriate touching of a child is never the child's fault or responsibility. Say, "It is never your fault if someone tries to touch you in secret or touches your private body when they shouldn't do so."

I would add a sixth R that's just for key adults—**Repetition.** We want our kids to know this information and be able to generalize it to different areas of their lives—at school, in sports, at camp, in relationships, and online. While we don't want to sound like a broken record, reiterating these prevention rules as your children mature can give them the confidence to speak up when necessary.

Quick Tip

Make a List!

Who is on your child's "safe adults" list? Grandma? A teacher? A coach? A safe adult is someone who consistently demonstrates safe behavior, respects healthy boundaries, and genuinely cares for the well-being of the child. For many kids, it can be uncomfortable and scary to talk to their parent about inappropriate touching (especially if the abuser is a family member), and telling another adult might be easier. This is one of those many times when "it takes a village" really hits home.

🗩 *Scripts in a Pinch*

When my child doesn't want to talk to me about sex or sexuality:
According to sexologist and sex educator Logan Levkoff, don't be afraid
to put the onus on you.[46]

- "I know you don't want to have this conversation with me. I get it. You
  know a lot. You've gotten this information from your friends and a
  whole host of sources, but I really want to have these conversations
  with you, less for you than for me. Because when I signed up to become a parent, I made certain promises. One of them was that I was
  going to help create a generation of young people who felt empowered by their sexuality, who knew how to make good decisions—so
  that's on me. I have not done my job if I am not sending you into the
  world with the right tools."

To provide your child with some control and choice, I would add:

- "Would you prefer to start this conversation off with you reading a
  book about it, watching some videos designed for tweens, or jumping
  right into a discussion with me?"

When I've had some very negative experiences and don't feel
comfortable talking about these topics and I fear relaying my own
problems, insecurities, and experiences to my impressionable child:
Sometimes it's wise to allow someone else—someone whom you and
your child trust and love implicitly—to step in and fill in the gaps where
you are struggling. In my own family, due to extenuating circumstances, timing, and my close relationship with my niece, I was the one who
taught her about periods and sanitary products. That's okay! Using a
proxy instead of avoiding the possibility of conversation altogether can
be a sign of love and wisdom!

Talking about sex has gotten such a bad rap, but these discussions truly are
an opportunity to bolster clear and healthy messages to our children about

their bodies and their sexuality. Rather than think about the awkwardness we feel, we need to focus on this purpose and concentrate on the more positive goals:

I want my child(ren) to feel good about themselves.
I want my child(ren) to develop and have good and loving sexual relationships.
I want my child(ren) to understand the beauty of how their body works.

Let's answer their questions as they come. Let's get our values across. Let's try and be open-minded to what our kids have to say. One day, when my children are sixteen or eighteen or thirty, I hope they can conjure these conversations we've had together, not just about the mechanics of sex but about the respect and the love. The time is now to start the long process of building our children's confidence in their bodies and in their sexual decision-making.

Be honest. Be flexible. Be ready. *Be brave.*

◔ Talking Points

QUESTION	YOUR ANSWER
Which sex and sexuality conversations, if any, scare or concern me the most?	
What is the next conversation I want to have with my child about sex or sexuality?	

QUESTION	YOUR ANSWER
What key message(s) do I want to relay to my child about sex or sexuality?	
Is there a message I received (or did not receive) about sex or sexuality when I was younger that I want to make sure to correct when speaking to my own child?	
What else do I need, if anything, to prepare me to have this next conversation (i.e., children's book, age-appropriate video, etc.)?	
How do I hope this conversation will help my child/teen now or in the future?	

Chapter 4

How to Talk to Kids about Death

"Am I Gonna Die? Are You Gonna Die?"

When my daughter was four years old, she started asking me about death while we were driving to dance class. It was casual at first, just a few informational questions: "Do butterflies die?" and "Can they still fly when they die?" We talked about bugs, leaves, and the seasons. Easy peasy. But just when I was feeling pretty good about how the conversation was going, she asked me about people—you know, point-blank. "What about the people, Mommy? Do they all die too?"

Ugh. I could feel my stomach tighten and my jaw clench as I eyed that sweet face with the big eyes in the rearview mirror. Couldn't we just talk about *Sesame Street*, ballet, or, like, I don't know, *anything* else? I tried to keep it light and breezy as I answered, "Everyone is born, and everyone dies."

The words hung there for a moment, heavy in the air between us, as my little girl in her size 3T leotard put two and two together. "You mean my yiddle brother's gonna die?" She burst into tears, right there at the traffic light, about a quarter mile away from dance class.

The topic of death is inherently sad, isn't it? It's difficult. Confusing. Emotional. It makes us think about loss of what was and about losing out on what's to come. Our own memories can remain raw from experiences of personal grief just as our deep-seated anxieties about the end of life can become triggered. This, of course, is normal.

I tried to end the discussion on a positive note: "Oh, sweet love, I know we might wish that everyone we love could live forever and ever, right? But you know what? Your brother is healthy, and so are you and Mommy and Daddy. Most people die after they've lived their full lives and their bodies have gotten old and don't work anymore. You and your brother are just getting started!" She seemed satisfied with that, but it would be the first of many difficult—but necessary—conversations we would have on the topic.

Children Should Know That Death Is...

- **Irreversible, permanent, and final:** Death is the final stage of the life cycle. Once death occurs, it can't be reversed, and there's no return to this life. Say, "Just like being born is part of life, death is part of life. Birth is at the beginning, and death is at the end. In between is where we live, learn, grow, and make memories with our loved ones. And even though we might wish it were different, once someone or something dies, they can't come back to life."

- **Inevitable and universal:** Every living things dies eventually. Say, "All living things—whether we're talking about plants, animals, insects, or people—die. Nobody knows why this has to happen—not even the adults in your life like Mommy, Daddy, or your teachers. But just like each living thing is born or buds or hatches, every living thing eventually dies."

- **Applicable only to the living:** Nonliving things don't live, so they can't die. Say, "Nonliving things, like rocks or staplers or my set of gardening tools or your rain boots, can't die. Why? Because they were never alive."

- **A cessation of function:** When a living being dies, the body no longer functions and can't be fixed. Say, "When people die, it means their bodies don't work anymore. Their hearts stop beating, and they no longer breathe, eat, walk around, or go to the bathroom. They don't feel hot or cold, hungry or tired, angry or sad. When people die, their bodies can't come back to life again. Death is the end of life."[1]

Fear of Conversations about Death

Clinical psychologists and bereavement experts stress the importance of talking to children about death in an honest and informative way, starting from an early age.[2] This means it's essential to portray death as a natural part of the life cycle. Studies show that most children experience the loss of a loved one by the time they finish high school—90 percent will grieve the loss of a family member or close friend, and one in thirteen will lose a parent.[3] While the causes of these losses vary from potentially lengthy illnesses such as heart disease and cancer to something as sudden as a car accident, our children need us to support them through it—and prepare them *for* it.

However, many parents do not broach the subject until the issue is forced on them.[4] According to a recent study, many parents don't talk about death (especially as it relates to a significant adult in the life of a child) because they want to protect their children from upset and they aren't sure what to say.[5] A survey of 270 American parents of four- to six-year-old children revealed that parents were least comfortable talking with their children about death when compared to other biological topics, such as reproduction, aging, and illness.[6]

I can't blame them. It's not easy, but all people, even children, deserve to know and understand that the time we have to spend with one another on earth is valuable, even fleeting. That's why it's important that we say the things we want to say while our loved ones are still with us—and do the things we want to do while we're all still here to enjoy one another. We want our kids to feel like they got their chance to be fully present and to leave no sentiment unsaid or question unanswered, just as we would want for ourselves.

Many children know a little bit about death (perhaps more than you think!). They have probably noticed the leaves falling from the trees, seen a dead beetle or bird on the ground, read about the death of a character in a book, or witnessed it in a film. Still, children often have many questions, and left unanswered, a germ of misinformation might develop in place of the truth.

Some might believe that death is temporary and that someone who has died will come back, just like when someone returns from a vacation or a business trip—or like a zombie from *The Walking Dead*. Some might believe that death happens to others, that it's selective rather than universal, and that it does not happen to the people or pets they know and love. Others might believe they are actually at fault or have caused a death: children who were angry with a sibling before that sibling died or whose parent was out picking up pizza for their dinner before a fatal accident might blame themselves. Some may even become superstitious about death and believe that if they talk about it, it will happen to them or someone they love.

Therefore, when someone is dying or has recently died, our children need help sorting out these big feelings. Misunderstandings can grow, strengthen, and become exaggerated, leaving them more fearful and confused than before. We don't want perceived myths to govern their thoughts or to teach them to hold their concerns inside.

We also don't want them to think death is a taboo subject. If they do, they may fear talking to us about it when they have questions or need comfort. They may think, "If Mommy or Daddy won't talk about it, it must be bad or might make them too sad, so I won't talk about it either." Holding on to feelings and unanswered questions is not healthy for anyone.

Instead, gentle, age-appropriate conversation with a trusted adult is the answer. Research has shown that one of the top indicators of how well children will do after the death of a significant person in their life is directly related to the type of relationship they have with the surviving adults in their lives—and how well these adults are able to cope with their own grief. "Don't tell your children what they will need to unlearn later," notes Earl Grollman in *Talking about Death: A Dialogue between Parent and Child*. "Avoid fairy tales and half-truths. Imaginative fancy only gets in the way when they are having enough trouble separating real from the make-believe."[7]

Ages and Stages: How Kids Respond to the Death of a Loved One

AGE: ONE TO TWO YEARS

- **Perception:** No ability to conceptualize death, understand death, or attribute meaning to death.
- **Behavior/reaction:** Displeasure or depression when the key adult, who provides comfort and basic needs, is missing. Babies who may have been known as "happy" or "easy infants" may have trouble sleeping and self-soothing. (Yes, even infants can be sensitive to the stress level in other adults around them and can be reactive to the grief felt by immediate family members.)
- **Adult reaction:** Stay calm and reassuring. Create a tranquil environment with peaceful music, familiar beloved lovies or blankets, or deep tactile pressure from massage or other deep-pressure tools. We must engage the vagal system, the nerve that extends from the brain to the abdomen, because it has a direct impact on the parasympathetic nervous system that can ease big emotions. Pediatric psychologist Dr. Lynne Kenney, whom I spoke with on two episodes of *How to Talk to Kids about Anything*, advises calming remedies such as SSSS—sing, swing, swaddle, and sway. If we stay calm, children are more likely to stay calm too and be comforted.

AGE: TWO TO FOUR YEARS OLD

- **Perception:** Death is seen as temporary and reversible. It happens to "other people," and death is not personal. Animals and people who die can come back, bodies can be fixed with medicine, water, food, or magic, and death is like sleep—the person can be awakened.

- **Behavior/reaction:** Curious about death, may talk about death and have questions about death, particularly as it applies to bodily functions and everyday activities. They may ask the same questions over and over not because they don't understand the information but for reassurance that the answers have not changed. Questions may seem "rude" but aren't intended to be that way. May want to touch dead things, investigate. Regression to behaviors such as thumb sucking, sleep problems, or baby talk may be witnessed.

- **Adult reaction:** Allow your children to ask questions, and, if requested, let them touch the dead beetle or flower petal to help them see how death "feels" and how it is different from life. Answer them simply and patiently, reiterating that death is permanent and irreversible. Stay relaxed about questions that seem strange or insensitive. Know that regressive behaviors may be a cry for attention, comfort, or need for help in processing death.

AGE: FIVE TO NINE YEARS OLD

- **Perception:** Gaining a clearer understanding of death. Death is not reversible or temporary but only happens to some or other people. Still not personalized or seen as something that will happen to them or others they know and love until the distant future. By age five, they begin to grasp the idea that death means the body is nonfunctional.

- **Behavior/reaction:** Magical thinking may prevail such that they believe thoughts can cause things to happen—even death or accidents. Increased interest in the physical and biological aspects of death. Questions about the facts and details of death. Violent play, playing "dead," changes in sleep patterns, nightmares, regression, loss or change of appetite. Many children may deny that death has happened and may not want to talk about it at all. When they do, they may show concern mainly for themselves, not because they are selfish but because of their developmental age, and ask questions like "Who will take care of me?" and "Who will drive me to my sports practice?"

- **Adult reaction:** Keep answering their questions. Don't pressure them to talk if they don't want to do so. Encourage physical play and alternative expressions of grief such as through art, song, exercise, role-playing, dolls, and storytelling.

AGE: NINE TO TWELVE YEARS OLD

- **Perception:** Similar to that of an adult, they understand that death is irreversible, permanent. They have awareness that death can be personal and universal and caused by a breakdown in body function. Still, even though this age group has the cognitive awareness of the universality of death, there is a tendency toward denial of personal death.
- **Behavior/reaction:** They will have questions about the science of death and what happens to the body as well as an increased interest in death. Some may experience school problems, acting out, regression, changes in eating or sleeping behaviors, concerns about their own deaths or the deaths of their loved ones. You may also see withdrawal from key friends and less of a desire to be away from loved ones.
- **Adult reaction:** Let your children know that when someone has died, their grief is normal. Encourage them to express their feelings, whether sad, angry, confused, fearful, or any mix of emotions. Don't avoid talking about death, but don't push your children to talk—let them know you are there when they are ready.

AGE: TWELVE YEARS THROUGH ADOLESCENCE

- **Perception:** Death is viewed abstractly and subjectively. They still tend to think of themselves as immortal and shielded from death. Egocentric.

And they have a curiosity about the subjective nature of death and life: "What is the meaning of life? Why am I here?" Death may be romanticized and can be seen as easy to cope with due to how loose ends are tied up easily or theatrically on TV or in movies. Even though there is much philosophizing, death is still seen as something that happens to others.

- **Behavior/reaction:** Sadness, questioning, denial, regression, and temporarily pulling away from the family (and preference for friends) is normal. May notice increased risk taking, anger, depression, or acting out—and in some cases, suicidal thoughts or survivor's guilt. Some may attempt to take on the role of the person who died to fill the "gap."

- **Adult reaction:** Be available and present. Encourage them to talk about their feelings, if not to you, then to a therapist, friend, mentor, or teacher. Give them the gift of time and let them know that their grief is normal and warranted. Get them help, if needed, and allow them to grieve in their own way, even if different from the way you or your other children are grieving.[8]

When the Topic Finds You

Debbie walked over to me at a child's birthday party with what looked like a mixture of trepidation and purpose. "We just found out that my mother-in-law has stage IV cancer," she said solemnly as kids giggled and ran around us at a party place. "They can't operate. I wanted to ask you… What do I tell the kids? *Do* I tell the kids? What if they ask me if she'll die? What do I say when she does?"

Many parents don't know where to start when it comes to discussing death with children. Some stay clear of these kinds of unpleasant conversations and talk about death and dying under their breath and out of earshot— until there's no way to avoid it, as when a loved one passes away.

The truth is regular communication is what can help parents take out some of the scariness, mystery, and stigma often associated with death. After all, it's much more comfortable to talk about death when life is calm and the environment feels safe and constant than when the rug has been pulled out from underneath you, as happened to Debbie, whose children were nine years old and six years old at the time.

"Maybe I should just wait," she said.

The problem with waiting is that, eventually, you run out of time. And with a terminal illness, you're not only putting off the inevitable for a few months to a year, you're inadvertently shortening the time your children have to actively spend focused and desired quality time with the person who is dying. Whether you wait or not, the end is quickly approaching.

I took her hand and said, "This is hard stuff. It stinks. It's not fair, and it's not pleasant, but it's important to think about how you want your children to use this time they have with her."

"They'll want to spend time with her," she said, nodding. "It's so sad, and I hate to make my kids sad."

"Then start with that," I suggested. "Just as you said: 'I have some sad news, my loves. And I'm so sorry to have to tell you sad news because Mommy doesn't like to make you sad.'"

"Okay, but how do you explain cancer?" she asked. "Do you just say she's sick?"

"You can say, 'There's something growing inside Nona that shouldn't be there, and it's making Nona sick. It's called cancer. The doctors can't take it out of Nona because of her age and because it's in a lot of places in her body, so she's going to get sicker.'"

"But isn't there a chance they'll get scared that when one of us gets sick we'll die too?"

That's one of the reasons why it's so important for parents to *name* the disease when they talk about death due to a terminal illness—so it's not confused with a regular cold or fever that is contagious and keeps children home from school or parents home from work.[9] "You can ask if they've heard that word before—cancer—and they can tell you what they know. That gives you a starting place and helps you to address fears and concerns."

"What about the death part? We've really never discussed it." She smiled meekly.

"Keep it simple. You might say, 'Unfortunately, Nona's body isn't working well. The cancer is making her body weak and creating lots and lots of sick cells instead of healthy cells that keep people well. Eventually, and we aren't sure when—it could be months or even a whole year—her body won't be able to work at all. There will be too many sick cells. We are very sad, but while the doctors will do what they can to help Nona feel comfortable over the coming months, they can't get the cancer out, and they can't fix her body. Nona is dying.' You can stay open for questions and just let your kids talk. Remember, it's okay not to know all the answers, because you don't. It's okay to be sad too and tell them that you are, but also remember to tell them that knowing in advance means that Nona is still here. You get the special gift of being able to talk to her and ask her questions about her life and to spend time with her. You can ask them what they might like to do."

Afterward, Debbie told the kids about her mother-in-law and spent the next couple of months making sure they all spent time together. Nona got the chance to share all the special family recipes she had in her head. Debbie's youngest made a beautiful picture for her nona showing the family under a big sun and a rainbow, holding hands. Her oldest asked her nona to retell stories about when she was little. They spent the time. Talking about death allowed them to enjoy what was left of their nona's life.

When It Comes to Talking about Death, When Do I…

- **Take the lead?** Sometimes talking about death or dying becomes necessary before your child comes to you to discuss it, particularly when someone in your child's life—such as a teacher or a friend's parent—is dying or has died. Hearing information from you, a trusted source, makes it easier to understand than if your child hears it through the grapevine. Parents can look for the following signs that their child is having trouble coping with a death:[10]

- ○ **Changes in appetite:** Eating much more or much less?
- ○ **Changes in sleep patterns:** Sleeping much more or much less? Fear of sleeping?
- ○ **Changes in sleep content:** Nightmares or frightening images?
- ○ **Changes in school success:** Sharp drop in grades or an inability to focus?
- ○ **Changes in behavior:** Acting out with aggression, regressing to behaviors of a much younger child, or withdrawing from others?
- ○ **Changes in relationships:** Spending less time with favorite peers?
- ○ **Changes in reactivity:** Blowing up, becoming agitated, frequently crying?
- ○ **Changes in vigilance:** Watching out for family members, repeatedly making sure doors are locked, checking where family members and friends are located?
- ○ **Changes in separation:** Difficulties with being alone or separating from parents?
- ○ **Changes in play:** Repeated story themes and play around the topic of death?

- • **Wait for my child to come to me?** Once you have had a conversation or several conversations about death, you can tell your child that you're open for additional discussions and any questions they might have. You don't need to keep bringing it up—just stay available. You can do a simple check-in: "Do you have any questions related to what we talked about recently?" If your child says no, don't press it—the questions may come later. Sometimes admitting your own grief by saying something like "I have been feeling sad and distracted lately" can prompt them to talk.

⌂ *In My Home*

When my grandmother was diagnosed with cancer, I took it upon myself to interview her on her life—her likes, dislikes, childhood, and even what she wanted to say to each key person in her family. As she stroked her irksome-but-beloved bichon frise, she patiently answered each one of my questions and walked me through the pages of her youth: how her mother, my great-grandmother (whom we had called "Big Grandma" on account of her being just a few inches taller than my grandfather's mother, whom we called "Little Grandma"), made a different soup every night for dinner, how my grandfather took her dancing in nearby Montclair when they were dating, and how my mother was the most perfect-looking baby she had ever seen. She told stories of my uncle Steve and how he'd bring home every conceivable furry creature he could find and sneak them through the back door. I learned that her favorite times of life were moments she spent with family and that she always subscribed to the advice "never go to bed angry." (This advice, interestingly, was written on a small piece of paper and given to me by my grandmother on my wedding day.)

I recorded our interview on my husband's old video camera (this was before cell phones) and was so happy I did. I was able to get these answers far before she got really sick and passed away. It's a treasure.

When my dad was declared sick with liver cancer, I really couldn't face it that well. It felt like it came on suddenly even though it didn't. I had been down in New Jersey visiting from Massachusetts and told my mom that my father looked yellow. He went to the doctor that Monday and was diagnosed with stage IV liver cancer. He was gone a month later.

I had this nagging feeling one day, in the backyard of my childhood home, while sitting with my dad, that I should record him. But I didn't. *Damn it*, I didn't. And there go the wise, made-up stories he used to tell us, including his hilarious version of how the ramp was invented (where a caveman builds a rock-and-mud pile to propel himself out of the cave) and his amazing way of explaining life. Time is really a precious thing, and if we are brave and willing, we can use it to prepare and do the things we hope to do before our "someones" are gone. It's important to take advantage of time while we can.

Pre-Talks

There are opportunities all around us to broach the subject of death with children in a way that seems natural and kind. Your pre-talks might center around these topics:

- **The life cycle as it applies to nature and all living things in general:** You can discuss how various living things are born or come into being, what their life cycle looks like, and what happens when they die. You might say, "All living things live, and all living things die. The leaves on the trees, our goldfish in the tank, the animals in the woods, and people all across the world."

- **Less personally devastating yet specific deaths in your child's world:** Since living things are born and die each day around us, we can discuss these deaths with kindness yet without intense emotional attachment. Whether it's the neighbor's dog that passed away or the monarch butterfly in your yard, these occurrences can be used as springboards for discussion. You might say, "Do you see that butterfly on the sidewalk? Do you know why it's not moving? It's because its bug body is no longer working. A living creature can't live once its body stops working." You can even give more concrete detail: "The bug lived its life, and now it has died. It doesn't take in any food or play with its bug friends. It can't feel cold or warmth or pain. That bug is no longer a living bug. What you are seeing now is a bug that once was, a bug body without a life inside." You can also add the permanence component: "It can't come back to life again."

- **Movies, books, or TV shows where a character dies or the subject matter is grief:** From the parents in *Frozen* and the father in *The Lion King* to characters in children's books such as *The Goodbye Book* (Todd Parr), *Life*

Is Like the Wind (Shona Innes and Irisz Agocs), *The Memory Box* (Joanna Rowland), and *Charlotte's Web* (E. B. White), media can be helpful in talking about death. Studies show that media, such as Disney movies, expose children to on-screen depictions of death and should be discussed since they can incite worry. Although older children are more likely to be frightened by witnessing media coverage of real events, children under seven are just as likely to be frightened by unrealistic and even impossible events on-screen. Ask your child, "How do you feel about what happened to Simba's dad?" or "How do you think Wilbur must've felt when Charlotte told him that she was at the end of her life and dying?" This can be a way to talk about death in a way that feels safe and a little bit removed from "real life."

- **Furnishings, such as a shelf in your child's room with books and bookends that you can point to in order to describe what it means to live:** Show children how the middle space of a bookshelf is filled with all kinds of stories—*A Wrinkle in Time*, the Magic School Bus, Junie B. Jones—just like our own lives are filled with all kinds of adventures. Tell them that the bookends on the shelf hold the stories of our lives together. It's important that we fill that space in between with as many of our own stories and adventures as we can.

What to Say and What Not to Say

I know parents often have good intentions when they want to soften the impact of death, particularly the death of a loved one. They may use sweet stories based on their spirituality ("Grandma went to sleep with the angels") or obliquely address the issue ("Uncle Peter's gone away for a while") in an effort to spare their child unnecessary heartache or the "harsh realities of life." Yet children feel loss, even if it is unspoken. The heartache is there simply because the loved one is gone—and it may be compounded if that loved one is gone inexplicably. Studies have shown that bereaved children may be at risk for depression, prolonged grief disorder, or even post-traumatic stress disorder, and one of the risk factors is a poor surrounding protective environment, such as a home without an open expression of sadness.[11] It's best to speak plainly rather than use euphemisms, as they can be detrimental to young children's understanding and processing of a loved one's death.[12]

WORDS NOT TO USE		WORDS TO USE
passed away	→	died/death
went to sleep and didn't wake up	→	body stopped working
went to a farm	→	body was too broken to work anymore
went away to a better place	→	kidneys were too sick to work so he died
resting	→	isn't breathing anymore, heart not beating

When Words Aren't Enough

Marilyn Price-Mitchell, PhD, a developmental psychologist who founded Roots of Action as a way of nurturing positive youth development, recounted a story that has really stuck with me.[13] It was about her own difficulties with grief after the death of her husband, Richard.

A few months after Richard's death, needing some rest and recuperation, Marilyn and her three-year-old daughter, Sarah, took a trip to the beach, where Sarah built one of her first sandcastles. Marilyn watched Sarah work diligently on that sandcastle, taking great pride in shaping each room and tower, exhibiting such joy and accomplishment. Moments later, an enormous wave crashed onto the beach, demolishing Sarah's castle. Of course, Sarah reacted to the loss of her sandcastle like any preschooler—with shock and anger, tears streaming down her cheeks. She ran to Marilyn for comfort, vowing never to build a sandcastle again.

A friend was with Marilyn and her daughter that day: Diane, a preschool teacher. Diane walked over to Sarah and said, "Part of the joy of building a sandcastle is that, in the end, we give it as a gift to the ocean. That is what building sandcastles is all about. It lets us be gift givers."

Sarah loved this idea and immediately responded with enthusiasm to the idea of building another sandcastle—this time, even closer to the water so the ocean would get its gift sooner! My friend Marilyn also had a realization that day. She began to see a parallel to her husband's death. "I visualized the castle as his life and the crashing wave as his death," she told me. "I was so shocked and angry when his castle was abruptly washed away. What I had missed until that moment was the concept that grief could be a gift-giving process, just as the sandcastle was a gift to the ocean. That day, I realized that although our lives are eventually washed away, the granules of our lives remain on the shoreline—like granules of sand. They do not disappear."

Grief is a difficult and deeply personal experience. However, it serves a common purpose—to help humans deal with loss and to develop a new normal, a new future, without the ones they love and cherish. Joe Primo, chief executive officer of New Jersey–based Good Grief, an organization that provides support to children and families after the death of a loved one, recently told me during a podcast episode, "Death is the thing that implodes your life, but grief is the thing that puts it back together. It helps us integrate our relationships with the person who died into our future."[14]

Discussing our feelings allows us to share our pain as well as remember the good times, but sometimes words aren't enough—and particularly for children who are learning to articulate their feelings, words can be elusive. That's okay. There are many ways to help your children cope with big feelings after someone they care about has died.

- Draw pictures of feelings/memories. Art can help children, particularly young ones, get their thoughts out on paper.
- Write feelings down in a special journal. Your children can keep this private or share it with you or others in the family. Sometimes it's easier to write the words than speak them.

- Write letters or make videos "speaking" to their loved one. Even though the person who died will not be able to read the letters or see the videos, the act of your children expressing what they want their loved one to know can be a comfort.

- Make a memory box or scrapbook. Keepsakes like special photos, ticket stubs, favorite books read together, letters, or notes can be looked at again and again in a collection that's portable and organized.

- Use puppets or dolls that allow your children to act out how they are feeling, make up stories, or show you what they miss, worry about, or fear.

- Keep that person's memory alive by carrying out a wish/project. Continue to do the charity 5K they always ran in, work at the dog/cat shelter where they devoted their time, or travel to their beloved country of origin as they had wished to do.

- Celebrate that person's life and the good they brought to others by doing something special on their birthday every year, planting a memorial garden, or having a party or dinner on a day that was significant to them. My friend and her children celebrate her mother's birthday each year (she died when the kids were pretty young), and they talk about her—they named it "Nana's Day."

- Fill out a kids' "Remembering Page" as suggested in *Talking with Children about Loss: Words, Strategies, and Wisdom to Help Children Cope with Death, Divorce, and Other Difficult Times* by Maria Trozzi and Kathy Massimini.[15] Include facts about the special person along with favorite memories, what your children will miss most, and what they liked to do with the loved one before that person died.

- Keep trinkets, poems, and quotes—or even a file of text messages, videos, and photos on your phone—that remind you of the person who died. You don't have to surround yourself with these things—you can keep them in a special place so you have control of when you take them out and experience them.

Q&A

WHAT IF I CRY WHEN I MISS THE PERSON WHO DIED?

"It's okay to cry when you're sad. Sometimes I cry too because I'm sad. In those times, you can ask to be alone for a while, or you can crawl up next to me and cuddle and talk. Some days, you may even want to run around, exercise, draw, listen to music, or dance! The best thing is to get those feelings out instead of leaving them shoved down inside you—that can make us feel sick or bad. Letting them out in positive ways can make us feel better."

Funeral and Memorial Services

Funerals are human rituals bringing together generations of people just like graduations and weddings—and yet many people wonder if it's appropriate to bring a child to a funeral.

The answer is yes. It is appropriate—and healthy.[16]

Children's attendance at a funeral or memorial service can help them work through their grief because they will be surrounded by friends and family who feel just as they do. Shared grief may be difficult, but it is also helpful to those who experience it. "Throughout life, we experience joy, sorrow, and new beginnings," Joe Primo told me on the *How to Talk to Kids about Anything* podcast. "Rituals are the things we do to highlight all of these moments. They're the expression of feelings that can't be easily spoken. So perhaps the most important rituals are those that acknowledge death and grief. And that is exactly the reason why it's important for children to take part in funerals and memorial services. Excluding children denies them the opportunity to mourn, be with others who are hurting, and to grieve."[17]

Funerals, even though we might initially think otherwise, are not just for adults. (There is a current movement—spurred by an increasingly secular, nomadic, and casual society—to toss out the old rules about funerals and turn them more into a bona fide celebration or party, putting a sense of "fun" in funerals.) They provide closure and comfort for children just as they do for the grown-ups in their lives.[18] In a study of a hundred children who experienced the loss of a parent during childhood, two-thirds reported that attending the funeral was a helpful or positive event. In contrast, over 75 percent of those who did not attend the funeral, many because they were forbidden or didn't know it was occurring, later wished they had. Over a third of children who did not attend had feelings of regret, while others felt anger, hurt, and frustration that they were not included in this important ritual.[19]

That said, children should never be *forced* to attend. They should be given a choice (and the option to leave a service if they find it too overwhelming, scary, or upsetting once they arrive). If you find they are showing reluctance to attend, find out what might be concerning to them. Ask them:

- "Are you worried or nervous about going to the funeral service?"
- "What do you think you might see or experience?"
- "How can we make this less scary for you?"

Children who are very close to the deceased may want to bury something with that loved one—a small token or gift, a drawing or photo, or a stuffed animal. That can be a wonderful nonverbal way for your child to release some of their pent-up grief and send a message of what they might perceive as comfort to the person lost.

Funeral Preparation

To alleviate some of the anxiety around the funeral, funeral directors advise key adults to prepare their children for what they will see when they enter the funeral home, from the decor to the funeral director and even the casket.[20] Keep it simple and honest:

"Marcus, the funeral director, will greet us at the door, where there'll be a big bouquet of flowers and a special book for guests to write their name in as they enter. We'll see many friends and family members as they come to the funeral home, like Grandpa and Aunt Jen as well as Mrs. Garvel from next door and many more people who loved and respected your grandma. When we go into the sanctuary where we'll have the service, the closed casket will be in front of the room." Correct any misinformation they might have about the funeral service or the funeral home.

You may also want to prepare your children for the types of sentiment they might see, how people will be sad and cry but may also laugh at a story told about your loved one as a way of remembering and celebrating that person's life. Explain that death brings a mix of emotions—sometimes very intense and consistent, other times light and fleeting.

"Funerals are about mourning," Primo notes, "and mourning is a core component of a child adapting to their new norm, expressing their grief, and getting support from their community." This is how children build resilience and learn they are not alone in their grief—they have friends and family supporting them and grieving with them. Funerals allow people to say goodbye to those they love.

Your child may choose to take a role in the funeral beyond simply attending—but this, of course, isn't necessary. They can create a slideshow or photo boards, sing, or even give the eulogy. As someone who eulogized my own father and grandmother, I can say with confidence that while it was difficult, it was also an honor.

If there will be a viewing or your children will be attending a burial, they should be prepared for that as well:

"Your grandpa's body will be in a wooden box called a casket. There will be an opportunity to see the casket when it's open, and you'll be invited to go see Grandpa and say goodbye if you would like to do that. Grandpa will look like he's just sleeping, but as we discussed, he's not sleeping. He died. You won't see him moving or breathing, and he may even look a little different, but he'll also look peaceful and no longer in pain." Answer any questions they have beyond the information you provided.

If your child isn't ready to attend, isn't able to attend, or doesn't want to attend a memorial or funeral service, you can come up with some other ways of saying goodbye that can help them move forward. Sharing memories with other family members, having a smaller remembrance service with close friends, or celebrating a loved one's life through art, dance, singing, poetry, planting a tree, or even viewing favorite movies and old videos are all simple ways children can say goodbye in their own way.

Q&A

WILL WE EVER SEE THIS PERSON AGAIN?
"Once a person dies, that person can't come back to life, but their memory will always live in our heads, our hearts, and our dreams. Some people believe they'll see that person again in an afterlife. We believe _____ . What do *you* believe?"

The Death of a Pet

Losing a pet is something that many adults, families, and kids experience in their lifetimes. We personally had to say goodbye to our beloved Casey, a fuzzy, blond-furred dog we rescued from a shelter seventeen years ago as he barked his way out of his crate and into our hearts. We joked, "We'll take the loud one," but truly, as most people seem to say, our pet, as he buried his wet nose into our necks, picked us just as much as we picked him.

The loss of a dog, cat, hamster, bird, etc., brings grief just like losing a friend or family member because they *are* our best friends and our family members, particularly for children.[21] Who could be a better listener than a pet? Who can be comfier and cozier to lean on than a pet? Therefore, it's critical that we don't trivialize the death of a pet because it's not human—"oh, it's just a pet"—and that we discuss its death as openly and honestly as we would the death of a human.

Years after Casey's death, we were painting my daughter's room a new color and bought her new bedding in a nice calm blue green. I started taking photos of her bright raspberry-pink rug to post on the internet for sale, and Tallie burst into tears! She said it was Casey's favorite rug. She didn't want to get rid of it, so we talked about other options—keeping it in her room or putting it in the basement to use when playing, for instance. Those feelings were still so raw after all that time. That's how grief works sometimes.

Wendy Van de Poll, a certified end-of-life and pet-grief support coach and founder of the Center for Pet Loss Grief, suggests parents continue to talk about the happy times they had with pets and there's no need to despair if they try to discuss a pet's death with a child and, at first, don't get a positive response. "You're not going to rush," she told me during a podcast episode, "but know that the child is probably going to hear that, and you're going to put a positive memory in that child's head. And positive is healing. Eventually, you will start to see some reaction or that little gleam in their eye or smile, and they start to laugh. Then you can add, 'What do *you* remember?' Then you can play back and forth. All these little cues that we get are ways to teach and express love."[22]

Here are some additional ways to have a dialogue with children about the death of a beloved pet.

- Exchange happy memories. One time, it was raining, and my children were talking about Casey, who, to put it mildly, did not like the rain…or cats. I said, "Maybe he's playing around right now and backing a cat into the pool," and they laughed. "Maybe he's getting the cat a little wet." They thought that was a great idea.
- Read books like *Dog Heaven* and *Cat Heaven* by Cynthia Rylant.
- Perform a special ritual to honor your pet. Van de Poll suggests writing a letter to your pet or drawing a picture. Because Casey loved the backyard so much, we decided, as a family, we were going to plant a tree. We buried

his collar by the tree. And when we say our "I love yous" at night, my daughter has said, "I love you, Mom. I love you, Dad. I love you, Noah. I love you, Casey," and my two children will look to the heavens. It's hard not to smile a little through the sadness.

Quick Tip

Don't rush to get another pet right away to "replace" your child's deceased pet.[23] Rather, get a pet when the family is ready to welcome a new family member into the home. When it's the right time, you'll know it. When we found ourselves giggling over photos of adorable puppy faces online and playing the what-if game as we went through our typical day—"What if a dog were here to help clean up the carrots you dropped on the floor?"—we knew we were ready. We adopted Bentley a little over three years after Casey died. We would always remember our Casey, but we were looking forward rather than focusing on the past.

When a Sibling Dies

When people hear that one of my dearest friends suffered the loss of her thirteen-year-old son, Gavin, they often say something like, "No parent should experience the death of a child." And they're right. But there's a secondary loss that many don't often consider to the same degree, and that is the loss of a sibling. My friend's teenage daughter, Jadyn, is now an only child, the death of her only brother ending one of the longest and most consistent relationships of her life.

Studies tell us that when a sibling passes away during childhood, it can have a profound impact on surviving children.[24] The development of independence from parents, romantic relationships, educational attainment, and even career paths can be stunted or affected, as growing children feel the need to stay close to home or fill the space their sibling left.[25] The death of a sibling has also been associated with increased diagnoses of mental disorders such as anxiety, depression, and disordered eating.[26] This is especially true among teenage siblings, who, caught between childhood and adulthood, feel responsible for their parents' well-being and yet are dealing with great emotional strife themselves.[27] How can we best support surviving siblings as they cope with their enduring grief?

- Let them grieve in their own way. "I think it's important to ask the person who is grieving, 'What do you need?'" fifteen-year-old Jadyn told me in a podcast interview.[28] "Sometimes I want to talk about memories, look at pictures, and remember my sibling with someone. Sometimes I want to grieve by myself and listen to music in my room or wear something that belonged to him, like his hockey jersey, to be close to him. But other times I just want to block it all up." Let them do what works for them, as long as their method of coping is healthy and safe, rather than what you think should work for them.

- Let them express a wide range of emotions. Joe Primo of Good Grief says grief is not a linear process. On the *How to Talk to Kids about Anything* podcast, he explained, "Grief is like a roller coaster. It's up, down, all around… For kids and adults alike, every single day is different. And as the grieving person, you have no idea how your day is going to unfold."[29]

- Give them some slack. Jadyn and her mom came up with their own lingo to explain their forgetfulness, sensitivity, and fear that comes with losing an immediate family member. They call it "grief brain." Grief brain can go on for several weeks, months, or even years as there is no time limit on grief. Memories and emotions have a way of creeping up on you when you least expect it.

- Offer healthy outlets and relief. "I used to hit walls in the bathroom because I just wanted it to hurt differently," Jadyn said. "I know so many kids who have done hurtful, unsafe things, like cutting. Hurting yourself is physical pain instead of emotional pain. The thing is…the physical pain doesn't make the emotional pain go away. That feeling of control is so fleeting. You have control over your pain for a second, and then—now you're just hurting in two ways." Talk to your children about healthy ways of coping, whether it's through talking, exercise, art, music, or being out in nature.

Most of all, be present and patient. Children who have someone who can "listen to their story" and "empathize," according to researcher Dr. Jan-Louise Godfrey, tended to cope a lot better in the long run.[30]

"Will You Die Too, Mom?"

After her brother, Gavin, died, Jadyn worried that her parents would get so depressed that they would want to end their own lives. Studies have shown that siblings worry about their parents and their well-being after the death of a sibling. Dehra, Jadyn's mom, addressed this fear directly. She told Jadyn, "It is my whole goal in life to stay on this planet as long as possible with you."

"Are You Okay? Will You and Daddy Still Love Each Other?"

Many people mistakenly believe that after the death of a child, marriages have an extremely high divorce rate. This is actually untrue. While studies show that marriage disruption is more likely in couples who have experienced such a loss, the divorce rate is actually closer to 12 to 16 percent, with more than half those who divorced saying the death of their child was not a contributing factor to the breakdown of their marriage.[31] Still, it's important to reassure siblings of deceased children that the way you are grieving is not a reflection of how you feel about your partner but rather how you are expressing your emotions around the loss of your child. You can say, for example:

"While Daddy likes to talk out his sadness, I like to be alone when I'm sad. And you know we're all seeing someone to talk about how we can help one another through this. Even though I sometimes like to grieve alone, it doesn't mean I don't love you and Daddy. We're doing everything we can to make sure we all know we care about one another and about what each person needs, and one of those ways of showing love and care is allowing the other person some space to grieve the way they need to during this really hard time."

Death, whether it's sudden or expected, can make you feel as if the ground is falling out from under you. I once saw death described as a horrible magic trick—how we're here one minute, gone the next, with no one responsible and no one to blame. There's a 1983 children's picture book titled *Lifetimes: The Beautiful Way to Explain Death to Children* in which the authors state, "There is a beginning and an ending for everything that is alive. In between is living. All around us, everywhere, beginnings and endings are going on all the time. With living in between."[32]

I like that.

Let's help our children interpret death not just through the lens of void but also through the lens of meaning. What shall we gain from this individual's life? What do we learn about how we conduct our lives from the experience of knowing, loving, and interacting with one another? This moves us from a conversation simply about loss to a discussion about life—how to spend it, honor it, and celebrate it—even when it's over.

Q&A

MOMMY, IS IT OKAY TO FEEL ANGRY WHEN SOMEONE DIES?

"It's okay to feel all different ways when someone dies. We can have big feelings that fill us up inside and little feelings here and there throughout the day. We might feel sad one day, angry the next, scared today, and confused tomorrow—or we might feel a combination of all different feelings at once. In the beginning, you might have lots of sad or angry moments all in a row with just a few happy moments in between, but eventually you'll have more happy times—all strung together like beads on a necklace, with just a few moments of sadness or anger in between."

🗩 *Scripts in a Pinch*

When a beloved grandparent or family elder has died after a long life or long-term illness:

- "Sweetheart, remember Grandma's been very sick? And we talked about how Grandma lived such a long and wonderful life that her body grew old and was having trouble fighting off germs? Well, Grandma's body couldn't fight anymore. Grandma died this morning, and those who loved her are very sad. I'm sad. It's okay to be sad. But we should know that she died feeling very lucky to have lived for such a very long time on this earth and to be your grandma. We will miss her, and we will keep her in our thoughts as we live our lives, which will help keep her memory alive in us."

When a valued young friend has died after a long illness:

- "Honey, I have some upsetting news. Remember we talked about the little boy in your school who couldn't come to class because his body was so weak? Well, he was very sick, and the doctors did all they could to help him get better, but he had a disease, and that disease was very strong. He died, honey. I'm so sorry. Can I hug you? I'm here to help you with whatever you need. Maybe we can do something to help his mommy and daddy. Maybe we can tell them how very special their son was to us and how we will remember him. Would you like to go to the funeral with me?"

When a death occurs suddenly:

- "Darling, I have to tell you something very sad. Mr. Smith who lives down the block died. I know you just saw him yesterday and that he smiled at you while you were at the bus stop, but sometimes bad things happen to good people. He was in a car accident this morning." For some kids, this might be enough for now. It can take time to process. For others (and you know your kids best!), you may need to continue. "Are you all right? How are you feeling? Let's see if we can do something special in Mr. Smith's honor. Maybe we can draw a picture of Mr. Smith smiling, since that's the present he left for us before he died, and bring it to his memorial service."

When there is a death by natural disaster:

- "There was an earthquake that happened in the ocean near a country that's very far from here, but it caused an enormous wave to crash onto the shore and hurt a lot of people. Some people died. Many of the people who live there lost their homes and need food and water. We can help. Would you like to contribute to the collection and be a helper?"

When there are deaths due to a school shooting and they are old enough that they may hear about it (keep it simple, listen to your child, and answer questions in an age-appropriate way):

- "You might have heard or you might be hearing about a situation that happened in another school. Did you hear anything?"

  "Yes, I think so."

  "I was shocked and sad when I heard about it. How are you feeling about what happened?"

  Or:

- "You might have heard or you might be hearing about a situation that happened in a school in _____ . Did you hear anything?"

  "No. What happened?"

  "A person who had a lot of hate in [his] heart and whose brain wasn't healthy went into a school and hurt a lot of people. Some of them died. I was shocked and sad when I heard about it. I'm here to answer any questions you have or research them with you. Do you want to talk about anything?"

"I don't know..."

"I know this is scary. I was feeling scared too when I heard about it, and it's normal to feel that way—scared or sad, confused or even angry. The people who are working on these cases learn how to keep everyone even safer each time something like this happens, and your school is doing [XYZ] to ensure you're all safe. I feel safe with you going to school. How are you feeling?"

Every family will experience the death of someone they know or hold dear in their lifetime. Preparing our children in a way that helps them to understand and process what's happening is an act of love. While it can feel like a daunting task at first, talking to kids about death and dying can, ironically, help us live more purposefully. It can also help open the door to more difficult conversations in the future.

✐ *Talking Points* ....

QUESTION	YOUR ANSWER
What do I need to do, read, consider, figure out, discuss, or practice before I feel ready to have a conversation about death with my child(ren)?	

QUESTION	YOUR ANSWER
What are my biggest concerns?	
What do I want to make sure to say or cover during my conversations about death?	
At the end of the first conversation(s) about death, what do I want my child(ren) to know, feel, or do?	
What conversation starter or method would I like to use to bring up our first conversations about death?	
When and where would I be the most comfortable discussing death with my child(ren)?	
Is there something I've said or haven't said about death that I'd like to correct or explain further?	
What do I want to make sure to discuss next time?	

Chapter 5

How to Talk to Kids about Diversity and Inclusion

"Are We All Equal?"

At the culmination of the film *My Big Fat Greek Wedding*, the staunch but lovable Greek father, Gus Portokalos, gives a uniting toast in honor of his daughter's marriage to his notably non-Greek son-in-law, Ian Miller—a wedding he originally opposed.

"You know, the root of the word 'miller' is a Greek word," Mr. Portokalos begins in his characteristically strong Greek accent. "'Miller' comes from the Greek word 'milo,' which is mean 'apple,' so there you go. As many of you know, our name, Portokalos, is come from the Greek word 'portokali,' which mean 'orange.' So, okay? Here tonight, we have apple and orange. We all different, but in the end, we all fruit."[1] This affectionate dad stumbles on something that we all need to do—recognize our differences while connecting through our similarities.

For many years, parents, caregivers, and educators wrapped up conversations about diversity with this simple statement: don't judge a book by its cover. Full stop. The end. But that declaration doesn't allow our children to recognize that how our friends look on the outside may profoundly impact how they are treated, how they identify, and how they exist on the inside.

Diversity means we are all different in many ways. We might differ in age, height, appearance, ability, gender, age, ethnicity, and more! When we understand our differences, we learn that we can appreciate others for who they are and appreciate ourselves for who we are too. In other words:

- Instead of simply saying, "Don't judge a book by its cover," try, "Don't judge a book by its cover. Open the book, and get to know its contents, but also remember that for many people, their outside—their hair, skin, disabilities, style of dress—is very important to their identity and can't be separated from who they are on the inside. See the entire person, and refrain from making assumptions."

- Instead of generalizing with "disabilities are just different abilities," be specific: "She has a disability—it's called dyslexia." (Note: Some people like the term "disabled" as it's an identifier, acknowledges a person's disabling situation, and shows there is nothing shameful or wrong about it.[2] Other people may prefer "differently abled,"[3] although some find it offensive or patronizing,[4] so it's best to ask.)

- Instead of giving a platitude like "gender doesn't matter," say, "Gender doesn't matter when it comes to the friends you like, the toys you want to play with, or the jobs that interest you, but gender is often an important part of how people like to describe themselves. Some people think they know how you think, feel, and act just by knowing your gender, and that's just not true, right?"

The key to having a conversation about diversity is to avoid relying on clichés and to send the overarching message that it's important to get to know people beyond how they appear on the surface. We won't get to know them until we open our minds and hearts and find out right from the source.

Glossary

Microaggression: A subtle, everyday instance of (sometimes unintentional) discrimination or bias in the form of racism, homophobia, sexism, or ableism that leaves the affected marginalized groups feeling insulted, uncomfortable, or misunderstood.

Ally: A helper; someone who provides support, assistance, and their voice to a group that is oppressed or marginalized.

💬 Script in a Pinch

When your children point out differences, from skin color to gender to disability, refrain from shushing them. After all, differences are perfectly normal! When we make it okay to notice what make us all unique, it helps us to appreciate our differences and get to know each other better. It also sends the message that differences are nothing to be embarrassed about and don't need to be mentioned under our breath or admitted with apology.

Script: "You are right! You have long straight brown hair and use the traditional swing on the playground, and your friend Tasha has lots of tiny black braids and uses the wheelchair-accessible swing on the play-ground. All these little details and differences are part of what make you who you are and Tasha who she is! And don't forget what also makes you the same—you both love to swing on the swings!"

Grit-to-Glory Stories

There are many stories of diverse people rising against barriers and succeeding against all odds. Rosa Parks, John Lewis, and Martin Luther King Jr.

fought racism, challenged laws, and helped further the cause for civil rights. Helen Keller, both deaf and blind, became a notable writer, public speaker, and activist. Albert Einstein, whose name is synonymous with "genius," is said to have had dyslexia, autism, and/or ADHD (he struggled with spelling, grammar, and delayed speech), and Harvey Milk, during a time of great discrimination, was the first openly gay politician to be elected in California and fight for LGBTQ+ rights. The following are more examples of people doing important work with passion and succeeding regardless of the barriers in their paths—some from the past and some from the present.

GENDER BIAS/RIGHTS

- **Examples:** Malala Yousafzai, Billie Jean King, Patsy Mink, Sojourner Truth, and the U.S. women's soccer team.
- **Script:** "While you get the right to attend school each year, many girls around the world are not given the right to education. Malala Yousafzai, as a young teen, was very vocal about the right for all girls to go to school in her birth country, Pakistan. She was very brave and spoke out, and she was targeted and hurt by the Taliban, an extremist group that didn't agree that girls should go to school. Luckily, she didn't let that stop her. She continues to challenge policies so girls can go to school! She even became the youngest-ever Nobel Peace Prize winner for her brave work."

PHYSICAL DISABILITIES

- **Example:** Desmond Blair, Amy Purdy, Helen Keller, Stephen Hawking, Frida Kahlo, Judith Heumann, Maysoon Zayid, Peter Dinklage, and Bethany Hamilton.
- **Script:** "I watched this really cool segment on TV about a gifted young artist named Desmond Blair who was born without hands![5] He taught himself how to hold pencils, pens, and paintbrushes by pinching them between his fists, and he does incredible work. His paintings were just displayed in a gallery! Would you like to see the short video and look at

some of his paintings? It really showed me that when you are passionate about something, you find a way to do it even if you have challenges."

RACE/RACISM

- **Examples:** Marley Dias, Cynthia Choi, Mary White Ovington, Althea Gibson, Jackie and Rachel Robinson, and Tarana Burke.
- **Script:** "Did you know that Marley Dias was only in elementary school when she became really frustrated that she didn't see diversity in the books she was reading? She started something called #1000BlackGirlBooks and collected a thousand books with Black female protagonists in them from all over the world. She gave the books to schools! Before she knew it, that number doubled and tripled several times over! She tells young people just like you, 'Use your passion as fuel for change.'"[6]

INTELLECTUAL DISABILITIES

- **Examples:** Jamie Brewer, Chelsea Werner, Sujeet Desai, Collette Divitto, Pablo Pineda, and Chris Burke.
- **Script:** "I think it's great that your friend Kasie wants to become an actress! There are several entertainers who have Down syndrome like Kasie. In fact, there's a woman named Jamie Brewer who has been on TV, in film, and in plays, and she was even the first woman with Down syndrome to walk in New York Fashion Week. She also advocates for people with intellectual disabilities to be included in society and seen for their gifts rather than just for their challenges."

NEURODIVERSITY

- **Examples:** Simone Biles, Michael Phelps, Michelle Carter, Cammi Granato, Anthony Hopkins, Sir Richard Branson, Jim Carrey, Lisa Ling, and Emma Watson.
- **Script:** "Did you know that Olympic gold medalist Simone Biles has ADHD? She even says not to think of ADHD as a downfall or problem

in an interview with *Understood*: 'Think of it as a superpower.'[7] And she's not the only one who has ADHD—there are also people like Olympic gold-medal swimmer Michael Phelps, hockey player Cammi Granato, and Olympic shot put athlete Michelle Carter. While there is no doubt that neurodiversity can sometimes pose challenges in a world that is set up for neurotypical people, it can also be a unique strength. Clearly, it's been a superpower to many very successful neurodiverse people! How do you think ADHD can be a superpower? How do you think ADHD can be a superpower for you?"

LGBTQ+

- **Examples:** Jason Collins, Pete Buttigieg, Sally Ride, Harvey Milk, Mark Takano, Laverne Cox, Helen Zia, Sue Sanders, Menaka Guruswamy, and Arundhati Katju.

- **Script:** "I know sometimes it can be difficult to feel like the first person to say, 'This is who I am,' especially when you feel different or when people react in a negative way. Have you ever heard of Jason Collins? He was the very first openly gay NBA player. He broke a taboo and took the lead. He's a trailblazer. Pete Buttigieg was the first openly gay man to launch a major presidential campaign. And Sally Ride? She was the first female astronaut, and she was gay. How can we help you feel safe and supported as you step out as the first in your grade to say, 'I'm a part of the LGBTQ+ community'?"

Telling kids about real people who are doing great work on a small and large scale can help them understand the struggles people face and how they are working to transcend those struggles. It also helps children who identify with these champions to see how they are paving the way for those who come after them. As Dr. Thema Bryant, clinical psychologist and president of the American Psychological Association, mentioned on the *How to Talk to Kids about Anything* podcast, "If the only thing people hear is the negative, they would, of course, feel negative about their identity. If we, as parents and teachers, are silent, and yet from others, kids hear terrible things about who they are, where are they getting the positive messages about their sexuality, gender, disability, religious background, or race?"[8] Let us be a source of positive stories and a clearinghouse of examples that defy stereotypes and misinformation.

Truth Bomb!

Demographers project that white people will become the minority in the United States around the year 2045—and if we just focus on those under eighteen years old, currently nonwhite children account for most of the nation's seventy-four million children.[9]

Talking to Kids about Race

On April 5, 1968, the day after the assassination of Martin Luther King Jr., educator Jane Elliott began a class lesson that has become widely known as the "Blue Eyes, Brown Eyes Experiment." After asking her all-white third-grade class what they knew about Black people and hearing that they had heard every negative stereotype, she decided it was time the children learned what it felt like to be judged negatively simply by the way they looked—in this case, the color of their eyes.

On that first day, Elliott instructed that "blue-eyed people aren't as smart, clean, or civilized as brown-eyed people."[10] She told them that brown-eyed students would get all the advantages—like being the only ones with permission to use the drinking fountain or play on the playground equipment or receive seconds for lunch. On the second day, the experiment was switched so the blue-eyed students were in the favored position with all the perks of privilege.

The results of the experiment were eye-opening: The class of mostly friends became divided. Immediately, the students began to internalize and assume the characteristics they were told they had based on the color of their eyes. Elliott even found that the children deemed inferior performed worse academically in class on that day, while the children who were told they were superior felt emboldened. They turned on one another and physically fought and hurled insults. "I watched what had been marvelous, cooperative, wonderful, thoughtful children turn into nasty, vicious, discriminating little third graders," Elliott said.

Empathy became a powerful turning point. When the experiment was over, the children reconvened in relief as one unified class again. The pressure of discrimination was off.

"There is only one race on Earth, and that's the human race," Elliott, who is ninety years old and continues to be passionate about her work, wrote to me recently. "You can't change skin color, but you can change attitudes."[11]

That starts with us. We need to help our children to step into others' shoes and develop empathy for those who are different from them. Research shows that high levels of empathy mean low levels of discrimination, bullying, and bias.[12]

Yet a recent report by Sesame Workshop (based on more than six thousand parents of children ages three to twelve, along with more than a thousand teachers from preschool to fifth grade) revealed these facts:

- Only about 10 percent of parents say they discuss race "often" with their children.
- A little over 20 percent of Black parents say that they discuss race "often" with their children, while only 6 percent of white parents do.
- Less than a third of parents who have children ages three to five discuss race and ethnicity "sometimes" or "often."
- Over 60 percent of parents rarely or never discuss race, ethnicity, or social class with their children.
- And yet 99 percent of parents admit that a child's race/ethnicity impacts their ability to succeed.

Why is this topic avoided? Parents may feel unqualified or uncomfortable, as they often do with difficult or complicated conversations, or they think kids don't process race until they are older. However, research tells us otherwise. According to a recent study out of Boston University, regardless of whether the participants in the study were Black or white, parents were, on average, 4.5 years off base about when kids notice race.[13] The truth is this:

- Infants as young as six months can notice differences in skin color and have been shown to prefer faces of people of their own ethnic background.[14]

- Between the ages of two and five, children detect messages and ideas about race, use racial categories to identify themselves and their peers, and can internalize racial bias based on both subtle and overt messages about the desirability of different social groups.[15]

- By elementary school, kids can define race fairly accurately and tend to demonstrate a strong affinity to their own racial group.

Research also tells us that silence on this subject provides room for stereotypes and biases to form and for racism to be covertly reinforced.[16] Even if we think our open-minded values will seep into our children's minds by osmosis, kids can pick up negative views from other sources. As Christia Spears Brown, professor and associate dean of diversity, equity, and inclusion at University of Kentucky, told me, "If parents don't talk to kids about bias and the historical reasons people often categorize others based on race, kids will absorb the idea that skin color has a real meaningful difference and categorize others accordingly."[17]

Bullying and Race

In a study of nearly four thousand high schoolers in Pittsburgh, almost 10 percent reported race-based bullying, and nearly 6 percent bullied someone because of their race. Those with multiple stigmatized identities were at the greatest risk of being bullied. That is, gender-diverse Black and Hispanic youth reported the highest rates of identity-based bullying among all the study participants. Another study found that school diversity increased the likelihood of bullying by white and Latine kids—an unexpected result, as one might assume that increased diversity would provide a much-needed buffer for bullying behavior as students might be more used to navigating a variety of different racial and ethnic groups.[18] Professor Nadine Connell and her colleagues at the University of Texas and Rowan University in New Jersey explain that this increase in racial bullying among the 3,965 middle schoolers they surveyed may be a result of vying for social status or, conversely, due to outside influences such as neighborhood disorganization and community violence.

▣ Script in a Pinch

"What is race? What is racism?"

- "Usually, when people are talking about 'race,' they are referring to grouping people based on what they look like on the outside, like the color of their skin. There are so many different colors of skin that range from very, very pale, light colors to very, very dark, rich colors. Even my skin color is different from yours, and yours is different from your friend Sierra and from your teacher Mrs. Wong. While all our skin colors are different, everyone should be treated equally—not worse or better because of what they look like, right? But sometimes people do treat others differently because their skin color is different. When people treat others unfairly or meanly because of their skin color or ethnic appearance, that's called racism."

Gain Traction with Action

When speaking to kids about race, racism, and acceptance of people who look different from them, make sure your behavior backs up your words.

- **Walk the walk:** A study on the racial socialization of European American parents found that their children's racial attitudes were unrelated to their mothers' attitudes about race but rather to the prominence of their mothers' cross-race friendships.[19] Children whose mothers had diverse friends and a high percentage of nonwhite friends showed lower levels of racial bias than those who had mothers with a low percentage of diverse and nonwhite friends.

  As Ibram X. Kendi, author of *How to Raise an Antiracist*, asked on the *How to Talk to Kids about Anything* podcast, "If everyone you bring to your home in a loving capacity—a friend—is white, what are you saying to your kids, without saying, about who's valuable to you?"[20] This modeling opportunity encourages children to embrace cross-ethnic friendships, which, according to a large body of research, can reduce prejudice.

- **Representation matters:** According to work out of the Children's Television Project at my alma mater, Tufts University, although the number of diverse characters on TV and in film has improved in recent years, of their research sample of more than fifteen hundred characters in the most popular children's series,
  - Only 5.6 percent of the characters were Black.
  - 11.6 percent were Asian American.
  - 1.4 percent were Latine.[21]

  And a portion of these characters were portrayed in a negative light or as tokens and sidekicks, according to educator and founder of the Antiracism Academy, Brandee Blocker Anderson—which can drive low self-esteem and confusion in children of color[22] and also subtly teach all children that Black, Indigenous, and people of color (BIPOC) are "not as valuable, interesting or relatable," she says.[23]

  The situation with books seems to be improving—slowly. The University of Wisconsin's Cooperative Children's Book Center (CCBC), which compiles data on books by and about BIPOC for children and teens, shows a steady increase in racially diverse characters since 2014.

Given that more than half of U.S. children K–12 are BIPOC, according to the U.S. Census, there's still work to be done to increase representation.[24] Madeline Tyner, librarian at CCBC, wrote to me that in 2021, 36.47 percent of the books received at the CCBC were about BIPOC characters or subjects (BIPOC here includes Arab, Black, Asian, Indigenous, Latine, Pacific Islander, and characters with brown skin but no specified heritage/race), up from 34.65 percent in 2018.[25] We are going in the right direction.

- **Point out disparities:** If you see low or no diversity on TV or in books and films, say, "I've noticed in this series we've been watching that there are no people of color besides the one person who works as the school lunch lady. What do you think about that? Is that how things look in your school—in most schools? I wish they'd show more diversity on TV and more interracial friendships since friends don't all have to look the same!"

- **Welcome diverse entertainment:** Look at the books you have around your home. What children's books do you read to your kids? What dolls and toys do you have for your children to select? When my daughter, Tallie, went through a "fashion doll" phase, instead of just purchasing a bunch of blond-haired, blue-eyed Barbies, I bought her dolls with all different skin tones and body sizes. And when the 2023 live-action version of *The Little Mermaid* came out, starring Halle Bailey as Ariel, the whole family went to see it.

- **Watch your natural biases:** Even when books and toys reflect a more diverse world, our natural biases can step on our own toes. Dr. Kendi pointed out on the *How to Talk to Kids about Anything* podcast that when Black and white parents show their kids diverse books, they tend to focus on the characters of their own race.[26] Instead, switch the lens. Point out cross-ethnic characters and ask, "How do you think this person feels right now?" and "How do you think race plays a role in this story, if at all?"

- **Call out a demeaning joke:** Model for your children that they don't need to sit idly by or laugh along with a belittling or inappropriate joke—in fact, such behavior can encourage biased actions. We might say, "While jokes are supposed to be funny, laughing at a joke that spreads hate and discrimination is anything but. If you hear a joke like that, one idea might be to try disrupting the joke and changing the course of the conversation. For example, 'Hey, not another joke about that. I don't think that's funny, but how about that one you started to tell the other day about the three dogs and the chicken?' What other ideas might you have to send the message about how that kind of joke isn't all right to tell?"

- **Stamp out misinformation:** There is much false information readily available to our children based on outdated viewpoints, prejudice, and groupthink. We can teach our kids to be "disruptors for good,"[27] as Luvvie Ajayi Jones, author of *Rising Troublemaker*, told *Chicago Tonight: Black Voices*—or, as Catherine Sanderson calls it in her book *Why We Act*, "moral rebels."[28] These are people willing to call out truth distortions or propaganda even when they are the only ones around them courageous enough to do it. Liz Kleinrock, ABAR (antibias and anti-racism) educator and author of the ABAR guide *Start Here, Start Now*, suggests children (and parents!) use this powerful "thinking stem": "I used to think…but then I learned…and now I know."[29] That might sound like, "I used to think [this information about this group was correct], but then I learned from [book, person, article, etc.] that it's actually wrong and offensive, and now I know that [this is actually the right information]." Such an approach delivers the information tactfully and shows growth—without cramming it down anyone's throat with a virtue stick!

Asking Questions Leads to Acceptance

"I don't want to hold Katelyn's hand! Her skin is brown!"

Parents are often embarrassed when their child says something like this and might reflexively shush their child, sharply state, "Don't say that—it's rude!" or even pretend their child didn't say the offensive remark (with the hopes that giving it no attention might result in their child not saying it again). Of course, it's not the fault of the young child for picking up on social bias, which, according to research, is primed to happen from the time they're in preschool. That means we need to discuss it so our children adopt our antibias values rather than leave it up to chance.

One of the ways to do this is by asking inductive questions, as Ibram X. Kendi discusses in *How to Raise an Antiracist* and on my podcast,[30] such as, "How do you think Katelyn feels right now?" while also using restorative questions like, "How do you think we can help Katelyn feel better?" Try these actions:

- **Show curiosity:** Starting from a place of curiosity rather than blame or shame lays the foundation for good conversation instead of defensiveness and embarrassment. "Can you tell me more about why you don't want to hold her hand because it's brown?"

- **Elicit empathy:** Say, "Let's look at Katelyn's face and the expression she's showing. How do you think it makes her feel that you won't hold her hand because of the color of her skin?"

- **Create perspective:** Flip questions around to create perspective-taking opportunities, like Jane Elliott did in the blue eyes, brown eyes exercise. You might say, "Ask your heart, how do you think it would make *you* feel if someone wouldn't hold your hand because your skin color is [peach/white/tan]?" Dr. Kendi explained on the *How to Talk to Kids about Anything* podcast that empathy allows children to "step into the shoes of people who don't look like them so that they can think critically and ask themselves questions." Once we go through the empathy and perspective-taking door, Dr. Kendi adds, "We can then move to discussing that all skin colors are equal and beautiful."

- **Reveal misunderstandings:** Ask questions like, "Do you know why her skin color is darker than yours?" or "When someone is darker or lighter on the outside, can you tell what the person is like on the inside?" or

"What do you think might happen when you hold her hand?" You don't need to get into a long science lesson about melanin (unless that's your kids' jam!) or the history of oppression, but these moments are perfect for bite-sized nuggets of information that kids carry with them and become part of the fabric of who they are and how they make decisions.

By asking questions and discussing answers, we can create a pattern of behavior that is expected and reflective of the allies we are looking to create in our children in relation to race. And while these conversations may feel a little uncomfortable, as Dr. Kendi says, "It's okay for our children to experience constructive discomfort" since it's how they learn, grow, and evolve—and it's how we do too.

Talking to Kids about Disabilities

Nate was getting bored of people in school asking him why he "walked funny," so he headed them off at the pass. He created and gave a PowerPoint presentation to explain what cerebral palsy was and how it affected his gait. The kids stopped asking questions about his walk and started asking him questions about what it was like being a twin. Problem solved.

I loved that Nate took such a proactive approach, but it didn't surprise me that he did. His mom, one of my closest friends, had been going in on the first day of school since kindergarten to explain why Nate wore a helmet on the playground at the time. Once Nate was old enough, it was normal for him to follow his mother's lead.

I asked him, "If you could tell parents one thing to make sure they talked to their kids about when it came to disabilities, what would it be?" He answered quickly, "It would be best to tell kids that people with disabilities still have a body that works—it just works differently than their bodies. And it may surprise them that we might even be smarter or better at something than they are!"[31]

According to the United States Census, there are about three million children under the age of eighteen who have a disability.[32] Of children five to seventeen years of age,

- 172,000 boys and 134,000 girls have a hearing disability.
- 173,000 boys and 156,000 girls have an ambulatory disability.
- 235,000 boys and 237,000 girls have a vision disability.
- 1.6 million boys and 793,000 girls have a cognitive disability.

Therefore, it's likely that your children will know another child with some kind of disability. Here are some key truths they should also know:

- **No disability, just like no one person, is the same:** "There are lots of different kinds of disabilities. No one disability is exactly the same, and even when people are diagnosed with the same disability, they may experience it differently than other people. Because each person is different!"

- **People with disabilities are not "bad" or "worse" than other people:** "While your classmate Chris has a disability and has some different challenges in school than your other classmates, there's absolutely nothing that makes him 'bad' or 'worse' than you or your other friends, right? A lot of kids with disabilities and their parents really want us all to know that just like people who don't have disabilities, children with disabilities want to be included, befriended, and treated with kindness. How might you and your friends include Chris the next time you're out for recess?"

- **Use the right language:** Check in with friends to see what language they prefer, as words such as "disorder," "impairment," or "abnormality" may be considered offensive by some but not by others. Many people who have a disability embrace and use the word "disabled" over the term "special needs."[33] In fact, researchers from a 2016 study found people who are referred to as having "special needs" are seen more negatively than those referred to as having a disability.[34] "When we use euphemisms to avoid using the word 'disabled,'" McAlister Greiner Huynh, a teacher who refers to herself as an "accessibility specialist" in Raleigh, North Carolina, told *Good Morning America*, "what we are communicating is that being disabled is somehow a bad thing…but in reality, being disabled is just a perfectly valid way of being human…much like race, gender, or sexuality."[35] Lisette Torres-Gerald, board secretary for the National Coalition for Latinxs with Disabilities, has fibromyalgia, a chronic condition with no known cure, and puts a different spin on the issue: "I am disabled by society due to my impairment… My needs are not 'special'—they are the same human needs that everyone else has."[36] Indeed, and we should similarly avoid saying, "This is what is *wrong* with her" or mentioning a person's disability when it has no application to the story ("my friend, who has dyslexia, plays Anna in the musical").

- **If you make a mistake, own it and make it right:** Made an incorrect assumption about a person with a disability that you found out was just plain wrong? Used an outdated or offensive word by accident? Everyone makes mistakes when learning. Talk to your children about making it right by setting the example yourself or discussing how people they admire own up, such as American singer Lizzo who, after being called out online for including the ableist slur "spaz" in her song "GRRRLS," took swift action.[37] "Did you hear that when Lizzo found out she was using a harmful word in her new song, she apologized and changed the lyric? What do you think of that?"

- **When unsure or in doubt, ask for permission:** While it's natural to be curious, not all questions are appropriate or invited. Mackenzie Saunders, a disabled JD candidate at Harvard Law School, advises that we ask permission before asking.[38] We might encourage our children to say, "Would you be okay if I asked you a question about your disability right now?" And we can remind them to be empathetic: "It can be tough to understand what it's like to have a disability when you don't have one yourself. But before you ask your friend a question, ask yourself, 'Is it really important for me to know the answer beyond the fact that I'm curious?' and 'If someone were to ask me this type of question, would I be uncomfortable?'"

- **People with disabilities have strengths just like you do:** Sometimes, people look at those with disabilities and only see their challenges, not their strengths. But both are present, and it's important that we talk to our kids about the challenges *and* strengths. For example, Dr. Robert Melillo, author of *Disconnected Kids*, told me on the *How to Talk to Kids about Anything* podcast, "Some children with neurological issues like ADHD or autism spectrum disorder are four, five, six, seven, eight years ahead in certain skills."[39] Punctuating this fact, Dr. Devon Price, author of *Unmasking Autism* (and autistic himself), reminds us that "autistic people deserve acceptance, not because we can't help the brains we have, but because being autistic is good."[40] And how about those with physical disabilities who are notable artists, musicians, scholars, or athletes? This is a great time to pull out those grit-to-glory stories! "You've got to see these amazing videos of Ezra Frech, who has a prosthetic leg *and* became a Paralympian, competing in the Tokyo games at just sixteen years old. Look at how high he can jump!"

- **People with disabilities should not be blamed for their challenges:** Kids with mobility disabilities may need extra time to get down the hallway, while kids with ADHD or autism might tap their pencil repetitively or look away while you are talking to them—characteristics that are not their "fault." We must teach our children to be both gentle and patient. As Mona Delahooke, clinical child psychologist and author of *Beyond Behaviors: Using Brain Science and Compassion to Understand and Solve Children's Behavioral Challenges*, told me on the *How to Talk to Kids about Anything* podcast, "We must use love and compassion to help our vulnerable children instead of blaming them for challenging behaviors."[41] Let's remind our kids, "I know it can seem like Ashley is trying to hurt your feelings, but there is a completely different reason for her behavior. Ashley sometimes needs a few minutes alone in a calm space in the middle of a playdate—not because she's being rude or mean but because she needs space to manage her big feelings."

Ableist Language

Ableist language, or words and phrases that discriminate against people with disabilities, has become so ingrained in our lexicon that we may not even know we are using it—or modeling its use for our kids. Phrases like "that's lame!" are commonplace but may be derogatory and offensive to those who have mental or physical disabilities. There are easy alternatives!

Instead of saying...	Which actually means...	Try...
That's lame!	Trouble walking due to injury or illness.	• That's boring! • That's so dull!
You're being crazy!	Mentally impaired/deranged.	• You're out of control! • You're wild!
You're retarded.	Affected by an intellectual disability (outdated and highly offensive word).	• You're ridiculous (strange, absurd, silly, foolish, dense).
I'm ADHD/OCD about it.	• ADHD: A neurodevelopmental disorder, which includes challenges with attention, hyperactivity, and impulsiveness. • OCD: A pattern of unwanted thoughts (obsessions) that leads a person to engage in repetitive actions (compulsions).	• I have trouble focusing on that. • I have trouble paying attention to that. • I like my room really clean. • I'm a real stickler about that.
You're blind to it.	Trouble with being able to see, unable to see.	• You're overlooking it.
Are you deaf?	Without the ability to hear, hard of hearing.	• Are you listening to what I'm saying?
I'm being so spastic.	Related to muscle tightness or spasms, often experienced by people with cerebral palsy or multiple sclerosis.	• I'm not being careful. • I'm being so klutzy (incompetent).

Bullying and Disabilities

Children with disabilities are two to three times more likely to be bullied than those kids who do not have disabilities.[42] These kids may be especially vulnerable because they lack social power, may be seen as "different," and may not be able to respond as quickly as someone without a disability. According to UNESCO's review of more than three hundred international scientific articles, in comparison with their nondisabled peers:

- In rural schools in the United States, girls with disabilities were nearly four times as likely to be bullied.
- In rural schools in the United States, boys with disabilities were two and a half times as likely to be bullied.

UNESCO also found that learners with emotional and behavioral disabilities are more at risk of bullying than those with other disabilities.[43]

🗩 *Scripts in a Pinch*

"Why does Lucy talk like that?"

- **Define:** "Lucy has a stutter. Do you know what that means? It means she knows what she wants to say but can have trouble speaking her thoughts smoothly without repeating some of her sounds and words or getting stuck on a letter."
- **What it means for peers:** "When someone stutters, it's important to be patient and allow them to finish what they're saying, just like you would want someone to do for you. I bet she could use a kind and patient friend."
- **Show the importance:** "Did you know that seven to eight out of ten kids who stutter report being bullied for how they talk?"
- **And you can throw in a grit-to-glory story for good measure!** "Did you know that President Joe Biden, Ed Sheeran, Charles Darwin, Nicole Kidman, Shaquille O'Neal, Samuel L. Jackson, and Carly Simon all stuttered when they were growing up?"

"Why does Connor have braces on his legs and use those special crutches to walk?"

- **Give the facts:** "Some people's bodies work differently than yours and mine. For Connor to walk and play and do all the things he loves to do, he uses crutches and braces to balance and get around."

- **Connect it to different/same:** "He may walk a little differently than you do, but he does a lot of the same things as you too—like playing ball and doing arts and crafts!"

- **Open the door to talk:** "Do you have any more questions about Connor's braces or crutches?"

"Tilly says her family is going skiing over winter break. But Tilly uses a wheelchair, so she can't do stuff like that, right?"

- **Clear up the misconception:** "A lot of people who use wheelchairs play all kinds of sports—from hockey to basketball to skiing and more!"

- **More grit-to-glory stories!** "People who use wheelchairs [or braces, crutches, or prosthetic limbs] sometimes need special equipment or just adapt the way they use their equipment so they can participate. For example, one of the best archers in the world, Matt Stutzman of Iowa, was born without arms and shoots his bow with his feet! Amy Purdy, *New York Times* bestselling author of *On My Own Two Feet* and one of the best snowboarders in the world, lost both her legs to a rare infection and went on to win three medals in the Paralympic Winter Games! She uses a special snowboard and a specific kind of prosthetic foot to do the things she loves."

- **Revisit the original question with new knowledge:** "So how do you think your friend Tilly might ski with her family while using special equipment?" In this small exchange, perception-altering knowledge can lead to a whole new outlook on adaptive equipment, people with disabilities, and their involvement in physical activities.

Truth Bomb!

One in five children is neurodiverse, which, according to Harvard Medical School, includes those with autism spectrum disorder as well as other neurological or developmental conditions such as ADHD or learning disabilities.[44] According to Deborah Reber, *New York Times* bestselling author and founder of TiLT Parenting, a worldwide resource for parents of differently wired kids, it's best to talk to kids about neurodiversity in an easy, accessible, nonthreatening way. "When you do that, kids can stand up for these kids…and when we do this at a young age, our kids grow up thinking, 'This is just another piece of who this person is, and I can support and understand them instead of otherizing them.'"[45]

Talking to Kids about Gender

Many of us grew up as part of a "this or that" world. Girls or boys. Pink or blue. Dolls or trucks. Full aisles at stores were labeled with the words "For Girls" or "For Boys," drowned in either a pink or blue cloak and doused with frilly gowns, sparkly makeup, and baby dolls or dump trucks, robot monsters, and dinosaurs. As Lisa Selin Davis, author of *Tomboy*, said on the *How to Talk to Kids about Anything* podcast, "It's really insidious how gender is manufactured and sold and how it narrows the range of 'normal' for boys and girls."[46]

There are several problems with definitive gender boundaries:

1. **They may keep children from finding what they truly love.** Clearly, girls can like dinosaurs, and boys can like baby dolls. There are very gifted makeup artists who are men (12 percent in the United States, according to career site Zippia[47]) and robotics engineers who are women (19

percent in the United States, according to CareerExplorer by Sokanu[48]). If we tell kids that these toys and professions are "not for girls" or "not for boys," they may never find out where their true passions lie. In fact, according to a Deloitte survey of three thousand full-time U.S. workers discussed in *Harvard Business Review*, a mere 20 percent say they are passionate about their work.[49] Perhaps if we refrained from labeling a career "for men" or "for women," more people would find and follow their passion in life.

2. **They limit imagination, creativity, and skill development.** According to Lisa Dinella, a professor at Monmouth University, if we put children down a specific one-way track, they are likely to lose not just their ability to explore at a particular moment but also overall development.[50] If girls are predominantly given dolls, beauty tools, and domestic toys to play with, and boys are given trucks, science kits, and blocks, their imagination will be limited to those items.

    "Gendered toys adhere to a clear gender binary," Dr. Nawar Al-Hassan Golley, professor of literary theory and gender and women's studies at American University of Sharjah, told me recently.[51] That means they represent stereotypical masculine characteristics like strength, aggression, action, and adventure for boys and stereotypical feminine traits for girls such as softness, caring qualities, and certain standards of beauty based on physical attractiveness. "Over time," Golley says, "boys and girls are very likely to associate these stereotypical qualities with their gender and their roles in life," while also resisting "crossing over" or adopting beneficial qualities that are assigned to the opposing gender.

    When we refrain from creating gender boundaries in play, our kids are free to explore—making anything possible. (I used to love watching my son and daughter play with a mishmash of toys, like when Dora the Explorer drove the remote-control race car to the animal hospital to get her monkey, Boots, some treatment from "Dr. Tallie" and "Dr. Noah.") But research out of the Geena Davis Institute on Gender in Media shows we are fighting against stereotypes or what I call "gender boxing." Parents are

- ○ Two times as likely to encourage boys to engage in coding than girls.
- ○ Three times more likely to encourage girls to cook or bake than boys.
- ○ Three times as likely to encourage boys over girls to engage in programming games, sports, and LEGO play.
- ○ Six times as likely to think of scientists and athletes as men than women.
- ○ Over eight times as likely to think of engineers as men than women.[52]

By removing gender boxes from toys, careers, and skill development, we send the message to all children that there is no limit to what they can do or become.

3. **They create limiting beliefs.** When we provide only gender-specific toys, funnel kids into gender-specific activities, and tell kids, "That's for boys (or girls)," we convey contained beliefs about gender. While young children will play with just about anything, somewhere between the ages of three and five, they become much more susceptible to the "rules" of gender, as relayed to them by society.

4. **They can impact development.** A study out of Indiana University–Purdue University showed that if we want to help develop children's physical, cognitive, academic, musical, and artistic skills, the best way to do this is to stay away from strongly gender-typed toys.[53] The researchers warned that strongly gendered girls' toys were associated with physical attractiveness and strongly gendered boys' toys were associated with violence and aggression. The ones that fall more toward the middle (moderately masculine or moderately feminine) are likely to encourage children to develop special skills, science, building, nurturing, and domestic skills such as cooking and cleaning. Interestingly, another study out of Eastern Connecticut State University shows that toys that have traditionally been viewed as "for boys," like construction tools and toy vehicles, elicited the highest quality of play from girls.[54]

According to the World Economic Forum's Global Gender Gap

Report 2022, we still have a long way to go to reach gender parity in everything from leadership to wealth accumulation, political representation, care work, and STEM education.[55] However, the more access and opportunity we provide for our children, the more they make strides in their own development and the more they can positively impact the world around them. In other words, when we widen gender roles, we have a chance to narrow gender gaps.

Opening Up Gender Boxes

Every day, our children are getting consistent gender messages from society about who they should be, what they should like, and how they should behave. How do we help kids embrace a more moderate and less stringent view of gender roles, gender interests, and gender expectations so they don't box themselves in by a "difference" that may not be so different after all?

- **Separate gender from interest:** Say, "There are messages out there that tell you that certain toys, topics, and careers are 'for boys' or 'for girls.' This is not true. Do you think advertisers should be the ones who get to pick what is interesting to you? Or should you get to pick?"

- **Provide examples:** Say, "There are some very gifted movie-makeup artists who are men. Did you know that the person who did the makeup for Jim Carrey's *How the Grinch Stole Christmas* is a guy? In fact, Rick Baker earned eleven Oscar nominations (taking home the prize for seven) for his makeup artistry on movie sets. Let's look at the movies he was nominated for. Oh, look, *Harry and the Hendersons*! We saw that!" Or "I was watching this really cool movie called *Hidden Figures* that was based on a true story. It was so fascinating to discover that a woman named Katherine Johnson was so amazing in math that her computations got NASA's flight crew to land on the moon in 1969! Want to look her up with me?"

- **Call out stereotypes:** Say, "I was looking for a dinosaur building set for you and your sister. It's so strange to me that the only images they show of these sets on TV are of dads and sons playing with them. What do you think that means? If you were in charge of promoting that set, what might you do differently?" You might encourage your kids to take it a step further by encouraging them to write a message or letter to the company telling them directly, "I would like to see more gender diversity in your marketing." Or more simply, "I'm a girl, and I like dinosaurs. Show people that girls like your building sets too!"

- **Watch what you affirm:** Children do more of what we pay attention to and what we praise. If key adults exclaim, "Wow! Look at you! You're an awesome ninja!" to a boy but say nothing or negatively react when that boy picks up a doll, it's not surprising which interest that child will cultivate. You might make a point to say, "Thank you for baking with me, Charlie! I love the pink, yellow, and green sprinkles you put on the cake for Daddy. Did you know that some of the most amazing bakers can make their cakes look like anything? One famous baker named Duff Goldman made a cake look like a big box of crayons! Would you like to look it up with me?"

- **Connect the behavior to real-world appropriateness:** Say, "You are being very sweet with that doll, Asher. Have you seen Daddy holding the baby so nice like that too?" Or "Wow! You built this whole LEGO world all by yourself, Ella! I imagine some of the best architects and builders in the world started just like you."

- **Encourage boy-girl friendships:** While children learn important skills from same-gender friendships, research shows that gender-diverse friendships help create better attitudes and feelings about other-gender peers. Empathy, understanding, and respect become more possible. You might say, "It looks like Fiona likes playing Alien-Superhero Wars as much as you do. How about we invite her over for a playdate?" Or "I love that you and AJ both love to cook. That was a cool concept for a restaurant you both had at the play place today. Let's see when we can get together with him again." Let's send the message that kids' friendships can be based on mutual interests and respect rather than gender only. (Note: Avoid romanticizing these friendships. Nothing says "cringe," as my daughter and son would say, as much as pegging a different-gendered peer as your child's "boyfriend" or "girlfriend." Labeling a friend in this manner can unintentionally make children feel uncomfortable about pursuing a friendship outside their own gender confines.)

- **Create opportunities:** Go to the park, play places, ice-skating arenas, and other locations where it's likely all kids, of all genders, will come to play. Friendships may develop organically. You can also facilitate diverse gender play by getting cousins, neighbors, and the children of your own peers together. Sometimes when socializing isn't in your children's typical friend circles, they can feel freer to explore different sides of themselves, try new skills, and engage in new activities.

If we are purposeful about exposing the roots of false gender pretenses, our children can enjoy the benefits of being the fullest expression of themselves while gaining the advantages of new skills, passions, and friendships that can serve them for a lifetime. I can't think of anything more gender defining than that.

Talking to Kids about Gender and Sexuality

"Can you imagine being a mother and thinking your son was condemned to hell?" Sara Cunningham asked in a 2021 Upworthy interview.[56] Sara, who was raised in a church that preached that homosexuality was wrong, absorbed the teachings of that church until she couldn't—when her beloved son, Parker, came out as gay. It was time for a change.

In 2015, Sara donned a homemade "Free Mom Hugs" button that she pinned to her shirt as she stood with her son and his friends at the Oklahoma City Pride Parade. She offered a "free mom hug" to anyone who made eye contact with her. The first hug she gave was to a young woman who said it had been four years since she had gotten a hug from her mother. It was this spark that helped Sara both embrace her son and connect with others who also wanted to show kindness, affirmation, support, help, and acceptance to the LGBTQ+ community. The national movement and nonprofit Free Mom Hugs was born.

"Education is key to changing the social norm," Sara wrote to me. "Surround yourself with members of the LGBTQ+ community, read books, watch TV shows, and learn history that includes the LGBTQ+ community. We, as parents, must offer a safe space for our children to explore the LGBTQ+ spectrum and the vocabulary to express themselves."[57]

It is a matter of life and death. The Trevor Project reveals that suicide is the second leading cause of death in young people and that LGBTQ+ youth are four times more likely to consider, plan, or attempt suicide as compared to their cisgender heterosexual peers.[58] In fact, they estimate that at least one LGBTQ+ young person between the ages of thirteen and twenty-four years of age attempts suicide every forty-five seconds in the United States.[59] Additionally, the main findings in the 2022 National Survey on LGBTQ+ Youth Mental Health show that 45 percent of LGBTQ+ youth seriously considered attempting suicide in the past year but

- When these young people felt they had a supportive family, their rate of attempting suicide was less than half the rate of those with low or moderate support.
- LGBTQ+ youth who found their school to be affirming reported lower rates of attempted suicide.
- Those who lived in an accepting community reported significantly lower rates of attempted suicide.
- And most importantly, LGBTQ+ youth who report having at least one accepting adult were 40 percent less likely to report a suicide attempt than those who did not have an accepting adult in their lives.[60]

Understanding and knowing the critical state of our LGBTQ+ youth is imperative but only the first step. How we respond matters as well.

Dos	Don'ts
Educate yourself about the LGBTQ+ community and the struggles they face. From heightened homelessness and suicide to bullying, discrimination, and physical attacks, many LGBTQ+ youth are suffering and could use some understanding and support.	Don't use rude slurs or negative words that perpetuate hate and discrimination. Stop using outdated terms that reduce people to a singular label like "a gay" or "a transgender," as "gay" and "transgender" are adjectives that are just one descriptor of a person.
Ask questions regarding how your children feel about gender identity. Research out of England and the United States indicates that there has been a change in how young people think and talk about gender, including a shift in both vocabulary and awareness.[61]	Don't shrug off discriminatory comments, jokes, and misinformation. If someone says, for instance, "that's so gay," to refer to something that's uncool or boring, address it: "Can you tell me more about what you mean by that?" Or even the more direct "Do you mean 'uncool'?" Your kids are listening and watching.
Model kindness as you interact with and talk about people in the LGBTQ+ community. Regardless of where you stand or what your personal understanding is of being LGBTQ+, alienating, hurting, harassing, or belittling others who are different from you is wrong, and we must make that plain to our kids.	Don't wait to talk about gender identity until your children are older and you are talking about sex. Gender identity is not the same as sex and applies to all people throughout life. In fact, according to the Mayo Clinic, most children can categorize their gender by age three, so conversations about gender identity would be normal and natural.

Bullying & LGBTQ+

According to the 2019 GLSEN National School Climate Survey of more than sixteen thousand kids ages thirteen to twenty-one, the vast majority (86.3 percent) who identify as LGBTQ+ experienced harassment or assault based on personal characteristics, including sexual orientation, gender expression, gender, actual or perceived religion, actual or perceived race and ethnicity, and actual or perceived disability.[62]

Glossary

The concepts of gender and sexuality and how they're expressed are constantly changing. Remaining open to updates in how people talk about gender and sexuality and incorporating new terminology into our understanding help us to better relate to our children and the world they live in today. Keep in mind that while these are the terms people are using now, they could change. Let's keep rolling with the times.

LGBTQ+: Stands for lesbian, gay, bisexual, transgender, queer/questioning, and + for others who are not straight but whose gender identity or sexual orientation isn't included within the LGBTQ initialism. (Note: sometimes you will see extended version, LGBTQIA2S+, where I stands for intersex, A for asexual/aromantic, and 2S for two-spirit.)

Gender identity: One's personal concept of how they define their gender for themselves—male, female, somewhere in between, not on the gender spectrum at all, or a mix of genders.

Gender expression: The way in which a person chooses to outwardly present their gender identity—for example, through clothing, hairstyles, behavior, or body features.

Gender binary: A classification of gender that provides two strict gender classification options, male or female.

Cisgender: A term used for people whose gender identity matches the sex they were assigned at birth.

Transgender: An umbrella term for people whose gender identity differs from the gender they were assigned at birth.

Nonbinary: A descriptor for people who classify their gender as outside the binary. Some may feel they fall somewhere in between male and female, identify as being both, or describe themselves as completely outside the gender spectrum. Some nonbinary people also label themselves as "trans" but some do not.

Gender-fluid: A person who "flows" between various gender identifiers and has an unfixed gender identity that is not tethered to any specific classification.

Misgendering: Intentionally or unintentionally referring to a person with gender-identifying language that is contrary to their gender identity, such as referring to a person who identifies as a girl and uses she/her pronouns as "he" or referring to someone with long hair who identifies as a boy and uses he/him pronouns as "she."

Gender diverse: A way to describe gender inclusive of and beyond the binary framework.

Pronouns and Changed Names

Peyton, who had been assigned female at birth, told his mom that he was a boy from the time he was three years old, but all through preschool, his classmates continued to refer to him as a girl. By kindergarten, his mom noticed that he seemed depressed.

"When we started using he/him pronouns in the house and his classmates and teachers used them at his school," Peyton's mother confided in me over the phone, "Peyton became a lighter version of himself." He had already cut his hair short and opted for pants instead of skirts and Batman over Barbie underwear for years, "but any time people had referred to him as a girl or used female pronouns, he was miserable. This one small change made a huge difference. He was a new kid. He became comfortable with who he is."

Pronoun changes and name changes that reflect a gender transformation can be challenging for many people who grew up in an era when pronouns were fixed and assigned at birth. However, pronouns and names are deeply personal—they refer to who a person is and how they see themselves! And while they may seem like just words to some, for others they are an important way of showing respect while acknowledging gender identity. In fact, according to a research brief on gender-affirming care by the Trevor Project, using a child's chosen name rather than the name given at birth resulted in a 29 percent decrease in suicidal ideation and a 56 percent decrease in suicidal behavior.[63] Kristin Russo, coauthor of *This Is a Book for Parents of Gay Kids* with Dan Owens, put it this way on the *How to Talk to Kids about Anything* podcast: "Using your kid's name and pronouns is a very clear way of saying, 'I recognize you, I believe you, I accept you, I love you.'"[64]

The same is true between friends. If your cisgender child confides in you that a friend, like Peyton, has informed them of a change in pronouns and name, this is the perfect time to begin a discussion about gender and friendship. Interviews I conducted among friends and colleagues who have children who identify as trans and/or nonbinary or who identify as trans and/or nonbinary themselves suggest these strategies:

- **Get a baseline and open the conversation:** "What do you think of that?"
- **Explain the importance:** "For anyone who asks you to use their chosen name or pronouns, it's a very simple kindness to do just that. It takes so little on our part and makes a big difference to them."
- **Practice using the correct name and pronouns together at home:** "Can you ask your friend Vance if they will be going to the recital this weekend?" (Such practice, as Carolyn Hays, author of *A Girlhood: Letter to My Transgender Daughter*, noted on the *How to Talk to Kids about Anything* podcast, helps us to "reimagine that person" as they want to be seen.[65])
- **Let your child know what to do if they make a mistake:** "If you forget to use their chosen pronoun or name, you can just correct yourself and move forward as in, 'He said—I mean, she said her science notes were in

her back pack? New habits can take a little getting used to—and that's okay. Keep trying."

- **Remember, for some people, their gender identity is still evolving:** "Some people may decide to change their pronouns more than once as they figure out what feels comfortable and right for them. They're not doing this to annoy or inconvenience others—they're just finding what's best for them. The way to show kindness is to shift our language based on what they tell us."

- **If your friend is worried about how you'll accept them:** "Remind your friend that 'you're my friend because I like who you are—you're fun and like to go swimming and make funny jokes—not because you're a certain gender.'"

Language changes with the times—what is common today may be passé tomorrow. However, if we continue to put respect and kindness toward others before our own feelings of frustration, we will keep the lines of communication open with our children while helping the people around us feel understood and whole.

Microchanges That Make a Big Impact

According to the United Nations, gender-inclusive language is a way "to promote gender equality and eradicate gender bias"[66]—which sounds like a win for everyone! As it turns out, gender-inclusive language is pretty easy to incorporate by making the smallest shifts:

You guys	→	You all
Good morning, boys and girls!	→	Good morning, kids/everyone!
Do you have any brothers or sisters?	→	Do you have any siblings?
Tell me about your mom and dad!	→	Tell me about your parent(s) or caregivers!
Your parents must be proud of their son/daughter!	→	Your parents must be proud of you/their kids!

"Mom, I'm Gay"

"My son and I were always really close when he was younger," my friend Chrissy said to me once when we were taking a walk around the neighborhood, "but when he came out to me in sixth grade, I didn't know what to say. I was scared for him and worried for me, so my reaction, I'm embarrassed to say, was 'you're too young to know what you like, so maybe just keep that between us.'"

Chrissy's experience is not uncommon. Many parents are not prepared when their children make these kinds of intimate pronouncements. They may stumble on their words while dealing with the emotional impact of what their children are saying or, as one of my friends did, stand frozen in what she characterized as an "out-of-body experience," yelling at herself internally, "Say something! React!"

Here are a few dos and don'ts:

- **If your child comes out to you:** Don't say, "I knew it!" or "Are you sure?" We don't want this moment to be about us or feel like an interrogation but rather a moment to show empathy and connect. Instead, say something like, "Thank you for sharing this with me. I'm so happy you trusted me with this part of yourself, and I love you. I will always love you."

- **If you're worried about your child's safety:** Many parents express concern for their LGBTQ+ children due to discrimination and violence. However, according to Kristin Russo, consultant on LGBTQ+ issues, don't tell your child, "You can't tell anyone! It's not safe!" Instead, ask questions to explore their perception of safety: "Do you think you'll be safe [at school, in the neighborhood, etc.]? Do you feel safe? Are there other kids who also identify as LGBTQ+ at your school? What has their experience been? Do you feel like there are supportive adults at your school who have your back?"[67]

- **Looking for the perfect words?** No need. LGBTQ+ advocate and nonbinary bestselling author Jeffrey Marsh told me on the *How to Talk to Kids about Anything* podcast, "I never craved a mom who was perfect. I just craved a mom who was a little more frank—who could tell me, 'I don't know about all this LGBTQ+ stuff, and I'm a little scared.' You don't need to have all the answers—or even any of them. Perfection isn't the destination—communication, understanding, and support is."[68]

⬛ Scripts in a Pinch

"Molly says her mom and mommy are gay. What does that mean?"

"'Gay' means that a person is attracted to or has a romantic love for someone who is the same gender. When Molly says her mom and mommy are gay, it means they are attracted to and love each other just like Daddy and I [or a man and a woman] love each other and think of each other as attractive."

"Can two men or two women ever get married?"

"Yes, many gay couples are married."

"What does homophobic mean?"

"When someone is homophobic, it means that they have a fear of or a hate for people who are gay."

"If Alex is gay, will I become gay because we're friends?"

"No, it doesn't work that way. You can't 'catch' being gay (or being straight) like you can catch a cold. You are who you are! And I'd say the same thing to your friend Alex."

"Some kids are saying that Jordan is a girl, but he says he's a boy. Is he a boy or a girl?"

"Jordan is a boy. I don't know if you've ever heard the term 'transgender' before, but Jordan is a transgender boy. That means he was born into a girl body, but in his brain and heart, he is a boy. He lives his life as a boy and goes by he/him."

"Ari says he's nonbinary. What does that mean?"

"When someone is nonbinary, they can feel like they're not really a boy or a girl, or they might feel like they are a little bit of both. There's no one way to be nonbinary."

Truth Bomb!

It is important to trans kids that we don't ask, "What are your preferred pronouns?" This implies that pronouns are elective or optional. Instead, simply ask, "What are your pronouns?"

We Are All Different; We Are All the Same

Black. White. Male. Female. Nonbinary. Disabled. Non-disabled. Each of us is different and the same in many ways, making it easy to incorporate conversations on what connects us and what makes us all unique! Try using these suggestions:

BOOKS

Nonfiction and fiction can help shed light on the lives of multicultural characters. Not only do books help people gain perspective on how people with different skin tones, genders, and abilities experience life, but there is such power in seeing yourself reflected in books. As educator Alex Corbitt told me on the *How to Talk to Kids about Anything* podcast, "A good book should help us understand ourselves better."[69]

- "How are [you and I, you and your friends, you and these book characters] the same or different from one another?"
- "Have you ever felt different [like this character felt] from friends or classmates? How did that feel to you? How do you think it made [this character] feel when it was pointed out?"
- "When we look at characters in the books we've read over the past few weeks, what is the same or different about them across these books? Do these characters look like the many kinds of people in our world?"

ART/CREATIVE PROJECTS

Art, in all its forms, allows us to understand others and convey who we are. Through drawing, painting, collages, poetry, creative writing, dance, and more, kids can express themselves in unique and multifaceted ways that can defy everyday language. One fun idea: try using a large selection of skin-tone crayons (like Crayola Color of the World Skin Tone Crayons), various tones of yarn, stickers, magazines, and other materials, and have everyone in the family make a self-portrait!

- **Before:** "Draw and color a self-portrait, and write or cut out from these books/magazines all the words or images that reflect who you are and what you enjoy."

- **After:** "What made you choose this image of a violin?" Or "Tell me about the colors you chose here. Look, you colored your skin medium almond, I colored mine light rose, and your friends colored theirs medium deep almond and very light golden. We all have a different shade of skin. Those with darker skin have more melanin in it, and those who have lighter skin have less—and they are all beautiful. Who has the most melanin of all of us? Who has the least?"

FOOD

Food is like art on a plate! It provides yet another vehicle to talk about similarities and differences. When I was in high school, my friend Kristina and I decided we wanted to try a food from a different country once a month. What an adventurous year! We tasted paella from Spain, curry from India, fajitas from Mexico, and so much more.

- **Cook it!** Pick a food from a new place once a week or once a month, and make it at home. "How does this food taste similar to what we've eaten before? How does it taste different? In Spain, the people speak Spanish, along with some other languages as well. Do you know any words in Spanish? Let's learn a few together."

- **Visit a restaurant:** "I know how much you love rice. Last month, we had a rice dish called paella from Spain, and this week, how about we try a rice dish from China called fried rice? What looks and tastes the same? What looks and tastes different? Do you know your friend May was adopted from China? Her mom told me they eat fried rice as well as lots of other Chinese dishes at their home so they can all learn about Chinese food. Let's look at the menu together and see what else looks delicious!"

CULTURE

You don't need to travel to far-off lands to experience different cultures, abilities, and people. For many of us, opportunities for exposure can happen within a relatively short distance of our homes. From food truck events to multicultural festivals, theatrical performances, dances, sports, celebrations, parades, and holiday parties, there's an opportunity to learn about so many kinds of people. You can dig deeper into your own ancestry, expose yourself and your family to a new-to-you culture, or even help advocate for the rights of a marginalized group of people as an ally.

- **Attend cultural events:** "Asha's mom invited us to a Hindu festival of colors called Holi that's happening in this city this weekend. Let's learn about it and why it's celebrated so we understand why it's important before we go. Would you like to look online with me?"
- **Go to museums:** There are all kinds of exhibits that detail different cultural perspectives as well as history through the eyes of those who lived it. And if a museum isn't nearby, find out if they offer virtual tours! "You know how we talked about [racism, gender discrimination, ableism, diversity] the other day? There's an art exhibit dedicated to that topic not too far from here. How about we check it out this Saturday?"
- **Donate your time:** There are many causes, marches, and events that need volunteers to make them work. When my niece, Phoebe, and nephew, Owen, were in elementary school, they helped with a program in town that served children with disabilities. It was there that they befriended a

girl with Down syndrome and forged a friendship that continued outside the program. "We cannot create justice without getting close to places where injustices prevail," noted Bryan Stevenson, author of *Just Mercy: A Story of Justice and Redemption*, in a presentation at Texas Lutheran University. "We have to get proximate."[70]

While many of us were taught to overlook differences and talk about them only in hushed tones, let's instead celebrate our differences and appreciate them as the very things that make us who we are. Remember, differences don't negate our similarities. They make them stand out even more—and connect us all.

Constructive Discomfort

We are all so much more than the assumptions people make of us at first or second glance. "If we reduce people to the groups that we presume that they belong to," Irshad Manji, author of *Don't Label Me*, told me on the *How to Talk to Kids about Anything* podcast, "then we are overlooking the really unique and interesting things about them."[71]

Let's encourage our kids to go deeper. My hope is that we can move toward a more inclusive and accepting world, raising a generation cognizant of discrimination and bias and committed to rooting them out. I know that, as poet and activist Amanda Gorman explains in the PBS Kids program *Talking to Kids about Racism*, "Change doesn't happen all at once. It happens bit by bit,"[72] but if we can help kids see that we're all one big family of individuals who want to be seen, heard, loved, valued, and treated with respect, we can make progress.

It will take a lot of difficult conversations, a lot of callouts of unfair rules and owning up to our mistakes, and massive amounts of growth and empathy. This is what Ibram X. Kendi calls "constructive discomfort."[73] But moving toward a more inclusive and accepting world doesn't just help others who are different. It helps everyone. And that's worth a little constructive discomfort, isn't it?

⌀ Talking Points

QUESTION	YOUR ANSWER
Do my child and family presently have access to relationships with diverse people who represent different ethnicities, abilities, genders, and sexual orientations? What, if anything, would I like to change about that?	
Do I talk about, introduce, and insert the importance of kindness and openness to people who are different from us in conversation? In what ways?	
Which activities, events, or excursions do I want to do with my kids so they learn and grow with regard to diversity?	

QUESTION	YOUR ANSWER
In my home, how do I promote the idea that we need to celebrate differences and connect through similarities? If I have not done this yet with specific intention, what can I do over the next days, weeks, and months that would send this message?	
Am I purposeful about using inclusive and up-to-date language to refer to diverse populations? Do I shut down or discuss language that is biased, outdated, or cruel?	
On a scale of one to ten, how well do the books, movies, TV series, and other media that come into my house show diverse characters in positive lead roles? How can I improve that number by at least one point?	
Which conversations about diverse people do I want to make sure I have with my kids to ensure they have an understanding and get their questions answered in a way that is both kind and complete?	

Chapter 6

How to Talk to Kids about Divorce and Nontraditional Family Structures

"Why Don't We Look Like Other Families?"

When I was studying at New College of Oxford University in England, my social sciences tutor, whom I met with weekly to discuss psychology concepts, asked me to write a paper centered on a singular pointed question: What is family? At first, I wondered if I could really write a fifteen-page paper on such a small question, but as it turned out, there was much to explore.

I grew up in a "traditional family"—one with a dad, a mom, and a few kids, all related by blood or marriage and living under one roof.[1] And I lived in a world in which this definition was repeatedly reflected to me, unchallenged, in the children's books I read, the TV programs I watched, and in most of my classmates' families. It wasn't until middle school that I encountered families created by adoption (like my family now) as well as ones that included live-in grandparents who often spoke foreign languages and made unfamiliar foods. I began to meet single-parent families, blended families, families that included friends with affectionate relational terms like "Aunt Sally" and "Uncle Sam," and families led by two dads, two moms, or just one powerful grandma. There were even families created from scratch—cobbled together when original family members were no longer living or had stepped back from their children's lives. What I learned over time was, to paraphrase *Forrest Gump*, family is as family does.

As I detailed in my Oxford paper, "family" is defined as a group of two or more people related by blood, marriage, adoption, or mutual commitment and care for one another—regardless of gender, age, location, race, or ethnicity. Families have changed dramatically over the past fifty-plus years—they're smaller, and many of them don't reflect the "traditional" structure anymore. And although the majority (69 percent, according to the U.S. Census Bureau) of America's 73.7 million children under the age of eighteen live in families with two parents,[2] some of those are likely remarriages and blended families, two-dad families, two-mom families, or two-grandparent families. (The second most common family structure is the single-parent family—23 percent live with a single mom, for example.) Yet while TV, film, and online media are becoming better at highlighting different types of families, there is not yet a congruent reflection. The traditional family still seems to be the default.

"We have clung to this 'nostalgic' idea that Mom, Dad, two kids represents the ideal," says Professor Abbie Goldberg of Clark University and author of four books on family, including the recent *LGBTQ Family Building* and *Open Adoption and Diverse Families*. "Ironically, that may be the case even when what's going on in that 'ideal' family isn't so happy or healthy, and even though we have seen perfectly happy and healthy representations of diverse families all around us."[3]

When only one type of family structure is depicted and idealized, it sends a message about what is supposedly "normal," leaving others to feel less than. "We live in a world where everybody talks about nuclear families and biological children," Sue Cornbluth, PhD, a high-conflict family coach who focuses on divorce, fostering, and adoption told me on the *How to Talk to Kids about Anything* podcast. "It's just out there in the media and in society… When you find out you're different, it's like somebody digging a hole in you, and you start questioning yourself."[4]

Therefore, when speaking to our children about family, it's important to counter that narrowly defined narrative with what is scientifically and pragmatically accurate:

- "There are many different kinds of families, and they come in all shapes, sizes, colors, and backgrounds."
- "No one family structure is better than another—they are just different."
- "What's important is what happens *within* the family structure (not the family structure itself) and that, at its core, are principles such as love, support, acceptance, and connection."
- You might ask questions like these:
  - "Is the family warm and loving?"
  - "Is it supportive, communicative, and connected?"
  - "Is it safe and secure?"
  - "Is it predictable and reliable?"
  - "Is it positive and present?"

Reframing how we talk about families—what they *feel* like, rather than what they look like—can go a long way toward raising kids who embrace a more nuanced understanding of what family really means.

Talking about Divorce

After having a playdate with a new friend from kindergarten, my five-year-old daughter asked, "How come Abby's daddy doesn't live with her?" It was the first of what would be many questions about family and the different ways people build, live, and love together—in this case, the family created by divorce.

According to a wide array of robust data sources, the divorce rate has been falling in America (along with the marriage rate),[5] and about one in two children are still likely to experience the breakup of their parents' marriage.[6] The idea of divorce can be shocking to children because (1) they may have only seen or experienced a two-parent household, and (2) they have repeatedly been taught about "happily ever after" while being told to "hug it out" or "kiss and make up" when problems arise.

It's important to explain divorce in concrete and clear terms without allowing your own opinions (perhaps, for example, you think Abby's dad is a big jerk) to cloud the facts:

1. **Answer clearly.** "Abby's daddy doesn't live with her because her parents are divorced."

2. **Check in on level of understanding.** "Have you ever heard that word before? 'Divorced'?"

3. **Explain as needed.** "Divorce is when two adults who are married decide they are better off no longer being married and no longer living together."

4. **Answer questions.** "Why would they be better off not being married anymore?" You can say, "Marriage can bring a lot of happiness between two people. Of course, nobody is happy all the time, and many couples fight and get angry with each other from time to time. That's normal! But some couples find they're not happy with each other a lot of the time. They might fight a lot or stop being honest with each other. They realize that being apart, or divorced, means a lot less stress, a lot less fighting, and more calm times for the whole family. Sometimes it happens when the couple realizes they don't love each other in the close and caring way that couples need to in order to deal with the hard times together."

5. **When there's confusion, try a metaphor.** "Remember when you had that toy truck and the wheel came off along with that little piece of plastic? We couldn't fix it. We tried gluing it, taping it, and repositioning it, but the truck couldn't be fixed. Sometimes marriage is like that.

Sometimes something breaks, and it just can't be fixed. When a marriage breaks apart, and there's no way to fix it, the couple might choose to get a divorce and live separately."

6. **Stay open to further questioning.** "If you have any more questions about divorce, marriage, families, or anything we've talked about today, always know you can ask me. Even if it's been days or weeks since we talked about it, I am here for you."

It's normal for children to have follow-up questions when the concept of divorce is new to them. They may even wonder if their parents' marriage may end in divorce, if moms and dads can divorce their children, or if all conflicts can lead to divorce: "Since it happened to Abby's parents, is our family next?!"

Answering questions, as well as you can, can be both reassuring and illuminating: "While no marriage is perfect, and conflict is both healthy and normal, we have no plans to divorce and love each other very much. We're happy to be married to each other." Or "Even though your mom and I got a divorce and Abby's parents are getting a divorce, it doesn't mean all marriages end in divorce. Some couples, like Grammie and Grandpa, never got a divorce and were married their whole adult lives." And "When you're older and if you choose to be in a relationship, you will decide what's right for you. Everyone is different, every marriage is different, and every family is different—and that's okay!"

Quick Tip

Right around the time my daughter asked about divorce, *Sesame Street* came out with videos of "Abby Cadabby," the colorful fairy favorite who explained how her parents were divorced and that she lived in two different houses.[7] In order for Tallie to understand more about divorce and what her friend (coincidentally

also named Abby) might be experiencing, I had her watch these
videos so she could learn:

- Divorced and single-parent homes are one kind of family.
- Kids who experience divorce are loved just as much as kids
  who don't experience divorce.
- Divorce is never a child's fault.

When You Are Divorcing

The conversation changes when you're talking to your children about your
own impending divorce. Emotions can be intense—yours and theirs—and
you are trying to explain something personal, raw, and often painful while
also possibly juggling legal issues, working through grief, figuring out custody agreements, and establishing living situations for immediate family
members who will be touched by this decision.

During this time, kids are knee-deep in what Dr. Robert Emery, author
of *The Truth about Children and Divorce*, calls an "emotional stew."[8] They might
wonder, "Where does that leave me? What is going to happen to me? Do I
even have a family anymore?" Even though it's the parents who are divorcing, as clinical psychologist JoAnne Pedro-Carroll, PhD, author of *Putting
Children First*, writes, "With astonishing frequency, children refer to the end
of their parents' marriage as 'my divorce.'"[9] (My friend Karen explained to me
that once her parents divorced when she was nine years old, the hurt became
"fossilized" underneath her tough exterior, and she became untrusting, curt,
and closed off.)

Studies show that children from divorced families are two to three
times as likely to experience long-term adjustment problems—emotional
and physical health problems, peer relational issues, suicidal ideation—
than children who grow up in intact families.[10] Divorce has been shown
to increase the chances that a child will have difficulty in school and with
depression as well as engage in risky behaviors such as early sex and the use

of illicit substances.[11] Also, a recent longitudinal study out of Arizona State University's Research and Education Advancing Children's Health (REACH) Institute discovered that, after divorce or separation, kids experience fear of abandonment when their adversarial parents engage in conflict.[12]

Since you are your child's greatest asset, advocate, sense of security, and source of truthful information, how you talk with and listen to your child as you all process your divorce is vital to your child's well-being and mental health. According to the research, talking to kids about your divorce in clear and age-appropriate terms

- Opens the door to communication about feelings, concerns, or questions.
- Helps them learn that it's not their fault.
- Underscores that it's an adult problem and there's nothing they can do to make their parents stay married or get them back together again.
- Keeps children "in the know" about their family structure so anxiety about unknowns can remain more in check.
- Shows respect for how they are affected by the changes in the family too.

When It's Time to Begin the Conversation

1. **When should I tell them?** Plan a time. This conversation can't be rushed, even if it feels unpleasant. It's also important to do it when your child is not exhausted from a long day and isn't preparing for a big test or project that will take a lot of concentration.

2. **Who should be there?** If parents are having an amicable split and can cooperatively tell their children, this can be an advantage as it can show a united front and two committed parents. However, if parents are experiencing animosity and are having trouble communicating without arguing, it may be best for each parent to talk to their child independently of the other. In addition, if you have children of different needs, ages, or personalities, it may be best to tell them separately so you can be fully present for each one in the unique way they deserve.

3. **Where should I tell them?** Somewhere comfortable but not distracting to your child. It should be out of the way of screens, other people, and possible disruptions—a safe, private space where your child can be free to express emotions without having to curtail them or feel embarrassed by them. (For example, avoid telling them in a public place like a restaurant.)

4. **What should I tell them?** There is no perfect script, and emotions aren't linear. The key is to connect and be honest while remaining age appropriate. Research suggests that parents should try to maintain a balance between being clear and unambiguous and refraining from oversharing[13] (a tough line to walk, I know!). Remain present and responsive to your child's needs in the moment.

🗩 *Scripts in a Pinch*

A little background

- **Younger children:** "We have been having some big adult problems, and we haven't been able to fix them. That's why we've been fighting a lot. We are so sorry you had to hear us yelling. That must have been scary for you."

- **Older children:** "As you've probably noticed, we haven't been getting along very well lately, and we've been fighting a lot [or haven't been talking much at all]. We have some tough problems that we've been working on—and we have even gotten some help on them—but we haven't been able to fix them."

The main message

- **Younger children:** "We have had to make a hard choice that might make you feel lots of big feelings. It makes us have lots of big feelings too. We're going to get a divorce. That means we're not going to be married to each other anymore."

- **Older children:** "We realized that even though we really wanted our marriage to work, it's not working. In a successful marriage, both people need to be happy together, and unfortunately, we are no longer happy together. We really tried. We have needed to make a tough decision that will likely be very hard to hear. We've decided, together, that we are going to get a divorce."

What this means for your family

- **Younger children:** "[Mommy/Daddy] is going to live here in this house, and I will live in another home. You will have two places to live and a room in each home. You will get to see us both and spend time with us both. Even though [Mommy/Daddy] and I will be divorced, we will always be your parents, and we both love you very much—forever and ever."

- **Older children:** "As you know, this means that [Dad/Mom] and I aren't going to live together or be married to each other anymore. [Dad/Mom] is going to move into a different home, and I will stay here in this home. You will keep your room here in this house, and you will have another room—your room—in [Dad's/Mom's] home as well. [Dad/Mom] and I will create a schedule that will allow you to see and spend time with both of us."

Never forget

- "We both love you more than anything."
- "We are still a family even though we won't all live together in the same home."
- "We will always be your parents."
- "We will continue to take care of you and show up for you [and take you to your games and watch your piano recitals]."
- "This divorce is between us—as parents—not between us and you."
- "This divorce is not your fault. You are not to blame in any way."
- "We are here for you to listen, to hug you, and to answer any questions."

These conversations may need to be repeated and revisited as your children mull over what the change in the family means for them and the people they love. They may ask why this had to happen and inquire about the logistics: "Who will cheer me on at this weekend's track meet? The more reassuring, patient, and loving we can be, the more we can retain a strong connection with our children even as the marriage is ending.

When Safety, the Law, or Mental Stability Is in Question

Maintaining a connection with both parents may not be possible when discussing divorce. If one parent has done something illegal or inappropriate and can't safely be present for the conversation:

- **Emphasize *your* availability:** If you know your ex-spouse will not be in contact with your child for the foreseeable future, Dr. M. Gary Neuman advises that you only speak of yourself, as in, "I'll always be here for you" and "My feelings have never—and will never—change."[14] This is not an insignificant "throwaway" part of the conversation, as your children may likely feel unsettled and perhaps untrusting, given that someone significant in their lives has abandoned them physically or emotionally.

- **Consistently follow through with actions:** As Tina Payne Bryson, coauthor with Dr. Dan Siegel of *The Power of Showing Up*, told me on the *How to Talk to Kids about Anything* podcast, "Show up. It's what kids need most from you. When we provide experiences where kids feel safe, seen, and soothed in that predictable way, we achieve a fourth 's,' which is 'secure.'"[15] It's that sense of security that can help provide stability during this confusing, erratic time.

- **Stress safety:** We want our children to know that their well-being and security are always a priority. Say, for example, "I know you love Mom, and Mom loves you, but when Mom drinks too much wine, she doesn't make safe choices. Mom and I always want you to remain safe."

- **Remain objective and age appropriate:** While we don't want to sugarcoat explanations regarding parents who have disappeared or engaged in criminal behavior, we still need to be careful in how we phrase the information. Jean McBride, author of *Talking to Children about Divorce*, says, "State the facts without blaming or putting your children in the middle."[16] She advises telling young children that, for example, "Daddy has some big problems right now that he has to work on and he won't be back with us until he's better, which could be a long time."

Older children can hear more information regarding where the other parent is or what occurred. Remember, we are trying to inform, not turn our children against the other parent. No matter what has happened, this is still their mom or dad. You might say, "Your dad is suffering from alcoholism and will be attending a facility in New Jersey to help him get better. You'll stay with me one hundred percent of the time until he has a safe place for you to visit and everyone agrees that he's ready to have you there overnight. He wants to get better and loves you very much."

Quick Tips

When explaining divorce or why a marriage sometimes doesn't work:

- **Use what children already know:** Divorce coach Christina McGhee's book *Parenting Apart* asked a young child in her divorce group, "What's your favorite food?" He answered, "Doughnuts." McGhee shared with him that her favorite food was pizza, and she posed, "What would you think if we put our favorite foods together and made a pizza-doughnut sandwich?" The young child didn't think that pizza and doughnuts sounded good together (and I agree). McGhee suggested that perhaps it was the same between his parents.[17] You might say, "Just like pizza and doughnuts are not

> so great together—but are pretty awesome on their own—
> maybe your parents were not so good together and are
> better apart too."
>
> - **Use accurate words:** For example, say, "We are getting
>   a divorce," rather than, "We are taking a little break," and
>   refrain from lying to cushion the blow, as in, "Daddy just
>   needs to move closer to his job." Studies show that when par-
>   ents withhold information or are perceived as covering up
>   the truth, it can negatively affect the relationship between
>   the parents and children.[18] Ambiguity or a lack of informa-
>   tion also provides space for children to self-interpret what
>   went wrong—and blame themselves. Christina McGhee told
>   me on the *How to Talk to Kids about Anything* podcast, "Our kids
>   are going to go out into the world and need words to talk
>   about what's happening. 'Divorce' is not a bad word. It's a
>   change in a family."[19]

🗩 Scripts in a Pinch

"Will we still be a family even if you don't live here anymore?"

"We will always be your family. A family is a group of people who love and care for one another—no matter where they live! Grammie is part of our family, and she doesn't live with us, right? The important thing is that as your parents, we will continue to love you, care for you, and show up for you no matter what, no questions asked."

"Will you and Daddy/Mommy be getting back together?"

Clinical psychologist JoAnne Pedro-Carroll, PhD, author of *Putting Children First*, reveals that 79 percent of children feel that the family problems related to their parents' divorce are their fault.[20] Therefore, it's not surprising that many kids hold out hope that they can get their parents back together again. It's important that you don't give your child ambiguous messages or false hope. If the answer is no, say it outright: "We won't be getting back together, but we will always love you and we will always be your parents." (In a sweet exchange between Gordon and Abby Cadabby, who experienced her parents divorcing on *Sesame Street*, she says, "I wish there was something I could do to stop the divorce...maybe a magic trick?" Gordon explains, "Not even magic can change something like this. You can't fix it, and you can't wish it away."[21])

"Who will take care of me? Who will make my grilled cheese for me?"

Children in a two-parent household are used to a certain parent doing certain jobs. Changing to two one-parent homes can spark concern and confusion about how particular tasks are done. Children are looking for a sense of security and assurance that they will be getting their needs met. "Even though we won't be living together anymore, we will always be your parents. When you are with Dad, he will take care of you and make your grilled cheese, help you get ready for school, and tuck you in at night. When you are with me, I'll do all those things. We will always take care of you because we love you, and that will never, ever change."

"Will I have to leave my school and my ballet class?"

Children crave consistency and predictability. If it's possible to keep the rest of your children's schedules familiar, that can help with their adjustment to life during and after divorce. "Even though we all won't be living together anymore, you will be staying at the same school with your friends and the same ballet class with your teacher, Miss Lisa. On Tuesdays, I will take you to ballet class, and on Saturdays, Daddy will take you to ballet class." (If you aren't going to be able to keep the same schedule, talk about what can stay the same and which parts will be adjusted.)

Shared Parenting

Shared parenting, co-parenting, or "a two-home concept" is still a relatively new notion. Just a few decades ago, when a marriage ended, kids would typically stay with their mothers and visit with their fathers. This single-home arrangement was made with the hope that having one primary residence would help kids to have a more grounded foundation and sense of stability.

However, the idea of children "visiting" with their fathers would often relegate their father to "visitor" status and create distance between dads and their children.[22] It also often created a stressful, sometimes less affectionate dynamic between the child and the custodial parent, usually the mother. While this structure is still often used and sometimes with success, more parents are now opting for a shared-parenting model—one in which both parents spend more equal time with their children in two separate spaces.

Shared parenting may not be right for all families. I'm often asked, "But what if I can't stand the person I divorced?" I love what Jennifer Hurvitz, author of *One Happy Divorce* and host of *Doing Divorce Right*, said about this to *Oprah Magazine*: "When you are in a co-parent relationship, you have to love your children more than you hate your spouse."[23] However, research shows—when both parents are safe, secure, and loving options—that shared parenting offers many benefits for children, from better relationships and stronger academics to fewer risky behaviors and increased overall mental wellness.[24] Young people are also more likely to turn to both parents about concerns and problems when shared parenting is the chosen structure.

Household Rules in a Two-Home Concept

When engaging in shared parenting, consider talking to kids about rules and routines across households. This creates clarity and predictability and underscores that "we're all on the same team—the child's team!" While some common rules and routines will likely remain (like brushing teeth before bed), rules around screen use, lights out, and what kids can eat for snacks might be different. The most important thing about having separate rules and routines is to convey them clearly and stick to them:

1. Define the rules in child-friendly terms. For example, "We don't eat on the couch while watching movies in this house. I know this is different from the rule in our last place."

2. Why we follow the rules: "Eating in the family room creates crumbs, which can get stuck in the couch and bring lots of bugs. Remember what we found in the last couch? *Blech!* We don't want bugs in our family room, right?"

3. What we can do instead: "You are welcome to eat at the breakfast bar or kitchen table."

4. Consequences of what happens when the rules are not followed: "If you eat on the couch while watching a movie, you'll need to turn off the movie and vacuum the couch right away so we don't attract bugs. Does that make sense to you? Do you have any questions?"

Taking time to explain the rules can help kids understand what is expected and why each rule is important. Remember, if you set a family rule, it's important for each family member in the household (including you) to follow it.

For young children, it might be helpful to have a visual reminder of rules and routines to maximize the chance for success. You might say, "Let's check our chart for the rule about TV before we turn it on. Let's read it together: 'Maddie can watch one hour of TV per day.' That means that if it's nine a.m. now, you can watch two half-hour shows, and then the TV needs to be turned off by ten a.m. Or you can watch just one half-hour show now until nine thirty and watch another half-hour show after dance class at four p.m. What would you like to do?"

THE _____*Green*_____ FAMILY'S
TOP TEN FAMILY RULES

RULE 1
If you make a mess,
clean it up.

RULE 2
Maddie can watch one
hour of TV per day.

RULE 3
Finish homework
before playing.

RULE 4
Make your bed and take the
clothes off the floor each day.

RULE 5
Keep hands and
feet to yourself.

RULE 6
Above all,
be kind.

RULE 7
Speak in an inside voice
when inside the house.

RULE 8
Tell the truth,
even when hard.

RULE 9
Knock before entering
when door is closed.

RULE 10
All electronics must be in
Mom's room before bed.

As a member of the _____*Green*_____ family I hereby
acknowledge these rules as important and will work hard to
adhere to these rules as a sign of love and respect.

What if your child is struggling with the rule or exclaiming, "But Daddy lets me watch two hours of TV when I'm with him!"? Remember to "hold the boundary" and "okay the feelings" as Kristin Gallant and Deena Margolin of Big Little Feelings advise.[25] For example, you might say, "You wish you could watch another hour of TV like you get to do at Daddy's house. It's hard to turn off the TV when you're watching your favorite shows. At this house, we have one hour of TV watching per day. It's time to turn off the TV. Do you want to go to the park or read a story now?" If your young child still won't turn off the TV, don't let go of the boundary in favor of "keeping the peace." Instead, acknowledge the feeling and situation again, and enforce the rule. "You are having trouble turning off the TV because you're enjoying your favorite show. Turning off the TV is hard sometimes, but it's time to turn it off, so I will help you."

As children get older, they'll get used to different rules in different spaces, as long as you remain consistent, but you can still hold space for negative feelings and frustration around different rules for older children too: "It's hard to have two different sets of rules. This is the rule here, and it's a rule not because I want to make you mad or stunt your fun, but because I think it's best for your mental and physical health." You can also brainstorm different rules with your children and prompt discussion by saying things like, "What are your feelings about screen time?" and "Let's discuss bedtime rules." However, you, as the parent, get the final say.

Dual-Family Routines and Schedules

Whether your co-parenting schedule consists of alternating weeks, extended overnight stays, or special two-, three-, or four-night rotations, a physical dual-parent calendar can help your conversations along. You might try something like this, inspired by Elaine Wilson's co-parenting schedule, designed for the co-parenting series at the Oklahoma State University's Extension School.

You might say, "This is our calendar for February. As you can see by the big letter M, for Mom, you'll be here with me until Wednesday. On Sunday, we'll go to brunch with Gram, on Monday, I'll take you to basketball after school, and on Wednesday, I'll take you to guitar practice. Then, as you can see, on Thursday"—or, for younger kids, "in X sleeps"—"your dad will pick you up from school, and you'll be at his place on Thursday, Friday, Saturday, Sunday, Monday, Tuesday and Wednesday. Even though you won't be sleeping here that weekend, I'll see you at your basketball game on Saturday—cheering you on! You'll be back here next Thursday. Is that clear? Do you have any questions? You can keep this copy, and I'll have another copy up on the kitchen wall near the microwave. You can ask me or your dad about it anytime, and if something is confusing or makes you feel worried or concerned, let us know."

FEBRUARY

SUNDAY	MONDAY	TUESDAY	WEDNESDAY	THURSDAY	FRIDAY	SATURDAY
1 M Brunch with Mom & Gram	2 M 5pm Basketball	3 M	4 M 4pm Guitar	5 D	6 D History Test	7 D 10am Basketball
8 D Movies with Dad	9 D 5pm Basketball	10 D	11 D 4pm Guitar	12 M Spelling Quiz	13 M	14 M 2pm Basketball
15 M Riley's Skate Parrty	16 M 5pm Basketball	17 M Field Trip!	18 M 4pm Guitar	19 D	20 D Math Test	21 D 11am Basketball
22 D Dad's Birthday	23 D No school or practice	24 D	25 D 4pm Guitar	26 M	27 M Science Poster Due	28 M 10am Basketball

Bad-Mouthing

When emotions run hot, it's easy to get loose in the gums, as my husband's grandmother used to say. "See how your dad likes it when all this sugar he allows you to eat means thousands of dollars at the dentist's office!" Or "Of course, your mom allows you to stay up to all hours of the night. She couldn't care less about anyone's sleeping schedule!" But bad-mouthing the other parent can backfire or boomerang, making children feel a lack of closeness with the denigrator rather than the parent denigrated.

It also puts kids in the heartbreaking position of having to choose between their parents—or, as divorce coach Christina McGhee says, "where they need to become judge and jury, figuring out who is right and who is wrong."[26] Research tells us, again and again, that children should not be pressured, even subtly, into a "loyalty bind," in which they must rank one parent as better or worthier of love than the other. In addition, since many children think of themselves as "part Mom and part Dad," being critical of your ex can impact your children's view of that side of themselves.

Research by UC Santa Barbara's Tamara Afifi and colleagues tells us that when parents reveal information to a child that is negative, is hurtful to the other parent, is too sensitive given the child's age, and places the child in the inappropriate role of confidant or counselor, it can have adverse effects on the kid's physical and mental health.[27]

Therefore, before you send the biting email or the scathing text or dredge up past issues during drop-off, ask yourself these questions:

- What would my children think of what I'm saying?
- Is what I'm doing right now, in this way, in the best interest of my child?
- Is this issue a reflection of what my child wants, or is it what I want?
- Does this information reduce my child's anxiety or uncertainty?

We want to help our children better cope with a tough situation that has upended life as they knew it. Studies continually tell us that maintaining a positive relationship with both parents, when possible, is best for children's mental and physical health.

DOS AND DON'TS OF DIVORCE AND SHARED PARENTING

DO: **Carve out space at your new home for your children and allow them to have some say in the details.**

- **Science says:** While research across countries shows that children in dual-residence arrangements can often fare very well,[28] there is a caveat— aside from no ongoing conflict, kids do best when they have a say in the details of their living situations. With this in mind, help your kids carve out a space of their own.[29]

- Ask:
  - "What color would you like to make your room?"
  - "Where do you think we should put the couch?"
- Anything that conveys the messages "you belong here too" and "your opinion and comfort matter" is important to help your children transition to a two-home family.

DON'T: Say "my ex" when talking about your children's other parent.

- **Science says:** When we want the message for children to be "we are still part of your family," using "ex" to refer to their parent can subtly suggest that they are also an "ex-parent"[30] or "ex-member of the family."
- Instead, while being cognizant of your tone and body language, use their role, as in "your dad," or when talking about them within earshot of your child, "May's mom" or "Jill." Heed what parenting coach Meghan Leahy wrote in the *Washington Post* about divorce: "No matter what you decide to say or not say, your parenting North Star is to not divide."[31]

DO: Stay up to date with your children's important events and dates.

- **Science says:** Keeping life predictable, familiar, and stable during separation or divorce is critical to children's well-being. This will give your children a sense of security while family changes occur. Studies show that children tend to fare best, in normal and safe circumstances, when both parents remain involved.[32]
  - "Even though you won't be staying here at this house on your birthday, I'll still take you for birthday breakfast, before school, like always."
  - "How did your doctor's appointment go today for the recheck of your knee?"
  - "How did you feel about your math test today—less anxious than the last time?"

DONT: **Bring divorce drama to your kids' sports games and activities.**

- **Science says:** Sports and other extracurricular activities can give kids a respite from the emotional complexities associated with divorce in the home(s)[33] However, when parents bring conflict to these arenas, the benefit of these activities can be severely compromised.
- This script is between you and your child's other parent:
  - "We clearly don't agree on some scheduling things. I know we're going to see each other at Emma's soccer game today. Let's stay away from this topic and discuss it on the phone instead, at six p.m. or eight thirty p.m.?"

DO: **Start new traditions.**

- **Science says:** Divorce typically alters family traditions as most parents don't continue to celebrate holidays and mark milestones together once they've been divorced. Traditions are associated with comfort, meaning, and belonging,[34] so the loss of family traditions can be hard for children. Admit the loss and discuss new possibilities.
  - "Would you like to learn how to bake homemade bread with me that we can serve on our holiday table this year?"
  - "I know you always loved to throw the ball around with me each evening. How about we start a father-son football game in our neighborhood that meets on Saturdays?"
- From volunteering to taking a trip, establishing new traditions can be a gift to your children.

DONT: **Use a derogatory or demeaning tone or language when speaking about or to your ex-spouse.**

- **Science says:** Check yourself. Try slipping into a more formal "business relationship" tone, using a child-centered focus,[35] when talking to your child's other parent. When speaking to your child about your ex-spouse, ask yourself if you would be okay with the other parent using the same words or tone when speaking about you.

- Keep words like "visitation," "custody," "noncustodial parent," and "having contact" out of everyday conversation. Instead, incorporate more neutral language like "on-duty parent," "time with Mom/Dad," "Mom's/Dad's home," and "parenting time," to help support positive parent-child relationships across households.

Single Parenting

It's not only divorce that can create single-parent households. Some moms and dads parent by themselves, either because the other parent can't or won't be involved (for example, due to illness, death, abandonment, or incarceration) or because there was never another parent involved to begin with. One in four parents in America never married, and Pew Research Center shows that just over 50 percent of unmarried parents are solo mothers—those who are raising at least one child with no spouse or partner—and 12 percent are solo fathers.[36]

How do we answer children's pertinent questions about single-parent households?

- **"Why does Rose only have a daddy? Where is Rose's mom?"** If you know the simple answer, you can provide it in age-appropriate terms. "A few years ago, Rose's mom died. Sadly, her heart stopped working— she had something called heart disease Her heart was very sick." Or "Sometimes people have one parent, some have two, and some are raised by their grandparents or someone else who cares for them. Rose has a daddy who loves her very much. She doesn't have a mommy, and that's okay." If follow-up questions come, answer them! The more we can normalize single parenting (as it's become increasingly commonplace), the less likely kids will question it or see it as a deficit.
- **"When will I have a mom/dad too?"** In an interview with my friend and colleague Nefertiti Austin, author of *Motherhood So White*, she told

me a story of her son who, when he was in elementary school, told her, "I don't need any more Christmas presents, and you don't need to buy me any more birthday presents. I just want a dad. When can I get one?" As a single adoptive mother, she admitted, "It was painful."[37] These types of questions can be mistaken for resentment, triggering a parent's emotional response. Try these strategies instead:

○ **Acknowledge it:** You might say, "I know you'd really like to have a dad, especially now that you started Scouts. I hear that this is tough on you."

○ **Underscore that family differences are okay:** Nefertiti explained the situation matter-of-factly: "While everyone has a mother and a father, that's biology. Not every kid lives with one or both biological parents." You may point out families that are similar to yours and still others that have different family structures. Sometimes kids just need to know that a single-parent household is a family structure that many kids experience—and that they are not the only ones.

○ **Enlist some pinch hitters:** Whether in a single-parent or two-parent household, sometimes kids benefit from having another strong parental figure in their lives as a mentor or confidant. This can give them a different perspective or lend an alternative life experience as well as give them somebody to go with to a "daddy-daughter dance" or "mother-son dinner." (You can find mentors and/or parent figures within your extended family, school, sports teams, religious organizations, youth groups, etc.) You might say to your child, "I am always here for you, and if there's something you'd prefer to discuss with another adult, you can always call or text your aunt Denise!" Or "How about we FaceTime your uncle Scott to see if he can make it to the father-son camping event in a few weeks? Last month, you mentioned how much you enjoy spending time with him!"

Let's not forget, a single-parent family is headed up by a mom or a dad who is often working twice as hard while still providing all the love a child needs to thrive—and that is the message we all need to relay to our children in today's world.

Two-Mom or Two-Dad Households

As single parenting has become more common, so too have two-mom and two-dad households. According to the 2018 American Community Study out of the Williams Institute of UCLA, there are an estimated 16.2 percent of same-sex couples raising children (8.1 percent of same-sex male couples are raising children, and more than 20 percent of same-sex female couples are raising children, with higher rates of child-rearing among married same-sex couples).[38] The majority of same-sex couples were raising biological children (via surrogacy, sperm donation, or previous heterosexual relationships); however, two-dad and two-mom households were far more likely to be raising kids who were adopted or in the foster-care system than male/female couples.

As these types of family structures grow, your children may ask, "Why does Julia have two mommies?" or "Will I get to have two daddies like Jack?" You can answer like this:

- **Be straightforward:** "There are lots of different kinds of families. Some kids live with a mom and a dad, others live with one parent or a grandparent, and some live with two mommies or two daddies. There are families with kids who were adopted and some families with no children at all."

You may be able to stop here. However, if your child wants more information, you might try these strategies:

- **Stress commonalties:** "Jack and his daddies went to Disney World just like we did last year. And remember when we saw Jack's family at the movies last week? They love each other and like spending time together just like us." Or, if you know that Jack's dads are married, you might add,

"Just like a man can marry a woman, a man can marry another man or a woman can marry another woman in many areas around the world. Jack's parents are married just like Daddy and I are married."

- **Say "gay":** Don't make the word "gay" a bad word or one that needs to be uttered in hushed tones. "Julia's parents are gay. That's when a mommy loves another mommy or a daddy loves another daddy in the same way that a daddy and a mommy would love each other." If you make it weird, they'll get the message that they can't talk to you about this and that there's something wrong with their friend's family.

- **Realize that they aren't asking about sex here:** When kids ask this kind of question, they are asking about family structures, not about what happens between two people in the bedroom. (You might be wondering, "But what if my child *does* ask how they had kids?" You can explain, "People are able to add kids to their families in different ways. Sometimes parents who are gay adopt, while other times they get help from another person and a doctor." If you know how Jack's dads or Julia's moms added to their family, you might add, "Jack's dads had a surrogate help them—a surrogate is a woman who carries a baby inside her for nine months just like I carried you in my body for nine months. When the surrogate had the baby, Jack's dads became parents." Or "Julia's moms adopted her from foster care a few years ago, and they became a family.")

- **Let them know that sometimes people give families with gay parents a hard time:** Explain that LGBTQ+ parents and their families often face discrimination. "Sometimes when families are different from what others are used to seeing, people might think it's wrong or bad. It's not wrong or bad. It's just different. If you hear people saying mean things to Jack, stand by his side, say something, or let an adult know."

Remember, answer questions one by one in a clear and matter-of-fact way. Keep the door open for additional questions—but also don't be surprised if your child just accepts what you say about this and moves on.

Blended Families

Blended families have become incredibly common as divorced, previously single, and widowed parents date, remarry, and mesh their families together. According to the U.S. Census Bureau, about one in six kids are living in blended families—that is, a household with a stepparent, stepsibling, or half sibling. Hispanic, Black, and white children are uniformly likely to live in a blended family.[39]

Blended families have some unique challenges related to their family structure. They must deal with any pain from the divorce and past relationship, the complexities of new relationships, and the unique obstacles that come with creating one family from two. As parents and stepparents (or "bonus parents," if you are using family-positive language), we need to step up and have important conversations with our kids about fear, loss, inclusion, empathy, and connection that tie the binds between biological family members and new family members—all while dealing with our own frustrations and feelings.

"There's absolutely no blending, no co-parenting, no being a great person, unless you do the self-work," says Mashonda Tifrere, author of *Blend: The Secret to Co-Parenting and Creating a Balanced Family*, regarding how her family with ex-husband, Swizz Beatz, and his wife, Grammy Award–winning singer Alicia Keys, created a parenting team.[40] Of course, nobody says it's easy, but it certainly has its advantages when everyone works together for the good of the child. "Blending is a lifestyle," Tifrere said. "We all win if we can raise mindful, loving, and empathetic children," and "that process starts at home with parents and caregivers. By saving our families, we save our present and our future."[41]

In the *How to Talk to Kids about Anything* podcast, I spoke to Ron Deal, coauthor of *Building Love Together in Blended Families*, about two tough issues regarding blended families:[42]

- **As a stepparent or "bonus parent," I don't know what to do when the kids start talking about their deceased parent in front of me. Should**

I stay? Should I leave? Should I join in?

- ○ **Explanation:** While you may never have met your "bonus children's" deceased parent, being present while the kids talk about that special person can show kindness, affection, and empathy. In fact, it's a real act of love when you allow the kids to talk about the parent they lost in front of you.

- ○ **Sample script:** "Wow, he was a great guy. I really wish I could have met him. Tell me that story again about when he did that funny thing!" Sit with them when they are sad, and give them space when they want to be alone.

- ○ **Final word:** Deal says, "When you enter that sad place with them, they will see you as respectable, honorable, and worthy of being close to, as they can trust you with the hard stuff." In addition, you are showing them that what's important to them is also important to you. After all, their deceased parent is part of them and always will be.

- **My new spouse's daughter doesn't want to like me because she's loyal to her mom. I know this is hard for her. How do I extend an olive branch?**

  - ○ **Explanation:** In *Zen Parenting*, Cathy Cassani Adams writes, "If our children have a different perspective, we may immediately view them as disrespectful. If they ask questions, we perceive it as 'talking back.'"[43] This stops the conversation short before there can be any movement, understanding, or empathy. Additionally, some of the questions our children may ask can trigger our own pain and fear—the fear of not belonging and of being unloved or unlovable, for example. Find a moment when you have some private time together where there isn't a need for intense face-to-face connection, such as when you both happen to be in the car. Then build a bridge.

  - ○ **Show appreciation for the relationship.**
    - → Acknowledge the struggle and your commitment to working through it with her.

    → Solidify her mom's role and your role as different from her mom.

    → Say what you like about her and your unique relationship.

    → Let her off the hook for feeling differently than you.

    → Listen.

○ **Sample script:** On the *How to Talk to Kids about Anything* podcast, Ron Deal suggested that parents stress that they are not trying to compete. For example, "I just want you to know that I really care about you, and I appreciate our relationship. I also know this relationship might be hard for you because you love your mom. I want you to know that your beautiful relationship with your mom is good and right, and I would never get in the way of that relationship. I'm not trying to be your mom, but I'd love to have our own, different relationship, whatever it is. I really like you, and it's okay if sometimes you find it difficult to like me back." Then just listen and allow the child to talk openly.

○ **Final word:** When you take this initiative, you are working toward putting words to how children feel while also declaring that you are not trying to take the place of the child's parent.

Adoption

I started talking to my children about adoption before they were born.

My children's birth parents used to play a CD of my husband and me singing bedtime songs and explaining our adoption story to them when they were in utero. We all wanted them to know that they were loved from the beginning by all of us, their adoptive parents and their birth parents. Because we had an open adoption plan, my kids never had a need to wonder where they came from or why they were adopted. Once they were born, we displayed photos of us all together at ultrasounds and at the hospital, and I continued to discuss their adoption with them, even as infants. I know that might seem silly, but I wanted their story to roll off my tongue as easily as a recipe for peanut butter and jelly sandwiches.

Adoption is defined as a non-biological parent or parents legally taking a child into custody and bringing up that child as if the child were born to them. The non-biological parent might be related by blood or chosen through the foster-care system, adoption agencies, lawyers, or an informal kin agreement. There are more than a hundred thousand adoptions in the United States each year of varying types:[44]

- **Closed adoption:** The adoptive family and child are given little to no information about the biological parents or circumstances leading up to the adoption of the child. There is no contact between the biological and adoptive families.

- **Semi-open adoption:** The biological parents and the adoptive parents provide some nonidentifying information and communication to one another, usually through the adoption agency or lawyer.

- **Open adoption:** The biological parents and the adoptive parents provide identifying information and communication to one another and have ongoing contact during and after the adoption process. This type of adoption leaves a lot to interpretation; some families may visit with one another and take part in holidays and events together, while others may communicate via text or send photos from time to time.

When do you begin discussing your child's adoption? As early as possible. Amanda Baden, a professor at Montclair State University, highlights the negative consequences of waiting to tell your kids that they were adopted: psychological distress and feelings of anger, betrayal, depression, and anxiety. In particular, those kids who learned of their adoptions from age three and older reported more distress and lower life satisfaction than those who knew of their adoption at younger ages.[45]

Very young children may not be able to understand the nuances, but incorporating language, books, photos, and stories of adoption in the discussion helps to normalize it. "Just like you never have a moment when you know you learned your name, you don't want a moment when your kids suddenly learned they were adopted," says Carrie Goldman, a mom who adopted her eldest child and who is the author of the premier adoption blog, *Portrait of Adoption*. "Even when the children are young, you can throw in sentences here and there like: 'We are so glad we adopted you. We love being your parents.'"[46]

SAY THIS, NOT THAT	WHY?
SAY THIS • He was adopted. • They were adopted. **NOT THAT** • He is adopted.* • They are adopted.* *Unless that person has explicitly told you that is how they identify.	Traditionally, using past tense when speaking about adoption is a core example of "adoption-positive language." Adoption is considered a one-time event by many—something that happened in the past, like birth; hence the phrasing "I was adopted" as in "I was born." However, some children are viewing adoption as a defining moment in their lives and a way to describe themselves—part of their "I am" statement ("I am adopted"). In those cases, taking the cue from the child, "he is adopted" or "is an adoptee" would be acceptable.
SAY THIS • Birth mother (father, parent) **NOT THAT** • Real mom (dad, parent)	All parents are "real."[47] In the adoption community, people refer to the biological parent as the "birth parent" when they need to make a distinction between those who gave birth to the children and those who raise the children.
SAY THIS • Parent • Mom/Dad • Mother/Father **NOT THAT** • Adoptive parent	Unless a distinction needs to be made, in an everyday setting, a parent who adopted their children is simply the parent. This is the person who takes care of the child in every way!

SAY THIS, NOT THAT	WHY?
SAY THIS • Child • Son • Daughter **NOT THAT** • Adoptive child	Again, unless a distinction needs to be made between children who are biological and children who were adopted, children are just children, sons, and daughters.
SAY THIS • Biological children* *If there is a specific need to differentiate **NOT THAT** • Real children • Your own children	All children are real and fully part of their families.
SAY THIS • Children in the foster-care system **NOT THAT** • Foster kids	According to adoption expert Allison Maxon, coauthor of *Seven Core Issues in Adoption and Permanency*, it's important to use child-first language. "There is no such thing as a foster child" but rather a child who was in the foster-care system.[48]
SAY THIS • Placed for adoption • Made an adoption plan • Chose adoption **NOT THAT** • Gave up their children • Gave their children away • Their children were given up • Put up for adoption • Surrendered for adoption • Adopted out	Adoption is a thoughtful, loving choice made by birth parents who plan to place their children with parents who can take care of them and raise them as if the children were born to them. Many birth parents get to choose the people who will parent their children from detailed profiles with pictures and life details (my husband and I made one of these, and it's how our children's birth parents chose us). Children who were adopted are not given away or given up—these words can be hurtful and imply a cavalier and negative attitude toward innocent children, their birth parents, and everyone involved in their adoption.

SAY THIS, NOT THAT	WHY?
SAY THIS • Paid adoption **NOT THAT** • Bought/sold their children	In legitimate adoptions, parents who adopt do not buy children, and birth parents do not sell children. There can be many fees involved with the adoption process—from adoption lawyers and birth parent expenses to medical care and, at times, international travel. It takes a lot of people to help make an adoption possible.

"What If We Never Told Our Child That She Was Adopted?"

Perhaps you were scared about your child's reaction or you received bad advice about keeping adoption a secret. Whatever the reason, it's never too late to begin this tender and nuanced conversation. You may even want to request professional assistance to help plan. Here's some guidance:

- If you feel that you made a mistake, admit it. "I'm so deeply sorry that we didn't tell you sooner. It was a big mistake to keep this information from you, and we know now that it was the wrong choice."

- Detail the reasons you didn't tell your children sooner. While keeping adoption a secret is much less common now, according to Professor Abbie Goldberg, who studies family structures, in the past some people kept the information hidden because they were told it was best to raise a child as "completely their own" and as a "blank slate."[49] You might say, "We got some bad advice from [our adoption agency, our lawyer, our social worker] who told us it would be healthiest and easiest for you if you didn't know you were adopted. We only recently learned that this advice is wrong and damaging to you. We are so sorry, and we are glad you know now."

- Remain open and present. You might say, "We know this must be a shock to you, and you may have a lot of emotions about what we are telling you. We're here to listen, and we also have someone to help you process what we are telling you whom you can talk to as well. We love you very much."

You ultimately want to send the message "we didn't tell you sooner because we thought it was the right thing to do."

Origin Stories

Every child is entitled to their origin story—the account of who they are and where they came from. As renowned author Alex Haley wrote in his novel *Roots*, "Without this enriching knowledge, there is a hollow yearning; no matter what our attainments in life, there is the most disquieting loneliness."[50]

Studies show that psychological and physical well-being can be challenged when our children have no or very little information about their origin or are not allowed to ask questions or talk about it. And when kids who were adopted are lied to about their origins, according to the longitudinal research by Dr. Abbie Goldberg (as well as the extensive work of Sharon Kaplan Roszia and Allison Maxon[51]), "the discovery of such lies can prompt feelings of betrayal and amplify shame and guilt that often result from secrecy about adoption in the first place."[52]

It's best, as stated by Professor Goldberg, that children who were adopted know their full story, as much as their parents know, by the time they are an adolescent. Even divulging negative information such as unplanned pregnancy, poverty, addiction, sexual assault, or incarceration can strengthen the relationship between parents and children as well as children's relationships with themselves and their integrated past.[53] Such discussions also keep children who were adopted from filling in their own gaps with untruths or misconceptions.

Origin stories can involve the circumstances surrounding your child's birth; the birth family's heritage such as their special traditions, culture, holidays, and language; the birth parents' personal backgrounds; and your child's adoption story.

Children should be "at the center of their origin story," advises Professor Goldberg. You can incorporate your child's origin story into everyday occurrences: "It was snowing just like this on the day you were born!" or "Your birth dad loved to take apart alarm clocks and put them back together—I bet that's where you got your knack for building things and taking things apart too." Or do a retelling of their origin story each birthday or "gotcha day" (the day the child came to live with you), even if you aren't sure of all the details: "You were born on the Chinese New Year, so lots of people all around China were celebrating that day! I bet there were fireworks and decorations all over, just like the ones we have here in front of us. And of course, it was a new moon, which is why we call you Luna."

Kids who were adopted should be able to confidently talk about themselves, where they came from, and where they are going. As Dr. Jeanne Howard, professor at Illinois State University's Donaldson Adoption Institute, said in her presentation at the Rudd Adoption Conference, "Sometimes adoption is a big A, and sometimes it's a little a."[54] Whether playing a huge role in the moment or drifting to the background of their life, your child's origin story may not be their whole story, but it is always there, folded into their identity.

Origin Story vs. Adoption Story

Origin story: The story of who we are and how we came to be; our backstory. "Superman, the Man of Steel,[55] was born on Krypton, but when his home planet was in danger, his loving birth parents sent him in a special spacecraft to Earth where he serendipitously landed on the farm of Jonathan and Martha Kent."

> **Adoption story:** How a child became part of your family. "When a couple found Superman alone on their farm, they decided to adopt him and raise him as Clark Kent, with strong moral values and without the knowledge that he was adopted."

The Joys and Pains of Adoption

As a mom who adopted her children, I've always regarded our adoption experience as a beautiful, positive blessing, but assuming everyone, including our kids, feels one hundred percent happy about it all the time can invalidate a part of our children's existence.

Research introduced in 1982 by Deborah Silverstein and Sharon Kaplan[56] (and updated in 2019 by Sharon Kaplan Roszia and Allison Maxon)[57] tells us that there are seven core issues related to adoption: loss, rejection, shame and guilt, grief, identity, intimacy and mastery, and control. When parents of kids who were adopted allow for this dichotomy to exist—that is, for both positive and negative emotions about adoption to be expressed in a healthy way—kids become more at home with their identities as they grow and develop.

Adoptive mom and author Carrie Goldman, who conducts adoption workshops that focus on dialectics, suggests using the word "and" instead of "but" when discussing adoption, which can help to substantiate a child's full experience (as well as yours).[58] For example:

"I wish I knew my birth family BUT I love my mom and dad."	→	"I wish I knew my birth family AND I love my mom and dad."
"I am different from my family BUT we also have some similarities."	→	"I am different from my family AND we also have some similarities."
"I struggle with being adopted BUT I know my family will always support me."	→	I struggle with being adopted AND I know my family will always support me.

By acknowledging *both* conflicting feelings, parents tell their children

- "It's okay to feel both ways."
- "A lot of people who were adopted feel the exact same way."
- "You can tell me about these feelings anytime because they are part of you, and I love you."

My daughter has some dialectics of her own when talking about adoption, one of which is, "I feel fine about adoption, *and* I only tell my closest friends about it." When I asked her to tell me more about that, she said, "People are always so surprised when they find out and start asking annoying questions about where my 'real parents' are. You are my *real* parents!" These dialectics can open some very interesting conversations and perspectives, illuminating the nuances of adoption and, in turn, how your children think about themselves and their personal story.

⬛ *Scripts in a Pinch for Little Kids*

"Why didn't I come out of your tummy?"

- "Your birth mom, Brittany, gave birth to you, so you couldn't come out of my tummy. When you adopt, your biological mother gives birth to you and another parent raises you and takes care of you. I'm so glad Brittany gave birth to you! If you had come out of me, you wouldn't be you—you'd be someone else! We love you just as you are and wouldn't change a thing."

"Why didn't my birth parents keep me in their family?"

How you respond depends on your child's unique circumstance, but always try to answer simply and with age-appropriate language, even if your child's origin story is unpleasant.

- "Jay and Jasmine were very young and poor. They wanted to make sure you had food, a safe place to stay, and clothes to wear. They chose adoption because they loved you and wanted the best for you."

- "We don't know a lot of information, but from what we do know, your birth mom wasn't able to take care of you, so she placed you for adoption. I imagine she would be so proud of who you have become."
- "Your birth father wasn't safe around children, and your safety was the priority, so your birth mother chose adoption for you."

"Why does Sofie look like you, but I don't?"

- "Children often look like their birth parents or other people in their birth parents' families. Since I am Sofie's birth parent, she looks more like me with her green eyes and light skin. And since Kelsie and Marco are your birth parents, you look more like them, with your blue eyes from Kelsie and your olive-toned skin from Marco."

"Why did you adopt me?"

Again, how you respond depends on your child's unique situation.

- "There are many ways to make a family, and I wanted to build my family through adoption. Remember, my parents—your Grammie and Grandpa—adopted me, and I wanted to adopt too."
- "We wanted a family, and getting pregnant wasn't possible for me, so we decided to adopt. We're glad we did because we love you so much."
- "We always wanted to adopt, and when we met your birth mother, May, and learned she couldn't take care of you, we knew we wanted to adopt you. We are so happy you're part of our family."

"What do my birth mother and birth father look like?"

If you have photos of your children's birth parents, make sure your child has access to them and can look at them whenever they are interested. If you don't have access to photos, wonder together.

- "I wish I knew what your birth parents looked like, and I've often wondered about that too! I would imagine they might have your beautiful brown eyes and are tall like you! What do you think they might look like?"

Is Adoption Second Best?

There can be a negative connotation regarding adoption—the idea that because it is sometimes the "second way" a person or couple uses to create a family, it is somehow "second best" or "not as good." Of course, this couldn't be further from the truth! When reading articles about adoption, I often comb through the comments for insights from those who were adopted. I was very moved by one commenter, who captured this sentiment beautifully beneath an article by Creating a Family, a nonprofit for adoption education: "My parents were very upfront with me about trying for years to have a child the 'regular way' [before they] decided to adopt... Never once, did I ever feel as though I was the second choice, or second best. I was the baby they had dreamed of, the child that they wanted so much and worked so hard to get. They didn't 'settle' for adoption... Having me was a triumph, not a concession."[59] You might say to your child, "We want you to know that no matter how you came into our lives, you will always be our first choice, the child we have always wanted and will forever love."

Transracial Adoption

A longitudinal study by the Institute of Family Studies reports that 44 percent of adopted kindergarten students were being cared for by adoptive parents (mostly white) who were of a different race or ethnicity.[60] While other studies show the percentage as less, it's clear that the percentage is increasing.[61]

When children who are being fostered or children who were adopted are of a different race than their families, research shows that adds an extra layer of identity that must be integrated, combined, and celebrated in order for these children to thrive.[62] "Children need a sense of pride in their birth culture," said transracial adoptee and researcher Amanda Baden at a recent adoption conference, noting, for example, a child can see herself as "not just Korean, not just American, not just Korean American, but also an adoptee."[63]

The first step in helping a child integrate, combine, and celebrate their transracial adoptee identity is for parents to ask themselves introspective questions such as those outlined in the guidebook *Transracial Parenting in Foster Care and Adoption: Strengthening Your Bicultural Family* written by the Iowa Foster & Adoptive Parents Association:[64]

- Am I doing enough to help my Black child feel a sense of belonging in our family?
- How can I better connect my Chinese child to his culture, his racial roots?
- How can I prepare my daughter for the impending discrimination she will experience because she is Latina?
- How do I need to meet my Korean child's needs around race and culture?

When mothers or fathers are parenting a child of a different race, it's vital that they recognize that child's need to know, understand, and integrate those cultural roots.

TALK ABOUT DIFFERENCES SO THEY'RE NOT CONSIDERED WRONG OR TABOO

- Many parents, according to Amanda Baden, try to parent an adopted child in a "colorblind way"[65]—that is, without mentioning variation in looks and skin tone. Research shows that this is a mistake.[66] Aside from the fact that babies recognize race differences by the age of six months, transracial adoptees who grow up in this way have "very little language to talk about their ethnic experiences." Tonia Jacobs Deese, a clinical instructor with the University of North Carolina, Chapel Hill's School of Social Work, writes, "Minimizing racial differences won't make them disappear, and acknowledging them won't make your child self-conscious."[67]

- **You might say:** "Everyone has a different skin tone. Your skin is dark brown, and mine is peach. They are both beautiful colors." Or "Your hair is thick, dark, and tightly coiled, and your sister's hair is straight and red. You both have beautiful hair that is quite different from each other!"

CULTIVATE DIVERSE ROLE MODELS FOR YOUR CHILD

- Be sure to include mentors who also share your child's background and culture. According to a research report out of the Donaldson Adoption Institute, "Black children had a greater sense of racial pride when their parents acknowledged racial identity, moved into integrated neighborhoods, and provided African American role models."[68] It's important to create a community for your child that allows them to see themselves reflected. Many transracial adoptees report feeling like they "are the diversity" in their families, their communities, or their schools, according to Dr. Jeanne Howard, professor at Illinois State University's Donaldson Adoption Institute,[69] which can feel isolating and complicate the positive development of self. Transracial adoptee and mentor Angela Tucker advises white parents of transracial adoptees to "outsource some of their parenting duties"[70] to family friends who are of the same race as their child.

- **You might say:** "I am always here for you to talk about any topic you want to bring up. I also want to acknowledge that I'm not [Black, Latina, Chinese], and I don't want to pretend to have all the answers and best advice about race, racism, and some of the unique challenges you might be coming up against. You've known Jenette all your life, and she has told me that she's ready and waiting to talk with you about any of the frustrations you've been dealing with lately. She's lived it too, as a [Black, Latina, Chinese] girl and a [Black, Latina, Chinese] woman. She said you can call her up now, or you can plan to meet on Sunday."

PREPARE YOUR CHILD FOR PREJUDICE, RACISM, AND STEREOTYPING

- Children with black or brown skin (and defining characteristics outside of Caucasian) need to be prepared for ignorance and ugliness around race. "African American families tend to talk about this with their children regularly and coach them on how to respond," writes Deese.[71] Research shows that this provides a "buffer" that kids may need to skillfully cope with and navigate racism in their everyday lives.[72] Nikki Tennermann, LCSW, administrative director for Boston Children's Hospitals' Office of Health Equity and Inclusion, says to note that racism and bigotry exist ("you can tell them that it's not fair for people to make assumptions about them based on their race or color of their skin"[73]) but to focus on what's fair and just.

- **You might say:** "We are proud of our heritage and identity, and even if people say hurtful things, it doesn't affect who we are." Tennermann also advises that parents discuss with children how they can set the example with their own behaviors, as in, "Just as we don't want people to treat us differently because we're Black, we don't treat people differently because they're Asian."

EXPLORE YOUR CHILD'S BIRTH CULTURE THROUGH COMMUNITY RESOURCES, ORGANIZATIONS, BUSINESSES, AND MEDIA

- Whether you are enrolling your Chinese-born son in Chinese classes, getting your Black daughter's hair braided at a Black-owned hair salon, participating in multicultural events that celebrate your children's Native American heritage, or reading books and watching movies that showcase people who look like your children, your children are learning that who they are matters. This is vital to their self-esteem and identity development. As teacher Alex Corbitt said on the *How to Talk to Kids about Anything* podcast, "Kids need to be able to look into books and see themselves reflected back at them."[74] Classically, in school, the books kids read are by "authors who are white, male, dead, and straight... We need to explore different perspectives, cultures, and identities." From media to holidays, celebrating our children's background helps them to celebrate themselves.

- **You might say:** "While we are here at the grocery store, let's collect all the ingredients to make Jeonju bibimbap. It's one of the most popular dishes served in your home city and country of origin, Seoul, Korea, and is absolutely delicious!" or "I really hear you that learning Chinese is difficult, but keep at it! When we visit China next summer, it will be great for you to have a good foundation of the language so you can talk to—and understand—the people in your country of origin. It's part of who you are!"

GIVE YOUR CHILDREN THE TIME TO TALK ABOUT (AND ASK QUESTIONS ABOUT) THEIR BACKGROUNDS

- Many adoptees worry that they will hurt or offend their parents if they ask about their culture and background.[75] Don't just tell them that you are open to these discussions. Bring them up! While it can sometimes feel like a rejection when our children want to embrace the heritage of their birth family, think of it as a beautiful acceptance of a part of themselves.
- **You might say:** "You are many things! You are Chinese. You are American. You are Chinese American, and you were adopted. I love that we can celebrate all the different sides of who you are. I'm excited to learn about Chinese New Year with you. I see you were born in the Year of the Monkey! Let's read about what that means together."

Amanda Baden notes that when children embrace all components of their identity, they can have what she refers to as a "combined culture," welcoming the many sides of who they are and knowing that they can be proud of where they came from and where they are going. "You can think of yourself as a racial being," she says. "It's okay to see yourself in that way! You don't have to pretend that you are not any race in order to be accepted."[76]

Let's face it: Families look different—two parent, single parent, blended, fostered, adoption built, multiracial, multigenerational, and more. And because there are many ways to form a family, our conversations must follow suit. It is up to us to help kids understand that while different families may have different issues, they also have a great deal in common with ours.

"We don't know how our kids will grow up," noted Professor Abbie Goldberg on the *How to Talk to Kids about Anything* podcast. "We don't know if our kids will adopt, if our kids will be gay, or if our kids will decide that they don't want kids at all. So part of it is saying, 'Be kind, accept, empathize, be respectful to other families, don't judge.' Part of it is anticipating the range of possibilities that kids have for themselves. We don't want kids to foreclose any possibilities for themselves, so when we reinforce the idea of a particular kind of family that is valid, we are not only shaping how they treat other people, we are shaping what they can imagine for their own futures and for their own lives."[77]

When we raise children who contribute to and feel pride in their loving, supportive family, no matter its construction, they are more likely to grow up to contribute to and feel pride in a loving and supportive family of their own—and accept other families that may differ from theirs. A society made up of loving, supporting, and accepting families? What could be better than that?

✐ Talking Points

QUESTION	YOUR ANSWER
Which family structures have I discussed with my children and which family structures do I still need to discuss for my children to have a better understanding of family differences?	

QUESTION	YOUR ANSWER
What concerns do I have about discussing some of these family structures with my children, and how can I address these concerns to put myself and my children more at ease?	
Is there anything that I've said or another family member has said about different family structures that I would like to clear up, change, or underscore while talking to my children about this topic?	
What do I feel are the most important topics in this chapter, and what messages would I want my children to come away with?	
What questions do I want to ask my children regarding their perspectives on the topic of family structures?	
How can I use the exercises of "dialectics" or "origin stories" to help my own children feel more grounded in their family structures and how they came into this world/family?	

Chapter 7

How to Talk to Kids about Mistakes and Failure

"What If I Mess Up?"

It seems like yesterday when my five-year-old son, Noah, and I were driving to meet one of his friends and her mother for a playdate at the park. He was busily coloring in his Angry Birds coloring book when he looked up and said, "Mommy? I'm doing a good job coloring, but it's not *perfick*."

Every once in a while, I get this chill up my spine when interacting with my children—a knowing sign that tells me, "This is one of those times. This is my chance to talk to my child about something important." You know those moments?

I said, "Noah, it's okay to make mistakes. Mistakes are what make us interesting and weird and strange. Humans are not perfect. We were never meant to be. In fact, humans are wonderful because we're *not* perfect. That's what makes us special."

"Well, but machines are *perfick*, right, Mommy?" he said. "Machines do things *perfickly*."

I loved how his mind was thinking. He's always been such a scientist in his approach to life. "I suppose machines are made to be perfect," I answered. "But humans? Humans are made to be flawed. We are constantly learning, and the important part here is to love ourselves as people who learn, because each time we make a mistake, each time we have the courage to go out there and learn something new, we grow."

I could tell he was really listening to what I was saying, and I didn't want to lose this momentum—it's a rare time when parents have a captive audience with one of their children without the usual distractions of technology or food. And the car, where there's a lack of intense eye contact, can be a freeing environment for kids and parents to talk about serious things. "We all make mistakes," I continued. "Mommy makes mistakes, Daddy makes mistakes, Tallie makes mistakes, you make mistakes—we all do! We are all learning and making mistakes so we can become better."

"You make mistakes too?" Noah asked.

If he only knew... My mind raced over the past few days. Shrank my brand-new shirt in the dryer, check. Put the wrong name at the top of an email, check. Got snippy with one of my children, check. "Yes," I answered. "Mommy is learning how to be a better mom, better at her work, better at so many things! You are learning how to be a better son, a better friend, a better student, and a better colorer! We are going to make mistakes together as we learn. And that's okay."

🗩 Scripts in a Pinch

"Every one of us makes mistakes—parents make mistakes, brothers and sisters make mistakes, and teachers make mistakes too! No matter what age we are or how perfect someone seems, every person fails, in small and big ways, throughout their lives. Even the most successful and famous people in the world, from doctors to star athletes to scientists, make mistakes and fail. Failing and mistakes are part of life, part of learning, and part of success. It's okay to make mistakes and, in fact, we want you to make them because it shows you're trying—and trying is both brave and how we learn."

The Myth of Perfection

I still remember the shame I felt when I received a red F on a test paper, signaling that I'd failed—an embarrassing scarlet letter that alerted me, as well as my teachers, my parents, and my classmates, that I didn't measure up. After all, I can't think of any of my teachers who gave an F and exclaimed, "Congratulations, what a valuable lesson! You now have an opportunity to learn from your mistakes!" Nope. Most teachers are disappointed, and most students are grounded, chastised, or punished for failures once they get home. I folded that test in half and then in half again and put it on the very bottom of my bag, out of the light, out of sight, trying to make it less powerful and true.

As a culture, we are caught in this quest for perfection. We have gotten stuck in the mindset that making an error means we're lifelong members of detention—stupid, lazy, ignorant, careless, the class clown, the troublemaker—instead of seeing mistakes for what they really are: opportunities.

Anyone who has ever run a marathon, performed in a play or concert, written a book, or done anything that requires skill, hard work, patience, and determination knows that every mistake represents a step up the ladder to success. You don't make people powerful by pushing them to be perfect but by allowing them to develop the tenacity and passion about something that compels their interest. To focus on perfectionism robs them of enjoyment and can tie their sense of self and achievements with how well they do in a single moment in time. That's a lot of pressure.

Research shows that when we are driven only by how we perform rather than our effort, our experience, our growth, and our enjoyment, we can create what Canadian psychologists Gordon L. Flett and Paul L. Hewitt call "the perfection paradox":[1] by becoming hyperfocused on our mistakes, we undermine our performance. We perform at a level lower than our ability—and our expectations. This may create a need to

- Conceal mistakes
- Back away from opportunities
- Blame others for failings
- Be rigid and overly demanding
- Experiment with risky behavior, such as eating disorders
- Become overly self-critical[2]

This dark side of perfectionism, referred to as "perfectionistic concerns," happens when people consistently worry about making mistakes, letting other people down, or not measuring up to their own ridiculously high standards.[3] Researchers have found that perfectionistic concerns and the stress they generate can contribute to serious health problems, including depression, anxiety, eating disorders, fatigue, and even early mortality.[4] What often appears like intense self-control or "carefulness" can backfire.

According to researcher Andrew Hill, acting vice chancellor and professor of sport psychology at York St. John University in England, people with high perfectionism experience burnout and respond to failure with higher levels of shame and guilt than others.[5] These consequences of perfectionistic concerns can undermine effort and performance after that failure. In fact, he told me in an email, "Perfectionism is quite misunderstood. Because it can look desirable in some ways—for example, in sports or education—people often assume it is a good trait to have. However, we know from research that the more perfectionistic concerns people have, the more likely they are to experience a range of difficulties in the future."[6] In other words, perfectionism, while masquerading as an admirable quality, is more likely to hamper development, productivity, and achievement over time than promote them.

It's like we're all setting ourselves up to be dissatisfied. Think about it:

Don't we view very high achievement as a win? Don't we tend to clap the loudest at the flawless gymnast? Or for the baseball pitcher who has thrown a "perfect" game? If we continue to honor and celebrate perfection—rather than the work and mistakes that go into imperfect success—we create an impossible and a highly destructive path for our children, who can never measure up and are destined to disappoint us as well as themselves.

Is this the life strategy we want our children to have? Parents, coaches, and educators must celebrate mistakes as a normal and everyday part of our lives. In fact, research finds that, to be sure we're learning at the optimal rate, we should be aiming to fail around 15 percent of the time![7] That means we must fail in order to achieve. If we don't teach our children about the important role of failure, they may spend a lifetime running from it.

Failure should—*must*—always be an option.

Are You Creating a Perfectionistic Climate?

Research shows that a perfectionistic climate, an environment riddled with unrealistic expectations, harsh criticism, coercive control, conditional love and regard based on performance, and worry about mistakes can have profound negative effects on the well-being of young people.[8] Be sure to declare your home (or classroom or sports field) a safe place to fail. Ask yourself:

- Are my standards too rigid or unrealistic given this child's actual ability or situational constraints?
- Do I criticize this child too readily for even minor, inconsequential mistakes, despite their best efforts or progress?
- Do I manipulate or pressure this child to feel, think, and behave in a particular way to prevent minor mistakes, and do I threaten, punish, and reward this child to limit their autonomy?
- Do I treat this child more positively and kindly when they perform perfectly and treat them more negatively and harshly after imperfect performances?

- Am I overprotective and excessively vigilant regarding mistakes, irrationally preoccupied with imperfect performances, and averse to novel or uncontrollable circumstances where blunders are more likely?

Fixed Vs. Growth Mindset

Of course, we often don't grow out of this perfectionistic frame of reference; rather, we grow more heartily into it. To this day, I know of adults who don't hand in projects because they would rather get reprimanded by their bosses for being late than be told their work needed improvement. How many projects don't get finished? How many books, articles, or works of art go unseen? The theory is this:

- If I work really hard and I fail, people will know I'm not as good as I say I am.
- If I work really hard and succeed, then people won't think I'm just naturally great at what I do.
- If I don't try and I fail, I can simply say I didn't try.
- If I don't try and I succeed, people will think I'm a genius.

We wind up "self-handicapping,"[9] the strategy of avoiding effort with the goal of keeping potential failure at bay so we don't have to experience the perceived consequences of what we feel certain is a catastrophic blunder. Carol Dweck, a well-known psychology professor at Stanford, calls this concept the "fixed mindset," one in which we stop short at failure because we see it as the end of the road rather than a stop along the path to learning. What we want to strive for instead is a "growth mindset," which posits that we can continue to try and stretch ourselves even when things aren't going well and that each attempt, whether failed or not, is a learning opportunity.[10]

Now you might be thinking, "But what if my kid has a fixed mindset? Is a fixed mindset...well, fixed?" Actually, no. Recent research out of Michigan State University shows that children with a fixed mindset can retrain themselves to bounce back from mistakes if they are encouraged to pay attention to the errors, something that kids with fixed mindsets typically want to brush under the rug.[11] Parents and key adults can help! The lead investigator, Hans Schroeder, directs us to change our language from "it's okay, you'll get it next time," which provides no room to dissect where things went off track, to "mistakes happen, so let's try to pay attention to what went wrong and figure it out," which normalizes errors and sees them as clues for how to get better, smarter, and more masterful at the task.

FIXED MINDSET		GROWTH MINDSET
I don't do it well.	→	What can I improve?
I will never do it as well as they do.	→	What can I learn from them?
It's too hard.	→	I need more time to practice and learn.
There's nothing I can do to make it better.	→	What can I change on my next try?
I suck at this.	→	I have a lot of room for improvement.
I can't do it.	→	I haven't mastered it yet.

Quick Tip

When Sara Blakely, the founder of the megasuccessful apparel company Spanx, was growing up, her father used to ask her, "What did you fail at this week?"[12] He didn't inquire about grades, scored goals, or contests she won. He set the tone that it's not only okay to fail—it's expected and rewarded. In fact, she would receive a high five from him when she would give her report! Today, at fifty years old, she's worth $1.1 billion and pays millions of dollars forward each year by supporting, inspiring, and elevating women globally and helping them to take the risks on their own business endeavors. You can try a similar prompt with your child each week, such as "The mistake that taught me the most this week was..."

What's the Beef with Mistakes?

Paul Schoemaker, research director at the University of Pennsylvania's Wharton School and coauthor of *Brilliant Mistakes*, told *Harvard Business Review* in 2018 that when people make mistakes, they often "make an asymmetric evaluation of gains and losses so that losses loom much larger than gains."[13] That is, they make a big honking deal of the failure and tend to blow things completely out of proportion—minimizing the good and maximizing the perceived bad.

When I was a graduate student at Tufts University, my advisor returned a much-anticipated third draft of my dissertation to me. Judging from the amount of red ink from page three to page eighty-one (it was a very long paper), I figured he must have thought I was an idiot. Our brains are hardwired to focus more on the negative than the positive—even *only one* negative comment in a sea of positive ones grabs our attention and can govern our mood and how we perceive our mastery, reach, and self-worth. In her book *Being Wrong*, Kathryn Schulz captures this feeling beautifully when she says, "Certain mistakes can kill us, but many, many more of them just make us want to die."[14] Therefore, it becomes critical that we teach our kids that mistakes might feel uncomfortable and make us feel bad about ourselves, but if we use them to catapult (or even creep quietly) forward, they can be seen simply as growing pains and sure signs of learning.

🗩 *Scripts in a Pinch*

"Failing doesn't make you a failure. FAIL just stands for 'first attempt in learning!' And sometimes 'first' is actually 'fifth' or 'fifteenth' or 'fiftieth!'"

Conversation #1: Everyone Fails Sometimes

Even though some are better at hiding it, nobody is infallible. The star baseball player swings and misses. A parent misses her child's doctor's appointment (I can tell you from personal experience). A principal calls a student by the wrong name.

Yes, we see perfection online, but that is often facilitated by the meticulous crafting of setting, hairstyle, lighting, angle, outfit, expression, etc. And it's not just the celebrities. Don't believe me? Many teens have admitted to me that they take up to two hundred versions of the same picture just to be able to choose the very best of the best—and then they add a filter, crop, and change it in key ways to make it look that much better.

Life does not need Photoshop. It's messy because we are human, and humans are flawed. As it's been said and repeated, "fallor ergo sum" (I err, therefore I am). While many children learn that their parents aren't perfect somewhere along the line, few kids are taught that some of the world's most famous visionaries and inventors are fallible. In 2016, Columbia University researcher Xiaodong Lin-Siegler found that when high school students learned about the life struggles and the intellectual challenges faced by, for example, Albert Einstein (who flunked the entrance exam to the Zurich Federal Polytechnic School and was said to have possibly struggled with ADHD and autism spectrum disorder) or "Father of Electricity" Michael Faraday (who was known to have struggled with math and failed to make glass, though he tried) or Marie Curie (who had many of her experiments end in failure), their grades actually *improved*. For low-performing students, this effect was even more dramatic. And when students learned only about the successes of these scientists, their grades declined![15] The lesson here: we must tell the whole story, struggles and triumphs included, if we want kids to feel inspired, connected, motivated, and willing to take the risks to achieve their goals.

Grit to Glory Story

Telling our children stories that link mistakes to mastery helps to both humanize failure and demonstrate that failure is, indeed, part of success—and part of some of the biggest success stories there are. "Theodore Geisel, also known as Dr. Seuss, was rejected twenty-seven times before someone said yes to his first book,[16] and did you know that Walt Disney was fired from his newspaper job because he 'lacked imagination and had no good ideas'?[17] And what about media executive and billionaire philanthropist Oprah Winfrey? She was fired from her first job as a TV anchor in Baltimore (and told she was 'unfit for television news') before making it big with her own show, her own magazine, and her *own* TV channel! In fact, her failure, which she marked as 'the greatest growing period' of her adult life, sparked her often-quoted sentiment: 'There is no such thing as failure. Failure is just life trying to move us in another direction.'[18] Look at what these highly recognizable people did because they kept trying! Keep failing, and you'll keep learning and getting better and better."

Conversation #2: Dealing with Shame

Mistakes aren't fun. They can be demoralizing and embarrassing. Every time we make a mistake, we have a choice: we can either wallow in what we did wrong, or we can learn where we missed the mark, regroup, and try again.

What seems to trip us up is shame. According to famed "shame expert" Brené Brown, author of *Daring Greatly*, *The Gifts of Imperfection*, and *Rising Strong*, when people are making mistakes and learning, they often get into a shame cycle: every frustrating hurdle or failure is a reason to shower themselves with shame.[19] You might hear phrases from your children like, "How did I not know this?" or "How did I make this mistake?" or "I'm not good enough." The problem is that each time we ruminate about our current shortcomings, we feel worse! And when we feel worse, we do worse. Then we feel, well, "worser." It's like feeding that man-eating plant in *Little Shop of Horrors*—you are just feeding your own demise.

In a rare recording on guilt and shame, Albert Ellis, the founder of cognitive behavioral therapy, pinpoints shame-based sentences that prevent us from learning, put us in crisis mode, and lead us down the shame path.[20] For example, an initial sentence that invokes guilt or frustration, such as "I made a mistake," is often followed by a sentence that translates those feelings into shame: "This means that there's something wrong with me" or, even more denigrating, "I am a mistake."[21] Brown attributes this kind of shame-based language to fear of disconnection stemming from "being perceived as flawed and unworthy of acceptance and belonging."

Shame, in fact, has an inverse relationship with learning[22]—when shame is taken out of the equation, it leaves room for growth. Dr. Dehra Harris, who works with elite performers and happens to be a dear friend, a trained psychiatrist, and a leadership team member with the Toronto Blue Jays, has seen firsthand what happens when people *don't* get sucked down the rabbit hole of shame. The difference between elite performers and regular performers, she said in a presentation on "The Secrets of High Performance" at my husband's Systems Success mastermind group, has to do with how they deal with mistakes. Instead of getting caught in shame cycles, elite performers remain in a constant learning phase. They see each action to gain expertise as a "singular attempt to attain a learning outcome." That means they don't see the failed attempt as a reflection of themselves and their talent or worthiness but rather about this one attempt—if it failed, the attempt must be altered, so they persist. They move on to the next attempt.

If you take the time to learn from your failures, they are no longer failures at all:

- Your son leaves his homework on the counter and then writes himself a reminder for the next day to remember it. Success.
- Your daughter spends money on a hyped-up toy that breaks on the first day and then becomes a more discerning shopper. Success.
- You burn dinner because you put the stove on high and then shift the temperature for the next time. Success.

Mistakes are just lessons that allow us to grow and make changes for future attempts.

How Can We Keep the Shame Cycle from Persisting?

- **Prompt children to express the emotion:** Bring shame out of the shadows. A 2017 study published in the *Journal of Behavioral Decision Making* says that instead of burying shameful feelings about failure, it's most helpful to discuss the sensations in your body.[23]

  Ask questions that help capture the feelings: "Can you tell me how you are feeling? Where are you feeling the [tightness, butterflies, heat]? What thoughts are coming to mind? What does your body feel like doing right now?"

- **Ask them to voice the story they are telling themselves:** Sometimes children (and adults) can tell themselves untrue stories to explain why they failed. Brené Brown explains that storytelling, even if it's not based on real information, can help us to create order out of the emotional chaos we feel.[24] It can also shift our attention to anger rather than more painful feelings such as vulnerability, hurt, or fear.

- **Give them a new sentence structure:** "The story I'm making up/telling myself is…" as Brené Brown advises, or "I am imagining that…" or "I'm jumping to the conclusion that…"

- **Help them to move the mistake from a noun to a verb:** When we "mess up," it doesn't make us a disaster or a disappointment. In other words, we may have "screwed up" but we are not "a screwup." This seemingly small shift defines the current circumstance as specific, which—according to Marty Seligman, the father of positive psychology, and his vast studies on optimism and pessimism—gives us more control over changing the situation in the future.[25] Amy Morin, author of *13 Things Mentally Strong People Don't Do*, said it well in a podcast interview with me: "Mistakes don't need to be who we are. They may just be what we did."[26]

- **Help them reframe and make it specific:** Encourage children to transform permanent "I am" statements like "I am a failure" or "I am terrible at math" to more precise and temporary explanations such as "I failed this test" or "I didn't study well for this quiz."

Then you can ask them to add, "Next time, I can [get extra help, start studying earlier, etc.]" so that they can be more prepared.

FACT		FICTION
I failed the test.	→	I fail everything.
I made a mistake.	→	I always mess up.
I got six wrong on this quiz	→	I never get anything right.
I wasn't prepared for this project.	→	I am stupid.
When I start studying earlier, I perform better.	→	No matter what I do, I bomb.

Diverse Populations and Shame

While vulnerability and the willingness to make mistakes are "the birthplace of innovation, creativity, and change,"[27] as Brené Brown shares in her 2012 TED Talk, there may be children in your life who don't feel that they have the same permissions to be vulnerable as others. They may be struggling to be seen beyond their disability, for example, or to gain equal footing in this world because of their gender, their sexuality, or the color of their skin. Activist Tarana Burke, the founder of the #MeToo movement, recently joined forces with Brown on a collection of essays titled *You Are Your Best Thing*, in which she shines a light on the Black experience as it relates to shame, or "parts that we…feel we have to cover and hide and keep away from the world in order to survive, in order to exist."[28] We need to remember that, for those who historically have lacked societal or social power, embracing mistakes is not always simply about "mind over matter" but also about overcoming how others see you, judge you, and interpret you for the mistakes you make. We must make clear that there is room to fail—with you and without major repercussions. We need to say, unequivocally, "We know you are receiving messages that failure is not an option for you—and that you will be judged harshly or unfairly if and when you mess up—but here, in this family, in this school, in this neighborhood, you have a wide berth to make mistakes and to learn and grow from your missteps. While we may not be able to control what happens outside these worlds, we will be your safety net, your soft place to land, and your unwavering source of support." Then, and perhaps this is the most important part, follow through and honor those words.

Quick Tip

Worried about pointing out a negative pattern of self-criticism you are seeing in your child? Ask permission to provide some feedback. In a 2018 article titled "Using Neuroscience to Make Feedback Work and Feel Better," the authors explain, "Permission, it turns out, is hugely important for putting both parties in a psychological state that's ready for negative news. Without it, the brain begins to revert to a state that isn't conducive to growth, and that finds its roots thousands of years in the past."[29] In other words, when we say, "May I point something out to you that I've noticed?" you are preparing both your brain and your child's brain to receive and discuss the news in a way that will be more productive than if you just blurt it out.

Parenting Out Loud: Mistakes and Failure

Be direct: "Whoops, I made a mess! I'll just grab a sponge and wipe that up."

Be indirect (allow your children to overhear you talking on the phone, talking in person, etc.): "I'm sorry I forgot to bring the folder to you today at work. That must have been frustrating. I can run it over to your home right now or bring it into work tomorrow. Let me know which is best for you."

Conversation #3: Focus on the Process, Not Just the Product

Many schools have made grade checking an integral part of the parenting experience by making them easily accessible by a "parenting portal." Unfortunately, by putting grades online in a play-by-play fashion as each test or homework paper is marked, it's easy to get the idea that grades are the most important part of the school experience.

While overall grades might give you a window into understanding if and when your child needs additional help, where your child may have a passion or a gift, or even if there might be something causing an unexpected dip in your child's social or emotional life, having the ability to nitpick every score and grade can fuel unnecessary anxiety, perfectionism, and pressure.

A recent study of more than five hundred sixth graders published in the *Journal of Youth and Adolescence* reveals that when students face consistent academic expectations from grades to elite college admissions, the perceived parental pressure to achieve may impact a teen's well-being.[30] Additionally, in a recent Pew survey of teens, academic pressure tops their list of stressors: 61 percent say they face a lot of pressure to get good grades. By comparison, less than half say they feel pressure to look good (29 percent) or fit in socially (28 percent).[31] "When we focus our attention on real-time, up-to-the-second reporting on the portal," Jessica Lahey, author of *The Gift of Failure*, wrote in her 2017 article in the *New York Times*, "we elevate the false idols of scores and grades and devalue what really has an impact on learning: positive student-teacher relationships, relevance and student engagement."[32]

On the flip side, parents who emphasize kindness over grades have kids with less anxiety and depression, few behavioral problems, higher self-esteem—and better grades!

What did you do wrong?	→	What went right?
Why the heck did you do that?	→	What did you learn?
Why did you fail?	→	What will you try next time?

Failure	→	Trial
Bombed	→	Experiment
Fiasco	→	Attempt
Disaster	→	Learning opportunity
Flop	→	Investigation
Catastrophe	→	First crack

Arc: Attune, Reframe, Get Curious

When our child makes an error, we often respond in two ways: negatively (with disappointment or anger) or with positivity, as a way to show our children that, hey, mistakes happen. We may shout, "Mistakes are great!" or "Who cares if you messed up!" in the moment. Yet even rah-rah positivity can backfire. How? Your child may feel like you lack understanding. Instead of veering toward these two extremes, it can be more constructive to help your children figure out the right way to go or the skill they need to develop, while being empathetic to the frustration or negative feelings that often come with failure. Remember ARC:

1. **Attune:** Empathize with how your child feels. Heather Turgeon and Julie Wright called this "attuning" on my podcast. "When we attune, we need to pause and really take our children in," Wright said. "You are joining with how they are really feeling in that moment. Kneel down. Take a good look. It's a connecting moment, and they feel felt in that moment."[33] I think of it as getting on the same wavelength. Even if you don't think it's a big deal that they made a mistake or that they failed, let them know that they are heard and even reflect what you are hearing so they know you understand. For example, you might say, "I can really see that you're upset because you didn't make the team" or "I totally get that you're really sad that your toy broke when you stepped on it." It's a step that is often skipped—and then we wonder why our children don't want to talk to us or feel like we aren't listening to them.

2. **Reframe:** Offer a different way to view the blunder. Transform your focus from what has not been achieved to an emphasis on the process and what can move your child forward. Ask, "What can you learn from this?" rather than, "Why didn't you get an A?" or "Why did you get a D?" Think of mistakes not as character flaws but learning opportunities. They are not failures but first attempts.

3. **Get curious:** Brené Brown encourages us, in a viral 2019 article on "Rumble Language," to commit to leaning into vulnerability by staying curious, generous, and open to problem-solving. I love the language she offers to begin messy conversations:

   ○ "I'm curious."
   ○ "Tell me more."
   ○ "I'm wondering…"
   ○ "Walk me through that."[34]

   Without a bent of passive-aggressiveness or an agenda to tell our children what to do, we help them come up with their own solutions and gain their own understanding of the lesson in the mistake. This is a way to support autonomy in children so they learn how to cope with mistakes and move forward rather than crumble.

In the moment, it's completely normal to want to be encouraging. I do this too. As it turns out, attuning lets your child know that you are listening and "get them," which feels validating.

Consider the difference:

Child: "I totally messed up doing the routine today at the gym."
You: "You'll do better next time!"
Child: "I was so embarrassed, and my teammates kept pointing in my direction."
You: "Who cares? It'll come."
Child: "I care. Forget it."

versus

Child: "I totally messed up doing the routine today at the gym. I just can't do it!"

You: "Oh? That can be tough. What was going on?" **(Attune.)**

Child: "I was behind someone who was also making some mistakes, and I couldn't not look at her. I was in the back, and I couldn't really see the coach. I felt like I was stepping all over myself, and I didn't know what to do."

You: "That's really hard. **(Attune.)** Sorry to hear that it didn't go the way you wanted it to. It sounds like, from what you're saying, it's not so much that you can't do it but rather that standing in the back might not work best for you, especially when you don't know the material well yet. **(Reframe.)** I'm curious if there's a better place for you to stand in class that might help you to better see the coach. What do you think would work best for you?" **(Get curious.)**

As always, don't bash yourself if you think back to previous conversations and realize that you didn't follow the ARC—we are learning as we go! Believe me, I'm with you on this too. Thankfully, there will be many more opportunities like this, and with each one, we will learn and grow together.

Quick Tips

Instead of showering praise on our children for a desired result or reprimanding a child for a negative outcome, focus on what it takes to stick with a goal, bounce back from failure, and keep going. Ask them process-oriented questions:

1. What can you learn from this attempt for next time?
2. What is one task you can do right now that can move you forward?
3. What's your plan at this point?
4. What kind of reminder can you set for yourself for next time?
5. How can you repair/clean up (your relationship, the spill, the rip)?
6. What step can you take so the outcome is different when you try again?
7. What is the patient/kind/helpful action you can take at this point?
8. How can I help?

These kinds of questions shine light on the fact that failure is not the end but rather an opportunity to learn and grow on the path to self-awareness, clarity, goal achievement, and mastery.

Conversation Starters

- "You know what I've noticed? There's so much pressure to be perfect. Perfect grades. Perfect outfit. Perfect game. Do you or your friends ever feel that pressure to be perfect?"
- "I read a book that said a lot of people your age feel like they have to be perfect, and when they feel like that, they stop trying things that they don't know how to do because they might fail at them. What do you think of that?"
- "Which would you rather do: try new things even though you know you might make some mistakes, or only do what you think you can do really well?"

Quick Tip

Three Conversation Stoppers to Avoid

1. **Don't dismiss how your children feel.**

   Don't say: "You don't really mean that. There's no reason to be angry about something so silly."

   Do say: "I can really feel how angry you are about this. This felt like a betrayal of friendship to you."

2. **Don't punish them for admitting missteps.**

   Don't say: "I can't believe you did that! No iPad or phone for a week."

   Do say: "Thank you so much for coming to me. It took a lot of bravery for you to admit what you did. Let's discuss what happened and figure out what to do about it together."

3. **Don't give them unsolicited advice on how to fix their problems.**

   Don't say: "If it were me, this is what I'd do..."

   Do say: "What can I do to be the most helpful to you? Would you like some advice from me, or would you just prefer me to listen or give you a hug?"

   Often our children just want to be heard. If you aren't sure if they want you to simply listen or to speak your mind, ask.

Conversation #4: Offer Children a Do-Over

While we can't turn back the hands of time after a blooper, I like to have my kids run through a do-over. (Heck, I do them myself too.) Let me give an example:

Both my kids love reading. Since they're around the same age, just sixteen short months apart, they tend to read the same books. That means on "library day," when I bring home a bunch of new books from our local branch, there may be major negotiations about who gets to read what first.

Not too long ago, my daughter walked through the door and noticed that my son grabbed the brand-new Big Nate book she wanted to read. She said emphatically, "Noah, I want to read that book first!" Noah explained that he had already started the book and told her to read something else. My daughter screamed, "I'm reading it on the way to gymnastics, and I don't care what you say!" (Mistake #1) Noah said no. My daughter threw the book (Mistake #2) and shouted, "I hate you, Noah!" (Mistake #3) Then my daughter ran out of the room (Mistake #4) and slammed the door (Mistake #5) while Noah started crying that she made him lose his page. Yikes.

Now, my daughter can't unyell the yell, unthrow the book, unsay the mean words, or unslam the door. But she can have a do-over. There are two kinds: the organic and the theoretical.

In this situation, my son was uncharacteristically levelheaded for his eight-year-old self at the time. He asked my daughter, after she calmed down, if she wanted to look through the other books I brought, noting that I had brought some of her favorite comic books featuring Archie, Betty, and Veronica. Tallie then said, "Okay, but when I get home from gymnastics, can I read Big Nate?" He agreed. As she exited the door to the garage, she told her brother she loved him. This was an organic do-over.

But if it doesn't go that way (it often doesn't), you can also suggest a simulated do-over and have them do the entire exchange again using different words, actions, and attitudes. Or, if tempers are running high, you can facilitate a theoretical do-over afterward. For example, while I was in the car with my daughter, we discussed it:

"Tallie, I'm curious, if you were to do that whole situation over again, what would you have done differently?"

"I would have gone through the other books first to see if there was something else I wanted."

"And if you found other books you wanted to read, what would you have done or said?"

"I would have said, 'Can I read Big Nate after you?'"

"And if there weren't any books in the bag that you wanted to read?"

"I could have said, 'Can I read the other book you picked out while you read Big Nate? Because I wanted to read that one too.'"

Having this conversation doesn't make all the errors made in the heat of the moment disappear, but there is movement. One week later, my daughter and son got into my car and immediately started to argue about books. (Believe me, it was frustrating for all of us.) But about three-quarters of the way through the argument, the learning revealed itself when my daughter said, "Can we have a redo?"

Quick Tip

Jessica Lahey warned on my podcast, "We tend to pay lip service. 'You know, sweetie, what I really care about is that you're learning.' But then we put the report card on the refrigerator, and we check into the parent portal, and we ask them how the French test went as soon as they get in the door."[35] Make sure your actions match your words!

Conversation #5: Teaching Accountability

Accountability is not about punishment. It's about taking responsibility for what went wrong. When the mess is made, you clean it up. When the jacket is ripped, you offer to repair or replace it. When you forget to attend your friend's birthday party, you apologize and see how you can make it up to the other person.

Seems simple enough. But many parents don't want to hold their children accountable because they want to avoid confrontation, they feel that it's too time-consuming, or they find it easier and quicker to fix the problem themselves. Of course, when we do this, we are doing a disservice to our children who must, as Julie Lythcott-Haims, author of *How to Raise an Adult*, told me, "have the skills, mindset, and wherewithal to fend for themselves"[36] when they become adults. Being accountable for one's mistakes is one of those skills we need to sharpen.

Does this mean we are to talk to our children about how we're going to hold them accountable when they make a mistake? Not exactly. The discussion isn't about how we are going to hold our children accountable when they make a mistake but rather how part of being responsible and making mistakes is holding *oneself* accountable. We want our children to learn agency over what went wrong and, through their own efforts and learning, work to make the situation right again. This starts with teaching how to give a sincere apology.

The Anatomy of a Sincere Apology: The Five Rs

Two words: "I'm sorry." They have such power. While forgiveness and repairing a relationship can take time, taking action and showing accountability can offer immediate healing. And it all starts with a sincere apology that reflects ownership of the mistake, empathy, and accountability:

1. Be **real**: No fake apologies. Say what you mean and mean what you say.
2. State your **role**: Admit the mistake you made.
3. **Recognize** their feelings: Show empathy and imagine how the other person feels.
4. Take **responsibility**: Be accountable, don't blame others, and do what you can to repair the situation.
5. Ask for **release**: Request forgiveness or confirm that you've done what you can to make things better.

The script for the above might look like:

"I'm sorry for ＿＿＿＿＿＿＿＿ . That must have made you feel ＿＿＿＿＿＿＿＿ . I'd like to make it up to you by/make things better by ＿＿＿＿＿＿＿＿ . Will you forgive me?/Would that help?/What do you think of that idea?/Would that make things right again?"

An apology might sound like this:

- "I'm sorry for messing up and forgetting your birthday. That must have made you feel like I don't care about you when I really do. I'd like to make it up to you by having a special ice cream playdate with you, and we can stick a candle in your sundae and sing 'Happy Birthday'! What do you think of that idea?"

- "I'm sorry for yelling at you yesterday. That must have made you feel really cruddy. I'd like to make things better by letting you know how sorry I am and that I know you don't deserve to be yelled at. I will try very hard not to do that again! Will you forgive me?"

Whoops! Are You Sending the Wrong Messages?

Who doesn't love to see a big ol' A+ with stickers that say "wow!" on your child's work? We are programmed to cheer when our kid makes the grade, but when we glorify the outcome (the trophy, the ribbon, etc.) over the effort, perseverance, commitment, and sacrifice that it took to pursue or achieve that end, we can unintentionally convey that as long as the endpoint is achieved, it doesn't matter how you got there. Whether purposefully or inadvertently, parents teach their children that the gift is in the success and that if there is a chance for a slipup or embarrassment, then it's not worth pursuing. Let's look at how these messages may get delivered.

- **"Your grades are *my* grades."** Imagine your child gets the blue ribbon for their performance in a show. It is human nature for you to feel proud and, at the same time, partly responsible—sometimes we see our children's grades or performance as a reflection of our parenting. And when our children show us a poor report card, it's also easy to heap on the self-blame and wonder what we've done wrong. Jessica Lahey, author of *The Gift of Failure*, told me in a podcast interview that parents really need to be honest about why they are so focused on how their children perform and why their mistakes and failures feel so personal. "I think we just need to get a grip and realize that our children's grades have almost nothing to do with us as human beings," she said.[37]

- **"I love you more when you get good grades."** During her school presentations, Lahey asks students to "raise your hand if you truly believe your parents love you more when you bring home high grades and love you less when you make low ones."[38] She has consistently found that, among middle school students, approximately 80 percent raise their hands. (In high school, it's closer to 90 percent!) This is serious. Our children should never feel that we love them more and care about them more when they perform better—or love them less and care for them less when they fail or make mistakes. As Alfie Kohn, author of *Unconditional Parenting*, told me in an interview, "Children need to be loved for who they are, not what they do. There should never be strings attached to our level of care."[39]

Many times, our parenting behavior around failure and mistakes comes from our own experiences and unfulfilled goals or our own desire for our kids to always be "perfect." Yet if we are to pass on a healthy view of failure and mistake making, it's vital that we take a hard look at the messages we are passing down, how we behave when our children fail, and what we praise our children for each day.

Parenting Out Loud : Cheering on Positive Risk-Taking

Publicly praise kids for taking a risk, such as when they volunteer incorrect answers. For example, you may be taking a road trip with your family and playing a car game where you ask, "How many miles do you think we'd have to drive to get from San Francisco to New York City?" Encourage everyone in the car to take a guess, including Mom, Dad, or Grandma (if no one knows, you can consult Google for the right answer). Six or seven people are likely to yield six or seven different answers, and you can cheer those who guessed incorrectly with "good try, Grandma!" or "you were close this time, Daddy!" or "I'm so proud of you, Timmy, for knowing the number was in the thousands!"

A Conversation with Ourselves: Why and How to Back Off

I get it. As a parent myself, I know that tasks often can be done faster, bigger, bolder, and just plain better when parents take over. I mean, how many times have we quickly tied our children's shoes or packed their bags because we knew we could do it more skillfully? There are moments when I have to tell myself, "Stop. Let them do it. If they fail, they can recalibrate and try again." After all, how else will they learn how to tie their own shoes more tightly?

Many parents I know have been making a conscious effort to teach their kids some new life skills lately. Laundry. Feeding pets. Making meals. In my home, we gave our kids full ownership over cleaning the dinner table dishes, putting them in the dishwasher, wiping down the counters, and putting away leftovers in the fridge. We answered questions and demonstrated the skills but then stepped back. The process was slower—sometimes painfully so—and some pots and pans could have used a little more attention, but they were learning! We had to remind ourselves and each other to allow the struggle to happen—*theirs and ours*. It's easier if we take over, for certain, but what's easier isn't always the right move.

It's hard to let go, but if we want our children to grow up to become responsible, self-reliant, confident adults who bounce back from failure instead of being derailed by it, we need to allow them to make their own mistakes and learn from them. They need to dress themselves poorly before they dress themselves well. They need to forget their homework before they create a system to remember it. They need to mess up the brownie recipe before they cook like a star. So how can we keep ourselves from becoming overprotective micromanagers? We need to talk to ourselves!

- **Ask key questions:**
  - Look outward and ask, "Are my children doing something profoundly unsafe or unfair that can put them or others in harm's way?"
  - Look inward and ask, "Why am I doing this? Am I taking over because I want this done better, my way, on my timeline, or to look good to the neighbors/friends/family?"
  - And then ultimately ask, "Which will lead to my child's skill development and long-term success—my taking over, *or* my backing off in the short term?"
- **Talk out fears with friends:** Are you nervous that your child won't make the team without you pressuring her? Are you worried your child may fail if you don't do his homework with him each night? Discuss your concerns with someone you trust so you can get your nerves out without allowing your children to see that you may be full of unhealthy doubts.
- **Move into a new role:** If you want your children to take a lead role in their lives and their choice making, ask yourself: Am I acting more like a coach, consultant, and sounding board or more like a manager, conductor, or director? Phyllis Fagell, author of *Middle School Matters*, said it well on *How to Talk to Kids about Anything* when she remarked, "Parents need to see themselves as a coach, not a manager, a momager, or a dad who manages—a coach who is watching their child make decisions, asking follow-up questions, helping them debrief and come up with potential solutions."[40] In other words, you are there to assist and guide as needed,

but your children need to be the ones who are the CDMs (chief decision makers).

- **Say the words and provide the opportunities:** Are you conveying, in no uncertain terms, that you want your children to make mistakes and learn from them? Are you giving them the chance to make decisions, mess up, get back up, and try again? It can be affirming and confidence building to say to your kids, "I want you to practice running your own life. I want you to make decisions. I want you to make mistakes. I want you to learn from them." William Stixrud, coauthor of *The Self-Driven Child*, advised parents on the *How to Talk to Kids about Anything* podcast, "You are the expert in you. Nobody knows you better than yourself."[41] Most importantly, you want your children to know: "I have confidence in your ability to make choices about your life, to learn from your mistakes, and to apply what you learned the next time you are presented with similar choices. You are and will continue to become a competent decision maker."

- **Ensure that you are giving your children the opportunities to try, fail, and try again:** If your child is used to looking to you to take the lead, start shifting the role:
  - "What do *you* think?"
  - "What would *you* do?"
  - "What do *you* want to do first?"
  - "How do *you* see this going?"

⌂ *In My Home*

When I take Tallie to New York City, I ask her to get us to the right train. "What do the signs say?" I ask.

"We need to take the one, two, or three train."

"Which way should we head?"

She now applies the same strategies at the airport when looking for our gate or the baggage claim area. You want your children to get in the mindset of being watchful and processing what they see so they can make a good choice. Even if you would behave differently, step back and allow your children to see how the situation unfolds. There is more than one way to do things! And even if it's the "wrong" decision, there is wisdom gained from experience and, yes, bad decisions.

Remember, we are parenting, as Jess Lahey says, "for the long haul"[42] even while we are parenting in the moment. How do you want your children to face failure and mistakes in the future? As Vicki Hoefle, author of *Duct Tape Parenting*, said to me so beautifully, "Parent the child who will be twenty-four in a hot second… Ask yourself: Is this going to help my child create a satisfying, fulfilling, enriched, happy life between the ages of eighteen and eighty? If it isn't, then reassess what you are doing."[43] The most successful parents teach their children how to handle failure rather than handling the failure for their children.

When it comes to our children and failure, advise from a place of belief—belief in them, belief in their abilities, and belief in the process. Then expect mistakes. In fact, hope for mistakes while stakes are low, the chance for do-overs is high, and the learning curve is long. When we focus on the process and discuss the necessity of failure on the path to success, our children learn to take healthy risks and develop the character to withstand frustration and keep going when the chips are down. They discover that mistakes are pivot points, not quitting points. The aim is for them to sharpen their skills, not to become flawless, and, of course, for them to realize that hidden in each failure is the gift of learning, growing, and becoming more of oneself, which is what it means to be truly successful.

The thing that many of us don't realize about success and failure, especially when we're stuck in the thick of it, is that they aren't opposing forces. They work simultaneously. There is a give-and-take along a continuum of learning. If you think about it, many of our experiences are not utter failures or perfect successes. There are always lessons to be learned. We say the truth, but we express it too harshly. We speak our mind, but we forget to listen. We share our perspective but don't take the time to see someone else's. And so we learn. We try again. We do better. And we learn some more. In each experience, there is success, there are areas that need improvement, and there may even be failure—but we, ourselves, are not failures. If we are willing to saddle ourselves in a position of lifelong student, then that, in itself, is success. We are all learning.

✐ Talking Points

QUESTION	YOUR ANSWER
Do I allow my child to fail? Or do I tend to swoop in and correct them to avoid failure?	
Do I use shame-based language at home?	
How can I change my language or behavior so my child understands that failing doesn't make them a failure?	
In my home, do I promote the idea that failure and mistakes allow us to learn? If not, what changes can I make to my language or behavior?	
Do I believe that the process is just as important, if not more important, than the product?	

QUESTION	YOUR ANSWER
How can I encourage positive risk-taking to help expand my children's comfort zone?	
When I see my child's performance, grade, or outcome:	
• Do I focus on the result or the effort?	
• Do I see what is marked wrong as failures or as learning opportunities?	
• Do I reprimand my child when they fall short or reward them when they shine?	
• Do I ask my child, "What did you do wrong?" instead of, "What did you learn?" or "What went right?" or "What will you try the next time?"	
• Is "not perfect" missing the mark?	
• Do I find myself saying things like, "You got a nine out of ten—what happened on that last one?" or "Too bad you didn't get them all right!"	

Chapter 8

How to Talk to Kids about Friendship

"Why Won't Anyone Play with Me?"

One day, I got a call from the mother of one of my daughter's friends. Let's just say it wasn't exactly a social call.

"B came home crying today. She said your daughter wouldn't let her play with the group at recess, and she didn't know why."

Ugh. The girls were in third grade, and "in group, out group" was the name of the game. Being "out" never felt good.

I could feel my heart beating a little faster than normal. No parent wants to hear that their child made someone cry. What the heck had happened? They had just played together the other day. I took a breath and told myself not to go into Tallie's room with guns a-blazing. After all, that had never worked before.

When I sat down with my daughter, I said, "B's mom said that B came home really upset because she wasn't included in the game at school." I was purposeful about not placing blame or accusing my daughter, since I really didn't know what had happened. I left the discussion open-ended, so she could reply without being judged.

"B is so bossy!" she told me. "We were all ready to play house, and she came over and said, 'I don't want to play house. Let's play tag!' She was calling everyone over, and we told her a bunch of times that we were already playing house, but she didn't care, so I told her she couldn't play with us."

Childhood playground rules can feel a little black-and-white. The social finesse of compromise, letting kids down easy, taking turns, or finding common ground has not been fully developed in most kids during the elementary school years. But I knew, at that moment, it wasn't a good idea to yack on and on about give-and-take. When it comes to friendship matters, children tend to be emotionally charged (as do adults), and even the wisest words can fall on plugged ears, so being gentle is imperative. After all, what could be more heartfelt than friendship?

What Is Friendship?

There's a reason they say a good friend is hard to find. Requirements for a friend vary by person and change through life experience, making friendship difficult to define. What we *do* know is that when we call someone a "friend," it's saying something definitive about our connection to this person as well as our behaviors, expectations, and feelings about that connection.

Friendships are relationships we *choose*. They are often based on mutual interest, care, respect, and trust. As Lydia Denworth, author of *Friendship: The Evolution, Biology, and Extraordinary Power of Life's Fundamental Bond*, told me, "A good-quality friendship has three minimum requirements: it's long-lasting, positive, and cooperative."[1] But it has other extensive benefits as well:

- **It develops social skills:** Friendships can teach kids how to compromise, nurture others, show empathy, listen, problem-solve, share, make good choices, take turns, and speak their minds.[2]

- **It improves self-esteem:** Research out of University of Texas at Austin shows that self-esteem and friendships are mutually reinforcing, such that having strong support and acceptance in friendships translates into having higher self-esteem (the opposite is true too).[3]

- **It helps us to feel like we fit in:** An MIT study showed that our desire for social interactions is hardwired into our brains and resides in the same area where we crave food! What's more, we experience social exclusion in the same area of the brain where we experience physical pain.[4] No wonder being cast out hurts.

- **It offers support:** Research shows that having close, supportive friends can help kids through a variety of difficult circumstances. One study out of the UK revealed that kids from low-income backgrounds who had a strong supportive friendship could get through life's toughest hardships more successfully than someone who went without a best buddy.[5]

- **It reduces stress:** University of North Carolina, Chapel Hill, professor Claire Yang and her team analyzed four large databases, including that of *the* National Longitudinal Study of Adolescent to Adult Health (Add Health). They found that friendships are linked with specific measures of well-being such as lower blood pressure and lower levels of inflammation—helping people to have a better chance of staving off long-term health problems like heart disease, stroke, and cancer.[6]

- **It provides protective social power:** Janna Juvonen, developmental psychologist at the University of California, stated that "friends can be buffers" when dealing with peer pressure, social isolation, and bullying. She has found that for kids who have been victimized, banding together makes them feel less isolated or abandoned and less likely to be targeted.[7]

- **It makes us happier and healthier:** "The good life is built with good relationships," says psychiatrist Robert Waldinger at the end of his TED Talk detailing the longest-running Harvard study on happiness and life satisfaction.[8] According to research, people with good relationships (defined as warm, affectionate, and close) are happier and physically healthier. In fact, research shows that good friends are as important to health and longevity as quitting smoking and twice as beneficial as physical exercise![9]

Perhaps that's why Columbia University psychiatrist Dr. Kelli Harding, author of *The Rabbit Effect*, told me, "I wish I could prescribe friendship to all my patients."[10]

Friendship Stew

One easy way to talk about friendship with your children is to brainstorm the "ingredients" that would go into a thick friendship stew. Get your whole family in on the action! Ask, "What ingredients would you need to make the best friendship stew?" Go around the table or room and have everyone add a few components. Answers might range from a quarter cup of kindness and a heaping teaspoon of honesty to two dashes of silliness, a can of trust, and a gallon of dependability. You can even do an art project on construction paper where your children fill their friendship pots with their preferred ingredients (symbolized by words, photos, or drawings) and then hang it up for all to see.

Friendship through the Years

Friendship looks different at different stages of our lives. According to Beverley Fehr, author of *Friendship Processes*:

- **Preschoolers** tend to define friends by observable things that they do ("a friend shares toys with you") and do not do ("A friend doesn't hit you"), and even by how they look or what they possess ("She has red curly hair," or "He has lots of big blocks").
- **Elementary school kids** emphasize physical or observable details less often and instead focus on affection and support ("They help me with my math," or "They share their chips with me").

- **Tweens and teens** focus more on relational and abstract features of friendship, such as loyalty, intimacy, help, support, and hanging out.
- **Adults** view friendship through common interests, trust, reciprocity, and enjoyment of each other's company.[11]

What Are "Good Friends"?

Randi and I met when we were just toddlers in strollers. Three months apart in age, we spent our childhoods living two houses away from each other and have been there for each other ever since: through fickle friendships, bad breakups, car accidents, weddings, babies, family deaths, and infuriating parenting challenges. She and I have what authors Ann Friedman and Aminatou Sow would refer to as a "big friendship"[12]—nuanced, complex, deep, and one, as they explained to Julie Beck of *The Atlantic*'s Friendship Files, "that you have had for a long time and that you want to keep in your life for a long time."[13]

What are the qualities of a good friend? As mentioned, this can be individualized, and the numbers of characteristics can be endless. However, if we revisit that a good friendship is "long-lasting, positive, and cooperative," then some of the key words we might want to break down for kids might be as follows:

DEPENDABLE

- Dependability is the *ability* to show others that they can rely on you and trust you. When you are dependable, you are saying to your friends, "You can count on me!"
- **Brainstorm with your kids!** For example, "What would a dependable friend do?" (Keep promises, show up for their friends, clean up after a playdate, keep their word, fulfill their commitments, show accountability for mistakes.) You can also explore its opposite: "What would an undependable friend do?"

SUPPORTIVE

- Supportive people are there for their friends when they are going through a tough time—to lift them up or just sit with them when they're in need. Supportive friends also encourage their buddies when they have a dream or a goal. When you're supportive, you're saying to your friends, "I'm here for you in good times and bad!"

- **Try the beanbag game!** Sit in a circle with your family, and toss a small beanbag to each person. Each time the beanbag is received, the recipient has to compliment or say words of encouragement to someone else in the family. Then they throw the bag to the next person. Or start a "Supportive Stickies" campaign! Use sticky notes to distribute words of encouragement or support to friends on tough or worrisome days. For example, "Good luck on the test!" or "I'm thinking of you!" Model the idea by putting one in your child's lunch box!

CONSISTENT

- When we are consistent, our friends know what to expect from us. We're not there one day and gone the next. We send the message "I won't just drift in and out of your life. I'm here for the long haul!" (It's also important to stress that friends can have a bad day every once in a while. "A bad day doesn't make a bad friend. Sometimes a little space and time is all we need!")

- **Create a friendship chain!** Ask your children, "Which qualities do your friends almost always show that makes them a consistent, good friend? Get specific!" Then build a chain with slips of paper, each with one friendship characteristic written on it. (Display it in a playroom or anywhere you want them to see it!) Then ask, "What qualities do you almost always show that make you a consistent, good friend?" Help children see that the combined qualities make a friendship strong and long.

COOPERATIVE

- A cooperative friend is "one that reciprocates," Lydia Denworth told me on an episode of the *How to Talk to Kids about Anything* podcast. "That is, there's a back-and-forth."[14] In other words, "If your friend helps you when you need it and supports you when you're feeling down, to be a good friend, you need to do the same for your friend! You need to *be* a good friend if you want to *have* a good friend."

- **Point out cooperation when you see it!**

  ○ "That was so kind of Cullen to share his toy with you. When we take turns with our friends, everyone can have fun. What a good friend!"

  ○ "I love how you and Mackayla worked together to make that big block tower. That's some great cooperation among good friends!"

  ○ "I see that Michael and Max are working together with Raj to clean up the spill. What good friends!"

  ○ "What kind friends! You hugged Sofia when she got hurt today, and she gave you a drawing when you were feeling sad the other day."

Quick Tip

"What three words would you use to describe a good friend?" is a question I pose to children across the country when presenting on the power of friendship. It allows kids to come up with descriptors such as "loyal," "kind," and "trustworthy"—whatever they feel is most representative of how they would characterize friendship. Once they have their three words, I pose the clincher: "When you think of your closest friends, do they embody your definition of friendship?" The question can prompt a good deal of conversation about which friends are good friends and which ones fall short.

🏠 *In My Home*

At dinnertime, I like to use a bunch of exploratory questions, presented on strips of paper that are placed in a jar at the center of our table, for our "Table Time Talks." The kids love pulling out a question for the whole family to answer. This would be the perfect time to share something like, "What do good friends do?" and other questions that get to the heart of strong relationships.

How to Make Friends

As a social species, humans have an inherent need to feel connected to others and feel like we belong. Once your child knows what a good friend is and does, it's easier to talk about how to make and maintain those connections. Still, while many kids want to make friends, some can struggle with the first steps. Beyond saying "hello" to signify to the other person that you notice them and are interested in connecting, here are some starting points:

1. **Ask a question:** People love to talk about themselves! Let them. Also, asking questions shows curiosity. Say to your child, "Let's brainstorm some questions you can ask someone you'd like to become friends with at school or at one of your activities." Questions can range from "How are you?" to "What was the last TV show you watched?" You or your kids can write down your favorites and even role-play for practice.

2. **Notice something good:** I'm a big fan of giving sincere compliments— and it also happens to be a great way to show interest. Ask your child, "What do you like about _____? What do they do well? What's interesting, fun, or awesome about them?" Answers might range from "I love her style" to "He's great at basketball" or "They draw well." When we take note of someone's strengths and impart what we see, it makes the other person feel good and lets them know we appreciate them.

3. **Share a little about yourself:** Teaching kids to share about themselves with a new friend takes some finesse—disclosing too much without

allowing others to talk about themselves can feel overwhelming and self-centered, and asking potential friends to share about themselves while not divulging anything about yourself can seem a little shady and guarded. There needs to be a balance. Our goal is to help our child look for common ground on which to build a friendship rather than to look for ways to impress or conduct an in-depth investigation. Try teaching your child to

- Share something about who they are. "I really like making jewelry during my free time. I especially like making bracelets with beads." Disclosing a little bit about yourself invites people in and gives them the impetus to share too.

- Ask a related question. "What do you like to do during your free time?" This shows interest and helps kids build on commonalities between themselves and potential friends.

4. **Find the overlap:** Encourage your children to be detectives and determine where their interests intersect with peers in their class, neighborhood, or after-school program. How are the potential friends similar? That's the sweet spot! Eileen Kennedy-Moore, coauthor of *Growing Friendships: A Kids' Guide to Making and Keeping Friends*, says that where the two kids overlap is "where friendship begins."[15] For example, your child might notice that a classmate shares a unique interest and can say something like, "I saw you were picking up rocks during recess. Do you collect them? I do too!" or "I heard you went camping on Falls Lake this weekend. Our family loves to do that too! What did you do there?"

5. **Ask to get together:** This one can be a toughie for shy kids, but kids who have interests, activities, or hobbies in common can benefit from time together outside school or after-school programs or group meetups. It may take some guts, but your child can learn to ask, "Do you want to come over after school and play with my train set?" or "Do you want to meet at the park on the weekend?" This concentrated time together can help to deepen the friendship and form a stronger bond.

Truth Bomb!

Does your child want to make more friends? Tell them to "assume people like you"! According to the "acceptance prophecy,"[17] this simple shift in thinking becomes a self-fulfilling prophecy. That is, thinking in this positive way can make us "friendlier, warmer, and more open," helping us to attract more friends into our lives, explained bestselling author Dr. Marisa Franco of *Platonic: How the Science of Attachment Can Help You Make—and Keep—Friends* on the *Ed Mylett Show*. The opposite is also true. "When we fear that someone will reject us, we get closed up and withdrawn."[18] It's very hard for our kids to make friends when they assume in advance that they are unlikable and will be rejected.

ASK Steps

How can parents help their kids work up the nerve to ask? Science of People founder Vanessa Van Edwards told me that she advises people to "find their diving board," where a person can use something they have in common with the other person to help them broach the topic.[16] Although she was referring to adults, the same principle can be applied to kids in a slightly different way, with what I call the ASK steps:

1. **Approach** with a topic in mind: Bring up a place or activity you and the other person might share.
2. **Share** some emotion: Add some potential excitement regarding how cool, amazing, or fun the experience will be.
3. **Keep** it simple and casual: No need to make it a big thing. "You're not a salesperson," said Van Edwards. "Never be pushy or make them uncomfortable."

Putting all the steps together might sound like "I heard there's a new

Marvel movie coming out this weekend. It's supposed to be awesome! Wanna come with us?"

Remind kids that they show bravery when they ask someone for a playdate, and as they do it again and again, it gets easier. This is a skill that takes practice and can have wonderful rewards in the end when they find the right people to adopt as friends!

Quick Tip

When I am presenting on barriers that get in the way for people (e.g., procrastination), I do a section called "That's Me!" I yell out a barrier to success, and everyone who thinks that barrier describes them yells, "That's me!" It makes things fun and finds the commonality among people. For kids, I have heard of a similar game where one person shares something about themselves ("I do gymnastics!" or "I like video games!"), and the potential friends say, "That's me!" or "Me too!"—a fun way to find where common interests intersect.

🗩 Scripts in a Pinch

Preparing for a Successful Playdate

Hosting a playdate is a great way to exercise social skills and strengthen friendships in a place that is familiar and comfortable. It also gives you the opportunity to work through consistent sticking points, like trouble with sharing or compromising, in real time.

When children are hosting their first playdates or have had trouble having successful playdates in the past, you can ask them some pre-playdate questions:

- **Sharing is caring:** "What toys and games would you like to share with your friend? Let's take those out. And which toys/games are you not quite ready to share? Let's put those away." Leaving favorite toys where everyone can play with them can cause conflict if your child feels overly attached to those items.

- **Food for thought:** "What kind of fun snacks should we make or have here for you and your friends to enjoy when you're all together? What do you think everyone might like?" Given the number of allergies and food sensitivities, it is a smart idea to find out what the other children can eat and what foods will show them that someone thought of them and wanted to include them. My son, Noah, has celiac disease, and I can tell you that when a new friend has gluten-free snacks for him, it makes a difference!

- **Welcoming a new friend:** "Sometimes it can feel a little funny to come to a new friend's home for the very first time. How can you greet your new friends when they come over so they feel relaxed and at ease? What can you ask or say that can let them know this is a welcoming, fun place to be?"

- **Being a good host:** "How can you figure out if your new friends feel comfortable? How might you know from looking at their facial expressions or body language? Sometimes, when kids are uncomfortable, they might fold their arms, get really quiet, and move away from you."

- **Playing mutually satisfying games:** "How might you know if your friends are no longer interested in what you were playing and want to move on to something else? Often, when someone isn't interested anymore, they start fidgeting, looking at other options, or even asking outright to move on to another activity. If that happens, what can you say or do?"

- **Saying goodbye:** "Sometimes it can be hard to say goodbye when you've been having a great time with a new friend. How can you end on a happy note? It can be helpful to have a countdown at fifteen, ten, or five minutes left so you and your friend can have time to clean up and say goodbye without feeling rushed. Would you like me to give you a warning that your time is almost up?" Additionally, Eileen Kennedy-Moore suggests that you say, "When it's time to go, accept the end of the playdate calmly. Don't make a fuss or try to drag things out because that will annoy the adults and might upset your friend too."[19] As my mother always told me, "You always want to leave in a way that lets you be invited back." Or, in this case, in a way that your friend will want to return!

Six Steps to Joining a Group

Let's face it: joining an established group of peers can be challenging—at any age. You can feel like an intruder and an outsider at the same time. Rather than abruptly interrupting others or interjecting yourself, the key is to blend in or *merge* rather than *change* (see "In My Home" below). Dr. Kennedy-Moore suggests that group joiners try these strategies:

1. **Listen and watch:** Say to your child, "Let's listen in quietly. They sound friendly and like they are having a good time, don't they?"

2. **Move closer:** Proximity allows our children to move into the sight lines of the potential playmates. Say, "Let's move closer so we can see how best to blend into what they are already doing or discussing. What do you hear or see?"

3. **Help out:** Let potential friends know, through action, that you are a helpful person and a potentially positive contributor to the group. Say, "Their ball is rolling toward you. Maybe you can bring it to them?"

4. **Compliment what you see:** If someone in the basketball group makes a nice basket, urge your child to say, "Good shot!" Say, "That can be a way of letting them know you're friendly and kind, and you want to connect."

5. **Make an offer:** This is when the merge moves from words to action. Say, for example, "One of the boys just said he wishes they had another ball to

play with in addition to the one they have. You have another ball in the car! You can say, 'I can share my ball with you if you want!'"

6. **Get in line for a turn:** This is when the merge is completed. You might say, "Hand the ball to the person and say, 'Here you go!' and get in line to take a turn." Children learn to match what others are doing and join the fun.[20]

🏠 In My Home

Remember the story from the beginning of this chapter? My daughter's friend B tried to *change* what the group of friends was playing. She wasn't blending and merging—she was "breaking and entering" and received the message, courtesy of my daughter, that she couldn't play.

I said to my daughter, "Oh, B didn't want to play what the group already discussed? She was trying to get everyone to play tag instead? That sounds frustrating."

"It was!" my daughter agreed. "She was like, 'Come here, J! K, we're gonna play tag instead!' It was so annoying. She never listens to anyone, and she only cares what she wants to do. It's not fair!"

Not fair. Fairness is very important during the school-age years and is an ever-present theme in friendship. "It's totally normal to feel irritated by that," I said. "I wouldn't like it if we all had plans to play a game and someone else told us that we needed to play her game instead." Bridging the gap while validating the friendship issue can build rapport and let your child know you get it. "I know you are annoyed right now. I also know you like B and you had a good time playing with her at her house this past weekend, so this must be extra hard for you."

"I don't like it when she's bossy."

"What I'm hearing from you is that when she tells you what you can and can't do or when she tries to change what you and your friends are planning to play, you don't want to play with her," I reiterated.

"Yeah. She can't be in charge all the time. She's such a pain!"

"Right. That really bothers you. Can I share something with you? When B's mom called, she said that B didn't know why you didn't want her to play. She thought you didn't like her anymore, but what I'm getting from you is that it's not that you don't like *her*, it's that you don't like *what she was doing*, when she was taking over and being the boss. I wonder if you can tell her how you feel."

"Ugh, do I have to?"

I sometimes wonder why this process has to be so difficult. "Well, let's flip it for a second," I said. "If you did something that made your friend tell you that you couldn't play, but you didn't know what you did, would you want someone to tell you?"

"I guess I would." She thought for a little bit. "Okay, fine."

I called the mom back, and the girls got on the phone and talked it out. I'm not saying it was easy or that the news of her friend's bossiness was delivered in anything but the characteristically uninsulated, matter-of-fact way of a young school-age child ("I don't really like it when you're bossy and tell everyone they need to play what you want"). But the intention was received fairly well. The conversation soon turned to talk of B's cat, who was, at that moment, trying to fit herself into B's backpack.

The next day, the group was together again at recess and played a completely different game that seemed amenable to everyone. Practice makes progress.

Quick Tip

By the time your children are about four years old, they develop "theory of mind," an understanding that other people's thoughts, interests, and feelings might differ from their own. This capacity to be empathic can "help children make friends," says Eileen Kennedy-Moore, because when we "imagine someone else's perspective," it can "fuel more intimate friendships."[21]

Michele Borba, author of *UnSelfie*, told me in an interview that we can use empathy, or "the power of *we, not me*," to help kids get perspective during conflict by having them take these actions:

1. Stop and think about how the other person would feel if the roles were reversed.

2. Talk about the problem as if they were the other person:

   "What would the other person say?"

   "How would you feel if you were the other person?"

   "What do you think the friend would want to do?"

   "If you were in your friend's shoes, what would this friend want to tell you?"

   You can also use role-playing, with you taking the role of your child and your child taking the role of the friend, to allow your child to hear this practice in action.[22]

Friendship Makers and Breakers

Researchers have found that children who are rejected or neglected (due to their lower sociability and lack of engagement) by peers are often the ones who are less competent with how to communicate with potential friends. For children with ADHD and other neurological differences, in particular, the social skills needed to make and maintain friendships might not come as naturally (or as early in development) as they do for neurotypical kids. Learning and actively working on the skills that help to build friendships while becoming aware of what destroys them can be helpful to all kids who struggle.

The following Friendship Makers and Friendship Breakers game can help children strengthen their communication skills. Use the examples given or brainstorm your own! You might ask, "What kinds of honest compliments can you give to your new friends Mateo and Manny?" or "How do you think your new friends would react if you told a mean joke about them? What could you do instead that might make them laugh?" (Quick tip: you can use a board game to move forward with each skill that makes the friendship stronger and backward with each behavior that makes the friendship weaker so your children have a concrete way of seeing how these actions can impact their relationships.)

Friendship Makers	Friendship Breakers
Giving an honest compliment.	**Being the rule police.**
"Cool shoes!" "You're a fast runner!" "I love the colors in your drawing."	"The teacher said to hang your jacket up in your cubby, *not* put it on the back of your chair, Sam!"
Asking open-ended questions that show interest and allow answers beyond yes/no.	**Refusing to participate; sitting out; complaining about the activity, weather, snacks, etc.**
"What kinds of activities do you like to do after school?" "What's your favorite movie?" "What did you do during break?"	"Why do we have to do this stupid meetup at the park? I don't want to play kickball! I'll just read my book."
Looking people in the eye and greet them when you see them.	**Not being adaptable when plans or activities change.**
"Hi, Jack! Did you have a nice weekend?!" "Hey, Paige, how are you?"	"You said we were going to play *Minecraft*! I don't want to play that other dumb game!"
Checking in; remembering things about your friends and following up.	**Telling jokes at other people's expense.**
"Hi, Rose! How's your grandmother doing? Is she feeling better?" "Hey, Liam! How did the competition go?"	"Did you see Parker drop his lunch on the floor? So funny! Hey, Parker? I'm gonna call you 'Butterfingers'! Ha!"
Sharing and showing kindness.	**Correcting everyone.**
"Wow! You've got a lot to carry into school today. Would you like some help?" "Do you want me to help you to the nurse?"	"You're saying it all wrong! It's not *breffast*, it's breakfast!" "Nate, you have to stand here, not there... *Duh!*"

Friendship Makers	Friendship Breakers
Building on commonalities. "Aqua is my favorite color too!" "You play soccer? Me too! Want to play together at recess?"	**Acting like a poor sport.** "You cheated! That ball was *not* in. It was out! I'm not playing with you ever, CHEATER!"
Being inclusive. "Want to play with us?" "You can sit with us. We'll make room!"	**Bossing others around.** "Follow me and don't talk to her—we never talk to her." "Pick that up and come over here!"
Showing flexibility in plans and the ability to compromise. "How about we play your game first and then mine?" "I'm bummed you can't make it today, but I'll see you this weekend!"	**Not picking up on people's "stop" cues, allowing a joke to go on too long, teasing, inserting oneself.** Potential friend: "Stop calling me Shortie! It's so annoying!" Child: "Okay, Shortie! Or how about Short Stack!" (laughs)
Inviting a new friend on a playdate or get-together. "It was fun playing with you at recess today. Want to come over on Sunday?" "I was wondering if you wanted to hang out after school tomorrow."	**Bragging, trying to impress, being all about yourself, comparing, putting others down.** "You can only do a cartwheel? Well, I can do a back handspring! I've been the best in my gymnastics class for three years now!"
Giving a new friend "space"; not overwhelming or dominating. "You're playing jacks with Everly today at recess? Okay, I'll go do four square with Jaden. Maybe tomorrow or Friday, we can do sidewalk chalk together again!"	**Monopolizing one person and not allowing them to be with other people.** "You're *my* friend so you have to play with *me* every day before school, at recess, and before we go home. Want to sleep over this weekend? Just us. Nobody else!"

The Friendship Tango: Red Light, Green Light

To maintain healthy friendships, our kids need to understand the delicate balance of stepping up and stepping back: like a dance. They should show that they value, have fun with, and care for their friend but don't want that person to feel stifled, overwhelmed, or annoyed by them.

For some kids, this is easy. They can sense when someone wants or needs additional attention, when they need a little space, and when they don't like what the other person is doing.

But for other kids, this dance isn't so straightforward. Many times, less socially adept kids "step on each other's toes": they have trouble picking up on a peer's "stop" signals that tell them when to knock it off, so they unintentionally wind up continuing the offensive or irritating behavior, with unfortunate results.

Former public school teacher and author of *Me and My Friendships* JoAnn Crohn points out that the "stop" cues might be subtle, so it's important to tell kids, "Sometimes it's a little change. It could be [your friend was] smiling before, and now their mouth is a thin, straight line."[23] In other words, teach your children to look for the signals just as they would when crossing the street. Say, "Are you getting a green light that means go? Or a red light that means stop?" For example:

Behavior / Intention	Possible Problem	Green Light / Red Light
Making a joke Getting my friend to laugh	The joke goes on too long, is not funny, or has mean undertones.	**Your friend is laughing and/or joining in.** Your friend is saying, "Stop! That's not funny!" or tries to change the subject.

Behavior / Intention	Possible Problem	Green Light / Red Light
Talking to, making sure I'm next to, telling my friend, "I'll be your partner/I'll sit with you/spend free time with me." .... Connecting, having fun, and using what time we have to hang out, talk, or play.	Overpowering or monopolizing my friend so they don't have time to talk to anyone else.	Your friend is responding as enthusiastically as you! .... Your friend is approaching other people, telling you, "I'm busy," asking others to sit nearby at lunch, and making plans with others.
Telling my friend the intricate details of my vacation or the play-by-play of the ballgame I watched. .... Sharing what I did or what interests me.	Going on too long, not letting the other person share, not listening to the other person.	Your friend asks follow-up questions, urges you forward with "Tell me more!" .... Your friend looks away and fidgets. They grunt or roll their eyes.

Play a modified version of Red Light, Green Light with your child to make it fun. Give them a scenario such as the ones provided here and role-play what a green-light response or a red-light response would look like. You can demonstrate both big and subtle responses. When they hear a positive response, they can call out, "Green light!" And when they recognize the stop signals, they can shout, "Red light!" Then switch roles! Have your child show that they can exhibit stop signals as well. Tell your child, "Once you notice these stop signals, it's important to stop right away." For many kids, especially when first learning, they can be their best coach by simply stating out loud so their own ears can hear it, "Sorry, I'll stop now." That lets the other child know that your child has picked up on the stop signal.

Steps to Success: Building Your Child's Social Skills

When children repeatedly engage in behaviors that might alienate potential friends or keep them from having long-lasting friendships, working on social skills with intention can be helpful.

1. **Practice:** Set a practice playdate with a cousin or an old friend. Caroline Maguire, author of *Why Will No One Play with Me?* suggested on the *How to Talk to Kids about Anything* podcast that we approach friendship in real time with someone who will be forgiving and patient.[24]

2. **Assign a mission:** Together with your child, come up with something that might challenge them but where success is possible and meaningful. For example, if your child tends to be bossy, your mission might be to teach them to let a potential playmate choose a movie or pick a game they will play.

3. **Come up with a cue:** Have a secret cue when a familiar problematic behavior rears its ugly head. Maguire suggests that we might say, "Hey, would you like some popcorn?" in place of, "You are letting the joke go on too long, and your friend is getting annoyed."

4. **End on a good note:** Take a lesson from the most successful sitcoms in history (*Seinfeld*, anyone?): end when it's going well! Leave friends wanting more. That means keeping playdates short, especially early on, so there are fewer chances for them to get derailed. As your child gets more skilled, playdates can be extended.

5. **Debrief:** After the playdate, discuss what went right and what needs improvement. For example, "When did you feel like the playdate was going well?" or "When did you sense that your friend was not as interested in what you were saying or wanted you to stop doing an action?" This is what Richard Lavoie, author of *It's So Much Work to Be Your Friend*, calls "social skill autopsies," which help to determine what behaviors were received well and what the child could (as opposed to "should") do differently next time.[25]

Quick Tip

When our kids are little, it's easy to guide them toward certain friends, since they are exposed to the people we purposely aim to see. But what about picking "the right friends" for your school-age child, tween, or teen? Don't. I know it's challenging, but as Michelle Icard, author of *Middle School Makeover* and *Fourteen Talks by Age Fourteen*, told me, "Who your kid is friends with is their choice, not yours."[26] While we can ask our kids what they want in a friend and guide them, ultimately, who they spend their time with (barring if they're in harm's way) is up to them. "It's important for parents to practice curiosity and listening with their kids as they navigate challenging friendships," Rachel Simmons, author of *Enough as She Is*, told me. "If we come in with strong opinions and judgments, our kids will start to conceal what's really happening from us."[27]

Diversifying Your Friendship Circles

When children are very young, they tend to play with whoever crosses their path. But as children get older, interests develop, and play styles appear, friendships (or lack thereof) become more apparent. We see our children join forces with their teammates who are also in gymnastics or art class or playing football.

But what if your children have exhausted the options in school or in their usual neighborhood wheelhouse? These kids often begin to feel that something is wrong with them because they don't fit in or they stand out in a way that isn't valued by others in their path. These kids may find that they have two choices: (1) make friendships that don't quite feel right, or (2) remain aloof and alone. Neither option seems optimal. What can we do?

During interviews with teens and young adults, I have discovered an interesting thread. It's not just that diversifying social circles provides more options for friends, but for those kids who have struggled with being rejected or neglected, diversification also *diminishes the importance* of those kids who have not accepted them or who refuse to include them. As Dr. Marisa Franco, bestselling author of *Platonic: How the Science of Attachment Can Help You Make—And Keep—Friends*, explained on the *Ed Mylett Show*, the science shows that the more close friendships you have, the less triggered or devastated you become by any one relationship.[28] You get a double dose of benefit—you gain the support from the other positive friendships and the resilience from experiencing the breadth of friendships in your life.

Years ago, I interviewed a go-getter named Kyle Maynard, now a speaker and author, whose physical disability (he was born without arms and legs) and move to a new area made him feel like an outsider. "I was in elementary school, and I just didn't have a sense of belonging. It wasn't that I was picked last…it was that I wasn't picked at all."

Some even made ugly comments or tried to provoke him. For Kyle, the key to finding friends was his mother's commitment to diversifying his friendship circles.

"My mother was like a social butterfly," he told me. "She would just invite kids over. We didn't have a whole lot, but she saved up and bought us a Super Nintendo just so kids would want to come over and play. She would organize hockey games in our neighborhood. We had Sunday school. We got together with a group called 'Winners on Wheels' for kids with disabilities. And my mom thought nothing of driving somewhere if it meant meeting new people and more opportunities to make friends for all of us. So when that one kid didn't want to be friends with me, it was like, 'Screw you, dude. Someone else will.'"[29]

Kyle's mom had the right idea—if the friends aren't coming to your child, you can take your child to the friends. Here are some activities and places to get started.

The Friend Zones	Examples
Noncompetitive activities where "talking while doing" is possible	Art class, chess club, Sunday school, coding class, music/band lessons, robotics, scouting, cooking class, youth groups, nature walks.
Individual sports that provide group opportunities	Martial arts class, swim team, track and field club, archery.
Book clubs based on mutual interest	Have a manga fan? A kid obsessed with the I Survived series? A child who loves to read just about anything by a particular author? Locate a book club or create one that rotates homes or meets at a local library or coffee shop.
Park/play place	Trampoline parks, playgrounds, community pools, nature walks. Connect with some parents in the area, and bring kids together who wouldn't have met before.
Sports lessons or recreational play	Having your child join a team that pulls from many surrounding areas can be an amazing way to expose them to different people. From area baseball and county-wide volleyball to table-top role-playing games (like *Dungeons & Dragons*) or team-based project programs like *Odyssey of the Mind*; whatever looks interesting to your child can be a vehicle for introductions.
Volunteering and activism	Whether it's to get behind a local crisis like homelessness, helping a family in need due to a fire or an illness, spreading the word about recycling and clean water, or cleaning up the neighborhood, volunteering and activism have all the good feels and attract many people who wear their hearts on their sleeves.

The Friend Zones	Examples
School or neighborhood social media pages	If you have a larger neighborhood, moved to a new neighborhood, or your children are entering a school where they don't know anyone, don't be afraid to post if anyone is interested in getting a group of same-age kids together. You can even band together with another local parent to get the word out to more people. If your child likes a certain kind of activity—such as Pokémon cards, crafting, or Scouts—this can be a great way to find common interests.

When Friendships Go South

Contrary to what many kids believe, friendships don't always last forever. In a meta-analysis of friendship stability in the six- to seventeen-year-old range, only about 50 percent of relationships remain stable over time.[30] And as it relates to middle school, when there is a huge disparity between developmental levels of same-age kids and interests are widely varied, friendship finality is the *rule*, not the exception. A study funded by the National Institutes of Health and the National Science Foundation in 2018 showed that over two-thirds of friends were either lost or gained during the first year of middle school.[31]

Phyllis Fagell, author of *Middle School Matters* and a school counselor at Sheridan School in Washington, DC, told me in an interview that her students are always surprised to learn that—and to discover that only 1 percent of seventh-grade friendships are still intact in twelfth grade.[32] "Every single one of you is going to get rejected at some point, and it's not because there's something wrong with you," she tells them. "This is just a time when kids are figuring out how to choose—and be—a good friend."[33]

Still, the end of a friendship is painful, particularly when your child is the one who is being "dumped." Epic heartbreak. As parents, we want to go into repair mode, but this is a time for listening and empathy, not problem-solving and taking over. Some dos and don'ts:

THIS	NOT THIS
Say Now • "That sounds really painful." • "This is so hard." • "I am so sorry you're going through this." • "I can only imagine how sad you are right now. You have a right to be upset."	**Say Now** • "I never liked her anyway." • "You can just hang out with X, Y, or Z instead." • "This is a complete disaster!" • "I told you this would happen!" • "What did you do to her?" • "What's the big deal?"
Do Now • Be there. • Show empathy. • Listen. • Reflect what you hear. • Comfort.	**Do Now** • Call/email the ex-friend's parents, the school, or the other child and tell them what you think about it. • Laugh, roll your eyes, or tune out. • Criticize the other child.
Do Later • Allow some time to pass. • If your child is worried about who to sit with at lunch, give your child an opportunity to build up relationships with others. "Would you like to invite X or Y to laser tag?" • Keep the door open for more conversations about this.	**Do Later** • Tell your child to do whatever it takes to work it out with the friend. • Push your child to move on, pretending it's no big deal and demanding that they just "find some other friends." • Tell your child, "Stop talking about it" or "Stop thinking about it." • Take over and micromanage a reconciliation.

Keep in mind that just because your child is having difficulties with a friend does not mean it's the end of the friendship. Conflict is normal—and we need to normalize it with kids by telling them that "conflict is part of relationships."

Also, while it's easy to get caught up in the blame game ("Who started it?"), it's important to note that there are two sides to every relationship. "The eyes point outward," Eileen Kennedy-Moore told me, "so it's always much easier to see what other people might be doing wrong." When your children are ready, consider asking them about their own role in what worked well and what did not work well in a friendship. Kennedy-Moore suggests posing perspective-bending questions that can be revealing and allow for new understanding.[34] For example, you might ask:

- "Do you feel like you're consistent about telling your friend what you want or need when you are together?"
- "How often do you share what you're thinking and feeling with your friend?"
- "Everyone makes mistakes. Would you say you're consistent about accepting your friend's apologies? Forgiving your friend when a mistake is made? Letting go of old arguments?"
- "What would your friend say you might do that upsets them or annoys them?"
- "What would your friend say you do that lifts them up and makes them feel good?"
- "When your friend wants you to stop doing something upsetting or annoying, do you feel like you change what you are doing right away?"
- "What do you do to show your friend that they matter to you?"
- "What do you say or do when your friend is feeling angry, sad, or scared?"
- "What do you say or do when your friend tells you about a goal or something that went well?"
- "What do you most enjoy doing with your friend, and what would your friend say is most enjoyable to do with you?"

Perspective taking may sting a little, but taking time to see things through the eyes of your child's friends can be both reparative and a learning opportunity. For example, your child may realize that their own jealousy took a toll on the relationship and that, in the future, they can "feel jealousy, without acting on that jealousy," as Lisa Damour, author of *Under Pressure: Confronting the Epidemic of Stress and Anxiety in Girls,* said on my podcast.[35]

Try role-playing some scenarios with your child, depending on which areas need to be "exercised." For example, if your child has trouble communicating needs or wants with a friend, you might say, "Let's pretend I'm your friend and I want to do an activity you don't like to do, and you tell me how you feel, ask for what you want, and give some ideas of what we can do instead." If your child isn't sure what to say, you can switch roles so you can model the conversation first. Role-playing is a safe place to try new communication patterns, mess up, determine what feels right, and try again.

Quick Tip

When counseling your children about speaking to their friends regarding frustrations or hurt feelings, advise them to speak in person rather than through text or social media. That way, what they are saying and how they are saying it doesn't get twisted or misinterpreted. Written messages are left up to the inferred tone of the reader (e.g., "She must be saying this sarcastically," or "He's practically yelling at me here") while the tone of spoken words is controlled by the speaker. In addition, let your child know that it's best to speak to friends in private, rather than in front of others, so other people's presence or opinions don't influence the conversation in a negative way. Issues between two friends should stay between the two friends.

Resume, Repair, Reprioritize, or Remove?

After assessing why a friendship went south, our kids have an important decision to make. Do they resume the friendship, like my daughter, Tallie, and her friend B? Do they need to repair it due to hurt feelings? Or has the friendship fundamentally changed such that it must be reprioritized or removed? Research tells us that sometimes the disparities between friends are just too great to bridge.[36] You can guide your child to consider which of these actions to take:

- **Resume:** "Now that everything is out in the open, listen to your heart: Do you want to continue the friendship where you've left off? Are there any changes you feel need to be made? What would be most helpful now?" Sometimes there's a circumstance out of everyone's control that impacted the friendship (e.g., the isolation caused by a pandemic), and once acknowledged, friends can move forward without any real changes.

- **Repair:** "Are there any apologies that need to be made? Do you need to say you're sorry for what you said or did that might have caused some hurt feelings? Do you need to hear an apology in order to move forward?" Repairing a friendship takes time, commitment, humility, and work.

- **Reprioritize:** Sometimes there isn't a desire to repair damaged relationships. Instead, your child might choose to "demote" the friend: spend less time together but still stay connected in casual, less-intimate ways. British anthropologist Robin Dunbar, author of *Friends: Understanding the Power of Our Most Important Relationships*, describes friendship as a series of seven concentric circles, from "inner-circle" intimate confidants to the outer rings of casual acquaintances and known names.[37] You might ask your child, "Who would you like to spend more time with?"

- **Remove:** After some time away, your children might realize that people they once considered close friends repeatedly discourage, bully, devalue, or hurt them (of course, some friends simply drift apart due to lack of common interests or geographic relocation). If their overall experience is negative, it may be time to cut their losses. You might ask, "If you met this person today, would you still want to be friends?" or "When you're around this person, do you typically feel better or worse?" or "If you didn't spend time with this friend, would that feel like a punishment or a relief?" Just as positive relationships are good for us, negative ones can harm our physical and mental health.

Truth Bomb!

Friendship takes time. Research shows that you need forty to sixty hours to move someone from an acquaintance to a casual friend and then eighty to a hundred hours to create a solid friendship. Best friends are cultivated and nurtured over two hundred hours![38]

How to Break Away from a Bad Friendship

My most toxic friend was half bully, half bestie. While in school, she ignored me and spoke badly about me with sweeping intention. I was often alone and in tears. On the weekends, we slept over at each other's houses and spent our time laughing, playing, and making up choreographed dances. (You should have seen our moves to Madonna's "Material Girl" and Lionel Richie's "All Night Long"!) But from Monday to Friday, I was worse than dead to her.

A toxic relationship, where one friend is emotionally harmed, abandoned, or used by the other, can do a number on our self-esteem and self-worth.[39] It has been linked to increased levels of inflammation in the body, which can be precursors to depression, hypertension, heart problems, diabetes, and cancer. Toxic friendships can also make a person feel pressured to engage in risky behaviors such as speeding, drinking, or taking drugs.[40]

When you think of such a friendship, the need for a clean break might seem like an obvious solution. For me, circumstances such as sleepaway camp, separate classrooms the next school year, and separate schools a year later allowed the friendship with my bully/bestie to dissipate. (Years later, when we were older teens, I bumped into her at a store, and she asked me point-blank, "Why didn't you dump me? I was awful!" Oh, the gift of perspective, age, and time!)

Letting go of an established friendship is a hard concept for kids who feel like their worth and their very existence are dependent on the friends they keep—they may even feel that being without friends is a worse fate! However, it's important to relay to our kids that letting go is not only okay but also healthy.

- **Quality trumps quantity:** "Having one or two good friends is better than several unkind or hurtful friends."
- **Letting go gives you space:** "When you say no to a relationship that isn't right for you, you're leaving room for a friendship that's good and healthy for you."
- **You get to draw your own boundaries:** "A boundary is like a fence you draw around yourself, and you get to decide who comes in and who has to stay out. When someone is continually hurting you, it's brave and healthy to leave them on the other side of the fence."
- **You have yourself to depend on:** "You have family and friends who love you—but you also have yourself!" As bestselling author Ashley C. Ford said on the *We Can Do Hard Things* podcast, "Every time I put effort into myself, there is a growing confidence within me that I will take care of me."[41]
- **You can be your best self:** "Even when other people around you are choosing to be mean or behave in underhanded ways, remember who *you* are, and don't stoop to their level. Don't allow other people's behavior to govern how you act."

- **Forgive and learn:** "You can forgive her for what she did without forgetting how it made you feel. By doing so, you're less likely to get into a similar friendship." Past relationships can be wonderful teachers. That's the silver lining.

Remember, you don't have to wait until your kids are in a toxic relationship to talk about this topic. In fact, it's best to talk about it *before* it happens so your child is prepared. Use books, movies, and even your own situations to broach the topic so kids can talk about it in a less personal way.

And be patient. In the movies, ending a friendship can look like cutting off an arm—quick, violent, and with a lot of loss. But it doesn't need to be this way. Instead, it can be gradual and kind. "In the same way that it can take time for a child to make a friend," says Phyllis Fagell, author of *Middle School Matters*, "it can take time for them to end a friendship."[42]

Top Six Toxic Friends

Aside from my half bully, half bestie, there are several types of friends who rear their toxic heads. Here are a few of the ones we see the most.

THE CONTROLLER

- **Red Flags**
  - *What they say:*
    - → "You can't wear that."
    - → "You can't play with her."
    - → "You have to give me that, or I won't be your friend."
  - *What they do:*
    - → Boss your child around, give your child ultimatums, make rude comments.

Message We Want to Send to Our Children: "You are the boss of you. Good friends don't 'make' you do anything. You get to decide how you can be the best version of yourself."

THE FLAKE

- **Red Flags**
  - *What they say:*
    - → "I never got your text."
    - → "I ran into X and just forgot to call you back."
    - → "I didn't remember we had plans."
  - *What they do:*
    - → Promise to call, get together, or text and then…don't. Ditch you for better plans. Cancel last minute. Conveniently exclude you from plans.
- **Message We Want to Send to Our Children:** "Being dependable is a crucial part of being a good friend. We need to be able to trust our friends. We all mess up once in a while, but perpetually flaking leaves us guessing and uncomfortable."

THE TWO-FACED BACKSTABBER

- **Red Flags**
  - *What they say:*
    - → "What do you think of Eden? I won't tell her."
    - → "Did you hear what April, Sam, and Cole said about you?"
    - → "Bye, Jake! Good to see you!" After Jake leaves, say, "Jake is so annoying. Let me tell you what he told me!"
  - *What they do:*
    - → Gossip behind your back. Belittle. Go along with the crowd when they're talking trash about you and then are nice to your face. Talk down about people to you and then are nice to their faces.
- **Message We Want to Send to Our Children:** "Good friends stand up for you and say kind things about you, whether you're there or not. When someone is nice to a person's face and then says mean things about that person to you, that's a red flag. What they do *with* you, they often do *to* you."

THE USER AND THE TAKER

- **Red Flags**
  - *What they say:*
    - → "Can I copy your homework?"
    - → "I need another favor.
    - → "You have to do something for me."
    - → "I need you to read this/listen to this/help me solve this."
  - *What they do:*
    - → Ask for tons of favors but are never around when you need help. Unload on you but don't allow you to talk things out in return. Sap energy. Only show up in need
- **Message We Want to Send to Our Children:** "While friendships are not always even, one person shouldn't be doing all the giving/taking. A friendship isn't about one person. You shouldn't feel like you're running on empty and never being heard."

THE HURTFUL KIDDER

- **Red Flags**
  - *What they say:*
    - → "I was just kidding!"
    - → "Hey, Clumsy! Walk into any walls lately?"
    - → "You're so sensitive!"
    - → "You know I didn't mean it!"
    - → "Look at this horrible photo of you! Classic!"
  - *What they do:*
    - → Make jokes at your expense and then excuse it by saying "just kidding" or turning it around to make it your sensitivity, not their insensitivity.
- **Message We Want to Send to Our Children:** "A joke that makes you feel bad is not a good joke. While humor is fun in a friendship, kidding at the expense of others is toxic. When good friends know they hurt you, they apologize and change their ways right away."

THE BULLY-FRIEND

- **Red Flags**
  - ○ *What they say:*
    - → "I'll hang out with you on Saturday but don't talk to me at school."
    - → "'**Wah, wah, I'm Josh—stop being mean to meeeee**!' You know I'm joking, Josh!"
    - → "Congrats on your 'award' for being a such a nerd, Billie!"
    - → "Don't talk to Ty, or I won't be your friend."
  - ○ *What they do:*
    - → Make you feel inferior, don't listen to you when you ask them to stop, call you names, laugh at you, mock you for what you say or do, exclude you from get-togethers, boss you around, tease in a hurtful way.
- **Message We Want to Send to Our Children:** "A person who makes you feel unsupported, undervalued, disrespected, and small is not a friend. You have the right to be around kindhearted people who speak and behave in ways that make you feel uplifted and important and who treat you with dignity."

What If My Child Wants to Be Alone?

There's a difference between being alone and being lonely. A child can have many friends and still feel alone. Conversely, a child can have no or few friends and not feel lonely.

"It's the kids who want peer interactions, that is, who aren't isolated or neglected by choice that we need to be concerned about," Mitch Prinstein, author of *Popular: The Power of Likability in a Status-Obsessed World*, told me on the *How to Talk to Kids about Anything* podcast.[43] Research shows that lonely kids are approximately three to seven times more likely to report distress—from anxiety to headaches—than peers who don't report being lonely or having trouble with friends. When the solitude is not by choice it can be linked with social anxiety, depression, and loneliness.[44]

Sometimes asking specific questions can reveal whether your child might be feeling lonely and needs help connecting with others or just enjoys spending time alone. Here are some examples:

- "Being alone can be a wonderful time to do cherished solitary activities without anyone interrupting. What do you love to do while you're alone? When do you like to be alone?"
- "Do you ever wish you had more time to be alone? How much more time do you wish you had?"
- "It can be fun to be with friends and do some activities together. Which friends do you love to spend time with, and what do you like to do?"
- "Who did you sit with at lunch (or play with at recess) today? Did they say anything that made you smile, laugh, or feel good or bad? What was it?"
- "Did you have any free time before class started or in the middle of your classes? What did you do during that time? What made you choose to do that?"
- "Which friends did you talk to at school today? Would you be interested in meeting any of these classmates outside school?"
- "Did you tell anyone about your weekend/day yesterday? Did anyone share their weekend/day stories with you?"
- "Do you ever feel lonely? When you do, who can you turn to for help or support?"

The answers to these questions can reveal if your children are having trouble making friends or if they feel overwhelmed and wish for more "solo time." As always, listen, validate, and determine whether your children need help or if they just need to be left...alone.

When Your Child Is Being Bullied by a Friend

Surprisingly, tweens and teens are more likely to be bullied by friends than classmates they don't know well. A collaborative study out of Penn State, UC Davis, and Northeastern University, which utilized data from more than three thousand students, found that close friendship and familiarity encouraged the behavior. In fact, while schoolmates whose friendships ended during the year were three times as likely to bully or victimize one another in the spring, those whose friendships continued over the school year were over *four times* as likely to bully those friends! The study also found that many bullies act as they do to gain status among their peers, and in trying to climb the social ladder, they will often target their own friends.[45]

According to the National Bullying Prevention Center, "If you are experiencing treatment from a friend that hurts you and you have asked that friend to stop, but it still continues, then that is not friendship. That behavior could be bullying."[46] Studies show that when kids are bullied by their own friends, they suffer from increases in anxiety and depression as well as lower levels of school attachment.[47] The opposite is also true: kids who bully others suffer mental health consequences as well.[48]

Our children need to relay to their friend that the way they're being treated is hurtful and unacceptable. If the peer is remorseful and commits to changing, then the friendship may have a chance of being repaired and resumed. However, if the peer persists even while knowing that their actions are hurtful, your child needs to know what to do next.

- **When your child comes to you and describes what sounds to be friend-bullying behavior:** "Thank you for coming to me. This sounds like it's really upsetting you and hurting you deeply—especially because it's coming from a friend. It takes a lot of courage to admit what's going on. I'm here for you. Would you like my advice, or would you like me to simply listen and support you quietly?"
- **When your child wants to know how to approach the friend about the situation:** "If someone—a friend or otherwise—is stripping you of your dignity, making you feel small, or telling you that you don't matter, you deserve to be heard. It takes courage—and I know you can do it! You're more powerful than you think. Let's talk about how you might approach your friend."

Rosalind Wiseman, in her *Owning Up* curriculum, has a great format
to teach kids how to approach a peer who is being socially aggressive:
SEAL.[49]

- **S = Stop.** Ask, "What is this situation really about? When and where
  can you discuss it with the other person?"
- **E = Explain.** Say, "What, specifically, do you not like, and what do you
  want instead? How can you relay this to _____?"
- **A = Affirm/Acknowledge.** Say, "You have a right to your dignity. Let's
  practice telling _____ that you shouldn't be ridiculed, dismissed, or
  harmed [at school, online, etc.]." Make sure they use their own words
  so it sounds natural.
- **L = Lock it in/out.** Help your child decide: "Do you want to repair or
  resume this relationship? Do you want to resolve the issue and keep
  this friend, drop it and not be friends anymore, or take a break and
  see if you can reestablish it later?" Your child might choose to demote
  the friendship.

Role-play the entire SEAL strategy so that, as Traci Baxley, associate professor at Florida Atlantic University and author of *Social Justice
Parenting*, said in an interview with Harvard's *Education Now*, "If the situation comes up…they have words that they can say, they have some action
they can take because we've already practiced it…and they can respond
more automatically."[50]

Additionally, I like to suggest adding ER to SEAL to make SEALER:

- **ER = Evaluate/Reflect.** Follow up with: "How are you feeling now?
  What went well/what would you have changed if you could? Is there
  anything else that you need for you to feel that this issue has been
  fully handled?"

The ER step is often missed, and yet it's one of the most important. If
your child is coming to you about a pervasive or consistent problem, it is
unlikely that it'll stop right away. Kids often need our support for more
than just one or two days. Check in periodically to ensure they're okay.

- **When your child wants you to get involved:** "You can always count on me. How can I best help? Would you like me to contact _____'s parents or call a meeting with the teacher or principal so we can talk to them together? Or something else?"

On the *How to Talk to Kids about Anything* podcast, Rosalind Wiseman cautioned, "When approaching another parent about bullying, pick one or two things or a pattern of behaviors that the child is exhibiting rather than a laundry list of all the ways the other person's child is being a brat."[51] It's easier to address a small, finite number of issues than everything all at once. Plus, parents can be a bit sensitive when discussing matters that involve their children—especially negative ones—so sticking to the facts helps to avoid emotional pitfalls that can derail positive resolutions.

Friends to the End

Childhood friendships are far from child's play. Research has found that— unequivocally—when people have good, positive friendships during childhood, they are more likely to have greater success later in life:

- Better social competence.
- Stronger romantic relationships.
- Increased self-worth.[52]

These friendships are foundational as much as they are transformational. They teach our kids everything from sharing to compromise, assertiveness to empathy, and who they are to what they want in a relationship with others.

As we graduate from childhood, often leaving behind old habits, retired decor, and academic notebooks we'll never pick up again, we take our friendships with us—or at least the lessons they've taught us.

✐ Talking Points

QUESTION	YOUR ANSWER
Are there any lingering issues I have regarding my own past friendships that I need to address in order to talk to my kids about healthy friendship?	
What are the most important messages I want to underscore about friendship to my children?	
Which areas of friendship are ones in which my children struggle and need some help? (Making friends? Social skills? Maintaining friendships? Breaking off toxic relationships?)	
Which tips, strategies, and scripts would I like to use from this chapter to best help my children thrive?	
To practice the social skills my children still need to exercise, I can ask these people for practice playdates:	
When it comes to friends, the most important message I want my kids to know is:	

Chapter 9

How to Talk to Kids about Money

"Can You Buy Me This, Pleeeeeease?"

At six years old, Warren Buffett, who would become one of the most successful investors of all time, bought a six-pack of Coca-Cola for twenty-five cents and then sold each individual can for a nickel.[1] The "Oracle of Omaha," as he's been called, also bought gum from his grandfather's grocery store and sold it door to door to neighbors.[2] These side hustles, along with several others, led Buffett to accrue $53,000 by the age of sixteen,[3] the equivalent of about $750,000 today.[4] The person he credits for inspiring his financial success? His dad.[5]

"What I learned at an early age from him was to have the right habits early," he told CNBC in 2013. "Savings was an important lesson he taught me."[6] Indeed, well before young Warren was born, the Buffett ancestors lived by the mottos "spend less than you make" and "don't go into debt," as Alice Schroeder writes in her biography *The Snowball: Warren Buffett and the Business of Life*, and these lessons were adopted by the future billionaire early on.[7] What is the biggest mistake this money master thinks parents make when it comes to kids and cash? "Sometimes parents wait until their kids are in their teens before they start talking about managing money when they could be starting when their kids are in preschool."[8]

He's right.

According to a survey by the American Institute of CPAs, more parents had spoken to their kids about good manners, their grades, and healthy eating habits than how to handle their money.[9] And while the pandemic pushed more parents to have meaningful—and even weekly—money conversations with their kids (47 percent in 2021 vs. 35 percent in 2017), many parents were still resistant to engage in these discussions.[10] In fact, the thirteenth annual Parents, Kids & Money Survey issued by T. Rowe Price in 2021 showed that 36 percent of parents were either very reluctant or extremely reluctant to talk to their kids about financial matters.[11]

So what stops us? Research tells us that the reasons fall into one of six buckets:

1. We've often been told from a very young age that talking about how much money we earn, save, spend, or share with others is rude, pretentious, and nobody's business.

2. We have an awkward relationship with money,[12] either because of a challenging childhood or because of ugly financial experiences as young adults that have left us shamed, stunned, and scarred. Carl Richards, a certified financial planner and author of *The Behavior Gap*, wrote in the *New York Times* that even though money is "supposed to be rational, cold, and calculated," it's actually "an incredibly emotional subject…[which makes our] conversations about money kind of like running into an electric fence…shocking, to say the least."[13]

3. We don't think we have enough money to impart knowledge on the topic, or we are embarrassed about the state of our finances.[14] We wonder, "Who am I to say anything about a topic in which I show little or no success or mastery?" Or we think, "When I have X amount, then, maybe,

I'll talk to my kids about it," always waiting for *someday*—but the day is off in the future or never comes at all.

4. We worry that a conversation about money will *unmotivate* our children. Paul Sullivan, the Wealth Matters columnist for the *New York Times* and the author of *The Thin Green Line: The Money Secrets of the Super Wealthy*, writes that if parents have accrued any wealth, they "don't want the kids to think they have a free ride" and derail their career path.[15]

5. We don't think children will understand financial concepts. The 2021 money survey by T. Rowe Price shows that 56 percent of parents of eight- to fourteen-year-old children who didn't like to talk about money with kids believed that kids were too young to learn about finances.[16]

6. We were not taught the concepts of money by our own parents, so we don't have the model or the words to talk about it ourselves. This one is usually coupled with the sense that our own children will learn money management at some point from someone else, but we aren't sure at what age, by whom, and through what means.

It doesn't have to be this way. We can talk about money with our children now—and in fact, we should. Research out of the University of Wisconsin–Madison reports that even preschool children have the cognitive capabilities to support some rudimentary financial literacy education, particularly in the concepts of sharing, saving, and purchasing—habits that can lead the way to creating wise spenders and savers in the future.[17] Beyond preschool, a University of Cambridge study by Dr. David Whitebread and Dr. Sue Bingham showed that many of our kids' key money habits are set, at least in a basic way, by age seven.[18]

The time to talk is now.

Shouldn't Schools Teach Kids about Money?

Some of you might be thinking, "What about schools? Isn't it their job to teach kids about money?" In a recent large-scale survey, 74 percent of parents felt that kids should be taught financial literacy in school.[19] After all, kids learn how to divide fractions in school, so it would seem likely that learning about finances would be included in their education.

Sometimes it is! In the United States, a financial literacy class is required, or at least provided as an elective, in twenty-one states during the high school years.[20] Still, Mac Gardner, a certified financial planner and children's book author of *The Four Money Bears*, says if money concepts are secured by age seven, and we are waiting until age sixteen or seventeen to teach money concepts in school, "Then that's a ten-year gap of either misinformation about money or no information about money!"[21]

Also, according to a recent study by MoneyRates.com, while those who received personal finance education, on average, have less credit card debt (yay!), they also have higher bankruptcy rates (boo!).[22] Therefore, having personal finance education in school might not be a cure-all for the money knowledge problem. Says Paul Golden, managing director of media and communications for the National Endowment for Financial Education, "Research tells us that above all else, above having some kind of formal financial education in school, over having a part-time job where you have money coming in, it's parents who have the most influence over how kids will wind up managing their money."[23]

Early Money Concepts

Researchers Dr. David Whitebread and Dr. Sue Bingham explain that while children under the age of seven are unlikely to develop a sophisticated understanding of financial practices, they do gain a rudimentary grasp of why they're done and how they're effective.[24] As a foundation, we can start with some of the following basic money concepts:

COUNTING

Distinguish between counting words and other words;[25] successfully count a set of objects in order, counting each object once.[26]

- **Opportunity**: Use the world as your classroom. Ask your child to count items you both see during the day, on the way to Grandpa's home, or outside on a walk. Have fun with it!
- **Scripts**:
  - "Let's count the number of crayons in the box!"
  - "How many plates do we need to set for our family?"
  - "Are *these* six pennies, or are *those* six pennies?"

CONSERVATION

Learn that the value of a number doesn't change when the objects you are counting are rearranged. Also, four pennies are *not* more than one nickel, even though you have more of them.

- **Opportunity**: In a classic Piagetian experiment called the "Conservation of Number Task,"[27] line up five red beads in a row, and directly under it, line up five blue beads. See if your child understands that these beads retain their value even when shifted or spread.
- **Scripts**:
  - With the five red and five blue beads lined up right underneath each other: "Do these lines have the same number of beads or a different number of beads?"
  - With the blue beads spread out wider than the red: "Do these lines still have the same number of beads or a different number of beads?"

EXCHANGE AND EQUIVALENCE

Money, in the form of cash, check, credit card, or digital money, can be exchanged to buy goods. Sometimes we don't have enough; other times, we give more than enough and receive change back.

- **Opportunity:** Go to the store with your child and have them help
  - count out the money needed for an item,
  - give the money to the cashier,
  - receive correct change, if needed.
  - Practice in a "make-believe" store at home too.
- **Scripts:**
  - "We need two dollars to buy this toy. We have one dollar. Do we have enough? Let's pick something that's one dollar."
  - "I have a five-dollar bill, and these berries are four dollars. How much should the cashier give back to me?"
  - "When I pay with this debit card, it'll take the twenty dollars I owe to the store out of my bank account."

EARNING AND INCOME

People work in exchange for money. Money is often earned (unless gifted) by doing work and completing jobs. Children learn that an agreed on job can earn them money if they put in time and effort to complete it.

- **Opportunity:** Allow your children to take on small jobs around the house (beyond an expected family contribution) so they can earn money (see "allowance" section). Connect what they earn to the completion of the task. Show them that money they earn can be put toward desired items and that they can earn more with more work.
- **Scripts:**
  - "Uncle Marc needs someone to help him weed his garden. He'll pay fifteen dollars for your work. Are you interested in earning some money?"
  - "You can earn some extra money for the game you want by watering our neighbor's plants and feeding their cat while they're away."
  - "I go to work so I can earn the money we need to live here, buy food, and pay for karate lessons."

BUDGETING

Budgeting is a way of "planning ahead" for what we want to spend our money on before we spend it. We need to plan so we're purposeful about saving and allocating the funds for the item/experience that we need or want.

- **Opportunity:** Encourage your children to allocate some money for specific things they want or need. The teachers at YNAB (You Need a Budget) explain that kids need to (1) determine how much money they have, (2) decide what they want their money to do, and (3) follow the plan so they have enough money for what they want and need.[28]

- **Scripts:**
  - "I know you want to collect these special toys. How about we count your coins and dollars so you can see how much you have and write it down? Then we can see how much each costs, and you can determine how much you can budget for them."

DELAYED GRATIFICATION

Children must master delayed gratification (choosing a long-term reward over immediate indulgence) and learn that by delaying spending, they can get something that is more desirable and costs more money.[29]

- **Opportunity:** There are many opportunities to talk about waiting! We wait for birthdays, vacations, and movies to come out. We also wait to spend money. Ask your children to set a goal to purchase. Print out a picture of the item and allow them to track what they have and need to buy it over time (see Seeing Is Believing box below).

- **Scripts:**
  - "Would you rather have this small toy now or wait and buy the big one in a week when you have more?"
  - "Let's look at your chart! You saved twenty-two dollars for the skateboard you want—and you need twelve dollars more. If you keep saving three dollars per week, you'll have enough to buy your skateboard in four weeks!"

MONEY IS FINITE

There isn't an unlimited amount of money. While some people have more than others, when money is spent or given away, it's no longer yours.

- **Opportunity**: Go to a store (or pretend store at home) with cash. Have your child see that after you purchase something, you have less money left over.
  - Show your child how you pay bills at home and how the amount of money you pay is deducted from your bank account.
- **Scripts:**
  - While "playing store" at home: "I have ten dollars. I'll buy these bananas for two dollars. Here's two dollars! I now have eight dollars. Is the two dollars I gave you still mine? No. I gave it to the store, so it's no longer mine."
  - While paying bills: "I have three thousand dollars in this bank account to pay our monthly expenses. When I pay for rent ($1,450) and bills ($1,050), I have five hundred dollars left to save, give, and spend."

Seeing Is Believing

Children are very visual, so it can be helpful for them to be able to see their financial goal. Print out a calendar where the goal per week is written and a spot is designated for where they can jot down how much they saved to put toward their goal. For young children, money expert Chelsea Brennan suggests printing out a chart so they can see their progress.[30] For example, if they're saving for a big stuffed bear over ten weeks, you can print out a picture of a bear and separate it into ten different coloring sections, each to be colored once the funds have been raised. Once the coloring sections are filled, it's time to go and buy the stuffed bear!

I am saving for: _____

My savings goal is: _____

This will take _____ weeks to save.

Say This, Not That

Sometimes changing the way we talk about money can inspire kids to save and regard finances differently.

Don't Say / Do Say	New Message
Don't Say • "You should save your money." • When we advise our children to save rather than use their money to buy the things they want now, it can be a hard sell. After all, kids often want what they want *now*! **Do Say** Chelsea Brennan, founder of Smart Money Mamas, suggested on the *How to Talk to Kids about Anything* podcast that parents put it this way: "Saving doesn't mean it stays socked away forever. Saving just means 'future spending'!"[31] You might say, "How cool that the next time you go to the store, you'll be able to buy those rainbow boots you've been wanting because you saved your money over the past five months!"	If children are patient, they can get things they never would have gotten otherwise because they waited, added money to the pot, and now can afford something more expensive and of superior quality that they truly want or need.
Don't Say • "We can't afford that." • When we tell kids we can't afford something they want, it can make them worry that we don't have the money for basic needs. **Do Say** Brennan advises parents to talk about differing priorities instead. You might say, "We're prioritizing saving for a vacation over buying more dollhouse furniture right now."	We're in control of our money and how we spend it. We can make decisions that are best for our families and adjust our strategy when our priorities change.

Don't Say / Do Say	New Message
Don't Say	You might not have the money in this moment to purchase something you want, but you can get creative and earn or find the money if you really want to do so!
• "I'm not sure you've saved enough money for that." • This kind of statement can be a conversation stopper rather than a conversation starter.	
Do Say	
Chad Willardson, author of *Smart, Not Spoiled*, suggested shifting the mindset on the *How to Talk to Kids about Anything* podcast: "That's a great idea! Wouldn't that be fun to buy? Let's figure out a way to earn some extra money, or let's figure out some options to cut back in one area so you can buy that."[32]	

Quick Tip

It's normal to get frustrated when our children are asking for more and more *stuff*, but if we discuss finances only when we're irritated or angry, then "children will begin to associate money with stress and anxiety," according to Paul Golden of the National Endowment for Financial Education. Instead, take advantage of "moments when our children seem inquisitive or interested," Golden said.[33] Maybe they want to know how much first-grade teachers get paid ("Do they work for free or a million-gazillion dollars?") or your opinion on the NFT that sold for almost seventy million bucks ("Do you think I could maybe do that one day?"). Listen for these moments of curiosity, as they're openings for financial lessons and skill development.

Should You Give Your Children an Allowance?

Allowance is more than just forking over money week after week so your kids can spend it on trinkets and candy. It's a weekly ritual that psychologist Dr. Barbara Nusbaum told New York 1 "gives you an opportunity to talk to your kids about money fifty-two times per year"[34] and provides your kids with a chance to gain important financial skills while still under your roof. Think of allowance as your children's financial "training wheels"—allowing them to learn how to balance saving, spending, and charitable giving while still under the safety of your tutelage.

OPTION 1: KIDS GET PAID AN ALLOWANCE INDEPENDENT OF CHORES

- **Making this option work:** Ensure payment is given at the same time/ day each week. Make a point to teach your children to separate money into save, spend, and share categories (see the Jar System on page 325) and provide opportunities for them to use their money wisely while planning for the future.
- **Pros:**
    - Separating the allowance issue from chores sends the message that chores are completed because your kids are part of your family and everyone has to pitch in, not because your children are getting paid for them.
    - Money is provided each week so your children learn how to spend, save, and share their finances. It's a consistent educational tool.
- **Cons:**
    - Children's financial experience doesn't mirror the "real world," since they're not earning money but getting it from the Bank of Mom and Dad. As Rachel Cruze, money expert and bestselling coauthor of *Smart Money, Smart Kids*, told me, "Children should work on commission rather than just being handed money. You work, you get paid. You don't work, you don't get paid."
    - Children may feel "entitled" to get money from their parents.

- **Sample script:** "We would love to teach you about how to save, spend, and give money to others in need. In order to do that, you'll need to work with real money! Each Saturday, we'll give you X dollars, and we'll help you learn what you need to do to handle it wisely so that when you're older, you'll be really good with managing your finances."

OPTION 2: KIDS GET PAID "COMMISSIONS" AFTER THE COMPLETION OF HOUSEHOLD JOBS

- **Making this option work:** Chores are assigned and inspected after completion, simulating a similar "real world" employee-employer relationship. While the jobs may not be done extremely well, they serve as a training tool to teach kids that when they do work, they get paid. Over time, children will learn how to do the jobs more skillfully, and the expectations will increase. They're not paid if jobs are not complete.
- **Pros:**
  - Children learn that money comes from work—not from Mom or Dad's back pocket.
  - They feel a sense of ownership. As money expert Rachel Cruze told me, "They have skin in the game. When kids earn their own money, they give it differently, they spend it differently, they save it differently, they interact with it differently."[35]
- **Cons:**
  - Parents might inadvertently send the message that children should be paid for any household-related labor they complete.
  - Kids might not be motivated to contribute or help out without monetary compensation. Daniel Pink, bestselling author of *Drive: The Surprising Truth About What Motivates Us*, states, "In the absence of a payment, no self-respecting child would willingly set the table, empty the garbage, or make her own bed."
- **Sample script:** "You know how [I/Mommy/Daddy] go to work each day so we can pay for all the things we need like food and clothes and some

of the things we want like our TV and your art lessons? We would like to
give you the opportunity to make some money too! We'll teach you how
to do some jobs around our home, and after those jobs are completed
to the best of your ability, we'll pay you for them. Then we'll teach you
how you can spend, save, and give your money to those in need so that
when you're older, you'll know how to handle your money really well."

OPTION 3: KIDS GET PAID FOR WORK-FOR-PAY JOBS, NOT CITIZEN-OF-THE-HOUSEHOLD CONTRIBUTIONS

- **Making this option work:** A hybrid of Option 1 and Option 2, this
  method separates chores into two sections work-for-pay jobs and citizen-
  of-the-household tasks. Neale Godfrey, author of fourteen money-related
  books, including *Money Doesn't Grow on Trees*, explained on the *How to
  Talk to Kids about Anything* podcast that citizen-of-the-household tasks
  are chores that everyone is expected to do, like making your own bed,
  cleaning up your own toys, or throwing away your wrappers from your
  snacks. Work-for-pay jobs are a series of commission-based chores that
  are independent from what is expected of your child as a contributing
  member of your home.[36]
- **Pros:**
  - Children learn how to separate work-for-pay tasks from helping out
    around the home because they're members of the household.
  - Must-do chores and contributions get completed because they're
    treated as something everyone should and must do prior to other
    desired activities.
- **Cons:**
  - There is more to manage as there needs to be a list of work-for-pay
    jobs and a separate known list of weekly chores.
  - Some of your work-for-pay jobs may not get done because they're
    optional. If your children don't want to do the work for pay, they may
    not have the chance to work with and learn about money.

- **Sample script:** "I want to thank you for working so hard to keep your room tidy, feeding the dog, and clearing the table after dinner. When we all pitch in, our home and those we love in it stay clean, healthy, and nice! I'd also like to give you the opportunity to make some money so you can learn how to save, spend, and give money to those in need. So aside from your regular contributions that you're required to do each day, you can do any of these extra jobs on this list for the amount noted. These are work-for-pay jobs that you can choose to do, but you don't have to do. Then we can talk about some ways to use the money you've earned."

Sample Allowance Contract

_____ will receive $ _____ per week/month, which will be given every Saturday morning. This allowance will be divided the following way: _____ (for example: $1 for spending, $1 for saving, $1 for giving/sharing). The money for allowance can be used for _____

(for example: toys, games, clothes).

Signed by: _____

Date: _____

If I Choose to Give Allowance, How Much Should I Give?

According to a survey by RoosterMoney, an allowance and chore tracking app, 70 percent of parents offer their children an allowance that totals, on average, $9.59 per week or $499 per year, which is up 6 percent from 2018.[37] Most money experts suggest paying a dollar for every year of life—i.e., a five-year-old child would receive $5 and a ten-year-old child would receive $10 (although one recent study showed that parents have been paying their children up to thirty bucks a week!).[38] Still, it's not the amount per week that holds the most importance but rather the values and fiscal skills that managing incoming money teaches. Choose an amount that works best for your family and your current financial situation.

Hands-On Learning = Minds-On Learning

Research out of Carnegie Mellon University has shown that learning is more effective when it's active and hands-on.[39] Here are some easy ways to get minds and hands moving while talking about money:

- **Play money-based games:** Want to broach the subject of diversifying your investments? The different paths you can take in life and how they can impact your financial future? That the most expensive items aren't always the best choices for long-term economic stability? Try Monopoly, Cashflow, the Game of Life, and other money-based board games.

- **"Pay" young kids for their pretend job:** Are you playing house or store with your kids? Pay them with Monopoly money for their "job" and allow them to go to the (pretend) store and use the money to purchase items they need. A brilliant idea courtesy of "Budgetnista" Tiffany Aliche, author of *Get Good with Money*, is to create a "bank account" shoebox for kids where they can stash their Monopoly money and make withdrawals, as needed, for items they want to "buy." And if they don't have enough for the item, they have to go back to work to make the money! Aliche used this idea when she was a preschool teacher and gave the kids classroom jobs (e.g., clean up the blocks, set the snack table), and the kids learned that "if they did a really good job, they'd get two dollars, if they did an okay job they'd get one 'dollar.' If they didn't do the job at all, they would get no money."[40] Kids could then use the "money" they earned doing their classroom job to purchase little items at her classroom store.

- **Read books that teach money-related lessons:** Books like *A Chair for My Mother* by Vera B. Williams, *Money Ninja* by Mary Nhin, *The Four*

Money Bears by Mac Gardner, and *Rock, Brock, and the Savings Shock* by Sheila Bair all provide money lessons with colorful illustrations to keep the attention of most children. Even books that aren't really about money can be used to discuss money. For example, *The Little Red Hen* tells the story of a hen who, without the help of her disinterested friends, invests time and energy in planting, watering, cutting, grinding, and baking the wheat for bread. Guess who gets the reward of delicious baked bread at the end of the story?

- **Play a game of Then and Now:** Many kids are shocked about the differences between how much items cost in the past when compared to the present. Say, "Can you believe that in 1953, a movie cost an average of fifty-one cents?! Today, the average movie ticket costs an average of eleven to fourteen dollars!" These kinds of comparisons open the door to discussions about inflation and the time value of money and can be a primer to discuss why investing, when done wisely, can help people cope with inflation since money can have an opportunity to grow over time. It's also a great way to get Grandma and Grandpa in on the money discussion!

The Jar System: Spend, Share, and Save

Beth Kobliner, author of *Make Your Kid a Money Genius (Even If You're Not)*, once talked to a very familiar—and very hairy—red monster about what he could do with the three quarters he got from his nana. The chat was part of an initiative from *Sesame Street*, along with PNC Bank, called "For Me, for You, for Later: First Steps for Spending, Sharing, and Saving" that aimed to help families gain financial basics that will impact children now and in the future.

"I have a suggestion for you," Kobliner told Elmo. "You can put [your money] into three different jars… In one jar, you put the money you want to spend. In another jar, you put money you want to save. And in a third jar, you put money to share with others who need it."[41] Children can fund their jars with a portion of their allowance, money that someone gave them, like part of the $10 they got from Grandma on their birthday, or money earned from doing small jobs.

Kids are concrete thinkers, so seeing, feeling, and interacting with their money helps them to learn financial skills. You can even write, or have them write, the vacillating numerical amount of money they have on the jars in dry-erase marker. That way, they can connect real numbers to the dollars and coins that go in and out of the jars as it's earned and spent. As money expert and author Neale Godfrey explained on the *How to Talk to Kids about Anything* podcast, "The little ones want to see their money, hold their money, and count their money. A piggy bank makes their money 'go away' and doesn't really help them understand it at all."[42]

You might introduce these concepts:

- **Spending:** "The money you put into your spending jar can be used for the things you really need or want now. Many of these things cost money, and we can't have everything! Therefore, it's important to spend wisely. That means we should stay aware of
  - How much money we have in our spending jar.
  - How much money we're planning to spend on an item.
  - How much money we have left in our spending jar after we buy the item.

It's a good idea to spend less than you have in your jar so you have money left over. Having leftover money means you have a little cushion in case something comes up later that you really want to buy."

- **Sharing (or giving):** "We can share money with
  - People who need it. When we give some of our money to those who need it, they can use it to purchase basic needs like food to eat or clothing to keep them warm.
  - Charities and nonprofits that help lots of people at once. The money we give these places allows many people to survive and live a healthier life.
  - Someone we like or love. We can get a toy for our best friend or a bag of chips for our little brother."
- **Saving:** "We save money for the things we want and need in the future [see box on wants vs. needs]. We can save money for things like
  - The stuffed bear you said you wanted when you saw it at the store last week.
  - A special trip to the local bookstore to buy a bunch of books we have had our eyes on.
  - Music lessons to learn how to play the piano or guitar.

  When you keep putting money into your savings jar, over time, you'll have a lot more than you started with, and that money can be used to buy something you've been really wanting but was at first too expensive. You can also save money *just in case* something happens and you need money. Remember when we were surprised that our sink faucet broke, and we needed to buy a new one? We used the money I put into savings for that. We don't always know when we might need a little extra money—and when we save, we'll always be ready!"

Talking to kids about saving, spending, and sharing through this three-jar system helps them to see that there is more to dollars and cents than money for money's sake. Money is not a pot at the end of a rainbow or the reward under the X on a pirate's treasure map. Money is a tool rather than a goal, as the value isn't in the dollars and coins themselves but rather in what they can be used for: gaining access to the items we need, the things that are meaningful to us, and the resources that may help others survive and thrive.

🏠 *In My Home*

When our children were in second and third grade, we moved to a four-jar system, as recommended by Neale Godfrey, to teach them about more in-depth savings.[43] We separated their savings into two parts:

- **Medium-term savings:** Money slated for items and experiences that take more than one week's allowance to pay for in full.
- **Long-term savings:** Money slated for bigger-ticket items or personal responsibilities in the future, such as payment for a car (or your share of the car), college (or your share of college), insurance, a phone, or trips and vacations.

Godfrey noted on the *How to Talk to Kids about Anything* podcast that a four-jar system allows children to see that some items might only take a few weeks or a couple of months to save for while other big-ticket items can take years.[44]

"HOW MUCH MONEY DO I PUT IN EACH JAR?"

- **Option #1: Let the kids decide.** Some financial experts urge parents to allow their children to decide how much money goes in each jar. According to financial advisor Chad Willardson, "As long as a child isn't spending 98 percent of the money coming in, it's not the percentage of money that they are saving that matters. It's the principles and the purpose behind each category."[45]

    What you might say: "You got five dollars for your allowance. You can put it into your jars! How much would you like to put into Spending? How much would you like to put into Saving? Remember, you're saving your money for the drum set toy you saw at the toy store two weeks ago, and it costs twenty-five dollars! And how much money do you want to put into Sharing? You can use your sharing money to buy something nice for a friend or to help the doggies in the shelter you said you wanted to get toys for during the holidays!"

- **Option #2: Save a set amount/percentage for every dollar.** Beth Kobliner suggests saving a dime or a quarter for every dollar.[46]

     What you might say: "Uncle Scott gave you two dollars in shiny quarters! Don't forget we need to save a quarter for every dollar we have. Let's group our quarters into four since there are four quarters in every dollar. Since you have two dollars, you can save one quarter from one dollar and another quarter from the second dollar. How many quarters will we save? Two! Put them in your jar! And that leaves six quarters to spend or share. Wow! How would you like to divide those into your other jars?"

- **Option #3: Split it up by percentages.** This method involves dividing the money into the jars the same way every time. Neale Godfrey, with her four-jar system, suggests a 30-30-30-10 percent split: putting 30 percent into "quick cash," or the spending jar as well as 30 percent into medium-term savings, and 30 percent into long-term savings. That leaves 10 percent for giving or sharing with others.[47] You might decide to do 25-25-25-25, 40-30-20-10, or something else!

     What you might say: "You have ten dollars. Let's put three dollars into spending, three dollars into medium-term savings, three dollars into long-term savings, and one dollar into your giving and sharing jar." (Provide kids with small bills for easy dividing!)

Quick Tip

Need Versus Want

Deciphering between needs and wants is imperative for learning how to handle money. Start by discussing needs as things that are necessary for survival and health and wants as things that are really nice to have. For example, you *need* to have shoes to protect your feet, but you *want* Air Jordan sneakers. A fun and effective way to make this point is to use baking as a metaphor! Try "Do these cookies *need* flour, or is flour just something we *want* in there? Do these cookies *need* chocolate chips, or do we *want* them to make the cookies taste better?" Of course, the flour is a *need* to make the cookies, but the chocolate chips are a *want*. You can even show your child what happens in a sample cookie that doesn't have flour or a sample cookie that doesn't have chocolate chips!

Let's Get Digital!

It's a new world! An increasingly cashless society means teaching kids about using digital money—or perhaps they may be teaching you! Don't be afraid to ask your kids about modern financial opportunities they are hearing about and interacting with online: Bitcoin, blockchain, cryptocurrency, non-fungible tokens (NFTs). There are even YouTube videos for kids or *by* kids (for example, "Easy Peasy Finance"[48] or a segment put out by the Mighty McClures[49]) that explain some of these new concepts in simplified language that you and your child can watch together. This will open dialogues where everyone is learning together.

In addition, you may want to think about teaching your kids how to use digital money once they've had experience with physical cash for several years. Digital debit cards, such as those from Greenlight and FamZoo, allow children and teens to put earned money from allowance, jobs, or birthdays into digital "jars" or categories such as spending, saving, and future goals. Some even allow kids to invest!

This past year, our twelve-year-old daughter started using a digital card, completely customized and funded by her, at the mall. She's been able to choose how to spend her available "cash"—from making immediate purchases like a Monster drink to what she wants to save for in the future. Right now, she has a savings goal for cool black boots with colorful heels that cost $30 (medium term) and, believe it or not, another savings goal for a black Jeep Wrangler that she wants when she turns sixteen (long term). She's also putting away money for charity and some investment opportunities. As so much of our society's money behavior is digital now, it's important for your children to learn how to use digital money responsibly while still under your tutelage.

⌂ *In My Home*

At eight years old, my daughter received a gift card from her grandparents. She made the choice to spend it on a toy that she saw advertised on television. Frankly, I thought the toy was going to be a piece of garbage—and she wanted to spend $30 on it!

"Let's scan the product reviews, honey," I said.

"Fine," she said, "but I want to buy it anyway."

"Look, a bunch of these reviewers say it's a waste of money. It doesn't do what it says it does, and it's a real hassle to clean up."

"I don't care," she said adamantly. "I've wanted it for so long, and now I can buy it!"

"Do you want to look at anything else?" I offered. "Maybe look at some other companies that put out something similar?"

"No. This is the only one I want."

She had made her decision, and I stepped back and let her buy it. After all, it wasn't my money, and this gift card was a teaching tool. The only way she was going to learn that some things we want to buy are not worth the money was for her to pay for it herself and see.

When the toy arrived, she set it up, played with it for a few minutes, and found out for herself what the reviewers had tried to tell her before she purchased it.

"This was a bad choice," she said to me.

"Sometimes that happens," I said. "I'm sorry you're disappointed."

"It was thirty dollars, and it doesn't even do anything fun! You just sit there! That's not what I thought it was going to be. I wish I never bought it. Those reviews were right!"

She learned a valuable lesson that day—one that wouldn't have made such an impact if I had insisted that she not buy it.

⚑ Scripts in a Pinch

"How much money do you make?"

Many parents balk at this bold question. "That's none of your business," "Enough!" or "I'll tell you when you're older" are common answers—but are they the right ones? In the spirit of being open and encouraging conversation around the topic of money, it's best to engage in meaningful dialogue rather than shut it down. Therefore, if your child wants to know how much you are paid, why you can't afford to put in a pool, or if you are "rich" or "poor," try these strategies:

Start by doing a little digging: Ron Lieber, author of *The Opposite of Spoiled*, writes in the *New York Times* that it's important to find out what's on your child's mind and why they're posing this question to you.[50]

- **Sample script:** "What makes you ask?" or "What has gotten you interested in our finances right now?" Lieber advises parents to find out what's prompting the need for this type of information without showing disapproval or defensiveness.

Put numbers into context: For young children, $20 might sound like a lot, so when you start mentioning numbers in the thousands, it can seem like all the money in the world. Beth Kobliner, author of *Make Your Kid a Money Genius*, suggests stating how much money is coming in as compared to the national average.[51] As your children get older, it may be helpful for them to know more details and how, specifically, the money is applied to expenses and costs of living.

- **Sample script:** "Half the households in America earn less than $70,900, and half the households in America earn more than that. We earn [less than, more than, about that much] in comparison."[52] If you want to get more detailed, you might say, "We bring in [about, more than, less than] _____ , and that money goes toward things like mortgage, school expenses, our utilities, medical bills, your ballet lessons, and groceries. What's leftover is put toward _____ ."

Once your child can comprehend the "true value of a salary," Kobliner says, it can inform an eye-opening "discussion of the family budget...[including] expenses that are entirely invisible to a youngster, like insurance and taxes" (see box below). In addition, extrapolating from what Jean Chatzky and Kathryn Tuggle write in *How to Money*, talking about money can provide context for what's possible (in terms of payment or salary) so our children know, when they start working, when they're being paid fairly or unfairly.[53]

Talking about Taxes

"But, Dad, I don't get it. If the toy is $3.99, why do I have to pay $4.33?"

Ahhh, taxes. Yes, all of us have to pay them. And being a kid doesn't mean you're exempt from needing to fork over the extra cash for certain purchases—even if it comes as a bit of a shock.

Chad Willardson, author of *Smart, Not Spoiled*, jokes that his children will never be surprised by taxes. To their utter dismay, he's been teaching them about taxes since they were young. How? By taking a big bite of their desserts before giving it to them. "I don't just take *a* bite. I take a *big* bite. The first bite," he says. "Because that's how taxes work!"[54]

There are two types of taxes in particular that we want to make sure young people understand early because they encounter them early:

- **Sales tax:** It can be upsetting to kids (and to adults too!) when they march into a store with a five-dollar bill to buy something that costs $4.99 that they don't have enough money. You might say, "When you buy items at the store, we often pay an extra amount of money called sales tax This extra charge is a percentage of the purchase price. Each state decides how much tax a person needs to pay and how much sales tax is added to things like groceries, food, and, yes, toys and games too. So when you plan to buy the new card game at the store, don't forget that you need to add in sales tax to what you save for that purchase."

- **Income tax:** As children get older and receive their first check at their first job, they can become frustrated that putting in ten hours of work at $15 per hour does not mean that they get paid $150. Try "You'll see that income tax is taken out of your paycheck when you get a job. Income tax is a percentage of the money that you make for working at that job. Your paycheck stub will show your gross pay, your total payment without taxes taken out, and your net pay, which is the amount you receive after taxes are taken out. Depending on where you live in the world, you pay different rates of federal or country income tax and sometimes also state and local income tax. And depending on how much you earn, you'll pay more or less income tax. People who make more money typically pay more income tax."

That "Other" Jar: Investing

My parents invested money for as long as I can remember. As a young kid, I remember that in the early morning, I would walk into the den, and my father would be watching the ticker tape going across the TV screen with interest. I didn't know what it all meant, but I knew that sometimes those little letters and numbers brought good news, and other times they brought a troubled look to my father's face. And while investments were occasionally talked about at the dinner table, the conversation didn't involve me, and to be honest, I really wasn't trying to figure out if it should.

"It's not uncommon for parents to avoid these conversations about money and investments," the National Endowment for Financial Education's Paul Golden told me. Research corroborates this sentiment.[55] One study out of the University of North Carolina and the University of Texas suggested that, according to the children interviewed, while some topics like saving, earning, and spending were regarded as safer "disclosed" topics, anything involving investing was off-limits. And if investments were discussed, parents were much more likely to discuss them with their sons over their daughters, likely because boys were seen by their parents as the future financial providers.

Well, as it turns out, teaching your child what investing is and getting them involved in the conversation is a very good idea *no matter their gender*. While a savings account will keep money safe, earning power and keeping up with inflation (the increase in price for goods and services over time) comes from investing. According to T. Rowe Price's fourteenth annual Parents, Kids & Money Survey, which sampled more than two thousand parents and their eight- to fourteen-year-old children, "Kids look to their parents for advice when it comes to investing, even more so than social media."[56] Here are some things to consider when introducing your children to investing:

- **What it means:** "Investing might sound intimidating, but it's simply an action you can take with your money that gives it an opportunity to grow over time. Some of the main options or categories you can invest in are stocks, bonds, real estate, and private businesses. You don't need a lot of money to start investing, and you can start when you're a kid. In fact, the earlier you start investing, the more time you have for your money to grow."

- **Risk vs. reward:** "Things like stocks and real estate go up and down in value, based on a variety of factors. Since we don't have a Magic 8 Ball, we don't know exactly what will happen. Doing research can often help us make a good, informed choice."

- **Kids learn by doing:** Chad Willardson, author of *Smart, Not Spoiled*, suggests, "Let's earn some money, let's open a small account for you, and let's let you pick some stocks and/or investment funds and see what it's like and get your feet wet."[57]

- **Start with companies kids know:** "How would you like to own a piece of the company that sells the Monster drinks you love?" That was Willardson's opening line to his daughter when talking about investing. Pocket Sun, cofounder of SoGal Ventures, adds her advice to her younger self in Jean Chatzky and Kathryn Tuggle's book, *How to Money*: "Start small…invest $1,000 in three to five of your favorite companies' stocks, and don't touch them until graduation."[58] Instead of talking about the elusive "stock market," when you boil investing down to something that your kids use and know, it makes it more accessible.

Even if your kids invest just a few weeks or months of their allowance into a mutual fund or a stock, they will likely see some change over time. Allowing children to make small mistakes with a small amount of money when they're young can help them avoid bigger mistakes with larger amounts of money when they're adults.

The Power of Compounding

Sometimes numbers can speak for themselves. Such is the case when it comes to compound interest which is the money you earn on your savings as well as the money you then earn on the accumulated interest (from your savings) over time. This is sometimes simplified as making interest on interest I am not a huge math lover, but I thought this was super-*interest*ing (sorry for the pun—had to do it).

There are calculators online that can make explaining the concept of compound interest real and fun for kids. My eleven-year-old son and I sat together on the couch inputting various numbers—yes, even ridiculous numbers—to see how money could accrue over time: "Hey, Mom, look what happens in fifty years when I put in an initial one-million-dollar investment, then put in a million dollars every month, and get a 50 percent return daily," he said. (By the way, the future balance on this pipe dream would be about $1,805,064,422,764,433,664)! In my son's words, "This is the cool kind of math."

Below, you can see what might happen if an investment is made early on in life and remains untouched, with no other contributions and a constant return, for twenty-five years or even fifty years, when your child is at or approaching retirement age. You can also see what happens when the same amount as the initial investment is paid into the account annually. From my own experience, the compound interest calculator was a fun way to open my kids' eyes to how even relatively small sums of money could work for them in a tried-and-true diversified portfolio of stocks while they're busy living their lives as working adolescents or adults. If they start young, even if they suffer a few bad years, there are many years that allow "corrections" and growth over time.

A one-time investment of this amount	1 year, with a 10% annual return	2 years, with a 10% annual return	10 years, with a 10% annual return	25 years, with a 10% annual return	50 years, with a 10% annual return
$100	$110	$121	$259	$1083	$11,739
$500	$550	$605	$1297	$5417	$58,695
$1000	$1100	$1210	$2594	$10,835	$117,391

And if they invest the same amount year after year and leave it untouched?

A yearly investment of this amount	1 year, with a 10% annual return	2 years, with a 10% annual return	10 years, with a 10% annual return	25 years, with a 10% annual return	50 years, with a 10% annual return
$100	$220	$331	$1853	$10,918	$128,130
$500	$1050	$1655	$9266	$54,591	$640,650
$1000	$2200	$3310	$18,531	$109,182	$1,281,299

See? That *is* fun math!

Giving Money to Others

As a parent volunteer with a background in fundraising, my friend Sarah asked the fifth-grade students at Carpenter Community Charter School in California to see how far their pocket change could go to make a big change in other people's lives. The children had been learning about kids and families halfway around the world who didn't have basic things like clean water, vitamins, and medicine and who were also in desperate need of ways to protect themselves against contracting malaria from dangerous mosquitos. The students contributed over $500 from their own piggy banks, jars, and stashed cash on the bottoms of their backpacks. "One child," Sarah recalled, "brought in his entire allowance. He said, 'It will help them much more than it will help me. I mean, saving lives *feels better* than buying a few candy bars and some dumb game for myself.'"

Science would agree. Researchers Elizabeth Dunn, Lara Aknin, and Michael Norton found that spending money on others or giving items away to charity puts a bigger smile on a person's face than buying things for oneself. This finding remained consistent across cultures, in both rich and poor areas.[59] In fact, when Lara Aknin led the team to examine the link between charitable giving and happiness across the world, she found a positive association in 120 out of the 136 countries, regardless of socioeconomic status.[60]

And the good news is that there are lots of ways to give—helping charities is just one of them! Some kids might give money to the local animal shelter, while others might want to assist a specific family in need. We can help children to discover where they'd like to contribute, who they'd like to help, and how they can make a difference.

Here are seven ways to inspire kids to make a habit of giving.

INTEREST

Meet them where their curiosity, care, and concern converge. What lights their fire?

- **Science says:** Interest can be a powerful tool that makes an experience more enjoyable and worth further exploration.[61] Studies show that interest drives engagement, focusing experiences so that a child wants to know more and do more.[62] Researchers have also found that when people are interested in whom a charity serves and the help they can provide, they're more likely to donate.[63] The key is to find a cause that matters to them.[64]

- Ask "Who or what might you want to help with the money from your share jar? You can do so much good! For example..." If your child

  - Loves animals? Have them buy food for a local animal shelter or adopt an elephant from the Sheldrick Wildlife Trust of World Wildlife Foundation.

  - Likes sports? In lieu of birthday gifts, request that friends purchase balls and bats for children who don't have any.

  - Loves knitting? Take them to the store to purchase yarn to knit squares for blankets or beanies for babies in need at the local hospitals.

IDENTITY

Help your children see that charitable giving is part of who they are—not just something they might participate in once in a while.

- **Science says:** To integrate giving as part of your children's identity, help them to see giving as something they *do* rather than something they *did*. Dr. Mark Wilhelm, a professor of economics and philanthropic studies at Indiana University, urges parents to attribute children's charitable engagement to their character. "They start to internalize it and think of it as part of their identity," he told CNBC.[65]

- Acknowledge their donation and charitable nature: "Thank you for being a kind and giving helper. When you gave to X charity, you made a real difference to the people/animals/cause."

- Have them overhear your praise: "Tallie gave fifty dollars to the women's shelter to help the moms and children. She is such a caring person."

- Make it an attribute rather than an action: Instead of saying, "That was a caring thing to do," say, "You really are a caring, charitable person."

IMPACT

Allow them to see the impact they can make. How and who, specifically, will they help?

- **Science says:** Research shows that when people understand the specific impact of their help, it makes them happier and more emotionally invested and can also inspire them to give more and keep giving, initiating a positive feedback loop between giving and happiness. Even hearing gratitude from those who are being helped can spur more generosity.[66]

- Instead of talking in generalities, discuss individualized impact. For example, the fifth-grade class at Carpenter Community Charter School received an appreciation letter regarding the impact of their charitable donation. It said that the money "preserved the sight of 154 children at risk for blindness with vitamin A, provided fifty-three families in Africa with a month of clean water, protected thirteen moms and babies from malaria with bed nets, and saved the sight of two children with trachoma medicine."

ILLUSTRATION

Have your children witness sharing and giving in action. What kind of charitable giving do you do in front of them?

- **Science says:** Charitable giving and sharing are contagious and can inspire others to contribute—multiplying the effect of giving. Studies suggest when parents model charitable giving, their children were more likely to follow suit in comparison to those who did not demonstrate charitable giving to their children.[67]

- Demonstrate giving in consistent ways: round up to the nearest dollar for the local food bank when checking out of the grocery store; donate a present to Toys for Tots, or "adopt a family" over the holidays; forfeit one present on a birthday/holiday, and use the money to donate to a favorite charity instead; buy or make dinner for a sick neighbor; and say, "We like to donate to X charity. Here's why..."

INFORMATION

Engage your children in conversations about charitable giving.

- **Science says:** Studies out of Indiana University's Lilly Family School of Philanthropy show that parents who talk to their children about charitable giving are significantly more likely to have children, regardless of sex, age, race, or family income, who are philanthropic than those parents who do not discuss charitable giving.[68] In addition, when parents both model and talk with their children about the importance of donating, children are much more likely to give as compared to those whose parents model charitable behavior alone.[69]

- Relay to your children:
  - "I give to [this cause] because…"
  - "Giving to others is crucial, in my opinion, because…"
  - "Did you know that there are kids who are sick in the hospital wishing they had some new games/books?"
  - "What do you think about sharing money with those in need?"
  - "What kinds of questions do you have about charitable giving and helping others in need?"
  - "What kinds of causes are you interested?"
  - "When I help [this charity/cause] the money goes to [this purpose], which is important to me. What do you think about that?"

INTERRELATIONSHIP

Help them make a connection with those they are helping, bringing humanity into the act of giving.

- **Science says:** Studies have found that when parents help their children imagine the feelings of others, they can foster empathy—and thus their generosity toward others.[70]

- "How do you think your friend feels about losing his home to a fire? How do you think he'll feel when he receives the money/toys you donated? You gave a gift from your heart to his heart!"

INVOLVEMENT

Get them integrated in charitable giving so they can feel the joy that comes from helping others—and get into the habit of giving.

- Science says: When kids experience the happiness that comes from giving, they will be more likely to keep contributing. Fidelity Charitable's national Family Giving Traditions Study found that children who were engaged in charitable activities while growing up were 27 percent more likely to give five thousand dollars or more to charity annually as well as 22 percent more likely to volunteer their time.[71]

- Involve your children in charities that cater to them as well to their interests:
  - Children's volunteer opportunities at the local food bank.
  - A fun run that benefits a cause that means something to them.
  - Putting together breakfast-to-go bags for a local family shelter.
  - "Adopting" their favorite wild animals in need from the World Wildlife Foundation.
  - Buying a favorite book and a warm pair of pajamas for a child in the foster-care system through the Pajama Program.

Foundation = Future

When we open a two-way dialogue with children about money, we bring it out of the shadows and give them the foundation they need to be fiscally responsible adults. Teaching them to spend, save, give, and invest wisely is a life skill that isn't learned unless it's taught early—and often. Both conversations and opportunities that allow kids to have a hands-on experience with managing money help them to understand not only the power of money but also their own power and ability to use it wisely. It is incumbent on us to teach our children how to achieve economic health and success. Their financial future depends on it.

✐ *Talking Points* ....

QUESTION	YOUR ANSWER
Have I spoken to my children about money so they have a basic understanding of what it is, how to use it, and ways to manage it wisely?	
Do I want to give an allowance, and if so, how much will I give, when will I give it, and what will it be given for?	
What message(s) do I want to relay to my kids about spending money?	
Which conversations do I want to have with my kids about saving money for the short term? For the long term?	
What do I want my kids to know about investing, and when do I want to ensure that I have these conversations with them?	
How am I showing and telling my children about the importance of charitable giving?	
What are the top tips and scripts that I want to take from this chapter and use with my children and family?	

Afterword

This book covers some of the most challenging conversations we have with our children, but it is by no means exhaustive. As any parent knows, conversations can pivot from questions about sex, money, or death to children asking, "What will happen to the people who lost their homes during the hurricane?" and "Why does Grandma act funny when she drinks wine?" With so much talking about so many tough topics, I want you to remember that the full scale of what we say often ebbs and flows with time. That means we need to be in a constant state of learning, reevaluating, and listening in order to see the truth in what we relay to our kids. To strive for informed communication fitness make sure to do your LAPS.

L: Listen and learn. There's a lot we don't know. Read books, listen to those who are studying the issues of our time, and talk to your children about what they know. Topics like bullying, discrimination, race, failure, money, and anxiety take on new lives when filtered through different lenses and those who are experiencing the subject matter directly. What stories are those lives providing? Which concerns are they expressing? How are they interpreting what they see and hear around them? Tune in even when (or especially when) their view is different from yours.

A: Ask questions. Find out what your children are thinking about. If you don't ask when it comes to, for example, the pressures they feel in school or how they interpret gender bias these days, you won't know. If you think back to the differences between your world and your parents' world when you were a kid, you'll realize there's probably a chasm between what your kids think and know and what *you* believe is the truth of today. Say, "I was reading this book about some tough issues kids face these days, and I was wondering: How do you feel about the pressure to get good grades?" Or "When I was a kid, boys got the message that they can't show their feelings. What do you think about that? Do you see the same thing today? Why do you think that's the case?"

P: Percolate. Take in everything your child says, and let it simmer in your mind. This can be the hard part, as we tend to become comfortable with our own ways of thinking about a topic. When there's conflict, ask yourself: Where did I get the notion that what I believe is true? Who told me this information? Is what I think *the truth* or *an opinion*? We see life through a lens of our own experiences and teachings—sometimes this lens is helpful in separating fact from fiction, and other times it can prevent us from seeing the truth objectively. The key is to figure out which is which.

S: Stay open. As we gain more information from science, true stories from those who have experience, and perspectives through the eyes of our children, our own perspectives begin to shift. We can talk to our children in more nuanced ways and in a constant state of change as we gain more insight and continue to grow. This will make you an even better resource for your children who are experiencing tough topics in real time.

Are My Kids Even Listening?

Virtually all of us wonder, at times, if our children tune out as soon as our lips start moving. I know I do, but then a funny thing happens. I hear my daughter telling her friend that "it takes time to make friends at a new school—you've got to put yourself out there and try." I hear my son report how unfair it is that his peers are being mean to a child with disabilities at school because "that's just how his brain is wired, and he can't help that he acts that way." I think to myself, "This talking stuff is actually working." And if these conversations were making an impact, maybe some of the other ones did too.

Believe me, I still mess up, say the wrong thing, wait too long, talk too much, and wonder if I'm getting this all right. I'm probably not. That's okay. Shoot for the moon, and you'll land among the stars, they say! Remember, it's not always about what you say but also how you show up. You may not have all the right words, but you will be creating a great communicator as you become one as well.

This Is Not Goodbye

I want to hear all about your parenting stories, triumphs, and questions. We are in this together! Visit me at DrRobynSilverman.com or on my social media pages and join the conversation. I look forward to seeing you there!

—Dr. Robyn

Acknowledgments

In 2017, I had this idea to start a podcast called *How to Talk to Kids about Anything*. I wanted to interview the many amazing experts exploring tough parenting topics and get their strategies out to those who needed them the most—the parents! So many of those voices are reflected in this book. Here is my (ridiculously corny) praise for you:

Well done for the experts in chapter one! My "big feelings" of gratitude overflow for Tina Payne Bryson, Alyssa Blask Campbell, Joanna Faber, Kristin Gallant, Janine Halloran, Dehra Harris, Celeste Headlee, Dawn Huebner, Katie Hurley, Ned Johnson, Lynne Kenney, Julie King, Deena Margolin, Laura Markham, Amy Morin, Dan Reidenberg, Dan Siegel, Jonathan Singer, Bill Stixrud, Andrea Umbach, Rosalind Wiseman, Karen Young, and Wendy Young.

Woo-hoo for chapter two! My most sincere praise for my esteemed colleagues who lent their expertise to the self-esteem and body image discussion: Sue Atkins, Julie Bogart, Michele Borba, Common Sense Media team, Destini Ann Davis, Devorah Heitner, Lexie Kite, Lindsay Kite, Charlotte Markey, Dannielle Miller, Melissa Wenner Moyer, and Rachel Simmons.

Yippee for chapter three! Sex can be a sensitive topic to broach with children. Thank you to Dina Alexander, Gail Dines, Logan Levkoff, Peggy

Orenstein, Bonnie J. Rough, Dae Sheridan, Richard Weissbourd, and Sandy Wurtele for your help in making it easier.

You have the floor, chapter four. Wow. Thank you for your gentle wisdom. Along with the incredible studies and books written on death and dying, your words were exactly what we needed: Jadyn Glueck, Marilyn Price Mitchell, Joe Primo, and Wendy Van de Poll.

High five for chapter five. Your viewpoints help us to become better people. I learned so much about diversity and the conversations we must have with our kids from Christia Spears Brown, Thema Bryant, Alex Corbitt, Sara Cunningham, Lisa Delin Davis, Mona Delahooke, Jane Elliott, Nawar Al-Hassan Golley, Carolyn Hays, Ibram X. Kendi, Liz Kleinrock, Irshad Manji, Jeffrey Marsh, Robert Melillo, Nate Popat, Devon Price, Deborah Reber, and Kristin Russo.

Amazing tips in chapter six! Thank you for helping us to see the varied definitions of family: Cathy Cassani Adams, Nefertiti Austin, Sue Cornbluth, Ron Deal, Abbie Goldberg, Carrie Goldman, Megan Leahy, and Christina McGhee

Thank heavens for chapter seven and all of you who showed us that it's okay to fail and make mistakes on the way to success (thank goodness, since I fell on my butt many times during this writing process): Phyllis Fagell, Andrew P. Hill, Vicki Hoefle, Alfie Kohn, Jessica Lahey, Julie Lythcott-Haims, Heather Turgeon, and Julie Wright.

Chapter eight, you were great! Consider us friends for life: Lisa Damour, Lydia Denworth, Michelle Icard, Eileen Kennedy-Moore, Caroline Maguire, Kyle Maynard, Mitch Prinstein, and Vanessa Van Edwards.

You towed the line, chapter nine. You are all worth more than a million bucks for your insight on money matters: Chelsea Brennan, Rachel Cruze, Mac Gardner, Neale Godfrey, Paul Golden, Beth Kobliner, and Chad Willardson.

Of course, it takes more than content experts to make a book, so please allow me to gush over the following people:

To my agent, Judy Linden at Stonesong, who has been cheering me on since we met in 2008. Your enthusiasm for this book idea has been unparalleled from moment one. Thank you for connecting me to the next person on my list.

Anna Michels, your kind and constant encouragement about this project has kept me on track throughout the process. I loved hearing how much you appreciated the tips and scripts in each chapter, not just as an editor but as a parent. The fact that you used some of the scripts in the book while giving me feedback always made me smile. And thank you for your incredible patience that allowed me to take the time I needed to make this book what we knew it could be. I feel so honored to work with the entire Sourcebooks crew, and I want each of you to know how much I appreciate you.

To my extraordinary writing coach, Dina Santorelli, I could cry with gratitude (I think I actually have) when I think about how lucky I am to know you. You are more than a coach—you are a friend. For over twelve years now, you believed in me and urged me forward when I got stuck in the muck of writer's block. You asked just the right questions so I could make each chapter the best it could be. But probably the most important gift (for a loquacious girl like me anyway) is that you know just when to use the scalpel…and when to take out the hatchet.

And to my family and friends, I wonder how I got so lucky. Your kindness means more to me than you could ever know.

To those friends who boost me up, make me laugh, and lend a listening ear, thank you. Heather Popat, your friendship before, during, and after the writing of this book has meant the world to me. Randi Fishman—that's forty-seven years and counting—your words lift my spirits when I need them the most. Thank you also to my friends who listened and talked and talked and listened: Lisa Marx, Carrie Goldman and my entire Bedford tribe, Powerful Words family, gym crew, POOG pals, gals from NC and NJ, and confidants from East Coast to West for your stories and check-ins. And to the Powerful Words Character Development community, who have been cheering this book on from the start, I am grateful for your enthusiasm and your unrelenting commitment to talk to kids about what's really important.

To my family, who have been nothing short of stupendous, it is not lost on me how truly fortunate I am to have you all in my corner. Your support has been unwavering, and I always knew that you believed in me even when this process got challenging…and easier…and challenging again. I love you so.

A special moment for my husband and my kids. Thank you for loving me through the stressful days and celebrating with me as I completed my deadlines or received "the best news!" from my editor. Believe me, I get that this book was a labor of love from all of us. For the "I'll just order a pizza so you don't have to cook" nights and the "how's your latest chapter going?" questions, I adore you. Tallie and Noah, being able to talk with you about these tough topics will remain one of the greatest highlights of my life. I hope the message you have heard loud, clear, and consistently is that I am always here to talk and listen—and that I love you no matter what.

To my husband, Jason, you deserve your own line. It takes a special person to support a writer who must go down every rabbit hole, read every book she can, peruse all the studies, interview as many experts as she can, *and* write all the words. So many words. You are remarkable. And you don't know this, but there have been times when I have woken up in the middle of the night while in the process of writing this book, as my mind churns and reminds and rewrites lines, when I have paused to look over at you in the deep quiet of the darkness to thank you, a hundred times thank you, for being by my side.

And to you, dear reader, I am grateful for you. This book has been a long time coming, and I have envisioned you taking in the words in this book for many years now. I have written this for you. For the tough moments, the hard questions, and the worrisome days. But also for the conversations that bring us closer and make life worth living.

Notes

Introduction: Can We Talk?

1   "The Developmental Assets Framework," Search Institute, accessed September 10, 2022, https://www.search-institute.org/our-research/development-assets/developmental-assets-framework/.

Chapter 1: How to Talk to Kids about Anger, Sadness and Other Big Feelings

1   Alan Watkins, *Coherence: The Secret Science of Brilliant Leadership* (London: Kogan Page, 2013), 125.

2   Susan David, *Emotional Agility: Get Unstuck, Embrace Change, and Thrive in Work and Life* (New York: Avery, 2016), 35.

3   Ralph Adolphs, "The Biology of Fear," *Current Biology* 23, no. 2 (2013): R79–93, https://doi.org/10.1016/j.cub.2012.11.055.

4   "Parenting," Gottman Institute, accessed October 25, 2022, https://www.gottman.com/about/research/parenting/.

5   Daniel Siegel and Tina Payne Bryson, *The Whole-Brain Child: 12 Revolutionary Strategies to Nurture Your Child's Developing Mind* (New York: Bantam, 2012), 37.

6   Daniel Goleman, *Emotional Intelligence: Why It Can Matter More Than IQ* (New York: Bantam, 1995), 12–13; Daniel Goleman, "Emotional Intelligence, Emotional Hijacks, and Systems Thinking," LinkedIn, July 21, 2022, https://www.linkedin.com/pulse/emotional-intelligence-hijacks-systems-thinking-daniel-goleman/..

7   Daniel Siegel, interview with the author, *How to Talk to Kids about Anything*, podcast, August 6, 2018, https://drrobynsilverman.com/how-to-parent-with-awareness-with-dr-dan-siegel/; Siegel and Bryson, *Whole-Brain Child*, 64.

8   Susan David, "The Gift and Power of Emotional Courage," filmed November 2017 in New Orleans, LA, TED video, 16:39, https://www.ted.com/talks/susan _david_the_gift_and_power_of_emotional_courage.

9   Danushika Sivanathan et al. "Vulnerable Narcissism as a Mediator of the Relationship between Perceived Parental Invalidation and Eating Disorder Pathology," *Eating and Weight Disorders—Studies on Anorexia, Bulimia and Obesity* 24, (2019): 1071–77, https://doi.org/10.1007/s40519-019-00647-2; Esther M. Leerkes et al. "Links Between Remembered Childhood Emotion Socialization and Adult Adjustment: Similarities and Differences Between European American and African American Women," *Journal of Abnormal Child Psychology* 36, no. 13 (2015): 1854–77, https://doi.org / 10.1177/0192513X13505567; Elizabeth D. Krause, Tamar Mendelson, and Thomas R. Lynch, "Childhood Emotional Invalidation and Adult Psychological Distress: The Mediating Role of Emotional Inhibition," *Child Abuse & Neglect* 27, no. 2 (2003): 199–213, https://doi.org/10.1016/s0145-2134(02)00536-7; Eni Becker et al., "Don't Worry and Beware of White Bears: Thought Suppression in Anxiety Patients," *Journal of Anxiety Disorders* 12, no. 1 (1998): 39–55, https://doi.org/10.1016/s0887-6185(97)00048-0; Kari Edwards and Tamara Bryan, "Judgmental Biases Produced by Instructions to Disregard: The (Paradoxical) Case of Emotional Information," *Personality and Social Psychology Bulletin* 23, no. 8 (1997): 849–64, https://doi.org/10.1177/0146167297238006; Lizabeth Roemer et al., "A Preliminary Investigation of the Role of Strategic Withholding of Emotions in PTSD," *Journal of Traumatic Stress* 14, no. 1 (2001): 149–56, https://doi.org /10.1023/A:1007895817502; Richard M. Wenzlaff and Danielle E. Bates, "Unmasking a Cognitive Vulnerability to Depression: How Lapses in Mental Control Reveal Depressive Thinking," *Journal of Personality and Social Psychology* 75, no. 6 (1998): 155971, https://doi.org/10.1037//0022-3514.75.6.1559.

10   Laura Markham, interview with the author, *How to Talk to Kids about Anything*, podcast, January 7, 2019, https://drrobynsilverman.com/how-mindfulness-can-positively -impact-the-way-we-parent-our-children-with-dr-laura-markham/.

11   Sara F. Waters et al., "Keep It to Yourself? Parent Emotion Suppression Influences Physiological Linkage and Interaction Behavior," *Journal of Family Psychology* 34, no. 7 (2020): 784–93, https://doi.org/10.1037/fam0000664.

12   Marc Brackett, PhD, interview by Brené Brown, *Unlocking Us*, podcast, April 14, 2020, https://brenebrown.com/podcast/dr-marc-brackett-and-brene-on-permission-to-feel/.

13   Gloria Willcox, "The Feeling Wheel," Positive Psychology Practitioner's Toolkit, accessed October 28, 2021, https://www.gnyha.org/wp-content/uploads/2020/05 /The-Feeling-Wheel-Positive-Psycology-Program.pdf.

14   "Plutchik's Wheel of Emotions: Exploring the Emotion Wheel," Six Seconds, accessed May 17, 2022, https://www.6seconds.org/2022/03/13/plutchik-wheel-emotions/.

15   Megan Saxelby, "Emotional Granularity: A Tiny Guide," Cultures of Dignity, accessed October 6, 2022, https://culturesofdignity.com/product/emotional-granularity-a-tiny -guide/.

16   Rosalind Wiseman, interview with the author, *How to Talk to Kids about Anything*,

podcast, July 7, 2020, https://drrobynsilverman.com/how-to-help-parents-kids-cope
-with-big-issues-during-tough-times-with-rosalind-wiseman/.

17 Alyssa Blask Campbell, interview with the author, *How to Talk to Kids about Anything*,
podcast, July 12, 2022, https://drrobynsilverman.com/how-to-talk-to-kids-about
-emotions-boundaries-transitions-conflict-with-alyssa-blask-campbell/.

18 Eran Magen, "How to Be Supportive," Character Lab, May 17, 2020, https://characterlab
.org/tips-of-the-week/how-to-be-supportive/.

19 William Stixrud and Ned Johnson, interview with the author, *How to Talk to Kids about
Anything*, podcast, August 17, 2021, https://drrobynsilverman.com/how-to-talk-with-kids
-to-build-motivation-stress-tolerance-a-happy-home-with-dr-william-stixrud-ned-johnson/.

20 Laura L. Sisterhen and Ann. W. Paulette, "Temper Tantrums," National Library of
Medicine, last modified February 4, 2023, https://www.ncbi.nlm.nih.gov/books
/NBK544286/; James A. Green, Pamela G. Whitney, and Michael Potegal, "Screaming,
Yelling, Whining, and Crying: Categorical and Intensity Differences in Vocal
Expressions of Anger and Sadness in Children's Tantrums," *Emotion* 11, no. 5 (2011):
1124–33, https://doi.org/10.1037/a0024173.

21 "Anger, Irritability and Aggression in Kids," Yale Medicine, accessed October 5, 2022,
https://www.yalemedicine.org/conditions/anger-issues-in-children-and-teens.

22 L. R. Knost, "When little people are overwhelmed by big emotions, it's our job to share
our calm, not join their chaos," Facebook, April 24, 2017, https://www.facebook.com
/littleheartsbooks/photos/when-little-people-are-overwhelmed-by-big-emotions-its
-our-job-to-share-our-calm/1449215911775675/.

23 Deena Margolin and Kristin Gallant, interview with the author, *How to Talk to Kids
about Anything*, podcast, forthcoming.

24 Dehra Harris, interview with the author, *How to Talk to Kids about Anything*, podcast, August 29, 2017, https://drrobynsilverman.com/how-to-talk-to-kids-about
-impulsivity-adhd-with-dr-dehra-harris/.

25 Wendy Young, interview with the author, *How to Talk to Kids about Anything*, podcast, June 6, 2017, https://drrobynsilverman.com/how-to-talk-to-kids-about-anger-big
-feelings-with-wendy-young/; Lynne Kenney, interview with the author, *How to Talk
to Kids about Anything*, podcast, April 27, 2017, https://drrobynsilverman.com/how-to
-talk-to-kids-about-big-feelings-calming-down-strategies-featuring-dr-lynne-kenney/.

26 Joanna Faber and Julie King, interview with the author, *How to Talk to Kids
about Anything*, podcast, April 30, 2019, https://drrobynsilverman.com/how-to
-talk-so-little-kids-will-listen-with-joanna-faber-julie-king/.

27 Celeste Headlee, interview with the author, *How to Talk to Kids about Anything*, podcast,
September 19, 2017, https://drrobynsilverman.com/how-to-talk-to-kids-about-having
-meaningful-conversations-that-matter-with-celeste-headlee/.

28 Kenney, interview.

29 Kyle Benson, "The Anger Iceberg," Gottman Institute, accessed October 25, 2022,
https://www.gottman.com/blog/the-anger-iceberg/.

30 Stephanie Watson, "Recognizing the Unusual Signs of Depression," Harvard Health

Publishing, February 27, 2013, https://www.health.harvard.edu/blog/recognizing-the-unusual-signs-of-depression-201302275938; "Depression and Headaches," National Headache Foundation, October 25, 2007, https://headaches.org/2007/10/25/depression-and-headache/; "The Gut-Brain Connection," Harvard Health Publishing, April 19, 2021, https://www.health.harvard.edu/diseases-and-conditions/the-gut-brain-connection; Sandro Marsala et al., "Pain Perception in Major Depressive Disorder: A Neurophysiological Case-Control Study" *Journal of the Neurological Sciences* 357, no. 1–2 (2015): 19–21, https://doi.org/10.1016/j.jns.2015.06.051.

31 Asma Hayati Ahmad and Rahimah Zakaria, "Pain in Times of Stress," *Malaysian Journal of Medical Sciences* 22, (2015): 52–61, https://www.ncbi.nlm.nih.gov/pmc/articles/PMC4795524/; Elizabeth Hartney, "How Emotional Pain Affects Your Body," Verywell Mind, updated November 10, 2022, https://www.verywellmind.com/physical-pain-and-emotional-pain-22421; Marcus Mund and Kristin Mitte, "The Costs of Repression: A Meta-Analysis on the Relation between Repressive Coping and Somatic Diseases," *Health Psychology* 31, no. 5 (2012): 640–49, https://doi.org/10.1037/a0026257; Michelle C. P. Hendriks et al., "Why Crying Improves Our Well-Being: An Attachment Theory Perspective on the Functions of Adult Crying," in *Emotion Regulation: Conceptual and Clinical Issues*, ed. Ad J. J. M. Vingerhoets, Ivan Nyklíček, and Johan Denollet (Boston: Springer, 2008), 87–96, https://doi.org/10.1007/978-0-387-29986-0_6; Debra M. Zeifman, "Developmental Aspects of Crying: Infancy and Beyond Childhood," in *Adult Crying: a Biopsychosocial Approach*, ed. Ad J. J. M. Vingerhoets and Randolph R. Cornelius (Milton Park, UK: Routledge, 2001), 37–54; Abigail Millings et al., "Holding Back the Tears: Individual Differences in Adult Crying Proneness Reflect Attachment Orientation and Attitudes to Crying," *Frontiers in Psychology* 7, (2016): 1003, https://doi.org/10.3389/fpsyg.2016.01003.

32 Hendriks et al., "Why Crying Improves Our Well-Being"; Zeifman, "Developmental Aspects of Crying"; Nelson, Seeing Through Tears; Millings et al., "Holding Back the Tears."

33 KJ Dell'Antonia, "Teaching Your Child Emotional Agility," *New York Times*, October 4, 2016, https://www.nytimes.com/2016/10/04/well/family/teaching-your-child-emotional-agility.html.

34 Paul Kivel, *Men's Work: How to Stop the Violence that Tears Our Lives Apart*, 2nd ed. (Center City, MN: Hazelden, 1998), 21; Rosalind Wiseman, *Masterminds & Wingmen: Helping Our Boys Cope with Schoolyard Power, Locker-Room Tests, Girlfriends, and the New Rules of Boy World*, reprint ed. (New York: Harmony, 2014), 28.

35 Brian Heilman, Gary Barker, and Alexander Harrison, "The Man Box: A Study on Being a Young Man in the US, UK, and Mexico—Key Findings," Equimundo, March 29, 2017, https://www.equimundo.org/wp-content/uploads/2017/03/TheManBox-KeyFindings-EN-Final-29.03.2017-POSTPRINT.v3-web.pdf/.

36 Michael Reichert, interview with the author, *How to Talk to Kids about Anything*,

podcast, May 28, 2019, https://drrobynsilverman.com/how-to-raise-boys-to-become
-good-men-with-michael-reichert-phd/.

37 Christina Caron, "8-Year-Olds in Despair: The Mental Health Crisis Is Getting Younger," *New York Times*, June 28, 2021, https://www.nytimes.com/2021/06/28/well/mind/mental-health-kids-suicide.html.

38 Katie Hurley, *The Depression Workbook for Teens: Tools to Improve Your Mood, Build Self-Esteem, and Stay Motivated* (Emeryville, CA: Rockridge Press, 2019), ix.

39 Saloni Dattani et al., "Suicide," Our World in Data, accessed May 13, 2023, https://ourworldindata.org/suicide.

40 M. S. Gould et al., "Evaluating Iatrogenic Risk of Suicide Screening Programs: A Randomized Controlled Trial," *Journal of the American Medical Association* 293, no. 13 (April 2005): 1635–43, https://doi.org/10.1001/jama.293.13.1635.

41 Dan Reidenberg, interview with the author, *How to Talk to Kids about Anything*, podcast, April 9, 2019, https://drrobynsilverman.com/how-to-talk-to-kids-about-suicide-with-dr-dan-reidenberg/.

42 Jonathan Singer, interview with the author, *How to Talk to Kids about Anything*, podcast, July 6, 2021, https://drrobynsilverman.com/how-to-talk-to-kids-about-suicide-risk-and-prevention-with-jonathan-b-singer-ph-d-lcsw/.

43 Eli Lebowitz, interview with the author, *How to Talk to Kids about Anything*, podcast, August 31, 2021, https://drrobynsilverman.com/how-to-talk-to-kids-about-breaking-free-of-anxiety-and-ocd-with-eli-lebowitz-phd/.

44 Dr. Dawn Huebner, interview with the author, email, July 9, 2021, and September 4, 2021.

45 B. D. Wright et al., "Clinical and Cost-Effectiveness of One-Session Treatment (OST) versus Multisession Cognitive Behavioural Therapy (CBT) for Specific Phobias in Children: Protocol for a Non-Inferiority Randomised Controlled Trial," *BMJ Open* 8, no. 8 (August 2018): e025031, https://doi.org/10.1136/bmjopen-2018-025031; American Psychiatric Association, *DSM-IV-TR: Diagnostic and Statistical Manual of Mental Disorders*, 4th ed., text rev. (*Washington, DC: American Psychiatric Association, 2000*), 78–85.

46 Amy Morin, interview with the author, *How to Talk to Kids about Anything*, podcast, September 12, 2017, https://drrobynsilverman.com/what-to-do-and-what-not-to-do-to-become-mentally-strong-parents-with-amy-morin-lcsw/.

47 Andrea Umbach, interview with the author, *How to Talk to Kids about Anything*, podcast, December 4, 2017, https://drrobynsilverman.com/how-to-talk-to-kids-about-fears-phobias-with-dr-andrea-umbach/.

48 "How Our Research Could Help Children Overcome Severe Phobias," University of York, November 22, 2017, https://www.york.ac.uk/research/themes/child-phobias/.

49 "Fear Ladder Building: Getting Started," Mayo Clinic, accessed February 25, 2022, https://anxietycoach.mayoclinic.org/anxiety/building-a-fear-ladder/.

50 Karen Young, interview with the author, *How to Talk to Kids about Anything*, podcast, May 22, 2018, https://drrobynsilverman.com/how-to-talk-about-anxiety-in-kids-with-karen-young-rerelease/.

51 Elizabeth Gilbert, *Big Magic: Creative Living Beyond Fear* (New York: Riverhead Books, 2016), 25–26.

52 Dell'Antonia, "Teaching Your Child Emotional Agility."

53 Janine Halloran, interview with the author, *How to Talk to Kids about Anything*, podcast, April 20, 2021, https://drrobynsilverman.com/how-to-talk-to-kids-about -coping-skills-with-janine-halloran-m-a-lmhc/.

Chapter 2: How to Talk to Kids about Self-Esteem and Body Image

1 Nathaniel Branden, *The Psychology of Self-Esteem: A Revolutionary Approach to Self Understanding That Launched a New Era in Modern Psychology* (San Francisco: Jossey-Bass, 1992), 18.

2 California Task Force to Promote Self-Esteem and Personal and Social Responsibility, *Toward a State of Esteem: The Final Report of the California Task Force to Promote Self-Esteem and Personal and Social Responsibility* (Sacramento: California Department of Education, 1990), 21, 60, https://files.eric.ed.gov/fulltext/ED321170.pdf.

3 Roy F. Baumeister et al., "Does High Self-Esteem Cause Better Performance, Interpersonal Success, Happiness, or Healthier Lifestyles?," *Psychological Science in the Public Interest* 4, no. 1 (May 1, 2003): 1–44, https://doi.org/10.1111/1529-1006.0143.

4 Dat Tan Nguyen et al., "Low Self-Esteem and Its Association with Anxiety, Depression, and Suicidal Ideation in Vietnamese Secondary School Students: A Cross-Sectional Study, *Frontiers in Psychiatry* 10, (2019): 698, https://doi.org/10.3389/fpsyt.2019.00698; Joseph M. Boden, David M. Fergusson, and L. John Horwood, "Does Adolescent Self-Esteem Predict Later Life Outcomes? A Test of the Causal Role of Self-Esteem," Development and Psychopathology 20, no. 1 (2008): 319–39, https://doi.org/10.1017 /S0954579408000151; Kali H. Trzesniewski, M. Brent Donnellan, and Richard W. Robins, "Stability of Self-Esteem across the Life Span," *Journal of Personality and Social Psychology* 84, no. 1 (2003): 205–20, https://doi.org/10.1037//0022-3514.84.1.205; Carol C. Choo et al., "What Predicts Medical Lethality of Suicide Attempts in Asian Youths?," *Asian Journal of Psychiatry* 29, (October 2017): 136–41, https://doi.org/10.1016 /j.ajp.2017.05.008; Jennifer Crocker and Connie T. Wolfe, "Contingencies of Self-Worth," *Psychological Review* 108, no. 3 (2001): 593–623, https://doi.org/10.1037//0033 -295X.108.3.593; Auden C. McClure et al., "Characteristics Associated with Low Self-Esteem among US Adolescents," *Academic Pediatrics* 10, no. 4 (July-August 2010): 238–44, https://doi.org/10.1016/j.acap.2010.03.007.

5 Baumeister et al., "High Self-Esteem."

6 Lea Waters, "StrengthBased Parenting and Life Satisfaction in Teenagers," *Advances in Social Sciences Research Journal* 2, no. 11 (2015): 158–73, https://doi.org/10.14738 /assrj.211.1651.

7 Ulrich Orth and Richard W. Robins, "Is High Self-Esteem Beneficial? Revising a Classic Question," *American Psychologist* 77, no. 1 (2022): 5–17, https://doi.org/10.1037/amp0000922.

8   Sue Atkins, interview with the author, *How to Talk to Kids about Anything*, podcast, January 29, 2018, https://drrobynsilverman.com/how-to-raise-happy-confident-resilient-kids-with-sue-atkins/.

9   Melinda Wenner Moyer, *How to Raise Kids Who Aren't Assholes* (New York: G. P. Putnam's Sons, 2021), 133.

10   Geoffrey L. Cohen and David K. Sherman, "The Psychology of Change: Self-Affirmation and Social Psychological Intervention," *Annual Review of Psychology* 65, (2014): 333–71, https://doi.org/10.1146/annurev-psych-010213-115137; David K. Sherman and Geoffrey L. Cohen, "The Psychology of Self-Defense: Self-Affirmation Theory," *Advances in Experimental Social Psychology* 38, (2006): 183–242, https://doi.org /10.1016/S0065-2601(06)38004-5.

11   Amy Cuddy, *Presence: Bringing Your Boldest Self to Your Biggest Challenges* (New York: Little, Brown Spark, 2015), 47.

12   James Clear, *Atomic Habits: An Easy & Proven Way to Build Good Habits & Break Bad Ones* (New York: Avery, 2018), 247.

13   Julie Bogart, interview with the author, *How to Talk to Kids about Anything*, podcast, February 1, 2022, https://drrobynsilverman.com/how-to-talk-to-kids-about-being-critical-thinkers-with-julie-bogart/.

14   "Where I'm From," George Ella Lyon (website), last modified 2022, http://www.georgeellalyon.com/where.html.

15   Destini Ann Davis (@destini.ann), "So many of US are disconnected from our needs walking around exhibiting inappropriate behaviors that are really just outward expressions of internal needs and emotions," Instagram, June 30, 2022, https://www.instagram.com/p/CfwjMKPNrLF/.

16   Jan E. Stets and Peter J. Burke, "Self-Esteem and Identities," *Sociological Perspectives* 57, no. 4 (2014): 40933, https://doi.org/10.1177/0731121414536141.

17   Albert Ellis Institute (website), accessed September 21, 2022, https://albertellis.org/.

18   Atkins, interview.

19   "8 Practices That Raise Caring, Empathetic Kids," Michele Borba, Ed.D. (website), August 1, 2016, https://micheleborba.com/building-moral-intelligence-and-character/8-practices-that-raise-caring-empathetic-kids/.

20   Lindsay LaVine, "Sheryl Sandberg Encourages Women Bloggers to 'Lean In,'" Entrepreneur, July 29, 2013, https://www.entrepreneur.com/article/227596; "Your Daughter Isn't Bossy, She Has 'Executive Leadership Skills': Lessons from Sheryl Sandberg," Women's Agenda, July 29, 2013, https://womensagenda.com.au/latest/your-daughter-isn-t-bossy-she-has-executive-leadership-skills-lessons-from-sheryl-sandberg/.

21   Brittany Packnett Cunningham, "How to Build Your Confidence—and Spark It in Others," filmed May 20, 2019, TED video, 13:21, https://www.ted.com/talks/brittany _packnett_cunningham_how_to_build_your_confidence_and_spark_it_in_others.

22   Tun Hayrettin, "The Relationship between Self-Confidence and Learning Turkish as a Foreign Language," *Educational Research and Reviews* 10, no. 18 (*September* 2015): 257589,

https://doi.org/10.5897/ERR2015.2445; Alia E. Meisha and Raghad A. Al-Dabbagh, "Self-Confidence as a Predictor of Senior Dental Student Academic Success," *Journal of Dental Education* 85, no. 9 (September 2021): 1497–503, https://doi.org/10.1002/jdd.12617.

23 Edwin A. Locke et al., "Effect of Self-Efficacy, Goals, and Task Strategies on Task Performance," *Journal of Applied Psychology* 69, no. 2 (1984): 241–51, https://doi.org/10.1037/0021-9010.69.2.241; Madhuleena Roy Chowdhury, "The Science & Psychology of Goal-Setting 101," Positive Psychology, May 2, 2019, https://positivepsychology.com/goal-setting-psychology/.

24 Jill Taylor and J. Clare Wilson, "Using Our Understanding of Time to Increase Self-Efficacy towards Goal Achievement," *Heliyon* 5, no. 8 (August 2019): e02116, https://doi.org/10.1016/j.heliyon.2019.e02116.

25 S. Mehrotra and U. Chaddha, "A Correlational Study of Protective Factors, Resilience and Self-Esteem in Premedical Dropouts," *International Journal of Humanities and Social Science Invention* 2, no. 9 (September 2013): 103–106, http://www.ijhssi.org/papers/v2(9)/Version-1/R029101030106.pdf; Budi Kurniawan, N. Neviyarni, and S. Solfema, "The Relationship between Self-Esteem and Resilience of Adolescents Who Living [sic] in Orphanages," *International Journal of Research in Counseling and Education* 1, no. 1 (2017): 47–52, https://doi.org/10.24036/0054za0002.

26 Sheldon Hanton, Stephen Mellalieu, and Ross Hall, "Self-Confidence and Anxiety Interpretation: A Qualitative Investigation," *Psychology of Sport and Exercise* 5, no. 4 (October 2004): 477–95, https://doi.org/10.1016/S1469-0292(03)00040-2.

27 Alessandro Rossi et al., "The Anxiety-Buffer Hypothesis in the Time of COVID-19: When Self-Esteem Protects from the Impact of Loneliness and Fear on Anxiety and Depression," *Frontiers in Psychiatry* 11, (2020): 2177, https://doi.org/10.3389/fpsyg.2020.02177.

28 Nguyen et al., "Low Self-Esteem."

29 Katty Kay and Claire Shipman, *The Confidence Code* (New York: Harper Business, 2014), xi.

30 Rick Carson, "Intro", Taming Your Gremlin, accessed October 31, 2022, https://www.tamingyourgremlin.com/.

31 Kelly Wallace, "How to Teach Girls to be Confident #LikeAGirl," CNN, July 9, 2015, https://www.cnn.com/2015/07/09/living/feat-teach-girls-confidence-likeagirl.

32 Matthew McKay and Patrick Fanning, *Self-Esteem* (Oakland, CA: New Harbinger, 2016), 13.

33 "GirlTip #21: Use Your BFF Voice," Rachel Simmons (website), accessed September 27, 2022, https://www.rachelsimmons.com/girltip-21-use-your-bff-voice/.

34 "GirlTip #21."

35 Carrie Goldman, interview with the author, Zoom, March 3, 2022.

36 Eddie Brummelman et al., "On Feeding Those Hungry for Praise: Person Praise Backfires in Children with Low Self-Esteem," *Journal of Experimental Psychology: General*

143, no. 1 (2014): 9–14, https://doi.org/10.1037/a0031917; Eddie Brummelman et al., "When Parents' Praise Inflates, Children's Self-Esteem Deflates," *Child Development* 88, no. 6 (2017): 1799–1809, https://doi.org/ 10.1111/cdev.12936.

37 Cynthia McFadden and Deborah Apton, "Psychology of Parenting: Why Praising Your Kids Can Hurt Them," ABC News, September 2, 2009, https://abcnews.go.com /Nightline/nurtureshock-parenting-tips-praising-kids-hurt/story?id=8475074.

38 Robin Parks Ennis et al., "Behavior-Specific Praise: An Effective, Efficient, Low-Intensity Strategy to Support Student Success," *Beyond Behavior* 27, no. 3 (2018): 134–39, https:// doi.org/ 10.1177/1074295618798587; Robin Parks Ennis et al., "Behavior-Specific Praise in Pre-K–12 Settings: Mapping the 50-Year Knowledge Base," *Behavioral Disorders* 45, no. 3 (2020): 131–47, https://doi.org/10.1177/0198742919843075; Kevin S. Sutherland, Joseph H. Wehby, and Susan R. Copeland, "Effect of Varying Rates of Behavior-Specific Praise on the On-Task Behavior of Students with EBD," *Journal of Emotional and Behavioral Disorders* 8, no. 1 (2000): 2–8, https://doi.org/10.1177/106342660000800101.

39 Carol S. Dweck, *Mindset: The New Psychology of Success* (New York: Random House, 2006), 71–72; Claudia M. Mueller and Carol S. Dweck, "Praise for Intelligence Can Undermine Children's Motivation and Performance," *Journal of Personality and Social Psychology* 75, no. 1 (1998): 33–52, https://doi.org/10.1037//0022-3514.75.1.33.

40 Carol Dweck, "Praise the Effort, Not the Outcome? Think Again," Student Experience Research Network, March 23, 2016, https://studentexperiencenetwork.org /praise-the-effort-not-the-outcome-think-again/#.

41 Jennifer Henderlong Corpus and Kayla A. Good, "The Effects of Praise on Children's Intrinsic Motivation Revisited," in *Psychological Perspectives on Praise*, ed. Eddie Brummelman (Abington, UK: Routledge, 2020), 39–46.

42 Jennifer Henderlong and Mark R. Lepper, "The Effects of Praise on Children's Intrinsic Motivation: A Review and Synthesis," *Psychological Bulletin* 128, no. 5 (2002): 774–95, https://doi.org/10.1037/0033-2909.128.5.774; Jennifer Henderlong Corpus, Christin Ogle, and Kelly Love-Geiger, "The Effects of Social-Comparison Versus Mastery Praise on Children's Intrinsic Motivation," *Motivation and Emotion* 30, no. 4 (2006): 333–43, https://doi.org/10.1007/s11031-006-9039-4; Carol S. Dweck, "The Perils and Promises of Praise," ACSD, October 1, 2007, https://www.ascd.org/el/articles /the-perils-and-promises-of-praise.

43 Henderlong Corpus, Ogle, and Love-Geiger, "Effects of Social Comparison"; Henderlong Corpus and Good, "Effects of Praise."

44 Jacinthe Dion et al., "Development and Aetiology of Body Dissatisfaction in Adolescent Boys and Girls," *International Journal of Adolescence & Youth* 20, no. 2 (2015): 151–66, http://doi.org/10.1080/02673843.2014.985320; Jessica H. Baker et al., "Body Dissatisfaction in Adolescent Boys," *Developmental Psychology* 55, no. 7 (2019): 156–678, https://doi.org/10.1037/dev0000724.

45 Marika Tiggemann, Yolanda Martins, and Libby Churchett, "Beyond Muscles: Unexplored Parts of Men's Body Image," *Journal of Health Psychology* 13, no. 8 (2008):

1163–72, https://doi.org/10.1177/1359105308095971; Anna Bornioli et al. "Body Dissatisfaction Predicts the Onset of Depression among Adolescent Females and Males: A Prospective Study," *Journal of Epidemiology and Community Health* 75, no. 4 (2021): 343–48, https://doi.org/10.1136/jech-2019-213033; Haleama Al Sabbah et al., "Body Weight Dissatisfaction and Communication with Parents among Adolescents in 24 Countries: International Cross-Sectional Survey," *BMC Public Health* 9, (2009): 52, https://doi.org/10.1186/1471-2458-9-52.

46 Ab Latiff Azmira, Juliawati Muhamad, and Razlina A. Rahman, "Body Image Dissatisfaction and Its Determinants among Young Primary School Adolescents," *Journal of Taibah University Medical Sciences* 13, no. 1 (2017): 34–41, https://doi.org/10.1016/j.jtumed.2017.07.003; "Get the Facts," National Organization for Women, accessed September 27, 2022, https://now.org/now-foundation/love-your-body/love-your-body-whats-it-all-about/get-the-facts/.

47 Charlotte Markey, Daniel Hart, and Douglas N. Zacher, *Being You: The Body Image Book for Boys* (Cambridge, UK: Cambridge University Press, 2022), 6.

48 Maja Batista et al., "Predictors of Eating Disorder Risk in Anorexia Nervosa Adolescents," *Acta Clinica Croatica* 57, no. 3 (September 2018): 399–410, https://doi.org/10.20471/acc.2018.57.03.01.

49 Dannielle Miller, interview with the author, *How to Talk to Kids about Anything*, podcast, June 5, 2018, https://drrobynsilverman.com/how-to-raise-confident-girls-with-dannielle-miller/.

50 Elizabeth McDade-Montez, Jan Wallander, and Linda Cameron, "Sexualization in U.S. Latina and White Girls' Preferred Children's Television Programs," *Sex Roles* 77, no. 1–2 (2017): 1–15, https://doi.org/10.1007/s11199-016-0692-0.

51 Deborah Tolman et al., "Looking Good, Sounding Good: Femininity Ideology and Adolescent Girls' Mental Health," *Psychology of Women Quarterly* 30, no. 1 (2006): 85–95, https://doi.org/10.1111/j.1471-6402.2006.00265.x; Maddy Coy, "Milkshakes, Lady Lumps and Growing Up to Want Boobies: How the Sexualisation of Popular Culture Limits Girls' Horizons," *Child Abuse Review* 18, no. 6 (2009): 372–83, https://doi.org/10.1002/car.1094; Alana Papageorgiou, Colleen Fisher, and Donna Cross, "Why Don't I Look Like Her? How Adolescent Girls View Social Media and Its Connection to Body Image," *BMC Women's Health* 22, no. 1 (June 2022): 261, https://doi.org/10.1186/s12905-022-01845-4.

52 Maddy Coy, "Children, Childhood and Sexualised Popular Culture," in *Exploiting Childhood: How Fast Food, Material Obsession and Porn Culture Are Creating New Forms of Child Abuse*, ed. Jim Wild (London: Jessica Kingsley, 2013), 149–63.

53 Michelle I. Jongenelis, Susan M. Byrne, and Simone Pettigrew, "Self Objectification, Body Image Disturbance, and Eating Disorder Symptoms in Young Australian Children," *Body Image* 11, no. 3 (June 2014): 290–302, https://doi.org/10.1016/j.bodyim.2014.04.002; Kathrin Karsay, Johannes Knoll, and Jörg Matthes, "Sexualizing Media Use and Self-Objectification: A Meta-Analysis," *Psychology of Women Quarterly* 42, no. 1 (2018): 9–28, https://doi.org/10.1177/0361684317743019.

54 Tolman et al., "Looking Good, Sounding Good"; Coy, "Milkshakes, Lady Lumps"; Papageorgiou, Fisher, and Cross, "Why Don't I Look."

55 Jean Twenge, Gabrielle Martin, and Brian Spitzberg, "Trends in U.S. Adolescents' Media Use, 1976–2016: The Rise of Digital Media, the Decline of TV, and the (Near) Demise of Print," *Psychology of Popular Media Culture* 8, no. 4 (2019): 329–45, https://doi.org/10.1037/ppm0000203.

56 Emily A. Vogels, Risa Gelles-Watnick, and Navid Massarat, "Teens, Social Media and Technology 2022," Pew Research Center, August 10, 2022, https://www.pewresearch.org/internet/2022/08/10/teens-social-media-and-technology-2022/.

57 Dr. Lindsay Kite and Dr. Lexie Kite, interview with the author, *How to Talk to Kids about Anything*, podcast, January 4, 2022, https://drrobynsilverman.com/how-to-talk-to-girls-about-body-image-with-dr-lindsay-kite-and-dr-lexie-kite/.

58 Mariska Kleemans et al., "Picture Perfect: The Direct Effect of Manipulated Instagram Photos on Body Image in Adolescent Girls," *Media Psychology* 21, no. 1 (2018): 93–110, https://doi.org/10.1080/15213269.2016.1257392; Georgia Wells, Jeff Horwitz, and Deepa Seetharaman, "Facebook Knows Instagram Is Toxic for Teen Girls, Company Documents Show," *Wall Street Journal*, September 14, 2021, https://www.wsj.com/articles/facebook-knows-instagram-is-toxic-for-teen-girls-company-documents-show-11631620739.

59 Marika Tiggemann and Isabella Anderberg, "Social Media Is Not Real: The Effect of 'Instagram vs. Reality' Images on Women's Social Comparison and Body Image," *New Media & Society* 22, no. 12 (2020): 2183–99, https://doi.org/10.1177/1461444819888720.

60 Katie Paradis, "Help Kids Fight the 'Selfie Effect' and Build Self-Esteem Instead," Boston Children's Hospital, November 16, 2021, https://answers.childrenshospital.org/selfie-effect/.

61 Rosalind Gill, "Changing the Perfect Picture: Smartphones, Social Media and Appearance Pressures," City, University of London, accessed March 5, 2021, https://www.city.ac.uk/__data/assets/pdf_file/0005/597209/Parliament-Report-web.pdf.

62 Hester Hockin-Boyers, Stacey Pope, and Kimberly Jamie, "Digital Pruning: Agency and Social Media Use as a Personal Political Project among Female Weightlifters in Recovery from Eating Disorders," *New Media & Society* 23, no. 8 (2021): 2345–66, https://doi.org/10.1177/1461444820926503.

63 Ieuan Cranswick, "Muscle Dysmorphia: Why Are So Many Young Men Suffering This Serious Mental Health Condition," The Conversation, October 9, 2020, https://theconversation.com/muscle-dysmorphia-why-are-so-many-young-men-suffering-this-serious-mental-health-condition-147706; Ann Rousseau, Steven Eggermont, and Eline Frison, "The Reciprocal and Indirect Relationships between Passive Facebook Use, Comparison on Facebook, and Adolescents' Body Dissatisfaction," *Computers in Human Behavior* 73, (August 2017): 336–44, https://doi.org/10.1016/j.chb.2017.03.056.

64 Alexandra R. Lonergan et al., "Social Media and Eating and Body Image Concerns among Men and Boys," in *Eating Disorders in Boys and Men*, ed. Jason M. Nagata et

al. (Cham, Switzerland: Springer, 2021), 307–16; Madeline Wick and Pamela Keel, "Posting Edited Photos of the Self: Increasing Eating Disorder Risk or Harmless Behavior?," *International Journal of Eating Disorders* 53, no. 6 (June 2020): 864–72, https://doi.org/10.1002/eat.23263.

65 Virgina Sole Smith, *The Eating Instinct: Food Culture, Body Image, and Guilt in America* (New York: Henry Holt, 2018), 38.

66 Hockin-Boyers, Pope, and Jamie, "Digital Pruning."

67 Devorah Heitner, interview with the author, *How to Talk to Kids about Anything*, podcast, January 9, 2018, https://drrobynsilverman.com/how-to-talk-to-kids-about-tech-milestones-digital-readiness-with-devorah-heitner-rerelease/.

68 Gill, "Changing the Perfect Picture."

69 "Is There Really Such a Thing as Snapchat Dysmorphia?," Newport Academy, October 8, 2020, https://www.newportacademy.com/resources/empowering-teens/snapchat-dysmorphia/.

70 Susruthi Rajanala, Mayra B. C. Maymone, and Neelam A. Vashi, "Selfies—Living in the Era of Filtered Photographs," *JAMA Facial Plastic Surgery* 20, no. 6 (2018): 443–44, https://doi.org/10.1001/jamafacial.2018.0486.

71 Nancy Redd, "How to Give Kids Good Body Image in the Age of Snapchat," Mashable, December 12, 2018, https://mashable.com/article/good-body-image-kids-snapchat.

72 "Screen Time and Children," American Academy of Child and Adolescent Psychiatry, last modified February 2020, https://www.aacap.org/AACAP/Families_and_Youth/Facts_for_Families/FFF-Guide/Children-And-Watching-TV-054.aspx.

73 "The Common Sense Census: Media Use by Tweens and Teens, 2021," Common Sense Media, March 9, 2022, https://www.commonsensemedia.org/research/the-common-sense-census-media-use-by-tweens-and-teens-2021; "Landmark Report: U. S. Teens Use an Average of Nine Hours of Media Per Day, Tweens Use Six Hours," Common Sense Media, November 3, 2015, https://www.commonsensemedia.org/press-releases/landmark-report-us-teens-use-an-average-of-nine-hours-of-media-per-day-tweens-use-six-hours.

74 Melinda Wenner Moyer, "Kids as Young as 8 Are Using Social Media More Than Ever, Study Finds," *New York Times*, March 24, 2022, https://www.nytimes.com/2022/03/24/well/family/child-social-media-use.html.

75 Daniel Talbot et al., "'She Should Not Be a Model': The Effect of Exposure to Plus-Size Models on Body Dissatisfaction, Mood, and Facebook Commenting Behaviour," *Behaviour Change* 38, no. 3 (2021): 135–47, https://doi.org/10.1017/bec.2021.7.

76 Kite and Kite, interview.

77 Charlotte Markey, interview with the author, *How to Talk to Kids about Anything*, podcast, February 15, 2022, https://drrobynsilverman.com/how-to-talk-to-kids-about-body-image-and-self-care-with-charlotte-markey-phd/.

78 "Toxic Influence: A Dove Film," Dove Self-Esteem Project, April 27, 2022, YouTube video, 3:49, https://www.youtube.com/watch?v=sF3iRZtkyAQ.

79   Eric Robinson and Angelina R. Sutin, "Parents' Perceptions of Their Children as Overweight and Children's Weight Concerns and Weight Gain," *Psychological Science*, 28, no. 3 (2017): 320–29, https://doi.org/10.1177/0956797616682027; Lauren C. Fields et al., "Internalized Weight Bias, Teasing, and Self-Esteem in Children with Overweight or Obesity," *Childhood Obesity*, 17, no. 1 (2021): 43–50, https://doi.org/10.1089/chi.2020.0150.

80   Markey, Hart, and Zacher, *Being You*, 22.

81   Samantha DeCaro, "5 Ways Parental Body Image Issues Potentially Harm Their Children," Renfrew Center, accessed September 7, 2022, https://renfrewcenter.com/5-ways-parental-body-image-issues-potentially-harm-their-children/.

82   Monika Bidzan, Omar Yousaf, and Małgorzata Lipowska, "How Health-Related Behaviors Predict Body-Esteem in Men," *American Journal of Men's Health* 12, no. 6 (2018): 1901–7, https://doi.org/10.1177/1557988318801634.

Chapter 3: How to Talk to Kids about Sex

1   "New Poll: Parents Are Talking with Their Kids about Sex but Often Not Tackling Harder Issues," Planned Parenthood, January 30, 2014, https://www.plannedparenthood.org/about-us/newsroom/press-releases/new-poll-parents-talking-their-kids-about-sex-often-not-tackling-harder-issues.

2   Amie M. Ashcraft and Pamela J. Murray, "Talking to Kids about Adolescent Sexuality," *Pediatric Clinics of North America* 64, no. 2 (2017): 305–20, https://doi.org/10.1016/j.pcl.2016.11.002.

3   Ashcraft and Murray, "Talking to Kids"; Laura Widman et al., "Sexual Communication between Early Adolescents and Their Dating Partners, Parents, and Best Friends," *Journal of Sex Research* 51, no. 7 (2014): 731–41, https://doi.org/10.1080/00224499.2013.843148.

4   National Campaign to Prevent Teen and Unplanned Pregnancy, "Teens Say Parents Most Influence Their Decisions About Sex," Cision PR Newswire, August 28, 2012, https://www.prnewswire.com/news-releases/teens-say-parents-most-influence-their-decisions-about-sex-167680825.html.

5   Ashcraft and Murray, "Talking to Kids"; Ellen K. Wilson et al., "Parents' Perspectives on Talking to Preteenage Children About Sex," *Perspectives on Sexual and Reproductive Health* 42, no. 1 (2010): 56–63, https://doi.org/10.1363/4205610.

6   Ashcraft and Murray, "Talking to Kids."

7   Dina Alexander, interview with the author, *How to Talk to Kids about Anything*, podcast, August 1, 2017, https://drrobynsilverman.com/how-to-talk-to-kids-about-sex-featuring-dina-alexander/.

8   Richard Weissbourd, interview with the author, *How to Talk to Kids about Anything*, podcast, May 18, 2017, https://drrobynsilverman.com/talk-kids-healthy-caring-romantic-relationships-dr-richard-weissbourd/.

9   Dalmacio Flores and Julie Barroso, "21st Century Parent-Child Sex Communication in the U.S.: A Process Review," *Journal of Sex Research* 54, no. 4–5 (2017): 532–48, https://doi.org/10.1080/00224499.2016.1267693; Peter S. Karofsky, Lan Zeng, and Michael R. Kosorok, "Relationship between Adolescent-Parental Communication and Initiation of First Intercourse by Adolescents," *Journal of Adolescent Health* 28, no. 1 (2001): 41–45, https://doi.org/ 10.1080/00224499.2016.1267693; Kim S. Miller et al., "Patterns of Condom Use among Adolescents: The Impact of Mother-Adolescent Communication," *American Journal of Public Health* 88, no. 10 (1998): 1542–44, https://doi.org/10.2105/ajph.88.10.1542; Maxine L. Weinman et al., "Risk Factors, Parental Communication, Self and Peers' Beliefs as Predictors of Condom Use among Female Adolescents Attending Family Planning Clinics," *Child and Adolescent Social Work Journal* 25, no. 3 (2008): 157–70, https://doi.org/10.1007/s10560-008-0118-0; Bianca L. Guzmán et al., "Let's Talk about Sex: How Comfortable Discussions about Sex Impact Teen Sexual Behavior," *Journal of Health Communication.* 8, no. 6 (2003): 583–98, https://doi.org/10.1080/716100416.

10 Claire Zulkey, "The Sex Talk: Earlier Is Better," *U.S. Catholic*, August 23, 2016, https://uscatholic.org/articles/201608/the-sex-talk-earlier-is-better/; "Talking with Your Children about Moral Purity," Church of Jesus Christ of Latter-Day Saints, last modified 1986, https://www.churchofjesuschrist.org/study/ensign/1986/12/talking-with-your-children-about-moral-purity?lang=eng; Mark D. Regnerus, "Talking about Sex: Religion and Patterns of Parent-Child Communication about Sex and Contraception," *Sociological Quarterly* 46, no.1 (2005): 79–105, https://doi.org/10.1111/j.1533-8525.2005.00005.x; Gary D. Bouma, "Young People Want Sex Education and Religion Shouldn't Get in the Way" The Conversation, September 5, 2018, https://theconversation.com/young-people-want-sex-education-and-religion-shouldnt-get-in-the-way-96719.

11 Amy O'Leary, "So How Do We Talk About This?," *New York Times*, May 9, 2012, https://www.nytimes.com/2012/05/10/garden/when-children-see-internet-pornography.html.

12 Weissbourd, interview.

13 Richard Weissbourd with Trisha Ross Anderson, Alison Cashin, and Joe McIntyre, "The Talk: How Adults Can Promote Young People's Healthy Relationships and Prevent Misogyny and Sexual Harassment," Making Caring Common Project, last modified May 2017, https://mcc.gse.harvard.edu/reports/the-talk.

14 "Azoospermia," Johns Hopkins Medicine, accessed September 26, 2022, https://www.hopkinsmedicine.org/health/conditions-and-diseases/azoospermia; "Ovulatory Dysfunction," Center for Human Reproduction, updated October 8, 2018, https://www.centerforhumanreprod.com/contents/understanding-infertility/causes-of-infertility/ovulatory-dysfunction; "Mayer-Rokitansky-Küster-Hauser (MRKH) Syndrome," Penn Medicine, accessed November 30, 2022, https://www.pennmedicine.org/for-patients-and-visitors/patient-information/conditions-treated-a-to-z/mayer-rokitansky-kuster-hauser-mrkh-syndrome; Shuai Qiang et al., "Congenital Absence of the Penis (Aphallia)," *Medicine* 98, no. 15 (April 2019):

e15129, https://doi.org/10.1097/MD.0000000000015129; Stephanie Dutchen, "The Body, The Self," Harvard Medicine, accessed October 26, 2022, https://hms.harvard .edu/magazine/lgbtq-health/body-self; Anna Brown, "About 5% of Young Adults in the U.S. Say Their Gender Is Different From Their Sex Assigned at Birth," Pew Research Center, June 7, 2022, https://www.pewresearch.org/fact-tank/2022/06/07 /about-5-of-young-adults-in-the-u-s-say-their-gender-is-different-from-their-sex -assigned-at-birth/.

15 Logan Levkoff, interview with the author, *How to Talk to Kids about Anything*, pod-cast, June 8, 2021, https://drrobynsilverman.com/how-to-answer-kids-toughest -questions-about-sex-with-logan-levkoff-phd/.

16 Christine M. Markham et al., "Patterns of Vaginal, Oral, and Anal Sexual Intercourse in an Urban Seventh-Grade Population," *Journal of School Health* 79, no. 4 (April 2009): 193–200, https://doi.org/10.1111/j.1746-1561.2008.00389.x.

17 "Youth Risk Behavior Surveillance System," Centers for Disease Control and Prevention, last modified April 27, 2023, https://www.cdc.gov/healthyyouth/data/yrbs/results.htm.

18 Melissa Pintor Carnagey, *Sex Positive Talks to Have with Kids* (self-pub., 2020), 26.

19 Alexander, interview.

20 Dae Sheridan, interview with the author, *How to Talk to Kids about Anything*, podcast, July 4, 2017, https://drrobynsilverman.com/how-to-talk-to-kids-about -suicide-sexual-assault-13-reasons-why-with-dr-dae-sheridan/.

21 Bonnie J. Rough, interview with the author, *How to Talk to Kids about Anything*, pod-cast, October 30, 2018, https://drrobynsilverman.com/how-to-talk-to-kids-about -sex-love-and-equality-with-bonnie-rough/.

22 Levkoff, interview.

23 "Tea Consent," Emmeline May and Blue Seat Studios, May 12, 2015, YouTube video, 2:50, https://www.youtube.com/watch?v=oQbei5JGiT8.

24 Peggy Orenstein, *Girls and Sex* (New York: Harper, 2017), 220.

25 Peggy Orenstein, interview with the author, *How to Talk to Kids about Anything*, podcast, February 18, 2020, https://drrobynsilverman.com/how-to-talk-to-boys -about-sex-with-peggy-orenstein/.

26 "The Impact of Pornography on Children," American College of Pediatricians, June 2016, https://acpeds.org/position-statements/the-impact-of-pornography-on-children.

27 "Impact of Pornography on Children."

28 Christina Camilleri, Justin T. Perry, and Stephen Sammut, "Compulsive Internet Pornography Use and Mental Health: A Cross-Sectional Study in a Sample of University Students in the United States," *Frontiers in Psychology* 11, no. 3870 (2021): 613244, https://doi.org/10.3389/fpsyg.2020.613244.

29 British Board of Film Classification, "Young People Pornography & AgeVerification," Revealing Reality, January 2020, https://www.revealingreality.co.uk/wp-content /uploads/2020/01/BBFC-Young-people-and-pornography-Final-report-2401.pdf; O'Leary, "So How Do We Talk."

30 Jill Manning, "The Impact of Internet Pornography on Marriage and the Family: A Review of the Research," *Sexual Addiction & Compulsivity* 13, no. 2–3 (2006): 131–65, https://doi.org/10.1080/10720160600870711; "Impact of Pornography on Children."

31 Gail Dines, interview with the author, *How to Talk to Kids about Anything*, podcast, June 12, 2018, https://drrobynsilverman.com/how-to-talk-to-kids-about-porn-with-gail-dines/.

32 "Watching Pornography Rewires the Brain to a More Juvenile State," Neuroscience News, December 29, 2019, https://neurosciencenews.com/neuroscience-pornography-brain-15354/.

33 Alexander, interview.

34 Dina Alexander, interview.

35 Levkoff, interview.

36 Diane Felmlee, Paulina I. Rodis, and Amy Zhang, "Sexist Slurs: Reinforcing Feminine Stereotypes Online," *Sex Roles* 83, no. 1–2 (2020): 16–28, https://doi.org/10.1007/s11199-019-01095-z.

37 "8th Grade, Objective 8.02," NC Comprehensive School Health Training Center, last modified June 20, 2019, https://resources.finalsite.net/images/v1561036709/issschoolwirescom/fddcvt0nm1wsuybrvqim/802-unintendedpregnancy.pdf.

38 "Adolescent Pregnancy," World Health Organization, September 15, 2022, https://www.who.int/news-room/fact-sheets/detail/adolescent-pregnancy.

39 Arik V. Marcell, Gale R. Burstein, and Committee on Adolescence, "Sexual and Reproductive Health Care Services in the Pediatric Setting," *Pediatrics* 140, no. 5 (2017): e20172858, https://doi.org/10.1542/peds.2017-2858.

40 Julie S. Downs et al., "Specific STI Knowledge May Be Acquired Too Late," *Journal of Adolescent Health* 38, no. 1 (2006): 65, https://doi.org/10.1016/j.jadohealth.2005.01.004; Arianna Strome et al., "Youths' Knowledge and Perceptions of Health Risks Associated with Unprotected Oral Sex," *Annals of Family Medicine* 20, no.1 (2022): 72–76, https://doi.org/10.1370/afm.2761.

41 Chelsea L. Shannon and Jeffrey D. Klausner, "The Growing Epidemic of Sexually Transmitted Infections in Adolescents: A Neglected Population," *Current Opinion in Pediatrics* 30, no. 1 (2018): 137–43, https://doi.org/10.1097/MOP.0000000000000578.

42 "Child Maltreatment Survey, 2016," Children's Bureau, an office of the Administration for Children & Families, last modified June 29, 2021, https://www.acf.hhs.gov/cb/report/child-maltreatment-2016; "Children and Teens: Statistics," RAINN, accessed June 29, 2022, https://www.rainn.org/statistics/children-and-teens.

43 Shanta R. Dube et al., "LongTerm Consequences of Childhood Sexual Abuse by Gender of Victim," *American Journal of Preventative Medicine* 28, no. 5 (2005): 430–38, https://doi.org/10.1016/j.amepre.2005.01.015; Sandy K. Wurtele and Maureen C. Kenny, "Primary Prevention of Child Sexual Abuse: Child- and Parent-Focused Approaches," in *The Prevention of Sexual Violence: A Practitioner's Sourcebook*, ed. Keith L. Kaufman (Holyoke, MA: NEARI Press, 2010), 107–19.

44 "Children and Teens: Statistics."

45 Wikipedia, s.v. "Sandy K. Wurtele," last modified April 11, 2023, https://en.wikipedia
    .org/wiki/Sandy_K._Wurtele; Wurtele and Kenny, "Primary Prevention."
46 Levkoff, interview.

Chapter 4: How to Talk to Kids about Death

1   Mark W. Speece, "Children's Concepts of Death," *Michigan Family Review* 1, no. 1 (1995):
    57–69, https://doi.org/10.3998/mfr.4919087.0001.107; Virginia Slaughter, "Young
    Children's Understanding of Death," *Australian Psychologist* 40, no. 3 (2005): 179–86,
    https://doi.org/10.1080/00050060500243426; David Schonfeld and Thomas Demaria,
    "Supporting the Grieving Child and Family," *Pediatrics* 138, no. 3 (September 2016):
    e20162147, https://doi.org/10.1542/peds.2016-2147.

2   Joan N. McNeil, "Young Mothers' Communication about Death with Their Children,"
    Death Education 6, no. 4 (1983): 323–39, https://doi.org/10.1080/07481188308252139;
    Joo Ok Lee, Joohi Lee, and Sung Seek Moon, "Exploring Children's Understanding
    of Death Concepts," *Asia Pacific Journal of Education* 29, no. 2 (2009): 251–64, https://
    doi.org/10.1080/02188790902859020; Sarah Longbottom and Virginia Slaughter,
    "Sources of Children's Knowledge about Death and Dying," *Philosophical Transactions
    of the Royal Society: Biological Sciences* 373, no. 1754 (2018): 20170267, https://
    doi.org/10.1098/rstb.2017.0267; Anya Kamenetz and Cory Turner, "Be Honest and
    Concrete: Tips for Talking to Kids about Death," NPR, May 28, 2020, https://www.npr
    .org/2019/04/24/716702066/death-talking-with-kids-about-the-end.

3   "Facts and Stats," Children's Grief Awareness Day, accessed August 25, 2022, https://www
    .childrensgriefawarenessday.org/cgad2/pdf/griefstatistics.pdf; Coalition to Support
    Grieving Students (website), accessed February 14, 2022, https://grievingstudents
    .org/; "Recognizing Grief Awareness Day at Your School," National Education
    Association, November 10, 2021, https://www.nea.org/professional-excellence/student
    -engagement/tools-tips/recognizing-grief-awareness-day-your-school.

4   C. Randy Cotton and Lillian M. Range, "Children's Death Concepts: Relationship to
    Cognitive Functioning, Age, Experience with Death, Fear of Death, and Hopelessness,"
    Journal of Clinical Child Psychology 19, no. 2 (1990): 123–27, https://doi.org/10.1207
    /s15374424jccp1902_3; Karl S. Rosengren, Isabel T. Gutiérrez, and Stevie S. Schein,
    "Cognitive Dimensions of Death in Context," *Monographs of the Society for Research
    in Child Development* 79, no. 1 (2014): 62–82, https://doi.org/10.1111/mono.12079;
    Andrzej Tarlowski, "If It's an Animal It Has Axons: Experience and Culture in
    Preschool Children's Reasoning about Animates," *Cognitive Development* 21, no. 3
    (2006): 249–65, https://doi.org/10.1016/j.cogdev.2006.02.001; Sandra Waxman and
    Douglas Medin, "Experience and Cultural Models Matter: Placing Firm Limits
    on Childhood Anthropocentrism," *Human Development* 50, (2007): 23–30, https://
    doi.org/10.1159/000097681; Jackie Ellis, Chris Dowrick, and Mari Lloyd-Williams,
    "The Long-Term Impact of Early Parental Death: Lessons from a Narrative Study"

Journal of the Royal Society of Medicine 106, no. 2 (2013): 57–67, https://doi.org /10.1177/0141076812472623; Sydney Campbell et al., "The Unspeakable Nature of Death & Dying During Childhood: A Silenced Phenomenon in Pediatric Care," *OMEGA—Journal of Death and Dying* 0, no. 0 (2022), https:// doi.org/10.1177/00302228211067034.

5   Elizabeth Rapa et al., "Experiences of Preparing Children for a Death of an Important Adult during the COVID-19 Pandemic: A Mixed Methods Study," *BMJ Open* 11, no. 8 (2021): e053099, https://doi.org/v10.1136/bmjopen-2021-053099; David Menendez, Iseli Hernandez, and Karl Rosengren, "Children's Emerging Understanding of Death," *Child Development Perspectives* 14, no. 1 (2020): 55–60, https://doi.org/10.1111 /cdep.12357.

6   Simone P. Nguyen and Karl S. Rosengren, "Parental Reports of Children's Biological Knowledge and Misconceptions," *International Journal of Behavioral Development* 28, no. 5 (2004): 411–20, https://doi.org/10.1080/01650250444000108.

7   Earl A. Grollman, *Talking about Death: A Dialogue Between Parent and Child* (Boston: Beacon Press, 2011), 3.

8   "Concepts of Death by Age Group," University of Maryland Employee Assistance Program, last modified September 22, 2015, https://umb-eap.org/wp-content/uploads /pdf/DeathByAgeGroup.pdf; "Children's Understanding of Death at Different Ages," Child Bereavement UK, accessed May 10, 2022, https://www.childbereavementuk .org/information-childrens-understanding-of-death; "A Child's Concept of Death," Stanford Medicine, accessed August 1, 2022, https://www.stanfordchildrens.org/en /topic/default?id=a-childs-concept-of-death-90-P03044.

9   "Talking to Children about Death," National Institutes of Health Clinical Center Patient Education Materials, accessed April 18, 2022, https://portal.ct.gov/-/media /SDE/Digest/2018-19/childdeath.pdf.

10 Institute of Medicine (US) Committee for the Study of Health Consequences of the Stress of Bereavement, *Bereavement: Reactions, Consequences, and Care*, ed. Marian Osterweis, Frederic Solomon, and Morris Green (Washington, DC: National Academies Press, 1984), chap. 5, https://www.ncbi.nlm.nih.gov/books/NBK217849/.

11 Ann-Sofie Bergman, Ulf Axberg, and Elizabeth Hanson, "When a Parent Dies—A Systematic Review of the Effects of Support Programs for Parentally Bereaved Children and Their Caregivers," *BMC Palliative Care* 16, no. 39 (2017): 39, https://doi.org/10.1186 /s12904-017-0223-y; Steven Pham et al., "The Burden of Bereavement: Early-Onset Depression and Impairment in Youths Bereaved by Sudden Parental Death in a 7-Year Prospective Study," *American Journal of Psychiatry* 175, no. 9 (2018): 887–96, https:// doi.org/10.1176/appi.ajp.2018.17070792; Kathryn R. Cullen, "Persistent Impairment: Life After Losing a Parent," *American Journal of Psychiatry* 175, no. 9 (2018): 820–21, https://doi.org/ 10.1176/appi.ajp.2018.18050572.

12 Longbottom and Slaughter, "Sources of Children's Knowledge"; Esther Heerema, "Euphemisms for Dead, Death, and Dying: Are They Helpful or Harmful?,"

Verywell Health, last modified January 30, 2022, https://www.verywellhealth.com
/euphemisms-for-dead-death-or-dying-1131903.

13 Marilyn Price-Mitchell, "Loss of a Loved One: Finding Meaning Through
Metaphor," Roots of Action, July 30, 2012, https://www.rootsofaction.com/loss-of
-a-loved-one-gift-of-a-childs-sandcastle/.

14 Joe Primo, interview with the author, *How to Talk to Kids about Anything*, podcast, August 8, 2017, https://drrobynsilverman.com/how-to-talk-to-kids-about
-death-dying-with-joe-primo/.

15 Maria Trozzi, *Talking with Children about Loss: Words, Strategies, and Wisdom to Help
Children Cope with Death, Divorce, and Other Difficult Times* (New York: TarcherPerigee,
1999), 113.

16 John Holland, "Should Children Attend Their Parent's Funerals,?" *Pastoral
Care in Education* 22, no. 1 (March 2004): 10–14, https://doi.org/10.1111/j.0264
-3944.2004.00281.x; Mireia Campanera Reig, Rebeca Izquierdo, and Maite Gamarra,
"Children Aren't Allowed at Funeral Homes: A Study on Grief in Childhood and
Adolescence," *Catalonian Journal of Ethnology* 43, (2018): 92–98.

17 Primo, interview.

18 Phyllis R. Silverman and J. William Worden, "Children's Understanding of Funeral
Ritual," *OMEGA—Journal of Death and Dying* 25, no. 4 (1992): 319–31, https://doi.org
/10.2190/0QMH-FR98-R7XW-18VY.

19 Holland, "Should Children Attend"; "Youth & Funerals," Funeral Service
Foundation, accessed October 20, 2022, https://www.funeralservicefoundation.org
/resources-for-professionals/youth-funerals/.

20 "Youth & Funerals."

21 Katherine M. Crawford et al., "The Mental Health Effects of Pet Death during
Childhood: Is It Better to Have Loved and Lost Than Never to Have Loved at All?,"
European Child & Adolescent Psychiatry 30, no. 10 (October 2021): 1547–58, https://
doi.org/10.1007/s00787-020-01594-5; Matthew T. Cassels et al., "One of the Family?
Measuring Young Adolescents' Relationships with Pets and Siblings," *Journal of Applied
Developmental Psychology* 49, (March-April 2017): 12–20, https://doi.org/10.1016
/j.appdev.2017.01.003.

22 Wendy Van de Poll, interview with the author, *How to Talk to Kids about
Anything*, podcast, May 23, 2017, https://drrobynsilverman.com/how-to-talk
-to-kids-about-the-death-of-a-pet-with-wendy-van-de-poll/.

23 Moira Anderson Allen, "How Soon Should You Adopt a New Pet?," Grief Support
Center at Rainbows Bridge, accessed January 22, 2018, https://www.rainbowsbridge
.com/grief_support_center/grief_support/how_soon_should_i_get_a_new_pet.htm.

24 Aaron E. Carroll, "When Children Lose Siblings, They Face an Increased Risk of Death,"
New York Times, July 31, 2017, https://www.nytimes.com/2017/07/31/upshot/when
-children-lose-siblings-they-face-an-increased-risk-of-death.html.

25 Jan-Louise Godfrey, "The Impact of Sibling Death on Adolescent Psychosocial Development

and Psychological Wellbeing" (PhD diss., Swinburne University of Technology, 2017), 53, 67, https://researchbank.swinburne.edu.au/file/ea74d804-5c86-4f58-aa31-d20788 f41079/1/jan_louise_godfrey_thesis.pdf; Jason Fletcher et al., "A Sibling Death in the Family: Common and Consequential," *Demography* 50, no. 3 (2013): 803–26, https:// doi.org/ 10.1007/s13524-012-0162-4.

26 Mikael Rostila et al., "Experience of Sibling Death in Childhood and Risk of Psychiatric Care in Adulthood: A National Cohort Study from Sweden," *European Child & Adolescent Psychiatry* 28, no. 12 (2019): 1581–88, https://doi.org/10.1007 /s00787-019-01324-6; Darlene E. McCown and Clara Pratt, "Impact of Sibling Death on Children's Behavior," *Death Studies* 9, no. 3–4 (1985): 323–35, https:// doi.org/10.1080/07481188508252527; Albert C. Cain, Irene Fast, and Mary E. Erickson, "Children's Disturbed Reactions to the Death of a Sibling," *American Journal of Orthopsychiatry* 34, no. 4 (1964): 741–52, https://doi.org/10.1111/j.1939-0025.1964 .tb02375.x; John E. Baker, Mary Ann Sedney, and Esther Gross, "Psychological Tasks for Bereaved Children," *American Journal of Orthopsychiatry* 62, no. 1 (1992): 105–16, https:// doi.org/10.1037/h0079310; James M. Bolton et al., "Bereavement after Sibling Death: A Population-Based Longitudinal Case-Control Study," *World Psychiatry* 15, no. 1 (2016): 59–66, https://doi.org/10.1002/wps.20293; Terrah L. Foster et al., "Changes in Siblings after the Death of a Child from Cancer," *Cancer Nursing* 35, no. 5 (September-October 2012): 347–54, https://doi.org/10.1097/NCC.0b013e3182365646; Margaretha Nolbris and Anna-Lena Hellström, "Siblings' Needs and Issues When a Brother or Sister Dies of Cancer," *Journal of Pediatric Hematology/Oncology Nursing* 22, no. 4 (2005): 227–33, https://doi.org/10.1177/1043454205274722; Abby R. Rosenberg et al., "Long-Term Psychosocial Outcomes among Bereaved Siblings of Children with Cancer," *Journal of Pain and Symptom Management* 49, no. 1 (2015): 55–65, https://doi.org/10.1016 /j.jpainsymman.2014.05.006; Godfrey, "Impact of Sibling Death."

27 Joanna H. Fanos and Bruce G. Nickerson, "Long Term Effects of Sibling Death during Adolescence," *Journal of Adolescent Research* 6, no. 1 (1991): 70–82, https:// doi.org/10.1177/074355489161006; Australian Psychological Society, "Silent GriefThe Overlooked Impact of Losing a Sibling," Psychlopaedia, September 12, 2016, https://psychlopaedia.org/family-and-relationships/silent-grief-the-overlooked -impact-of-losing-a-sibling/.

28 Jadyn Glueck, interview with the author, *How to Talk to Kids about Anything*, pod-cast, November 4, 2019, https://drrobynsilverman.com/how-to-help-kids-grieve -when-a-sibling-dies/.

29 Primo, interview.

30 Australian Psychological Society, "Silent Grief."

31 Wayne Loder, "Only 16 Percent of Bereaved Parents Divorce, New Survey Reveals," Cision PR Web, October 12, 2006, https://www.prweb.com/releases/2006/10 /prweb449794.htm; "To the Newly Bereaved," Compassionate Friends, accessed September 2, 2022, https://www.compassionatefriends.org/to-the-newly-bereaved/.

32 Bryan Mellonie and Robert Ingpen, *Lifetimes: The Beautiful Way to Explain Death to Children* (New York: Bantam, 1983), 1.

Chapter 5: How to Talk to Kids about Diversity and Inclusion

1   *My Big Fat Greek Wedding*, directed by Joel Zwick (Alliance Cinema, 2002), 1:35.

2   David Oliver, "'I Am Not Ashamed': Disability Advocates, Experts Implore You to Stop Saying 'Special Needs,'" *USA Today*, June 11, 2021, https://www.usatoday.com /story/life/health-wellness/2021/06/11/disabled-not-special-needs-experts-explain -why-never-use-term/7591024002/; Andrew Pulrang, "Here Are Some Dos and Don'ts of Disability Language," *Forbes*, September 30, 2020, https:// www.forbes.com/sites/andrewpulrang/2020/09/30/here-are-some-dos-and -donts-of-disability-language/?sh=955c4e8d1700.

3   Jessica Cox, "How to Help Your Child with a Disability Overcome Adversity," Possible Thinking, January 15, 2016, https://jessicacox.com/how-to-help-your -disabled-child-overcome-adversity/.

4   Allaya Cooks-Campbell, "Why You Shouldn't Use 'Differently Abled' Anymore," Better Up, June 18, 2021, https://www.betterup.com/blog/differently-abled.

5   "Texas Man Born without Hands on Creating Art," CBS Mornings, July 27, 2022, https://www.cbsnews.com/video/texas-man-born-without-hands-on-creating-art/.

6   "Teenage Activist Marley Dias on the Trailblazer Who Inspired Her," CBS Mornings, February 20, 2020, https://www.cbsnews.com/video/teenage-activist -marley-dias-on-the-trailblazer-who-inspired-her/.

7   Understood, "Simone Biles Inspires Two Sisters with ADHD to Be Unstoppable," Facebook, October 17, 2017, https://www.facebook.com/Understood/videos/20977 02430256112/.

8   Dr. Thema Bryant, interview with the author, *How to Talk to Kids about Anything*, podcast, August 23, 2022, https://drrobynsilverman.com/how-to-talk-to-kids-about -trauma-recovery-with-dr-thema-bryant/.

9   "Older People Projected to Outnumber Children for First Time in U.S. History," United States Census Bureau, March 13, 2018, https://www.census.gov /newsroom/press-releases/2018/cb18-41-population-projections.html; Rogelio Sáenz and Dudley L. Poston Jr., "Children of Color Projected to Be Majority of U.S. Youth This Year," PBS, January 9, 2020, https://www.pbs.org/newshour/nation/children -of-color-projected-to-be-majority-of-u-s-youth-this-year.

10 "Jane Elliott's Brown Eye/Blue Eye Test," University of Northern Iowa, June 19, 2020, YouTube video, 4:39, https://www.youtube.com/watch?v=yTYL7NK8j5Y; Frontline, season 1985, episode 9, "A Class Divided," directed by William Peters, aired March 26, 1985 on PBS, https://www.pbs.org/wgbh/frontline/documentary/class-divided/; Jane Elliott (website), accessed November 3, 2022, https://janeelliott.com/.

11 Jane Elliott, interview with the author, email, August 13, 2022.

12 Jennifer A. Kotler, Tanya Z. Haider, and Michael H. Levine, "Sesame Workshop Identity Matters Study: Parents' and Educators' Perceptions of Children's Social Identity Development," Sesame Workshop, accessed October 3, 2022, https://www .sesameworkshop.org/what-we-do/research-and-innovation/sesame-workshop -identity-matters-study.

13 Jessica Sullivan, Leigh Wilton, and Evan P. Apfelbaum, "Adults Delay Conversations about Race Because They Underestimate Children's Processing of Race," *Journal of Experimental Psychology: General* 150, no. 2 (2021): 395–400, https://doi.org/10.1037 /xge0000851.

14 Monica P. Burns and Jessica A. Sommerville, "'I Pick You': The Impact of Fairness and Race on Infants' Selection of Social Partners," *Frontiers in Psychology* 5, no. 93 (2014): 1–10, https://doi.org/10.3389/fpsyg.2014.00093; Naiqi G. Xiao et al., "Infants Rely More on Gaze Cues from Own-Race Than Other-Race Adults for Learning under Uncertainty," *Child Development* 89, no. 3 (2017): e229–e244, https://doi.org/10.1111 /cdev.12798; Naiqi G. Xiao et al., "Older but Not Younger Infants Associate Own-Race Faces with Happy Music and Other-Race Faces with Sad Music," *Developmental Science* 21, no. 2 (2017): e12537, https://doi.org/10.1111/desc.12537; David J. Kelly et al., "Three Month-Olds, but Not Newborns, Prefer Own-Race Faces," *Developmental Science* 8, no. 6 (2005): F31–F36, https://doi.org/10.1111/j.1467-7687.2005.0434a.x.

15 Phyllis A. Katz and Jennifer A. Kofkin, "Race, Gender, and Young Children," in *Developmental Psychopathology: Perspectives on Adjustment, Risk, and Disorder*, ed. Suniya S. Luthar et al. (Cambridge, UK: Cambridge University Press, 1997), 51–74, https:// doi.org/10.1111/j.1467-7687.2005.0434a.x; Erin N. Winkler, "Children Are Not Colorblind: How Young Children Learn Race," University of Wisconsin-Milwaukee, last modified November 13, 2017, https://inclusions.org/wp-content/uploads/2017/11 /Children-are-Not-Colorblind.pdf.

16 Katherine A. Lingras, "Talking with Children about Race and Racism," *Journal of Health Service Psychology* 47, no. 1 (2021): 9–16, https://doi.org/10.1007/s42843-021-00027-4.

17 Christia Spears Brown, interview with the author, email, August 6, 2022.

18 Nadine M. Connell et al., "The Intersection of Perceptions and Experiences of Bullying by Race and Ethnicity among Middle School Students in the United States," *Deviant Behavior* 36, no. 10 (2015): 807–22, https://doi.org/10.1080/01639625.2014.977159.

19 Erin Pahlke, Rebecca S. Bigler, and Marie-Anne Suizzo, "Relations between Color-Blind Socialization and Children's Racial Bias: Evidence from European-American Mothers and Their Preschool Children," *Child Development* 83, no. 4 (2012): 1164–79, https://doi.org/10.1111/j.1467-8624.2012.01770.x.

20 Ibram X. Kendi, interview with the author, *How to Talk to Kids about Anything*, podcast, June 14, 2022, https://drrobynsilverman.com/how-to-raise-and-antiracist -with-ibram-x-kendi/.

21 Julie Dobrow, Calvin Gidney, and Jennifer Burton, "Why It's So Important for Kids to See Diverse TV and Movie Characters," The Conversation, March 7, 2018,

https://theconversation.com/why-its-so-important-for-kids-to-see-diverse-tv
-and-movie-characters-92576.

22 Toni Schmader, Katharina Block, and Brian Lickel, "Social Identity Threat in
Response to Stereotypic Film Portrayals: Effects on Self-Conscious Emotion and
Implicit Ingroup Attitudes," *Journal of Social Issues* 71, no. 1 (2015): 54–72, https://
doi.org/10.1111/josi.12096.

23 Brandee Blocker Anderson, "Unlearning: Who IS the Main Character?," PBS
Teacher's Lounge, March 11, 2021, https://www.pbs.org/education/blog/unlearning
-who-is-the-main-character.

24 "Books by and/or about Black, Indigenous and People of Color," Cooperative
Children's Book Center, School of Education, University of Wisconsin-Madison, last
modified January 11, 2023, https://ccbc.education.wisc.edu/literature-resources/ccbc
-diversity-statistics/books-by-about-poc-fnn/.

25 Madeline Tyner, interview with the author, email, September 12, 2022.

26 Kendi, interview.

27 *Chicago Tonight: Black Voices*, "Author Wants You to Become a Professional Troublemaker,"
directed by Marc Shaykin, aired March 28, 2021, on PBS, https://www.pbs.org/video
/professional-troublemaker-hi1p1u/.

28 Catherine A. Sanderson, *Why We Act: Turning Bystanders into Moral Rebels* (Cambridge,
MA: Belknap Press, 2020), 171.

29 Liz Kleinrock, *Start Here, Start Now: A Guide to Antibias and Antiracist Work in Your School
Community* (Portsmouth, NH: Heinemann, 2021), 56; Liz Kleinrock, interview with the
author, *How to Talk to Kids about Anything*, podcast, forthcoming, DrRobynSilverman.com.

30 Ibram X. Kendi, *How to Raise an Antiracist* (New York: One World, 2022), 70–71; Kendi,
interview.

31 Nate Popat, interview with the author, July 25, 2022.

32 "Living with Disabilities," United States Census Bureau, September 30, 2021, last
modified October 8, 2021, https://www.census.gov/library/visualizations/2021/comm
/living-with-disabilities.html.

33 Oliver, "'I Am Not Ashamed.'"

34 Morton Ann Gernsbacher et al., "'Special Needs' Is an Ineffective Euphemism,"
Cognitive Research 1, no. 29 (2016): 1–13, https://doi.org10.1186/s41235-016-0025-4.

35 Genevieve Shaw Brown, "Special Education Teacher Explains Why She Wants
to Be Called 'Accessibility Specialist," *Good Morning America*, November 2, 2020,
https://www.goodmorningamerica.com/family/story/special-education-teacher
-explains-called-accessibility-specialist-73975480?.

36 Oliver, "'I Am Not Ashamed.'"

37 Sian Cane, "Lizzo Removes 'Harmful' Ableist Slur from New Song Grrrls after
Criticism," *Guardian*, June 13, 2022, https://www.theguardian.com/music/2022/jun/14
/lizzo-removes-harmful-ableist-slur-from-new-song-grrrls-after-criticism.

38 Mackenzie Saunders, "Why I Say 'Disabled Person' Rather Than 'Person with a Disibility',"

Spinal Cord Injury Law Firm (blog), accessed June 4, 2023, https://spinalcordinjury lawyers.com/blog/why-i-say-disabled-person-rather-than-person-with-a-disability/.

39 Robert Melillo, interview with the author, *How to Talk to Kids about Anything*, podcast, November 12, 2018, https://drrobynsilverman.com/how-to-help-kids-with-autism-adhd -and-other-neurological-disorders-gain-better-brain-balance-with-dr-robert-melillo/.

40 Devon Price, *Unmasking Autism: Discovering the New Faces of Neurodiversity* (New York: Harmony Books, 2022), 23.

41 Mona Delahooke, interview with the author, *How to Talk to Kids about Anything*, podcast, June 18, 2019, https://drrobynsilverman.com/how-to-look-beyond-behaviors-to -solve-childrens-behavioral-challenges-with-mona-delahooke-phd-rerelease/.

42 "Students with Disabilities and Bullying," PACER's National Bullying Prevention Center, accessed May 18, 2022, https://www.pacer.org/bullying/info/students-with-disabilities/.

43 UNESCO, "Violence and Bullying in Educational Settings: The Experiences of Young People and Children with Disabilities," UNESCO, 2021, https://unesdoc.unesco.org /ark:/48223/pf0000378061.

44 Nicole Baumer and Julia Frueh, "What Is Neurodiversity?," Harvard Health Publishing, November 23, 2021, https://www.health.harvard.edu/blog/what-is -neurodiversity-202111232645.

45 Deborah Reber, interview with the author, *How to Talk to Kids about Anything*, podcast, January 3, 2018, https://drrobynsilverman.com/how-to-talk-to-kids-about-differently -wired-children-with-debbie-reber/.

46 Lisa Selin Davis, interview with the author, *How to Talk to Kids about Anything*, podcast, September 15, 2020, https://drrobynsilverman.com/how-to-talk-to-kids -about-gender-and-identity-with-lisa-selin-davis/.

47 "Makeup Artist Statistics by Gender," Zippia, last modified September 9, 2022, https:// www.zippia.com/makeup-artist-jobs/demographics/.

48 "Robotics Engineer Demographics in the United States," Career Explorer, accessed October   5,   2022,   https://www.careerexplorer.com/careers/robotics-engineer /demographics/.

49 Jon M. Jachimowicz, "3 Reasons It's So Hard to 'Follow Your Passion,'" *Harvard Business Review*, October 15, 2019, https://hbr.org/2019/10/3-reasons -its-so-hard-to-follow-your-passion.

50 "Are Gendered Toys Impacting Child Development?," Creative Play, accessed February 22, 2022, https://creativeplayuk.com/gendered-toys-impacting-childhood-development/.

51 Dr. Nawar Al-Hassan Golley, interview with the author, email, September 1, 2022.

52 Geena Davis Institute on Gender in Media, "Ready for Girls," LEGO, accessed October 11, 2021, https://seejane.org/wp-content/uploads/LEGO-Ready-for-Girls -Infographic.pdf.

53 Judith Blakemore and Renee Centers, "Characteristics of Boys' and Girls' Toys," *Sex Roles* 53, no. 9–10 (2005): 619–33, https://doi.org/10.1007/s11199-005-7729-0; "What the Research Says: Gender-Typed Toys," NAEYC, accessed October 31, 2022, https:// www.naeyc.org/resources/topics/play/gender-typed-toys.

54 Jeffrey Trawick-Smith et al., "Effects of Toys on the Play Quality of Preschool Children: Influence of Gender, Ethnicity, and Socioeconomic Status," *Early Childhood Education Journal* 43, no. 4 (2014): 249–56, https://doi.org/ 10.1007/s10643-014-0644-7.

55 "Global Gender Gap Report 2022," World Economic Forum, July 13, 2022, https:// www3.weforum.org/docs/WEF_GGGR_2022.pdf.

56 "Upworthy Voices: The Story of Free Mom Hugs," Upworthy, June 1, 2021, YouTube video, 3:34, https://www.youtube.com/watch?v=blyxFoZAElo.

57 Sara Cunningham, interview with the author, email, September 9, 2022.

58 "Estimate of How Often LGBTQ Youth Attempt Suicide in the U.S.," Trevor Project, March 11, 2021, https://www.thetrevorproject.org/research-briefs/estimate-of-how -often-lgbtq-youth-attempt-suicide-in-the-u-s/.

59 "Estimate of How Often."

60 "2022 National Survey on LGBTQ Youth Mental Health," Trevor Project, accessed November 6, 2022, https://www.thetrevorproject.org/survey-2022/.

61 Emma Renold et al., "How Gender Matters to Children and Young People Living in England," Cardiff University, last modified December 18, 2017, https://orca .cardiff.ac.uk/id/eprint/107599/1/How%20Gender%20Matters.pdf; Kim Allen et al., "Trailblazing the Gender Revolution? Young People's Understandings of Gender Diversity through Generation and Social Change," *Journal of Youth Studies* 25, no. 5 (2022): 650–66, https://doi.org/10.1080/13676261.2021.1923674; Barbara J. Risman, "2016 Southern Sociological Society Presidential Address: Are Millennials Cracking the Gender Structure?," *Social Currents* 4, no. 3 (2017): 208–27, https:// doi.org/10.1177/2329496517697145.

62 Joseph G. Kosciw et al., "The 2019 National School Climate Survey: The Experiences of Lesbian, Gay, Bisexual, Transgender, and Queer Youth in Our Nation's Schools," GLSEN, November 20, 2020, https://www.glsen.org/research /2019-national-school-climate-survey.

63 "Gender-Affirming Care for Youth," Trevor Project, January 29, 2020, https:// www.thetrevorproject.org/research-briefs/gender-affirming-care-for-youth/.

64 Kristin Russo, interview with the author, *How to Talk to Kids about Anything*, pod- cast, May 5, 2020, https://drrobynsilverman.com/how-to-help-parents-understand -support-their-lgbtq-kids-with-kristin-russo-rerelease/.

65 Carolyn Hays, interview with the author, *How to Talk to Kids about Anything*, podcast, June 7, 2023, https://drrobynsilverman.com/how-to-talk-to-kids-about-transgender -people-with-carolyn-hays/.

66 "Gender-Inclusive Language," United Nations, accessed August 1, 2022, https:// www.un.org/en/gender-inclusive-language/.

67 Russo, interview.

68 Jeffrey Marsh, interview with the author, *How to Talk to Kids about Anything*, pod- cast, July 26, 2022, https://drrobynsilverman.com/how-to-talk-to-kids-about-self -esteem-gender-identity-being-yourself-with-jeffrey-marsh/.

69 Alex Corbitt, interview with the author, *How to Talk to Kids about Anything*,

podcast, May 1, 2018, https://drrobynsilverman.com/how-to-inspire-children -to-read-with-alex-corbitt/.

70   Ashlie Ford, "Bryan Stevenson: Get Proximate on Issues of Race and Injustice," Texas Lutheran University, June 6, 2020, https://www.tlu.edu/news/bryan-stevenson -get-proximate-on-issues-of-race-and-injustice.

71   Irshad Manji, interview with the author, *How to Talk to Kids about Anything*, podcast, January 18, 2022, https://drrobynsilverman.com/how-to-talk-to-kids-about -labels-and-diversity-with-irshad-manji/.

72   "Award-Winning PBS Kids Talk About: Race & Racism," PBS Kids, October 9, 2020, YouTube video, 28:00, https://www.youtube.com/watch?v=_fbQBKwdWPg.

73   Kendi, interview.

Chapter 6: How to Talk to Kids about Divorce and Nontraditional Family Structures

1   George P. Murdock, *Social Structure* (Oxford, UK: Macmillan, 1949), 1; Joel A. Muraco, "The Family," Noba, accessed June 6, 2022, https://nobaproject.com/modules/the -family.

2   "The Majority of Children Live with Two Parents, Census Bureau Reports," United States Census Bureau, November 17, 2016, https://www.census.gov/newsroom/press -releases/2016/cb16-192.html.

3   Abbie Goldberg, interview with the author, *How to Talk to Kids about Anything*, podcast, May 4, 2022, https://drrobynsilverman.com/how-to-talk-to-kids-about-diverse -family-structures-with-abbie-goldberg-ph-d/.

4   Sue Cornbluth, interview with the author, *How to Talk to Kids about Anything*, podcast, October 24, 2017, https://drrobynsilverman.com/how-to-build-self-esteem-in-kids -who-were-adopted-or-fostered-with-dr-sue-cornbluth/.

5   Leslie Reynolds, "Divorce Rate in the U.S.: Geographic Variation, 2019," Bowling Green State University, updated April 8, 2021, https://www.bgsu.edu/ncfmr/resources/data /family-profiles/reynolds-divorce-rate-geographic-variation-2019-fp-20-25.html; Leslie Reynolds, "Marriage Rate in the U.S.: Geographic Variation, 2019," Bowling Green State University, updated April 13, 2021, https://www.bgsu.edu/ncfmr/resources/data /family-profiles/reynolds-marriage-rate-geographic-variation-2019-fp-20-24.html; Krista K. Westrick-Payne, Wendy D. Manning, and Lisa Carlson, "Pandemic Shortfall in Marriages and Divorces in the United States," *Socius: Sociological Research for a Dynamic World* 8, no. 1–3 (2022): 1–7, https://doi.org/ 10.1177/23780231221090192.

6   "Children and Divorce," American Academy of Child & Adolescent Psychiatry, updated January 2017, https://www.aacap.org/AACAP/Families_and_Youth/Facts _for_Families/FFF-Guide/Children-and-Divorce-001.aspx.

7   "Sesame Street: Little Children, Big Challenges—Divorce—Sizzle Reel," Sesame Street, December 11, 2012, YouTube video, 2:26https://www.youtube.com/watch?v

=UXjmqfg0Iw8; "Dealing with Divorce," Sesame Street in Communities, accessed July 29, 2022, https://sesamestreetincommunities.org/topics/divorce/.

8   Robert E. Emery, *The Truth about Children and Divorce* (New York: Plume, 2006), 6.

9   JoAnne Pedro-Carroll, *Putting Children First: Proven Parenting Strategies for Helping Children Thrive Through Divorce* (New York: Avery, 2010), 13.

10   Ronald L. Simons et al., "Explaining the Higher Incidence of Adjustment Problems among Children of Divorce Compared with Those in Two-Parent Families," *Journal of Marriage and the Family* 61, no. 4 (1999): 1020–33, https://doi.org/10.2307/354021; E. Mavis Hetherington and Anne Mitchell Elmore, "Risk and Resilience in Children Coping with Their Parents' Divorce and Remarriage," in *Resilience and Vulnerability: Adaptation in the Context of Childhood Adversities*, ed. Suniya S. Luthar (Cambridge, UK: Cambridge University Press, 2003), 182–212; Rianne van Dijk et al., "A Meta-Analysis on Interparental Conflict, Parenting, and Child Adjustment in Divorced Families: Examining Mediation Using Meta-Analytic Structural Equation Models," *Clinical Psychology Review* 79, no. 101861 (2020): 1–15, https://doi.org/10.1016/j.cpr.2020.101861.

11   Paul R. Amato and Bruce Keith, "Parental Divorce and the Well-Being of Children: A Meta-Analysis," *Psychological Bulletin* 110, no. 1 (1991): 26–46, https://doi.org/10.1037/0033-2909.110.1.26; John P. Hoffmann and Robert A. Johnson, "A National Portrait of Family Structure and Adolescent Drug Use," *Journal of Marriage and Family* 60, no. 3 (1998): 633–45, https://doi.org/10.2307/353534; Frank F. Furstenberg Jr. and Julien O. Teitler, "Reconsidering the Effects of Marital Disruption: What Happens to Children of Divorce in Early Adulthood?," *Journal of Family Issues* 15, no. 2 (1994): 173–90, https://doi.org/10.1177/0192513X9401500200; Sharlene A. Wolchik, Clorinda E. Schenck, and Irwin N. Sandler, "Promoting Resilience in Youth from Divorced Families: Lessons Learned from Experimental Trials of the New Beginnings Program," *Journal of Personality* 77, no. 6 (2009): 1833–68, https://doi.org/10.1111/j.1467-6494.2009.00602.x.

12   Karey L. O'Hara et al., "Longitudinal Effects of PostDivorce Interparental Conflict on Children's Mental Health Problems Through Fear of Abandonment: Does Parenting Quality Play a Buffering Role?," *Child Development* 92, no. 4 (2021): 1476–93, https://doi.org/10.1111/cdev.13539.

13   Casey L. James, "Communication in Divorced Families with Children," *Hilltop Review* 10, no. 2 (2018): 83–90, https://scholarworks.wmich.edu/hilltopreview/vol10/iss2/11/.

14   M. Gary Neuman and Patricia Romanowski, *Helping Your Kids with Divorce the Sandcastles Way* (New York: Times Books, 1998), 31–32.

15   Tina Payne Bryson, interview with the author, *How to Talk to Kids about Anything*, podcast, February 3, 2020, https://drrobynsilverman.com/how-to-show-up-for-our-children-with-tina-payne-bryson-phd/.

16   Jean McBride, *Talking to Children about Divorce: A Parent's Guide to Healthy Communication at Each Stage of Divorce* (Berkeley: Althea Press, 2016), 23, 61.

17   Christina McGhee, *Parenting Apart: How Separated and Divorced Parents Raise Happy and Secure Kids* (New York: Berkley, 2010), 180.

18 James, "Communication in Divorced Families"; Tara G. McManus and Sandra Donovan, "Communication Competence and Feeling Caught: Explaining Perceived Ambiguity in Divorce-Related Communication, *Communication Quarterly* 60, no. 2 (2012): 255–77, https://doi.org/10.1080/01463373.2012.669328.

19 Christina McGhee, interview with the author, *How to Talk to Kids about Anything*, podcast, June 13, 2017, https://drrobynsilverman.com/how-to-talk-to-kids-about-divorce -with-christina-mcghee/.

20 JoAnne Pedro-Carroll, "Reducing Risk and Fostering Resilience in Children and Families," Werkplaats Samen, accessed August 28, 2020, https://www.werkplaatssamen .nl/wp-content/uploads/2019/02/Dr.-JoAnne-Pedro-Carroll.pdf.

21 "Reminding Kids It's Not Their Fault," Sesame Street in Communities, January 20, 2021, YouTube video, 1:14, https://www.youtube.com/watch?v=Px3a9B3o5KI.

22 Matthew M. Stevenson et al., "Fathers, Divorce, and Child Custody," in *Handbook of Father Involvement: Multidisciplinary Perspectives*, ed. Natasha J. Cabrera and Catherine S. Tamis-LeMonda, 2nd ed. (New York: Routledge, 2013), 379–96.

23 Sara Stillman Berger, "How to Co-Parent Successfully," Oprah Daily, June 20, 2019, https://www.oprahdaily.com/life/relationships-love/a28089403/co-parenting-tips/.

24 Robert Bauserman, "Child Adjustment in Joint-Custody Versus Sole-Custody Arrangements: A Meta-Analytic Review," *Journal of Family Psychology* 16, no. 1 (2002): 91–102, https://doi.org/10.1037//0893-3200.16.1.91; Linda Nielsen, "Joint Versus Sole Physical Custody: Children's Outcomes Independent of Parent-Child Relationships, Income, and Conflict in 60 Studies," *Journal of Divorce & Remarriage* 59, no. 4 (2018): 247–81, https://doi.org/10.1080/10502556.2018.1454204; Richard A. Warshak, "Social Science and Parenting Plans for Young Children: A Consensus Report," *Psychology, Public Policy, and Law* 20, no. 1 (2014): 46–67, https://doi.org/10.1037/law0000005; Emma Fransson et al., "Psychological Complaints among Children in Joint Physical Custody and Other Family Types: Considering Parental Factors," *Scandinavian Journal of Public Health* 44, no.2 (2016): 177–83, https://doi.org/ 10.1177/1403494815614463; Malin Bergström et al., "Fifty Moves a Year: Is There an Association between Joint Physical Custody and Psychosomatic Problems in Children?," *Journal of Epidemiology and Community Health* 69, no. 8 (2015): 769–74, https://doi.org/10.1136/jech-2014-205058; Emma Johnson, "Shared Parenting Research," Moms for Shared Parenting, March 27, 2019, https://momsforsharedparenting.org/shared-parenting-research/.

25 Margolin and Gallant, interview.

26 McGhee, interview.

27 Tamara D. Afifi et al., "Inappropriate Parental Divorce Disclosures: The Factors That Prompt Them, and Their Impact on Parents' and Adolescents' Well- Being," *Communication Monographs* 74, no. 1 (2007): 78–102, https://doi.org /10.1080/03637750701196870; Tamara D. Afifi and Paul Schrodt, "Uncertainty and the Avoidance of the State of One's Family in Stepfamilies, Postdivorce Single-Parent Families, and First-Marriage Families," *Human Communication Research* 29, no. 4 (2003):

516–32, https://doi.org/10.1111/j.1468–2958.2003.tb00854.x; Jonathon J. Beckmeyer, Melinda S. Markham, and Jessica Troilo, "Domains of Ongoing Communication Between Former Spouses: Associations with Parenting Stress and Children's Post-Divorce Well-Being," *Journal of Family Issues* 43, no. 6 (2021): 15791600, https://doi.org/ 10.1177/0192513X211029264; Paige W. Toller and M. Chad McBride, "Enacting Privacy Rules and Protecting Disclosure Recipients: Parents' Communication with Children Following the Death of a Family Member," *Journal of Family Communication* 13, no.1 (2013): 32–45, https://doi.org/10.1080/15267431.2012.742091; Konomi Asai and Keigo Asai, "A Pilot Study to Assess Positive and Negative Post-Divorce Parental Disclosures," *International Journal of Brief Therapy and Family Science* 11, no. 1 (2021): 14–25, https://doi.org/10.35783/ijbf.11.1_14; Kim Gale Dolgin and Nicci Berndt, "Adolescents' Perceptions of Their Parents' Disclosure to Them," *Journal of Adolescence* 20, no. 4 (1997): 431–41, https://doi.org/10.1006/jado.1997.0098.

28 Rakel Berman and Kristian Daneback, "Children in Dual-Residence Arrangements: A Literature Review" *Journal of Family Studies* 28, no. 4 (2020): 1–18, https://doi.org/1 0.1080/13229400.2020.1838317; Malin Bergström et al., "Preschool Children Living in Joint Physical Custody Arrangements Show Less Psychological Symptoms Than Those Living Mostly or Only with One Parent," *Acta Paediatrica* 107, no. 2 (2018): 294–300, https://doi.org/10.1111/apa.14004; Malin Bergström et al., "Mental Health in Swedish Children Living in Joint Physical Custody and Their Parents' Life Satisfaction: A Cross-Sectional Study" *Scandinavian Journal of Psychology* 55, no. 5 (2014): 433–39, https://doi.org/10.1111/sjop.12148; Malin Bergström et al., "Living in Two Homes—A Swedish National Survey of Wellbeing in 12 and 15 Year Olds with Joint Physical Custody" *BMC Public Health* 13, no. 1 (2013): 868–75, https://doi.org/10.1186/1471 -2458-13-868; Emma Fransson, Anders Hjern, and Malin Bergström, "What Can We Say Regarding Shared Parenting Arrangements for Swedish Children?," *Journal of Divorce and Remarriage* 59, no. 5 (2018): 34958, https://doi.org/10.1080/10502556.2018.1454 198; Stephen Gilmore, "Contact/Shared Residence and Child Well-Being: Research Evidence and Its Implications for Legal Decision-Making," *International Journal of Law, Policy and the Family* 20, no. 3 (2006): 344–65, https://doi.org/10.1093/lawfam/ebl016; Jani Turunen, Emma Fransson, and Malin Bergström, "SelfEsteem in Children in Joint Physical Custody and Other Living Arrangement," *Public Health* 149, (2017): 106–12, https://doi.org/10.1016/j.puhe.2017.04.009.

29 Rakel Berman, "Children's Influence on Dual Residence Arrangements: Exploring Decision-Making Practices," *Children and Youth Services Review* 91, (2018): 105–14, https://doi.org/10.1016/j.childyouth.2018.05.038; Monica Campo et al., "Shared Parenting Time in Australia: Exploring Children's Views," *Journal of Social Welfare and Family Law* 34, no. 3 (2013): 295–313, https://doi.org/ 10.1080/09649069.2012.750480; Gry Mette D. Haugen, "Children's Perspectives on Everyday Experiences of Shared Residence: Time, Emotions and Agency Dilemmas," *Children & Society* 24, no. 2 (2010): 112–22, https://doi.org/10.1111/j.1099-0860.2008.00198.x; Carol Smart, "Equal Shares:

Rights for Fathers or Recognition for Children?," *Critical Social Policy* 24, no. 4 (2004): 484–503, https://doi.org/10.1177/0261018304046673.

30 Earl Grollman, *Explaining Divorce to Children* (Boston: Beacon Press, 1969), 43.

31 Megan Leahy, "I'm a Divorced Parent: What's the Best Way to Talk to My Kids about My Ex?," *Washington Post*, February 9, 2022, https://www.washingtonpost.com /parenting/2022/02/09/divorced-parent-complains-kids/.

32 Nielsen, "Joint Versus Sole Physical Custody"; Warshak, "Social Science and Parenting Plans."

33 Molly C. Easterlin et al., "Association of Team Sports Participation with LongTerm Mental Health Outcomes among Individuals Exposed to Adverse Childhood Experiences," *JAMA Pediatrics* 173, no. 7 (2019): 681–88, https://doi.org/10.1001 /jamapediatrics.2019.1212.

34 Rebecca Fraser-Thrill, "How Family Traditions Help Form Stronger Bonds," *Verywell Family*, July 1, 2021, https://www.verywellfamily.com/family-rituals-meaning -examples-3288187.

35 Alexandra Stolnicu et al., "Healing the Separation in High-Conflict PostDivorce Co-Parenting," *Frontiers in Psychology* 13, (2022): 913447, https://doi.org/10.3389 /fpsyg.2022.913447.

36 Gretchen Livingston, "The Changing Profile of Unmarried Parents," Pew Research Center, April 25, 2018, https://www.pewresearch.org/social-trends/2018/04/25/the -changing-profile-of-unmarried-parents/.

37 Nefertiti Austin, interview with the author, *How to Talk to Kids about Anything*, podcast, June 23, 2020, https://drrobynsilverman.com/how-to-talk-about-racism-adoption-and -parenting-a-black-boy-in-america-with-nefertiti-austin/.

38 Shoshana K. Goldberg and Kerith J. Conron, "How Many Same-Sex Couples in the US are Raising Children?," UCLA School of Law: Williams Institute, July 2018, https:// williamsinstitute.law.ucla.edu/publications/same-sex-parents-us/.

39 "Parenting in America: Outlook, Worries, Aspirations Are Strongly Linked to Financial Situation," Pew Research Center, December 17, 2015, https://www.pewresearch.org /social-trends/2015/12/17/1-the-american-family-today/.

40 Michelle Darrisaw, "Mashonda Tifrere on Co-Parenting with Her Ex Swizz Beatz and His Wife, Alicia Keys," Oprah Daily, September 25, 2018, https://www.oprahdaily.com /life/relationships-love/a23368039/mashonda-tifrere-coparenting-advice/.

41 Mashonda Tifrere, "Mashonda Tifrere Breaks Down the Secrets to Co-Parenting in New Book," *Essence*, December 6, 2020, https://www.essence.com/entertainment /mashonda-tifrere-co-parenting-new-book-blend/.

42 Ron Deal, interview with the author, *How to Talk to Kids about Anything*, podcast, April 21, 2020, https://drrobynsilverman.com/how-to-talk-to-kids-about-step-families-and -blended-families-with-ron-l-deal-mmft/.

43 Cathy Cassani Adams, *Zen Parenting: Caring for Ourselves and Our Children in an Unpredictable World* (New York: Hachette Go, 2022), 3.

44 "U.S. Adoption Statistics," Adoption Network, accessed November 8, 2022, https://adoptionnetwork.com/adoption-myths-facts/domestic-us-statistics/.

45 Amanda L. Baden et al., "Delaying Adoption Disclosure: A Survey of Late Discovery Adoptees," *Journal of Family Issues* 40, no. 9 (2019): 115480, https://doi.org/10.1177/0192513X19829503.

46 Carrie Goldman, interview with the author, *How to Talk to Kids about Anything*, podcast, January 15, 2018, https://drrobynsilverman.com/how-to-talk-to-kids-about-adoption-with-carrie-goldman/.

47 Amanda L. Baden, "'Do You Know Your Real Parents?' and Other Adoption Microaggressions," *Adoption Quarterly* 19, no.1 (2016): 1–25, https://doi.org/10.1080/10926755.2015.1026012.

48 Allison Davis Maxon, "Words Matter!," LinkedIn, December 12, 2018, https://www.linkedin.com/pulse/words-matter-allison-davis-maxon/.

49 Goldberg, interview.

50 Alex Haley, *Roots: The Enhanced Edition: The Saga of an American Family* (New York: Da Capo, 2016), back cover.

51 Sharon Roszia and Allison Davis Maxon, *The Seven Core Issues in Adoption and Permanency: A Comprehensive Guide to Promoting Understanding and Healing in Adoption, Foster Care, Kinship Families and Third Party Reproduction* (Philadelphia: Jessica Kingsley, 2019) 51; Sharon Roszia and Allison Davis Maxon, *The Seven Core Issues Workbook for Parents of Traumatized Children and Teens* (Philadelphia: Jessica Kingsley, 2022), 17.

52 Abbie E. Goldberg, "I've Been Following Families in Open Adoptions for 15 Years, Observing Adoptive Parents' Struggles to Share Painful Origin Stories with Kids," The Conversation, May 26, 2020, https://theconversation.com/ive-been-following-families-in-open-adoptions-for-15-years-observing-adoptive-parents-struggles-to-share-painful-origin-stories-with-kids-138672.

53 Betsy Keefer and Jayne E. Schooler, *Telling the Truth to Your Adopted or Foster Child: Making Sense of the Past* (New York: Bergin & Garvey Trade, 2000), xiii; David Brodzinsky, "Family Structural Openness and Communication Openness as Predictors in the Adjustment of Adopted Children," *Adoption Quarterly* 9, no. 4 (2006): 1–18, https://doi.org/10.1300/J145v09n04_01; Santona Alessandra et al., "Talking about the Birth Family since the Beginning: The Communicative Openness in the New Adoptive Family," *International Journal of Environmental Research and Public Health* 19, no. 3 (2022): 1203, https://doi.org/10.3390%2Fijerph19031203; David Brodzinsky, "Children's Understanding of Adoption: Developmental and Clinical Implications," *Professional Psychology: Research and Practice* 42, no. 2 (2011): 200–207, http://doi.org/10.1037/a0022415.

54 Baden and Howard, "Adolescents and Identity," Rudd Adoption Conference, March 2012, YouTube video, 1:01:34, https://www.youtube.com/watch?v=CBnv7W0Vh38.

55 Jennifer Gilmore, "Is Superman the Greatest Adoption Story of All Time?," *Dame Magazine*, November 23, 2015, https://www.damemagazine.com/2015/11/23/superman-greatest-adoption-story-all-time-01/.

56 Deborah N. Silverstein and Sharon Kaplan, "Lifelong Issues in Adoption," Accord, accessed November 8, 2022, https://accordcoalition.org.uk/wp-content /uploads/2012/01/Lifelong-Issues-in-Adoption.pdf.

57 Roszia and Davis Maxon, *Seven Core Issues in Adoption*, 1.

58 Carrie Goldman, interview with the author, Zoom, March 3, 2022.

59 "Second Best or Second Choice: Adoption After Fertility," Creating a Family, last modified 2016, https://creatingafamily.org/adoption-category/choice-adoption-infertility/ .

60 Nicholas Zill, "The Changing Face of Adoption in the United States," Institute for Family Studies, August 7, 2017, https://ifstudies.org/blog/the-changing-face -of-adoption-in-the-united-states.

61 Allon Kalisher, Jennah Gosciak, and Jill Spielfogel, "The Multiethnic Placement Act 25 Years Later: Trends in Adoption and Transracial Adoption," Office of the Assistant Secretary for Planning and Evaluation, U.S. Department of Health and Human Services, December 2020, https://aspe.hhs.gov/sites/default/files/private/pdf/264526 /MEPA-Data-report.pdf.

62 Nicholas Zill, "Analysis of Data from the Early Childhood Longitudinal Studies of the Kindergarten Class of 2010–2011 and the Kindergarten Class of 1998–1999," National Center for Education Statistics, U.S. Department of Education, 2017, https:// nces.ed.gov/pubs2015/2015078.pdf.

63 Baden and Howard, "Adolescents and Identity."

64 "Transracial Parenting in Foster Care and Adoption: Strengthening Your Bicultural Family," Iowa Foster & Adoptive Parents Association, accessed November 8, 2022, http://www.ifapa.org/pdf_docs/transracialparenting.pdf.

65 Amanda L. Baden and Jeanne Howard, "Adolescents and Identity."

66 Sydney K. Morgan and Kimberly J. Langrehr, "Transracially Adoptive Parents' Colorblindness and Discrimination Recognition: Adoption Stigma as Moderator," *Cultural Diversity Ethnic Minority Psychology* 25, no. 2 (2019): 242–52, https://doi.org /10.1037/cdp0000219; Mariette Williams, "How to Talk to Your Transracially Adopted Child about Race," What to Expect, June 12, 2020, https://www.whattoexpect.com /family/adoption/talking-to-transracially-adopted-children-about-race/; Karen Valby, "The Realities of Raising a Kid of a Different Race," *Time*, accessed May 14, 2023, https:// time.com/the-realities-of-raising-a-kid-of-a-different-race/.

67 Tonia Jacobs Deese, "Parenting a Child of a Different Race," *Fostering Perspectives* 20, no. 1 (November 2015), https://fosteringperspectives.org/fpv20n1/Deese.htm.

68 "Finding Families for African American Children: The Role of Race & Law in Adoption from Foster Care Policy & Practice Perspective," Evan B. Donaldson Adoption Institute, May 14, 2008, https://www.nationalcenteronadoptionand permanency.net/post/finding-families-for-african-american-children.

69 Baden and Howard, "Adolescents and Identity," Rudd Adoption Conference, YouTube, March 2012, https://www.youtube.com/watch?v=CBnv7W0Vh38.

70 Michelle Li, "Transracial Adoptees Say Their Parents Need to Talk to Them about

Race," King 5, December 15, 2020, https://www.king5.com/article/news/community
/facing-race/transracial-adoption/281-724574f9-afc4-4d5c-842a-691270fae931.

71 Jacobs Deese, "Parenting a Child."

72 Colleen Butler-Sweet, "'Race Isn't What Defines Me': Exploring Identity Choices in
Transracial, Biracial, and Monoracial Families," *Social Identities: Journal for the Study of
Race, Nation and Culture* 17, no. 6 (2011): 747–69, https://doi.org/10.1080/13504630.
2011.606672; Gina E. Miranda Samuels, "Being Raised by White People: Navigating
Racial Difference among Adopted Multiracial Adults," *Journal of Marriage and Family*
71, no. 1 (February 2009): 80–94, https://doi.org/10.1111/j.1741-3737.2008.00581.x.

73 Ellen Greenlaw, "Talking to Your Child about Slurs: When Words Hurt," Boston
Children's Hospital, April 29, 2021, https://answers.childrenshospital.org/talking
-about-slurs/.

74 Corbitt, interview.

75 "Parenting Your Adopted Teenager," Factsheets for Families, Child Welfare Information
Gateway, Children's Bureau, November 2020, https://www.childwelfare.gov/pubPDFs
/parent_teenager.pdf.

76 Baden and Howard, "Adolescents and Identity."

77 Goldberg, interview.

Chapter 7: How to Talk to Kids about Mistakes and Failure

1 Gordan L. Flett and Paul L. Hewitt, "The Perils of Perfectionism in Sports and
Exercise," *Current Directions in Psychological Science* 14, no. 1 (2005): 14–18, https://doi.org
/10.1111/j.0963-7214.2005.00326.x.

2 Thomas Curran and Andrew P. Hill, "Young People's Perceptions of Their Parents'
Expectations and Criticism Are Increasing over Time: Implications for Perfectionism,"
Psychological Bulletin 148, no. 1–2 (2022): 107–28, https://psycnet.apa.org/doi/10.1037
/bul0000347; Martin M. Smith et al., "Perfectionism and Narcissism: A Meta-
Analytic Review," *Journal of Research in Personality* 64, (October 2016): 90–101, https://
doi.org/10.1016/j.jrp.2016.07.012; Sarah J. Egan, Tracey D. Wade, and Roz Shafran,
"Perfectionism as a Transdiagnostic Process: A Clinical Review," *Clinical Psychological
Review* 31, *no. 2 (March* 2011): 20312, https://doi.org/10.1016/j.cpr.2010.04.009.

3 Randy O. Frost et al., "Reactions to Mistakes among Subjects High and Low in
Perfectionistic Concern over Mistakes," *Cognitive Therapy and Research* 19, (1995):
195–205, https://doi.org/10.1007/BF02229694; Paul L. Hewitt and Gordon L. Flett,
"Perfectionism in the Self and Social Contexts: Conceptualization, Assessment, and
Association with Psychopathology" *Journal of Personality and Social Psychology* 60, no. 3
(1991): 456–70, https://doi.org/10.1037//0022-3514.60.3.456.

4 Thomas Curran and Andrew P. Hill, "Perfectionism Is Increasing over Time: A
Meta-Analysis of Birth Cohort Differences from 1989 to 2016," *Psychological Bulletin*
145, no. 4 (2019): 410–29, https://doi.org/10.1037/bul0000138; Andrew P. Hill and

Thomas Curran, "Multidimensional Perfectionism and Burnout: A Meta-Analysis," *Personality and Social Psychology Review* 20, no. 3 (2016): 269–88, https://doi.org /10.1177/1088868315596286.

5 Karina Limburg et al., "The Relationship Between Perfectionism and Psychopathology: A Meta-Analysis," *Journal of Clinical Psychology* 73, no. 10 (2017): 130126, https://doi.org /10.1002/jclp.224–35.

6 Andrew P. Hill, email to the author, February 21, 2020.

7 Robert C. Wilson et al., "The Eighty-Five Percent Rule for Optimal Learning," *Nature Communications* 10, (2019): 4646, https://doi.org/10.1038/s41467-019-12552-4.

8 Andrew P. Hill and Michael Grugan, "Introducing Perfectionistic Climate," *Perspectives on Early Childhood Psychology and Education* 4, no. 2 (2020): 263–76, https://ray.yorksj .ac.uk/id/eprint/4170/.

9 Malte Schwinger et al., "Why Do Students Use Strategies That Hurt Their Chances of Academic Success? A Meta-Analysis of Antecedents of Academic Self-Handicapping," *Journal of Educational Psychology* 114, no. 3 (2022): 576–96, http://doi.org/10.1037/edu0000706.

10 Carol Dweck, *Mindset: The New Psychology of Success* (New York: Ballantine Books, 2007), 6–7; Lisa S. Blackwell, Kali H. Trzesniewski, and Carol D. Dweck, "Implicit Theories of Intelligence Predict Achievement across an Adolescent Transition: A Longitudinal Study and an Intervention," *Child Development* 78, no. 1 (January/February 2007): 246–63, https://doi.org/10.1111/j.1467-8624.2007.00995.x.

11 Hans S. Schroder et al., "Neural Evidence for Enhanced Attention to Mistakes among School-Aged Children with a Growth Mindset," *Developmental Cognitive Neuroscience* 24, (2017): 42–50, https://doi.org/10.1016/j.dcn.2017.01.004.

12 Robert Frank, "Billionaire Sara Blakely Says Secret to Success Is Failure," CNBC, October 16, 2013, https://www.cnbc.com/2013/10/16/billionaire-sara-blakely-says -secret-to-success-is-failure.html.

13 Amy Gallo, "You've Made a Mistake. Now What?," *Harvard Business Review*, April 28, 2010, https://hbr.org/2010/04/youve-made-a-mistake-now-what.

14 Kathryn Schulz, *Being Wrong: Adventures in the Margin of Error* (New York: Ecco, 2011), 26.

15 Xiaodong Lin-Siegler et al., "Even Einstein Struggled: Effect of Learning about Great Scientists' Struggles on High School Students' Motivation to Learn Science," *Journal of Educational Psychology* 108, no. 3 (2016): 314–28, http://doi.org/10.1037/edu0000092.

16 "How Dr. Seuss Got His Start on Mulberry Street," *NPR*, January 24, 2012, https:// www.npr.org/2012/01/24/145471724/how-dr-seuss-got-his-start-on-mulberry-street.

17 Rachel Gillett, "How Walt Disney, Oprah, and 19 Other Successful People Rebounded After Getting Fired," Inc., October 7, 2015, https://www.inc.com/business-insider /21-successful-people-who-rebounded-after-getting-fired.html.

18 Colleen Walsh, "Winfrey: Failure Is Just Movement," *Harvard Gazette*, May 30, 2013, https://news.harvard.edu/gazette/story/2013/05/winfrey-failure-is-just-movement/.

19 Brené Brown, "Listening to Shame," filmed March 2012, TED video, 19:37, https:// www.ted.com/talks/brene_brown_listening_to_shame/transcript?language=en.

20 "Albert Ellis—On Guilt and Shame—RARE 1960 recording," ProfessorMystic, June 4, 2009, YouTube video, 10:00, https://www.youtube.com/watch?v=7yFxIjhdSlE.

21 "Albert Ellis."

22 Wenzhou Wang et al., "Shame on You! When and Why Failure-Induced Shame Impedes Employees' Learning from Failure in the Chinese Context," *Frontiers in Psychology* 12, (2021): 725277, https://doi.org/10.3389/fpsyg.2021.725277.

23 Noelle Nelson, Selin A. Malkoc, and Baba Shiv, "Emotions Know Best: The Advantage of Emotional versus Cognitive Responses to Failure," *Journal of Behavioral Decision Making* 31, no. 1 (January 2018): 40–51, https://doi.org/10.1002/bdm.2042.

24 Brené Brown, "Brené Brown on How to Reckon with Emotion and Change Your Narrative," Oprah.com, accessed November 8, 2022, https://www.oprah.com /omagazine/brene-brown-rising-strong-excerpt.

25 Martin P. Seligman, *Learned Optimism: How to Change Your Mind and Your Life* (New York: Vintage, 2006), 4–5; Catherine Moore, "Learned Optimism: Is Martin Seligman's Glass Half Full?," Positive Psychology, December 30, 2019, https://positivepsychology .com/learned-optimism.

26 Amy Morin, interview with the author, *How to Talk to Kids about Anything*, podcast, December 31, 2018, https://drrobynsilverman.com/how-to-talk-about-the-13-things -mentally-strong-women-and-girls-dont-do-with-amy-morin-lcsw/.

27 "Albert Ellis."

28 Tarana Burke and Brené Brown, "Introduction to 'You Are Your Best Thing': A Conversation," Tarana Burke (website), accessed November 8, 2022, https:// www.taranaburke.com/taranabrene.

29 David Rock, Beth Jones, and Chris Weller, "Using Neuroscience to Make Feedback Work and Feel Better," *Strategy and Business* 93, (Winter 2018), https://www.strategy -business.com/article/Using-Neuroscience-to-Make-Feedback-Work-and-Feel-Better.

30 Lucia Ciciolla et al., "When Mothers and Fathers Are Seen as Disproportionately Valuing Achievements: Implications for Adjustment Among Upper Middle-Class Youth," *Journal of Youth Adolescence* 46, no. 5 (2017): 1057–75, https://doi.org/10.1007 /s10964-016-0596-x.

31 Julianna Menasce Horowitz and Nikki Graf, "Most U.S. Teens See Anxiety and Depression as a Major Problem among Their Peers," Pew Research Center, February 20, 2019, https://www.pewresearch.org/social-trends/2019/02/20/most-u-s-teens -see-anxiety-and-depression-as-a-major-problem-among-their-peers/.

32 Jessica Lahey, "The Downside of Checking Kids' Grades Constantly," *New York Times*, August 22, 2017, https://www.nytimes.com/2017/08/22/well/family/the-downside-of -checking-kids-grades-constantly.html.

33 Julie Wright and Heather Turgeon, interview with the author, *How to Talk to Kids about Anything*, podcast, November 5, 2018, https://drrobynsilverman.com/how-to-attune -set-limits-and-problem-solve-with-children-in-difficult-moments-with-heather -turgeon-julie-wright/.

34 Brené Brown, "Let's Rumble," Brené Brown (website), May 1, 2019, https://brene brown.com/articles/2019/05/01/lets-rumble/.

35 Jessica Lahey, interview with the author, *How to Talk to Kids about Anything*, podcast, May 9, 2017, https://drrobynsilverman.com/how-to-talk-to-kids-about-the-gift -of-failure-with-jessica-lahey/.

36 Julie Lythcott Haims, interview with the author, *How to Talk to Kids about Anything*, podcast, December 4, 2018, https://drrobynsilverman.com/how-to-raise -a-confident-capable-resilient-adult-with-julie-lythcott-haims/.

37 Lythcott Haims, interview.

38 Jessica Lahey, "The Big Problem with Rewarding Kids for Good Grades and Punishing Them for Bad Ones," *Washington Post*, August 29, 2018, https://www.washington post.com/lifestyle/on-parenting/should-we-reward-our-kids-for-things-like-good -grades/2018/08/17/5910e896-9461-11e8–810c-5fa705927d54_story.html.

39 Alfie Kohn, interview with the author, *How to Talk to Kids about Anything*, podcast, June 11, 2019, https://drrobynsilverman.com/how-to-practice-unconditional -parenting-using-love-and-reason-with-alfie-kohn/.

40 Phyllis Fagell, interview with the author, *How to Talk to Kids about Anything*, podcast, August 6, 2019, https://drrobynsilverman.com/how-to-talk-to-middle -schoolers-about-what-matters-most-with-phyllis-fagell-lcpc/.

41 William Stixrud, interview with the author, *How to Talk to Kids about Anything*, podcast, May 14, 2019, https://drrobynsilverman.com/how-to-talk-to-kids-about-being -self-driven-self-motivated-self-controlled-with-dr-william-stixrud/.

42 Jessica Lahey, "Parenting, Not in the Moment, But for the Long Haul," *New York Times*, June 10, 2015, https://archive.nytimes.com/parenting.blogs.nytimes.com/2015/06/10 /parenting-not-for-the-moment-but-for-the-long-haul/.

43 Vicki Hoefle, interview with the author, *How to Talk to Kids about Anything*, podcast, April 16, 2019, https://drrobynsilverman.com/how-to-use-duct-tape-parenting-to-raise -respectful-responsible-resilient-kids-with-vicki-hoefle/.

Chapter 8: How to Talk to Kids about Friendship

1   Lydia Denworth, interview with the author, *How to Talk to Kids about Anything*, podcast, September 21, 2021, https://drrobynsilverman.com/how-to-talk-to-kids-about-the -lifechanging-benefits-of-friendship-with-lydia-denworth/.

2   Gary C. Glick and Amanda J. Rose, "Prospective Associations between Friendship Adjustment and Social Strategies: Friendship as a Context for Building Social Skills," *Developmental Psychology* 47, no. 4 (July 2011): 1117–32, https://doi.org/10.1037/a0023277.

3   Elian Fink and Claire Hughes, "Children's Friendships," British Psychological Society, February 5, 2019, https://www.bps.org.uk/psychologist/childrens-friendships; Michelle A. Harris and Ulrich Orth, "The Link Between Self-Esteem and Social Relationships: A Meta-Analysis of Longitudinal Studies," *Journal of Personality and Social Psychology*

119, no. 6 (December 2020): 1459–77, https://doi.org/10.1037/pspp0000265; Berna Güroğlu, "The Power of Friendship: The Developmental Significance of Friendships from a Neuroscience Perspective," *Child Development Perspectives* 16, no. 2 (June 2022): 110–17, https://doi.org/10.1111/cdep.12450; Laura Bechtiger et al., "Developmental Associations Between Sympathy and Mutual Disclosure in Friendships from Mid Adolescence to Early Adulthood," *Journal of Research on Adolescence* 31, no. 2 (June 2021): 36883, https://doi.org/10.1111/jora.12602; Neeltje P. van den Bedem et al. , "Interrelation between Empathy and Friendship Development during (Pre) Adolescence and the Moderating Effect of Developmental Language Disorder: A Longitudinal Study," *Social Development* 28, no. 3 (August 2019): 599–619, https://doi.org/10.1111/sode.12353.

4   Livia Tomova et al., "Acute Social Isolation Evokes Midbrain Craving Responses Similar to Hunger," Nature Neuroscience23, (2020): 1597–1605, https://doi.org/10.1038 /s41593-020-00742-z.

5   Rebecca Graber, Rhiannon Turner, and Anna Madill, "Best Friends and Better Coping: Facilitating Psychological Resilience through Boys' and Girls' Closest Friendships," *British Journal of Psychology* 107, no. 2 (May 2016): 338–58, https://doi.org/10.1111/bjop.12135; Isabelle Gerretsen, "How to Help Children Find Good Friends," BBC Family Tree, November 30, 2021, https://www.bbc.com/future /article/20211117-how-do-children-choose-a-best-friend.

6   Yang Claire Yang et al., "Social Relationships and Physiological Determinants of Longevity across the Human Life Span," *Proceedings of National Academy of Sciences* 113, no. 3 (2016): 578–83, https://doi.org/10.1073/pnas.1511085112; Courtney E. Boen et al., "Social Relationships, Inflammation, and Cancer Survival," *Cancer Epidemiology, Biomarkers & Prevention* 27, no. 5 (May 2018): 541–49, https://doi.org/10 .1158%2F1055-9965.EPI-17-0836.

7   Lydia Denworth, "The Outsize Influence of Your Middle-School Friends," *The Atlantic*, January 28, 2020, https://www.theatlantic.com/family/archive/2020/01 /friendship-crucial-adolescent-brain/605638/.

8   Robert Waldinger, "What Makes a Good Life? Lessons from the Longest Study on Happiness," filmed November 14, 2015, in Brookline, MA, TED video, 12:37, https:// www.ted.com/talks/robert_waldinger_what_makes_a_good_life_lessons_from_the _longest_study_on_happiness?language=en.

9   Julianne Holt-Lunstad et al., "Loneliness and Social Isolation as Risk Factors for Mortality: A Meta-Analytic Review," *Perspectives on Psychological Science* 10, no. 2 (March 2015): 227–37, https://doi.org/10.1177/1745691614568352; Julianne Holt-Lunstad, Timothy B. Smith, and J. Bradley Layton, "Social Relationships and Mortality Risk: A MetaAnalytic Review," *PLOS Medicine* 7, no. 7 (July 2010): e1000316, https://doi.org/10.1371/journal.pmed.1000316.

10   Kelli Harding, email to the author, November 21, 2021.

11   Beverley Fehr, *Friendship Processes* (Thousand Oaks, CA: Sage, 1996), 8–16.

12 Aminatou Sow and Ann Friedman, *Big Friendship: How We Keep Each Other Close* (New York: Simon and Schuster, 2020), 5.

13 Julie Beck, "How the Hosts of 'Call Your Girlfriend' Saved Their Friendship," *The Atlantic*, July 10, 2020, https://www.theatlantic.com/family/archive/2020/07/aminatou-sow-and-ann-friedman-on-big-friendship/613969/.

14 Denworth, interview.

15 Eileen Kennedy-Moore and Christine McLaughlin, *Growing Friendships: A Kids' Guide to Making and Keeping Friends* (New York: Aladdin/Beyond Words, 2017), 14.

16 Vanessa Van Edwards, interview with the author, *How to Talk to Kids about Anything*, podcast, January 29, 2019, https://drrobynsilverman.com/how-to-help-kids-succeed-with-peers-and-other-people-with-vanessa-van-edwards/; Vanessa Van Edwards, "Get More People to Like You Using These 5 Science Backed Strategies," Science of People, March 20, 2019, https://www.scienceofpeople.com/likable/.

17 Catherine Pearson, "How to Make, and Keep, Friends in Adulthood," *New York Times*, October 1, 2022, https://www.nytimes.com/2022/10/01/well/live/how-to-make-friends-adult.html.

18 "Are You Really a GOOD Friend?," *The Ed Mylett Show*, podcast, October 4, 2022, https://www.edmylett.com/podcast/dr-marisa-franco-the-science-of-amazing-friendships/.

19 Eileen Kennedy-Moore, interview with the author, *How to Talk to Kids about Anything*, podcast, July 18, 2017, https://drrobynsilverman.com/how-to-talk-to-kids-about-making-keeping-friends-with-dr-eileen-kennedy-moore-relaunch/.

20 Van Edwards, interview; Van Edwards, "Get More People."

21 Kennedy-Moore and McLaughlin, *Growing Friendships*, 25.

22 Michele Borba, interview with the author, *How to Talk to Kids about Anything*, podcast, May 23, 2017, https://drrobynsilverman.com/how-to-talk-to-kids-about-empathy-and-entitlement-with-dr-michele-borba/.

23 JoAnn Crohn, *Me and My Friendships: A Friendship Book for Kids* (New York: Rockridge Press, 2021), 33.

24 Caroline Maguire, interview with the author, *How to Talk to Kids about Anything*, podcast, October 15, 2019, https://drrobynsilverman.com/how-to-help-kids-learn-friendship-skills-and-avoid-social-isolation-with-caroline-maguire/.

25 Richard Lavoie, *It's So Much Work to Be Your Friend: Helping the Child with Learning Disabilities Find Social Success* (Miami: Atria, 2006), xlix.

26 Michelle Icard, interview with the author, *How to Talk to Kids about Anything*, podcast, July 27, 2021, https://drrobynsilverman.com/how-to-talk-to-teens-about-topics-that-matter-with-michelle-icard/.

27 Rachel Simmons, email interview with the author, May 18, 2020.

28 "Are You Really a GOOD Friend?."

29 Kyle Maynard, interview with the author, April 30, 2012.

30 Diana J. Meter and Noel A. Card, "Stability of Children's and Adolescents' Friendships: A Meta-Analytic Review," *Merrill-Palmer Quarterly* 62, no. 3 (2016): 252–84, https://doi.org/10.13110/merrpalmquar1982.62.3.0252.

31 L. M. Lessard and J. Juvonen, "Losing and Gaining Friends: Does Friendship Instability Compromise Academic Functioning in Middle School?," *Journal of School Psychology* 69, (August 2018): 143–53, https://doi.org/10.1016/j.jsp.2018.05.003.

32 Fagell, interview; Amy C. Hartl, Brett Laursen, and Antonius H. N. Cillessen, "A Survival Analysis of Adolescent Friendships: The Downside of Dissimilarity" *Psychological Science* 26, no. 8 (August 2015): 1304–15, https://doi.org/10.1177%2F0956797615588751.

33 Phyllis Fagell, "6 Ways to Help Your Child Thrive Socially in Middle School," *Washington Post*, April 14, 2020, https://www.washingtonpost.com/lifestyle/on-parenting/6-ways-to-help-your-child-thrive-socially-in-middle-school/2020/04/13/4dea1e32-7a70-11ea-9bee-c5bf9d2e3288_story.html.

34 Van Edwards, interview; Van Edwards, "Get More People."

35 Lisa Damour, interview with the author, *How to Talk to Kids about Anything*, podcast, February 12, 2019, https://drrobynsilverman.com/how-to-talk-to-girls-about-managing-stress-and-anxiety-with-dr-lisa-damour/.

36 Hartl, Laursen, and Cillessen, "Survival Analysis of Adolescent Friendships."

37 Robin Dunbar, *Friends: Understanding the Power of Our Most Important Relationships* (Boston: Little, Brown, 2022), Chapter 4.

38 Jeffrey A. Hall, "How Many Hours Does It Take to Make a Friend?," *Journal of Social and Personal Relationships* 36, no. 4 (2019): 1278–96, https://doi.org/10.1177/0265407518761225.

39 M. Janelle Cambron, Linda K. Acitelli, and Lynne Steinberg, "When Friends Make You Blue: The Role of Friendship Contingent Self-Esteem in Predicting Self-Esteem and Depressive Symptoms," *Personality and Social Psychology Bulletin* 36, no. 3 (2010): 384–97, https://doi.org/10.1177/0146167209351593.

40 Jason Chein et al., "Peers Increase Adolescent Risk Taking by Enhancing Activity in the Brain's Reward Circuitry" *Developmental Science* 14, no. 2 (March 2011): F1–F10, https://doi.org/10.1111%2Fj.1467-7687.2010.01035.x; Stefanie M. Helmer et al., "'Tell Me How Much Your Friends Consume'—Personal, Behavioral, Social, and Attitudinal Factors Associated with Alcohol and Cannabis Use among European School Students," *International Journal of Environmental Research and Public Health* 18, no. 4 (February 2021): 168–4, https://doi.org/10.3390/ijerph18041684; Steven A. Branstetter, Sabina Low, and Wyndol Furman, "The Influence of Parents and Friends on Adolescent Substance Use: A Multidimensional Approach," *Journal of Substance Use* 16, no. 2 (April 2011): 15060, https://doi.org/10.3109/14659891.2010.519421; Michael Windle, "A Study of Friendship Characteristics and Problem Behaviors among Middle Adolescents," *Child Development* 65, no. 6 (December 1994): 1764–77, https://doi.org/10.1111/j.1467-8624.1994.tb00847.x; Michael Windle, "Parental, Sibling, and Peer Influences on Adolescent Substance Use and Alcohol Problems," *Applied Developmental Science* 4, no. 2 (2000): 98–110, https://psycnet.apa.org/doi/10.1207/S1532480XADS0402_5; Thomas J. Dishion, Deborah M. Capaldi, and Karen Yoerger, "Middle Childhood Antecedents to Progressions in Male Adolescent Substance Use:

An Ecological Analysis of Risk and Protection," *Journal of Adolescent Research* 14, no. 2 (1999): 175–205, https://doi.org/10.1177/0743558499142003.

41   Glennon Doyle and Abby Wambach, "How to Love Yourself and Allow Yourself to be Loved," December 16, 2021, in We Can Do Hard Things, podcast, transcript, https://momastery.com/blog/we-can-do-hard-things-ep-52/.

42   Phyllis Fagell, email to the author, December 17, 2021.

43   Mitch Prinstein, interview with the author, *How to Talk to Kids about Anything*, podcast, September 3, 2019, https://drrobynsilverman.com/how-to-talk-to-kids-about-popularity-with-mitch-prinstein-ph-d/.

44   Audhild Løhre, "The Impact of Loneliness on Self-Rated Health Symptoms among Victimized School Children," *Child Adolescent Psychiatry Mental Health* 6, no. 1 (May2012): article 20, https://doi.org/10.1186/1753-2000-6-20; Rebecca A. Schwartz-Mette et al., "Relations of Friendship Experiences with Depressive Symptoms and Loneliness in Childhood and Adolescence: A Meta-Analytic Review," *Psychological Bulletin* 146, no.8 (August 2020): 664–700, https://doi.org/10.1037/bul0000239.

45   Robert Faris, Diane Felmlee, and Cassie McMillan, "With Friends Like These: Aggression from Amity and Equivalence," *American Journal of Sociology* 126, no. 3 (November 2020): 673–713, http://doi.org/10.1086/712972.

46   "Questions Answered," National Bullying Prevention Center, Pacer, accessed April 21, 2023, https://www.pacer.org/bullying/info/info-facts.asp.

46   "Et Tu, Brute? Teens May Be More Likely to Be Bullied by Social-Climbing Friends," Penn State Social Science Research Institute, February 24, 2021, https://ssri.psu.edu/news/et-tu-brute-teens-may-be-more-likely-be-bullied-social-climbing-friends.

47   Lauraliisa Mark, Airi Varnik, and Merike Sisask, "Who Suffers the Most from Being Involved in Bullying—Bully, Victim, or Bully-Victim?," *Journal of School Health* 89, no. 2 (February 2019): 136–44,https://doi.org/10.1111/josh.12720.

48   Rosalind Wiseman, *Owning Up Curriculum: Empowering Adolescents to Confront Social Cruelty, Bullying and Injustice* (Chicago: Research Press, 2009), 8–9.

49   "Education Now: The Healing Power of Friendships and Relationships," Harvard Graduate School of Education, October 20, 2021, YouTube video, 31:44, https://www.youtube.com/watch?v=56udEEJnRVw.

50   Rosalind Wiseman, interview with the author, *How to Talk to Kids about Anything*, podcast, April 27, 2017, https://drrobynsilverman.com/talk-kids-boyworld-girlworld-bullying-cultures-dignity-featuring-rosalind-wiseman/.

51   Joseph P. Allen et al., "The Connection Project: Changing the Peer Environment to Improve Outcomes for Marginalized Adolescent,s" *Development & Psychopathology* 33, no. 2 (May 2021): 647–57, https://doi.org/10.1017%2FS0954579419001731; Rachel Narr et al., "Close Friendship Strength and Broader Peer Group Desirability as Differential Predictors of Adult Mental Health," *Child Development* 90, no. 1 (January 2019): 298–313, https://doi.org/10.1111/cdev.12905; Holt-Lunstad et al., "Loneliness and Social Isolation"; Holt-Lunstad et al., "Social Relationships and Mortality Risk."

Chapter 9: How to Talk to Kids about Money

1   Tom Popomaronis, "Warren Buffet: This Is the No. 1 Mistake Parents Make When Teaching Kids about Money," CNBC, July 30, 2019, https://www.cnbc.com/2019/07/30/warren-buffett-this-is-the-no-1-mistake-parents-make-when-teaching-kids-about-money.html.

2   Drake Baer, "The Way Warren Buffet Sold Gum as a 6-Year-Old Reveals a Trait That Made Him a Billionaire," *Business Insider*, November 19, 2014, https://www.businessinsider.com/young-warren-buffett-sold-gum-2014–11.

3   Matt OKeefe, "8 Things Warren Buffet Did to Make $53,000 by Age 16," Lifehack, December 7, 2014, https://www.lifehack.org/articles/money/8-things-warren-buffett-did-make-53000-age-16.html.

4   "Value of $53,000 by Year," Saving.org, accessed November 10, 2022, https://www.saving.org/inflation/inflation.php?amount=53,000.

5   Alice Schroeder, *The Snowball: Warren Buffet and the Business of Life* (New York: Bantam, 2009), 55–96.

6   Popomaronis, "Warren Buffet."

7   Schroeder, *Snowball*, 37.

8   Popomaronis, "Warren Buffet."

9   "AICPA Survey Shows Parents Missing Opportunities to Teach Children about Personal Finance," *Journal of Accountancy*, November 1, 2012, https://www.journalofaccountancy.com/issues/2012/nov/aicpa-survey.html.

10 Cameron Huddleston, "How to Teach Your Kids Good Money Habits, *Forbes*, February 18, 2020, https://www.forbes.com/advisor/personal-finance/how-to-teach-your-kids-good-money-habits/.

11 "13th Annual Parents, Kids & Money Survey," T. Rowe Price, 2021, https://www.moneyconfidentkids.com/content/dam/mck/news-and-research/PKM_13thAnnual_2021_deck_Final.pdf; T. Rowe Price Group, "T. Rowe Price: Pandemic Impact on Financial Well-Being Compels More Parents Than Ever to Have Money Conversations with Their Kids," PR NewsWire, April 21, 2021, https://www.prnewswire.com/news-releases/t-rowe-price-pandemics-impact-to-financial-well-being-compels-more-parents-than-ever-to-have-money-conversations-with-their-kids-301273921.html.

12 Lynsey Kluever Romo, "Money Talks: Revealing and Concealing Financial Information in Families," *Journal of Family Communication* 11, no. 4 (2011): 26481, https://doi.org/10.1080/15267431.2010.544634.

13 Carl Richards, "How to Talk about Money," *New York Times*, accessed November 10, 2022, https://www.nytimes.com/guides/year-of-living-better/how-to-talk-about-money.

14 "13th Annual Parents, Kids & Money Survey."

15 Paul Sullivan, "4 Reasons Parents Don't Discuss Money (and Why They Should)," *New York Times*, August 2, 2019, https://www.nytimes.com/2019/08/02/your-money/parenting-wealth-discussions.html.

16 "13th Annual Parents, Kids & Money Survey."

17 Karen Holden et al., "Financial Literacy Programs Targeted on Pre-School Children: Development and Evaluation," University of Wisconsin-Madison, 2009, https://fyi.extension.wisc.edu/financialseries/files/2013/10/CUNA-Report-full-draft.pdf.

18 David Whitebread and Sue Bingham, "Habit Formation and Learning in Young Children," Money Advice Service, May 2013, https://mascdn.azureedge.net/cms/the-money-advice-service-habit-formation-and-learning-in-young-children-may2013.pdf.

19 T. Rowe Price, "2020 Parents, Kids & Money Survey Results," Money Confident Kids, December 4, 2020, https://www.moneyconfidentkids.com/us/en/news-and-research/research/2020-parents-kids-money-survey-results.html.

20 Richard Barrington, "States Where Financial Literacy Education Is Working," MoneyRates, updated October 14, 2022, https://www.moneyrates.com/research-center/financial-literacy.htm.

21 Mac Gardner, interview with the author, November 17, 2021.

22 Barrington, "States."

23 Paul Golden, interview with the author, December 8, 2021.

24 Whitebread and Bingham, "Habit Formation."

25 Karen Wynn, "Children's Understanding of Counting," *Cognition* 36, no. 2 (August 1990): 155–93, https://doi.org/10.1016/0010-0277(90)90003-3.

26 Rochel Gelman, Elizabeth Meck, and Susan Merkin, "Young Children's Numerical Competence," *Cognitive Development* 1, no. 1 (January 1986): 1–29, https://doi.org/10.1016/S0885-2014(86)80021-1; Barbara W. Sarnecka and Michael D. Lee, "Levels of Number Knowledge during Early Childhood," *Journal of Experimental Child Psychology* 103, no. 3 (July 2009): 325–37, https://doi.org/10.1016/j.jecp.2009.02.007.

27 Jean Piaget, *The Child's Conception of Number* (New York: Basic Books, 1952), 258.

28 "What Is a Budget?," YNAB Kids, May 12, 2020, YouTube video, 4:21, https://www.youtube.com/watch?v=gDMguO9wdM0.

29 Ning Ding et al., "Waiting for the Better Reward: Comparison of Delay of Gratification in Young Children across Two Cultures," *PLoS One* 16, no. 9 (2021): e0256966, https://doi.org/10.1371/journal.pone.0256966; Walter Mischel, Yuichi Shoda, and Monica L. Rodriguez, "Delay of Gratification in Children," *Science* 244, no. 4907 (May 1989): 93338, https://doi.org/10.1126/science.2658056; Michael J. Beran, "The Comparative Science of 'Self-Control': What Are We Talking About?," *Frontiers in Psychology* 6, (2015): 51, https://doi.org/10.3389/fpsyg.2015.00051; Jeffrey R. Stevens, "Evolutionary Pressures on Primate Intertemporal Choice," *Proceedings of the Royal Society B: Biological Sciences* 281, (2014): 1786, http://doi.org/10.1098/rspb.2014.0499; Patrick Burns et al., "More Later: Delay of Gratification and Thought about the Future in Children," *Child Development* 92, no. 4 (July/August 2021): 1554–73, https://doi.org/10.1111/cdev.13521.

30 Chelsea Brennan, interview with the author, *How to Talk to Kids about Anything*, podcast, May 4, 2021, https://drrobynsilverman.com/how-to-talk-to-kids-about-money-values-spending-giving-with-chelsea-brennan/.

31 Brennan, interview.

32 Chad Willardson, interview with the author, *How to Talk to Kids about Anything*, podcast, December 7, 2021, https://drrobynsilverman.com/how-to-talk-to-kids-about -money-skills-with-chad-willardson/.

33 Golden, interview.

34 "NY1: Teach Your Children How to Manage Money—Part 6," Beth Kobliner, October 17, 2016, YouTube video, 2:23 , https://www.youtube.com/watch?v=GIqQfi94Ux0.

35 Rachel Cruze, interview with the author, *How to Talk to Kids about Anything*, podcast, February 19, 2019, https://drrobynsilverman.com/how-to-talk-to-kids -about-smart-money-management-with-rachel-cruze/.

36 Neale Godfrey, interview with the author, *How to Talk to Kids about Anything*, podcast, May 16, 2017, https://drrobynsilverman.com/how-to-talk-to-kids-about-money -financial-responsibility-with-neale-godfrey/.

37 "Study: Nearly 70% of Parents Give Children Allowance," CBS19, January 28, 2020, https://www.cbs19.tv/article/news/local/study-nearly-70-of-parents-give-children -allowance/501-1980a787-658c-4267-baa2-a7e53a2495e1.

38 Jonathan Lynch, "Children's Allowance Pay Is Up—Amount Saved Alarmingly Low," AICPA, October 1, 2019, https://www.aicpa.org/news/article/childrens -allowance-pay-is-up-amount-saved-alarmingly-low.

39 Nesra Yannier et al., "Active Learning: 'Hands On' Meets 'Minds-On,'" *Science* 374, no. 6563 (September 2021): 26–30, https://doi.org/10.1126/science.abj9957.

40 The Budgetnista, "Easy Ways to Teach Your Kids about Money," Facebook, February 5, 2020, https://www.facebook.com/watch/live/?ref=watch_permalink&v=549512252357099.

41 "I Taught Elmo about Money!," Beth Kobliner (website), April 14, 2011, https:// bethkobliner.com/advocate/i-taught-elmo-about-money/; "Saving, Spending, Sharing," Sesame Workshop, accessed May 14, 2023, https://sesamestreetincommunities.org /activities/saving-spending-sharing/.

42 Godfrey, interview with the author, *How to Talk to Kids about Anything*, podcast, May 16, 2017, https://drrobynsilverman.com/how-to-talk-to-kids-about-money -financial-responsibility-with-neale-godfrey/.

43 Godfrey, interview with the author, *How to Talk to Kids about Anything*, podcast, May 16, 2017, https://drrobynsilverman.com/how-to-talk-to-kids-about-money -finacial-responsibility-with-neale-godfrey/.

44 Godfrey, interview with the author, *How to Talk to Kids about Anything*, podcast, May 16, 2017, https://drrobynsilverman.com/how-to-talk-to-kids-about-money -financial-responsibility-with-neale-godfrey/.

45 Willardson, interview.

46 Beth Kobliner, interview with the author, *How to Talk to Kids about Anything*, podcast, October 10, 2017, https://drrobynsilverman.com/how-to-talk-to-kids-about -becoming-a-money-genius-with-beth-kobliner/.

47 Godfrey, interview.

48 Rishi Vamdatt, Easy Peasy Finance, accessed November 10, 2022, https://www.easy peasyfinance.com/.

49   The Mighty McClures, "Explaining Cryptocurrency to the Twins," Facebook, July 21, 2021, https://www.facebook.com/mightymcclures/videos/494617358723949.

50   Ron Lieber, "Why You Should Tell Your Children How Much You Make," *New York Times*, January 29, 2015, https://www.nytimes.com/2015/02/01/your-money/why-you -should-tell-your-kids-how-much-you-make.html.

51   "Should I Tell My Kids How Much Money I Make?," Beth Kobliner (website), February 17, 2017, https://bethkobliner.com/conversation/tell-kids-much-money-make/.

52   Jessica Semega and Melissa Kollar, "Income in the United States: 2021," U.S. Census Bureau, September 2022, https://www.census.gov/content/dam/Census/library /publications/2022/demo/p60-276.pdf.

53   Jean Chatzky, Kathryn Tuggle, and the HerMoney Team, *How to Money* (New York: Roaring Brook, 2022), 18.

54   Willardson, interview.

55   Golden, interview.

56   "14th Annual Parents, Kids & Money Survey," T. Rowe Price, 2022, https://www.money confidentkids.com/content/dam/mck/news-and-research/14th%20Annual%20 Parents%20Kids%20%20Money%20Report%20-%20Full%20Results.pdf; "T. Rowe Price: Families' Excitement for Cryptocurrency Brings Risks and Opportunities," T. Rowe Price, April 5, 2022, https://www.troweprice.com/content/dam/trowecorp /Press%20Release%20-%20PKM22_release_FINAL%2004052022.pdf.

57   Willardson, interview.

58   Chatzky, Tuggle, and HerMoney Team, *How to Money*, 95.

59   Elizabeth W. Dunn, Lara B. Aknin, and Michael I. Norton, "Spending Money on Others Promotes Happiness," *Science* 319, no. 5870 (March 2008): 1687–88, https:// doi.org/10.1126/science.1150952.

60   Lara Aknin et al., "Does Spending Money on Others Promote Happiness? A Registered Replication Report," *Journal of Personality and Social Psychology* 119, no. 2 (November August 2020): e15–e26, https://doi.org/10.1037/pspa0000191.

61   Annie Murphy Paul, "How the Power of Interest Drives Learning," KQED, November 4, 2013, https://www.kqed.org/mindshift/32503/how-the-power-of -interest-drives-learning.

62   Paul J. Silvia, "Interest and Interests: The Psychology of Constructive Capriciousness," *Review of General Psychology* 5, no. 3 (2001): 270–90, https://doi.org /10.1037/1089-2680.5.3.270; Paul J. Silvia, "Interest—The Curious Emotion," *Current Directions in Psychological Science* 17, no. 1 (2008): 56–60, https://doi.org /10.1111/j.1467-8721.2008.00548.x.

63   Amornrat Apinunmahakul, Vicky Barham, and Rose A. Devlin, "Charitable Giving, Volunteering, and the Paid Labor Market," *Nonprofit and Voluntary Sector Quarterly* 38, no. 1 (2009): 77–94, https://doi.org/10.1177/0899764008315845; James Andreoni, "Philanthropy," in *Handbook of the Economics of Giving, Altruism, and Reciprocity, ed. L.-A. Gerard-Varet, Serge-Christophe Kolm, and Jean Mercier Ythier* (New York: Elsevier

Eleonor North-Holland, 2004), 2:1201–70,https://econweb.ucsd.edu/~jandreon /WorkingPapers/Philanthropy.pdf; Eleanor Brown and Hamilton Lankford, "Gifts of Money and Gifts of Time: Estimating the Effects of Tax Prices and Available Time," *Journal of Public Economics* 47, no. 3 (April 1992): 321–41, https://doi.org/10.1016/0047 -2727(92)90032-B; Matthew Smith, "Animal vs Human Charities: What Type of People Prefer Which?," YouGov, February 26, 2018, https://yougov.co.uk/topics/politics /articles-reports/2018/02/26/what-kind-person-would-rather-donate-animal-charit.

64 Alison Body, Emily Lau, and Jo Josephidou, *Our Charitable Children: Engaging Children in Charities and Charitable Giving* (Kent, UK: University of Kent, 2019), 1–36, https:// kar.kent.ac.uk/72169/1/OUR_CHARITABLE_CHILDREN_ENGAGING _CHILDRE-FINAL-2019.pdf.

65 Michelle Fox, "Here Are Creative Ways to Teach Your Kids about Charity," CNBC, November 17, 2020, https://www.cnbc.com/2020/11/17/here-are-creative-ways-to -teach-your-kids-about-charity-.html.

66 Daniel Västfjäll et al., "Compassion Fade: Affect and Charity Are Greatest for a Single Child in Need," *PLoS ONE* 9, no. 6 (2014): e100115, https://doi.org/10.1371/journal .pone.0100115; Tehila Kogut and Ilana Ritov, "The Singularity Effect of Identified Victims in Separate and Joint Evaluations," *Organizational Behavior and Human Decision Processes* 97, no. 2 (July 2005): 106–16, https://doi.org/10.1016/j.obhdp.2005.02.003; Lara B. Aknin et al., "Making a Difference Matters: Impact Unlocks the Emotional Benefits of Prosocial Spending," *Journal of Economic Behavior & Organization* 88 , (April 2013): 90–95, https://doi.org/10.1016/j.jebo.2013.01.008.

67 Katherine McAuliffe, Nichola J. Raihani, and Yarrow Dunham, "Children Are Sensitive to Norms of Giving," *Cognition* 167, (October2017): 151–59, https://doi.org/10.1016 /j.cognition.2017.01.006; Mark Ottoni-Wilhelm, David B. Estell, and Neil H. Perdue, "RoleModeling and Conversations about Giving in the Socialization of Adolescent Charitable Giving and Volunteering," *Journal of Adolescence* 37, no. 1 (January 2014): 53– 66, https://doi.org/10.1016/j.adolescence.2013.10.010; Jinhee Kim, Jaslean LaTaillade, and Haejeong Kim, "Family Processes and Adolescents' Financial Behaviors," *Journal of Family and Economic Issues* 32, (2011): 668–79, https://doi.org/10.1007 /s10834-011-9270-3.

68 Debra Mesch et al., "Women Give 2018: Transmitting Generosity to Daughters and Sons," Lilly Family School of Philanthropy, IUPUI Women's Philanthropy Institute, 2018, https://scholarworks.iupui.edu/bitstream/handle/1805/15451/women-give2018 .pdf; "Women Give 2013: New Research on Charitable Giving by Girls and Boys," https://philanthropy.iupui.edu/doc/institutes/women_give_infographic_9-12-20131 .pdf; Mark Ottoni-Wilhelm et al., "Raising Charitable Children: The Effects of Verbal Socialization and Role-Modeling on Children's Giving," *Journal of Population Economics* 30, no. 1 (January 2017): 189–224, https://doi.org/10.1007/s00148-016-0604-1.

69 Ottoni-Wilhelm, Estell, and Perdue, "RoleModeling and Conversations."

70 Elizabeth W. Dunn, Lara B. Aknin, and Michael I. Norton, "Prosocial Spending and

Happiness: Using Money to Benefit Others Pays Off: Corrigendum," *Current Directions in Psychological Science* 23, no. 1 (2014): 41 -47, https://doi.org/10.1177/0963721413512503; Frans B. M. de Waal, "Putting the Altruism Back into Altruism: The Evolution of Empathy," *Annual Review of Psychology* 59, (2008): 279–300, https://doi.org/10.1146/annurev.psych.59.103006.093625; Rene Bekkers and Mark Ottoni-Wilhelm, "Principle of Care and Giving to Help People in Need," *European Journal of Personality* 30, no. 3 (May-June 2016): 240–57, https://doi.org/10.1002%2Fper.2057; Louisa Pavey, Tobias Greitemeyer, and Paul Sparks, "Highlighting Relatedness Promotes Prosocial Motives and Behavior," *Personality and Social Psychology Bulletin* 37, no. 7 (2011): 905–17, https://doi.org/10.1177/0146167211405994; Mario Mikulincer et al., "Attachment, Caregiving, and Altruism: Boosting Attachment Security Increases Compassion and Helping," *Journal of Personality and Social Psychology* 89, no. 5 (2005): 817–839; Summer Allen, "The Science of Generosity," Greater Good Science Center, UC Berkeley, May 2018, https://ggsc.berkeley.edu/images/uploads/GGSC-JTF_White_Paper-Generosity-FINAL.pdf.

71 "Family Giving Traditions," Fidelity Charitable, accessed November 10, 2022, https://www.fidelitycharitable.org/content/dam/fc-public/docs/insights/family-giving-traditions.pdf.

Index

About the Author

© Heather C. Johnston Photography

Known as the "Conversation Doc," Dr. Robyn Silverman is a child and teen development specialist and host of the popular podcast, *How to Talk to Kids About Anything*, as well as the author of the book of the same name. She is a cofounder of the Powerful Words Character System, which gives educators the talking points they need to help children become kind, responsible citizens of the world. Dr. Robyn has appeared on the *Today Show*, *Good Morning America*, *CBS Early Show*, and *Nightline* and has been quoted in the *New York Times*, *Washington Post*, *Chicago Tribune*, CNN.com, and many other publications. She lives with her husband, two kids and rescue dog in North Carolina. Find out all about the book at DrRobynSilverman.com.